PARENT-INFANT HABILITATION

A Comprehensive Approach to Working with Hearing-Impaired Infants and Toddlers and Their Families

By

Valerie Schuyler, M.A.,
Deaf Education and Guidance
Co-Founder and Former Co-Director,
Infant Hearing Resource

And

Nancy Rushmer, M.A.,
Deaf Education and Guidance
Co-Founder and Director,
Infant Hearing Resource

With Foreword By

Marion P. Downs, M.A., D.H.S
Professor Emerita of Otolaryngology
University of Colorado Health Sciences Center

IHR Publications
Portland, Oregon

This book was developed and produced with funding from the following sources:

>   M. J. Murdock Charitable Trust
>   Good Samaritan Hospital and Medical Center Foundation
>   Infant Hearing Resource Board of Directors
>   and
>   Special Education Programs, U.S. Department of Education

>   The contents of this book were developed in part under Grant Number G008301650, Special Education Programs, U.S. Department of Education. However, the content does not necessarily represent the policy of that agency and endorsement by the Federal Government should not be assumed.

Photographs in the text were taken by:
>   Bruce Beaton
>   Bruce Bergman
>   Marjorie Newhouse

Library of Congress Catalog Card Number 86-83118
Main entry under title: Parent-Infant Habilitation

ISBN 0-9618297-2-9

Design, Production, and Typesetting by:
>   Richard Mort & Associates
>   Book Production Associates

Printed in the United States by:
>   EMP Design Printing and Publishing

This book is dedicated to
Donna Parsons
Administrative Coordinator,
Infant Hearing Resource

Your exceptional abilities,
warm personality, and
practice of going the extra mile
have been an essential part
of the accomplishments of IHR.

FOREWORD

Marion P. Downs, M.A., D.H.S.
Professor Emerita of Otolaryngology
University of Colorado Health Sciences Center

Long before other hearing professionals recognized the fact, the Infant Hearing Resource program had accepted the principle that the parents are the primary vehicle through which auditory and/or language learning can be transmitted. The very first program of this group was based firmly on a faith in the parents' ability to stimulate language learning in hearing impaired children.

How strange that workers in this field had ever lost sight of the great power of the parent-child bonding phenomenon to serve as the electric spark that passes learning on to the infant and older child! More, that this spark had not been utilized fully for the hearing impaired. But once understood, it has been accepted in a ground swell that characterizes today's planning for hearing habilitation of the young infant. Here and there one sees today some isolated islands of thought where professionals sit down once or twice a week with a child to impart a therapy that will be the only planned stimulation the child will have. But on the whole the field of educational audiology is totally committed to early childhood education of the hearing impaired through the parental medium. Names such as Freeman McConnell, Doreen Pollack, Hilde Schlesinger and many others are associated in the literature with programs dedicated to the parental principle of language stimulation. And since 1971 the Infant Hearing Resource program has been quietly and effectively developing and proving the methods of applying the principle.

The nature and complexity of the variables involved in evaluating parental involvement have made it all but impossible to quantify its impact. However, an analogy can be drawn here with the impact of parental involvement on normal hearing children who are at developmental risk. The sources for evaluating that impact are described in a chapter by Guinagh and Jester (1981), who looked at all the early intervention programs that have been reported in the United States. It was found that there was doubtful long-term gain resulting from programs that started at three years of age and took place in formal therapy or group training situations. But when the programs involved mother-infant stimulation beginning at birth, the cognitive gains were of acceptable duration. "The earlier the program and the more the parental involvement, the better are the results.'' That statement forms the keystone of any program designed to improve the child's chance to obtain his maximal potential development, regardless of what handicap is present, or even if none exists.

The Infant Hearing Resource program has honed the techniques of parent-child language interaction to a fine skill. They have refused to be bound by any traditional methodology, but have utilized whatever approach is suited to the individual child's needs. They have transcended the bounds of petty disputes over methods, and instead spent their energies sensing the paths that would best find their way through a child's neurological network for language learning. To tailor the program to the child is the highest form of professionalism, and that goal has been achieved in the program described herein.

It is a pleasure to see this manuscript published. Professionals should hail it, and hearing impaired children and their parents will be the ultimate benefactors of its publication.

Guinagh, B.J. and Jester, R.E.: Long-term effects of infant stimulation programs. *Advances of Behavioral Pediatrics,* 2:81-110, 1981.

ACKNOWLEDGEMENTS

This book is obviously the work of more than just the two of us: How could any two people generate so many words? We are indebted to many people for several different reasons. We hope we have included all these individuals below.

The staff and consultants of Infant Hearing Resource over the past 15 years deserve a great deal of credit for helping us learn about or conceive and test out many of the ideas and techniques included in this book. We are indebted to Arla Melum and Jayne Sowers for their work on the material from which the chapters on teaching vocal/speech skills and presymbolic communications are based. We are grateful to Carolyn Bullard and Carolyn Talbott who permitted us to include results of studies they conducted using families and children enrolled at IHR. Other staff members and consultants who have earned our gratitude for sharing their ideas and skills with us are: Roberta Arpan, Marlee McWain Dutli, Ed Fuller, Carol Greer, Nancy Hatfield, Russ Jackson, Norene Kennedy, Marlyn Minkin, Becky Moore, Dorothy Morgan, Rod Pelson, Caryl Purdue, Leif Terdal, and Norton Young.

Staff members Donna Parsons, Beverly Bowman, and Judy West have worked on agency administration and fund development activities that have kept Infant Hearing Resource alive and well. And finally, staff members Margie Arvidson and Becky Bergman typed their fingers to the bone through endless drafts of this manuscript. We appreciate their skills and patience.

Another group of people to whom we owe thanks is the professionals and parents who read all or parts of draft four of the manuscript. We are extremely grateful to Nancy H. Hatfield for her knowledgeable critique of the content and expert proofreading of the manuscript. We are also very grateful to the following field-readers whose many helpful suggestions made the book more accurate, readable, and, yes, longer!

Michael N. Prouty	Arla Melum
Cynthia Hooper	Norene Kennedy
Robert C. Rutten	Carol Greer
Mary McLean	Donna Parsons
Carolyn Talbott	Debbie Allen
Rodney O. Pelson	Peggy Dargan
Nancy Kosterlitz	Barbara Eck
Carolyn Bullard	Gene Reneau
Sandra Pemberton	Kathy Rodriguez
Jayne Sowers	Barbara Schrag

A long-time friend and professional colleague, Marybeth Longbine, volunteered many hours to the endless tasks involved in the final production of the book. We very much appreciate her help.

A special thank you goes to Thomas Behrens who, years ago, urged us to share with other professionals what we have learned about working with hearing-impaired infants and their parents. The content of this book is based on the Parent-Infant Specialist: Hearing-Impaired training program that we developed as a result of his encouragement.

Since 1976, 40 professionals have spent eight months each at IHR in the Parent-Infant Specialist: Hearing-Impaired training program. All of these people contributed their own ideas and feedback on techniques and procedures used in teaching families at IHR. We appreciate their assistance in refining and improving our habilitation services.

Finally, we are indebted to all the families who have been the heart of Infant Hearing Resource during the past 15 years. Parents and children have taught us what works and what does not work in our mutual efforts to meet the goals set for each family enrolled. These families have been strong supporters of IHR and their continued friendship is very important to us.

AUTHORS' NOTE

This book can be used in conjunction with *Parent-Infant Communication* (Infant Hearing Resource, third edition, 1985) and with any other parent-infant curriculum. A curriculum tells the parent-infant teacher *what* to teach; this volume tells *why* and *how*. We did not repeat herein the information contained in *Parent-Infant Communication* in the sequences of infant and parent learning objectives or in the 52 Parent Handouts. While each of these two Infant Hearing Resource publications stands on its own, the material in each supports and augments the other.

A 28-minute professionally produced color videotape based on the habilitation content and techniques described in *Parent-Infant Communication* and *Parent-Infant Habilitation* is available. Contact Infant Hearing Resource for more information.

PART I

COMPONENTS OF AN EFFECTIVE PARENT- INFANT HABILITATION PROGRAM

PART II

IDENTIFICATION AND AUDITORY ASSESSMENT OF HEARING-IMPAIRED INFANTS

PART III

PARENT INVOLVEMENT IN THE
HABILITATION PROCESS:
ESTABLISHING THE WORKING ENVIRONMENT

PART IV

HELPING PARENTS ACHIEVE PARENT OBJECTIVES

PART V

TEACHING PARENTS TO TEACH
INFANT OBJECTIVES

PART VI

WORKING WITH FAMILIES OF HEARING-IMPAIRED INFANTS WITH ADDITIONAL HANDICAPS

PART VII

GRADUATES OF INFANT HEARING RESOURCE

PART I

COMPONENTS OF AN EFFECTIVE PARENT-INFANT HABILITATION PROGRAM

CHAPTER 1

AN INTRODUCTION TO INFANT HEARING RESOURCE

Overview

What is Infant Hearing Resource?

Philosophy Behind IHR Services

The Impact of the IHR Program of
  Habilitation

OVERVIEW

"We're wondering if our baby has a hearing problem." Words like these frequently serve as our introduction to the parents of a hearing-impaired baby and to the start of a complex, rewarding, and unique process involving that baby, his family, and specially trained professionals at Infant Hearing Resource. This book is about this unique process which we call parent-infant habilitation. It is a process that involves the discovery of facts and feelings, the application of tried-and-true techniques, and the constant experimentation required when people work together to accomplish goals.

Infant Hearing Resource (IHR) is a private, non-profit agency which has been providing services in Portland, Oregon, since 1971. The agency was established with two purposes: 1) to promote attitudes and procedures which will lead to the identification of infants with hearing loss early in life, and 2) to provide parent-oriented services to families of hearing-impaired infants, 0-4 years of age. At the time IHR was established we, as co-founders, based our rationale for the need for early identification and family involvement on frustration, sensory deprivation studies conducted on animals, and untested logic! Our frustration evolved from our experiences in teaching hearing-impaired children who were identified and fitted with hearing aids shortly before enrollment in preschool at three or four years of age. During their preschool and kindergarten years these children did not acquire the listening and communication skills that enabled them to understand others and to express themselves, and that prepared them for a first grade curriculum. Parents of these preschoolers did not understand the implications of their child's hearing loss nor did they know how they could participate in the management of their child's educational career.

At a point when we were discussing our frustrations associated with late identification of hearing loss, a supportive neurologist, Dr. Robert Dow, provided us with information from studies which pointed up the deleterious effects of sensory deprivation imposed early in the lives of animals. These studies supported the idea of critical periods of development, a concept which asserts that there are times in the early development of an organism when sensory input is essential to the neural development of areas in the brain which receive and process that input. This information substantiated our intuitive feeling that getting started early with hearing aids and language input might be critical to the development of the hearing-impaired child.

The final element in our rationale, our untested logic, ran something as follows: "Parents are a baby's first teachers. Parents of normally hearing infants start the parent-infant bonding and communication processes with their infant at birth. Hearing-impaired infants need to follow the same steps in bonding and communication as do normally hearing infants. Hearing loss interferes with some aspects of these processes. Therefore, it seems logical to help parents learn to deal with their infant's hearing loss early on so that their relationship with their infant and their communication with their infant is not adversely affected."

We discussed our rationale with Portland audiologist, Dr. Norton Young, who had been testing the hearing of infants and young children for many years. He agreed with our hypothesis that providing hearing-impaired infants with auditory and language input during their first years of life and involving parents in the habilitation process would have a powerful and positive effect on the entire family. Bolstered by the support of Dr. Dow, Dr. Young, and Brian and Peggy Casey, parents of two hearing-impaired daughters, we opened the doors of IHR and began to work with three families of young hearing-impaired children.

A most gratifying aspect of our work with families during the fifteen years since those first days is that our original rationale has proven sound and that we can see clearly that the services our agency provides make a positive difference in the lives of the families we serve. The children graduating from IHR leave with a strong foundation of listening and language skills and we feel great about that fact. But as important to us as levels of child achievement is the warmth, love, and communication that exists between the parents and hearing-impaired children who graduate from IHR.

We have seen that parents who have had the opportunity to express and explore the feelings they experience as a result of their child's hearing loss can provide to their child the acceptance and support which is essential to the child's emerging self-esteem. Parents who have acquired knowledge and skills related to their child's hearing loss can be effective advocates for their child so that he can develop to his fullest potential. Knowledgeable, accepting parents provide benefits to the hearing-impaired child for a lifetime. The habilitation program at IHR is effective in meeting our goal of providing parents with the help they need to help their child.

Many talented and innovative people around the world have applied their expertise to the challenge of working with hearing-impaired children. We borrowed liberally from these experts in building the habilitation program at Infant Hearing Resource over the past 15 years. Based on what we learned from others and from our own work with hearing-impaired infants and their parents, we wrote the curriculum, *Parent-Infant Communication* (Infant Hearing Resource, Third Edition, 1985). *Parent-Infant Communica-*

tion serves as a guide to the specialist, telling her *what* to teach hearing-impaired infants, 0-4 years of age, and their parents.

In 1976, IHR was awarded the first of four three-year federal grants to train parent-infant specialists and to develop additional materials for teachers who work with hearing-impaired infants and their parents. In developing the eight-month-long training program for "Parent-Infant Specialists: Hearing Impaired" we borrowed knowledge and skills again, this time from experts in the fields of pediatric audiology, counseling, child development, multi-handicapped children, physical therapy, visual impairment, and developmental delay. We combined this information with what we knew — and continue to learn — about the children and their families with whom we work. We designed a series of courses to transmit this amalgamation of information to individuals who wanted to learn the skills and knowledge required by the specialist working with hearing-impaired infants and toddlers and their parents. We wanted these individuals to know not only *what* to teach, as delineated in *Parent-Infant Communication*, but *how* to teach.

As we have taught this "how to" material in courses, seminars, and practica over the past ten years, we have been told again and again that we should put the material into a book that would be available to parent-infant teachers in the field. The result is this book, *Parent-Infant Habilitation*. *Parent-Infant Habilitation* deals with the *"how to"* of teaching hearing-impaired infants, 0-4 years of age, and their parents. It describes the techniques and processes that have been used successfully by parent-infant specialists at IHR to achieve the goals set for infants and parents enrolled. The purpose of *Parent-Infant Habilitation* is to share with teachers and teachers-in-training techniques, processes, and procedures that specialists at IHR use effectively in their work with hearing-impaired infants and their families.

While it is very probably true that no one idea expressed in this book is new, many of the ways in which the ideas are combined, the environment in which we advocate that the ideas are applied, and the sequence in which the ideas are carried out are unique to Infant Hearing Resource. We feel it will be helpful to the reader to provide a brief description of Infant Hearing Resource as a background for the material which follows.

WHAT IS INFANT HEARING RESOURCE?

Infant Hearing Resource was established in 1971 to provide intensive, parent-oriented services to hearing-impaired infants. The first agency in the Pacific Northwest to address the needs of the very young hearing-impaired child and his parents, IHR has continued to focus on the identification and habilitation of infants with hearing loss, age 0-4, and on education and counseling for their parents. Founded by educators of the hearing-impaired, Nancy Rushmer and Valerie Schuyler, and by Brian and Peggy Casey, parents of two hearing-impaired children, IHR is a private non-profit agency governed by a volunteer Board of Directors. The agency has been affiliated with and located on the campus of Good Samaritan Hospital and Medical Center since 1972.

Infant Hearing Resource provides five major services: pediatric audiology, habilitation for hearing-impaired infants and their parents, training of professionals, development of materials for professionals, and informing medical personnel and the community of the need for early identification and habilitation of hearing-impaired infants.

Infant Hearing Resource employs four to five staff members who are trained "Parent-Infant Specialists: Hearing Impaired." These specialists have master's degrees in various fields of communication disorders and post-degree coursework and practicum in parent-infant habilitation. Each specialist has a range of responsibilities including teaching and managing a caseload of 4-6 enrolled families, instructing in the parent-infant specialist training program, presenting workshops, writing materials for dissemination, performing public awareness activities, and taking part in fundraising activities.

The director of IHR is Nancy Rushmer, a parent-infant specialist. She is responsible for carrying out the policies and activities mandated by the Board of Directors and for managing and supervising all agency programs and projects. The IHR pediatric audiologist works one day a week with children enrolled at IHR and with infants and toddlers referred for testing. Other staff members who are vital to the agency's ongoing programs are the administrative coordinator, secretary, and fund development coordinator.

PHILOSOPHY BEHIND IHR SERVICES

Families enroll at Infant Hearing Resource because they have been told that their baby has a hearing loss and most of them have no idea how to begin to help their child. The purpose of IHR is to help parents acquire information and skills that enable them to provide to their hearing-impaired child exactly what they provide to their other children: love, security, communication, positive self-esteem, and family values. The newly identified hearing loss is a barrier that can prevent many parents from successfully transmitting these important elements to their young child. IHR parent-infant specialists provide parents with roads and ladders around this barrier so that effective parenting can take place.

Families at IHR have chosen to enroll here. We are fortunate that in the Portland metropolitan area there are four programs which serve hearing-impaired infants and their parents. When specialists at IHR first meet parents of young infants, they encourage them to visit all the programs and to make an enrollment decision based on what program will best meet their

"More bubbles!" Her parents and older sister enjoy the bubbles blown by the parent-infant specialist as much as the baby does.

particular family's needs. When families elect to enroll at IHR, they have chosen to enter into a partnership with the parent-infant specialist, a partnership which will focus on, and take direction from, the needs of the family.

The parent-specialist partnership is the core of the habilitation process at Infant Hearing Resource. Both members of the partnership have clearly defined roles and responsibilities. Parents bring to the partnership their unique personalities, values, dreams, and aspirations for their child. Their responsibilities in the partnership include providing the specialist with information about their child's development and needs and with information about the dynamics and needs of their entire family. Parents retain the responsibility of making all decisions that affect their child and themselves.

The specialist brings to the partnership her expertise, her knowledge of hearing impairment and its effects on the child and family, her ability to transmit this expertise and knowledge to the parents, and her commitment to the belief that parents are their young child's most effective teachers. Parent-infant specialists at IHR retain the responsibility for keeping current on information relevant to the habilitation of infants, for guiding parents through the habilitation process, for presenting them with the options available at many of the steps in this process, and for hearing and responding to the needs of each family. Parents and specialist work together to uncover the unique characteristics and needs of the hearing-impaired infant and to establish and carry out a plan of action that will promote the infant's acquisition of communication skills and positive self-esteem.

IHR parent-infant specialists regard the habilitation process as one of discovery. We have tools — e.g., assessment and evaluation tools, curricula, books — that we use regularly but not slavishly. We have preferred routines for getting things accomplished, but we are flexible if the routine does not fit the situation. Every family introduces us to new complexities, satisfactions, and opportunities to learn and grow. In our work, we have repeated excuses to indulge the child within ourselves during play with infants and toddlers. We also have frequent opportunity to exercise our adult behaviors in our interchanges with parents and other professionals. All in all, we find this work to be fun, fulfilling, and growth producing. When we share these attitudes with the families, we create an energy that sustains all members of the partnership even through the hard times and that propels us toward attainment of our mutual goals.

THE IMPACT OF THE IHR PROGRAM OF HABILITATION

We think it is important to know what impact our program of habilitation has had on the lives of the children and families enrolled. Two educators of the hearing-impaired who have taught IHR graduates and four parents who were enrolled with their children at IHR describe this impact in the following statements.

A Teacher: "Over the past six years as a teacher of preschool-age hearing-impaired children, I have been fortunate to receive many graduates of Infant Hearing Resource into my classroom. I have often thought that, given no previous background information, I could have picked out IHR graduates on the first day of school based on factors such as expressive and receptive language skills, effective use of amplification, consistency of vocalization/speech, and readiness for a preschool setting (behavior-wise and academic).
"The most fundamental difference between IHR graduates and children from other parent-infant programs is family commitment to effective communication with the hearing-impaired child. The habilitation process that parents and families go through at IHR enables them to accept their child's handicap and move on to a positive approach to the child's future. Parents from other programs rarely show this level of emotional acceptance which allows them to direct their energy toward learning to communicate with their child, thereby beginning the habilitation process. It is this commitment to communication that then enables the IHR child to develop a strong foundation of self-esteem and a capacity to truly become a dynamic member of a family, a school, and eventually society.
"Based on effective communication in the home environment, the IHR graduate enters the preschool setting far beyond other classmates in language capabilities necessary to the develop-

ment of concepts, in readiness skills, and in the ability to mainstream with hearing peers."

A Teacher: "All in all, I saw my dreams come true when teaching the IHR graduates. There were marked differences between IHR grads and other children I taught. First, parents of IHR grads accepted their child's handicap more thoroughly. This acceptance gave them more freedom to 'get on with life' and to enjoy their children as they participated in their child's education and development. Second, parents' skills in communication development made a large difference in the rate of their child's language development. The IHR parents who used total communication and learned to portray the nuances of the English language in signed English had children who were using English word order, grammatical markers, and prepositions. These children who had more complete language input from their parents were able to develop their speech more readily because *what* they were saying was not the problem. Because of their good communication skills, I was able to work on their ability to reason and develop concepts. We had FUN learning.

A Parent: "When we came to IHR, we were a frustrated family. We did not know how to communicate with our 2½ year-old hearing-impaired daughter. Through the help of your excellent curriculum and well-trained staff, we soon broke through that frustration and saw a glimmer of hope. We learned what deafness is and how it can isolate — but that through patience and proper training it doesn't have to be a handicap that keeps a person from succeeding at whatever they choose to do in life. We truly expect as much from our hearing-impaired daughter as from our hearing children.

"The services IHR provided that we especially found helpful were sign language classes for the entire family, a family counselor who helped us express our feelings and gave us help in working through our concerns, bringing in panels of deaf teen-agers and adults that we could question, taking us to different programs that our child would be involved with upon graduating from IHR, and just caring enough to go above and beyond the call of duty.

"Our years at IHR were perhaps the most meaningful we've spent. IHR gave us a common goal to work for: To help our daughter become the delightful person she is becoming."

A Parent: "IHR was so important to us as we began the process of working with our hearing-impaired son. We knew nothing about hearing-impaired people, hearing aids, or even where to begin the education process. IHR was our support and guidance through the first few years. We left IHR with the confidence that we needed to take responsibility for and guide our son's educational experience.''

A Parent: ''I've just been thinking really how lucky and special our 2½ years were at IHR. I realize it more and more as time goes on. When I talk to and get to know other parents of deaf children, I realize how lucky we were to have gone to IHR. I always appreciated it at the time, but more now. I realize the strength and knowledge all of you shared with *all* our family and friends.

''I've always wondered if I had accepted our daughter's deafness. I can really say 'yes' and know that's true now, thanks to all the IHR staff. They exposed us to the deaf culture. We appreciate all the knowledge they shared and beat into our heads. These children can be educated and can succeed in life and will be someone in our world. They will show the hearing world that deaf people can and will succeed and be independent in life. IHR taught us to challenge ourselves, our children, and especially our schools and government, to make sure our children are educated. We learned to accept that we're not alone as parents and that we do indeed have a special challenge in life.''

A Parent: ''We were woefully ignorant about hearing impairment in general and specifically all that is involved in the rearing and training of a hearing-impaired infant. The help we received from IHR has been invaluable to us. The one-on-one approach of teaching parents and their infant children is extremely helpful.

''We found that our friends, family, and community were nearly as ill-informed about hearing loss as we were and their well-meaning comments at times could make the situation even more difficult. Our parent-infant specialist came to our home and shared an evening with all. She gave a film presentation showing the different teaching techniques used at Infant Hearing Resource; she showed a large diagram of the ear and explained each function of the ear. We looked at and discussed a hearing aid, and those present got a first-hand look at it. Finally, we had an open question and answer time. Our son has greatly benefitted from the information that was gained that evening by friends and family, and we have found they have made every effort to put into practice the helpful suggestions that were given to them.''

IHR specialists continue to acquire new information that affects our interactions with the families with whom we work. We are certain that other parent-infant specialists use techniques and procedures that would benefit the families enrolled at IHR. One of the fascinating and challenging aspects of this specialty is the wealth of knowledge that continues to be generated about young hearing-impaired children and their capabilities. We encourage the reader to learn about other parent-infant programs and about materials and curricula that are used in these other programs (see Ling, 1984, and Cole and Mischook, 1985, for a listing of many programs and curricula). Everyone, authors and readers alike, must continue to find ways to share knowledge and skills as these evolve. We hope this volume will contribute to this process of sharing.

CHAPTER 2

GETTING STARTED: ESTABLISHING A FRAMEWORK FOR HABILITATION

Establishing Program Goals
- Goals for Parents
- Goals for Hearing-Impaired Children

Content of the IHR Habilitation Program

The Curricula Used in Habilitation
- The Infant Curriculum
- The Parent Curriculum

The Habilitation Settings at Infant Hearing Resource
- Habilitation Activities at the Agency
- Habilitation Activities in the Families' Homes
- Habilitation Activities in the Audiological Suite

ESTABLISHING PROGRAM GOALS

Clearly defined goals are the foundation of a successful habilitation program. The goals that are set not only determine what services and activities will be offered by the program but they provide guidelines for the way in which these services and activities are conducted in order to assure achievement of the goals.

A parent-infant habilitation program needs goals both for the parents and for the infants enrolled. Once goals are established, curricula and habilitation activities that promote achievement of these goals can be selected. The goals, curricula, and activities of the habilitation program at IHR have proven to be extremely effective in addressing the needs of the infants and parents enrolled. A description of these elements of the IHR program follows.

GOALS FOR PARENTS

IHR has established four major goals for parents who enroll with their hearing-impaired infants:
  1. That parents experience and accept the feelings associated with the discovery and reality of hearing loss in their child.
  2. That parents acquire the information and skills they need to teach their child listening and communication skills.
  3. That parents acquire the knowledge they need to participate actively in the management of their child's educational career.
  4. That parents interact with their hearing-impaired child in ways that promote the development of the child's feelings of self-esteem and competency.

GOALS FOR HEARING-IMPAIRED CHILDREN

IHR specialists have three major goals for enrolled infants:
  1. That children will acquire a functional communication system

based on the English language that enables them to understand the information, feelings, and ideas conveyed by family members and friends and to communicate their own thoughts, feelings, and ideas to others.

2. That children, upon graduation from IHR at around four years of age, are functioning linguistically and cognitively at levels at or near those of hearing children of the same age.

3. That children will acquire the social skills, emotional well-being, and positive self-esteem that allow them to function effectively in their families, schools, and society.

CONTENT OF THE IHR HABILITATION PROGRAM

The habilitation program for enrolled families includes the 16 services listed below. Each of these services is discussed in detail later in this volume. These services, which are provided in a combination of agency and home settings, are:

1. Individualized assessment and developmental programming in listening, presymbolic and symbolic language, and speech skills for each infant.

2. Individualized instruction for parents in using play and daily activities to teach listening, presymbolic and symbolic language, and speech skills to their infant.

3. Individual counseling for parents on issues related to their child's hearing loss.

4. Regular hearing assessment and hearing aid evaluation for each child by staff audiologist and parent-infant specialists.

5. Training for parents in electro-acoustic monitoring of the function of their child's hearing aids.

6. Group educational and counseling sessions for parents two or three times each month.

7. Group activities for children with guided observation for parents two or three times each month (#6 and #7 occur simultaneously).

8. Use of videotape to give parents feedback on their interaction with their child.

9. Evening classes in manually-coded English for parents, siblings, extended families, and caretakers.

10. Saturday group meetings/workshops for fathers, extended family, and siblings.

11. Interpreter services for deaf parents.

12. Printed educational materials for parents from *Parent-Infant Communication* to build each family's personal notebook.

13. Access to educational materials from the Infant Hearing Resource

library.

14. Ongoing record-keeping of parent and child skill acquisition.

15. Videotaped record of each child's development of communication skills, continuing after the child enrolls in a school-age educational setting.

16. Comprehensive annual reports on child and family achievements in habilitation.

THE CURRICULA USED IN HABILITATION

Parent-Infant Communication, A Program of Clinical and Home Training for Parents and Hearing-Impaired Infants (Infant Hearing Resource, 1985) is used by IHR parent-infant specialists to assess levels of functioning and to plan habilitation objectives for both infants and parents. This curriculum, written by the IHR staff, was first published in 1977 and has been revised twice since that time.

THE INFANT CURRICULUM

The infant curriculum sections of *Parent-Infant Communication* contain a total of 309 objectives in three areas of infant development — Auditory, Presymbolic Communication, and Receptive and Expressive Language — and a section, Activities, for teaching these objectives. The objectives in each section are based on sequential communication behaviors acquired by normally hearing children, 0-4 years of age. The curriculum is derived from standardized scales of communication skill development, allowing for its use as a criterion-referenced assessment tool as well as a planning guide.

AUDITORY DEVELOPMENT

The Infant Auditory Development section of *Parent-Infant Communication* is divided into two parts:

1. *Auditory landmarks for the hearing-impaired child.* Landmarks are behaviors a) which are typical of a young hearing-impaired child who has just acquired hearing aids, or b) which signal the child's growing awareness of sound. These landmark behaviors, unlike auditory objectives, cannot or should not be taught. They are important behaviors to note and record, however, because many landmark behaviors give the parent and specialist significant information about the child's developing ability to use his residual amplified hearing.

2. *Auditory objectives for the hearing-impaired child.* Auditory objectives are designated either "NV," or "V" indicating that a non-voice stimulus (NV) or a voice stimulus (V) is specified in the objective. Examples of non-vocal stimuli are environmental sounds, noisemaking toys, and noise-producing activities such as hitting a spoon on a high chair tray. Examples of vocal stimuli are speech, songs, adult-produced animal sounds, and other vocalizations. Auditory objectives are not age-specific but occur in the sequence of acquisition demonstrated by hearing infants. Thus, the auditory objectives listed can be used with any child needing to acquire auditory skills if the activities used to teach the skills are appropriate to the child's developmental level.

A hearing-impaired child who achieves *all* of the landmarks and objectives in the Infant Auditory section of the curriculum is using his aided residual hearing to understand most of what is said to him during daily routines through audition alone. He is following conversation in a group of three to four people, and is acquiring information incidentally from overhearing the conversations of people talking near him. While the majority of children who have graduated from IHR at or near age four have not yet acquired these most advanced skills, a number of children with moderate, severe, and severe-profound losses have passed all the objectives in the Infant Auditory section of the curriculum prior to graduation.

PRESYMBOLIC COMMUNICATION

The Infant Presymbolic Communication section of *Parent-Infant Communication* delineates the sequence of behaviors that the infant uses to communicate his wants or needs before he can produce spoken or signed words. This section was added to the Third Edition of *Parent-Infant Communication* because of our growing recognition of the importance of presymbolic communication as the foundation for symbolic communication. Presymbolic Communication objectives trace infant communication from non-intentional communication, e.g., first cries, to intentional communication, e.g., gestures. Cooing, babbling, gestures, and vocal and motor imitation — all precursors of symbolic language, including speech — fall into the category of presymbolic communication. The objectives in this section demonstrate the importance of presymbolic communication interactions between the infant and his caregivers as the motivating force behind the infant's desire to learn to use symbolic language. Presymbolic communication usage leads into symbolic communication usage. However, all of us continue to use the gestures and vocalizations acquired as presymbolic communication to convey meaning throughout our lives.

RECEPTIVE AND EXPRESSIVE LANGUAGE

The Infant Receptive and Expressive Language section of *Parent-Infant Communication* begins with the acquisition of symbolic receptive language at nine months of age and with use of symbolic expressive language at 10-12 months of age. Objectives delineate the develoment of both receptive and expressive language as they are acquired by normally hearing children to four years of age. Receptive language refers to spoken or signed words that the child understands. Expressive language is the spoken or signed words that the child uses to express his ideas, desires, and feelings, and to ask questions. The receptive and expressive language categories are interrelated, with the child first demonstrating understanding of a word and then using it spontaneously (without prior modeling) and meaningfully to convey what he wants or thinks.

The objectives in the Infant Receptive and Expressive Language section of *Parent-Infant Communication* follow the sequence of English language development as it occurs in normally hearing and otherwise normally developing children. The hearing-impaired child can acquire understanding and production of language in this same sequence, although the age and rate at which language is acquired may be different from that of the normally hearing child. The sequence in which a child acquires both receptive and expressive language is similar whether a child is learning through the auditory-oral mode or through the auditory-oral with signed English modes if two important rules are observed.

First, children must be able to receive language through one or more sensory input channels before they can understand or use it themselves. Normally hearing children learn language because they hear it. A hearing-impaired child must receive language input through hearing or vision or both. It is not our purpose to argue the merits of communication modes here. **The point is that a child will not learn language if he does not have a consistent and reliable way to receive it.**

Second, non-handicapped children learn the symbolic language that is modeled for them. They learn Chinese, for example, if that is the language used in their environment. Hearing-impaired children learn symbolic language as it is *modeled for them* and as it is *received by them*. If the language that is modeled is incomplete or if the child can receive only a portion of what is modeled, that is what he will learn. If the hearing-impaired child receives complete English language through hearing speech, he will learn English (assuming there are no other handicapping conditions which complicate language acquisition). If he receives complete English language through hearing and seeing a combination of spoken and signed English, he will also learn English.

ACTIVITIES

The Activities section of *Parent-Infant Communication* contains 159 activities specific to curricular objectives. It also includes additional play activities, fingerplays, and body movement games that promote the child's cognitive skill development and acquisition and use of language. The activities are intended to suggest ways in which specific objectives can be taught. We rely on the specialists using the curriculum to be creative in developing additional teaching activities.

THE PARENT CURRICULUM

The parent curriculum sections of *Parent-Infant Communication* contain 325 information and skills objectives in four areas and 52 handouts which can be given to parents to teach and reinforce the objectives. The content of the four curricular areas is outlined below.

GENERAL INFORMATION AND SKILLS OBJECTIVES

1. Factors Which Affect Your Child's Acquisition of Skills.
2. Teaching Your Child Through Play and Daily Activities.
3. Becoming an Accurate Observer and Reporter of Your Child's Behaviors.
4. Modifying Your Child's Behaviors.
5. Family Involvement.
6. Coordinating Services for Your Multi-Handicapped Child.

DEVELOPMENT OF AUDITORY SKILLS

1. Hearing Aids.
2. Information About Audition.
3. Teaching Your Child to Listen.

DEVELOPMENT OF PRESYMBOLIC COMMUNICATION

DEVELOPMENT OF RECEPTIVE AND EXPRESSIVE LANGUAGE

1. Modifying Adult Language Directed to the Child.
2. Promoting Your Child's Receptive and Expressive Language Development.

The objectives in *Parent-Infant Communication* tell the parent-infant specialist *what* to teach parents. This volume, *Parent-Infant Habilitation*, is intended to tell the reader *how* these objectives are taught at Infant Hearing Resource. Each of the subject areas listed above has a corresponding section in Parts II through VI of this volume.

THE HABILITATION SETTINGS AT INFANT HEARING RESOURCE

Habilitation activities for IHR families occur at three sites: the agency, the families' homes, and the audiological suite. Family participation consists of two individual sessions per week and two or three group sessions per month at the agency, one session in the family's home each month, and audiological evaluations as needed. When a family enrolls at IHR, they are assigned a parent-infant specialist with whom they will work during individual sessions, audiological evaluations, and home visits.

HABILITATION ACTIVITIES AT THE AGENCY

INDIVIDUAL SESSIONS

Most families meet with their parent-infant specialist for two 50- minute sessions each week. One or both parents, a regular caregiver other than the parents, or an adult member of the extended family must accompany the child to sessions. Siblings can also come to sessions. During habilitation sessions parents, specialist, and child work together to achieve both parent and child objectives. Time during individual sessions is also spent in developing the parent-specialist partnership, talking about the parents' feelings and concerns, evaluating the function of the child's hearing aids, making new earmolds, and observing and evaluating the child's behaviors.

There is no set pattern of activities that occurs during every individual habilitation session. While the specialist does have several teaching activities planned for the 50-minute period, needs or questions expressed by parents upon arrival at the agency take precedence over planned activities. The specialist has the freedom to alter her lesson plan in response to the family's needs. The agency does not establish any schedule of objectives that must be accomplished during a set period of time for each family. It is a simple fact of life that dozens of variables affect the pace at which each family acquires information and skills. The job of the specialist is to help families learn and to present new information and skill objectives when previous objectives are met.

BENEFITS OF AGENCY SESSIONS

There are several benefits that come from holding individual sessions with each family at the agency. We have maintained agency-based sessions, rather than conduct all sessions in the families' homes, to take advantage of these benefits. These benefits are: access to equipment, materials, and supplies; observation by other staff; interaction with other families; limited distractions for parents; and efficient use of the parent-infant specialists' time.

Access to Equipment. Infant Hearing Resource has a hearing aid test box, an impedance audiometer, a pure tone audiometer with sound-field capacity, and videotape equipment on the premises. All of this equipment is used on a daily basis with families. Because properly functioning hearing aids are essential to the child's use of his residual hearing, parents are taught to test their child's aids on the hearing aid test box on a weekly basis. When there is a question about the function of the child's middle ear system, the parent-infant specialist can perform impedance testing to determine if middle ear function is normal. If results suggest middle ear dysfunction, the specialist can advise the parent to take the child to his physician for medical examination. Children enrolled at IHR are taught the skill of giving a conditioned response to sound when they are 18-24 months of age (Chapter 17). They are able to learn and practice this task using the audiometer and sound field speakers in one of the teaching rooms at IHR. The child who has acquired this skill is able to participate in play audiometry when being tested by the audiologist. Finally, videotape is frequently used during sessions with families for instructional purposes and to record child and parent progress. It would not be possible or practical for all the parent-infant specialists to carry these pieces of equipment with them on home visits.

There are also materials and supplies available at IHR which are readily accessible should the need arise. Materials for re-tubing an earmold, loaner hearing aids to substitute for malfunctioning aids, educational handouts for parents, and library books can be provided immediately when a problem or question arises.

Observation by other staff. Two of the teaching rooms at IHR have observation rooms from which staff and visitors can observe habilitation sessions in progress. Whenever a specialist has a question about a child or parent, she can ask other specialists to observe the session and give her feedback. Sometimes a specialist is feeling some resistance from a parent in carrying out a recommendation. Despite the specialist's best efforts to elicit the parent's feelings about the issue, a stalemate has been reached. Sometimes another specialist, after watching the parent-specialist interaction, can suggest other ways in which the issue might be approached. Sometimes a child's behavior or development is of concern to the specialist. Utilizing the expertise of other specialists can be very helpful in pinpointing causes of child behaviors. Every specialist at IHR has one or more areas of habilitation that are her own particular area of interest. Being able to draw on the knowledge and experience of more than one specialist is extremely valuable to families.

Interaction with other families. Almost every morning, from two to six families come for sessions at IHR. They congregate in the waiting room before and after their sessions. The children argue over whose turn it is on the rocking horse and the parents talk. These informal moments are very important to both parents and children. The children, who may have come to know each other in group sessions, have another opportunity to see their buddies. The parents have an understanding listener with whom to share their latest triumphs and challenges. Parents are a significant source of support to each other. Encounters at the agency give them access to that support.

Limited distraction for parents. When parents come to the agency with their child they can leave behind the unfinished business at home or at the office. They are now in an environment where the focus is on them and their child. They do not need to handle unexpected phone calls. They do not even need to supply the toys for their child! Habilitation sessions at the agency give the parents an uninterrupted period of time in which to focus on their own needs and the needs of their child. Some families report that there are times when making it to habilitation sessions is not easy, but they come in spite of the difficulties. We have had families attend IHR for two sessions each week when attendance required them to spend up to 1 1/2 hours in the car each way. Such commitment from parents is not rare when their needs and the needs of their child are being met by the habilitation program.

Efficient use of specialists' time. When sessions are held at the agency the specialist can use her time planning and carrying out activities related to habilitation rather than in driving from one home to another. Given that each session with a family requires at least one hour outside of the session to plan activities and record results, it is necessary for specialists to have adequate time for these essential parts of the habilitation process.

Habilitation at IHR is heavily weighted in the direction of agency- based sessions. Each family has a home visit once a month (discussed later in chapter). This formula works well for the families enrolled and for our staff. Families of hearing-impaired infants in the Portland metropolitan area can choose to enroll in one of several parent-infant programs that are available to them. If the habilitation schedule at IHR does not meet their needs, they can opt to enroll in another program. This is not to say that we do not adjust habilitation schedules for individual families; not every family enrolled attends three sessions a week. However, we do not serve any families through a schedule of home visits alone.

REGULARLY SCHEDULED GROUP SESSIONS

CHILD GROUPS

Hearing-impaired infants and toddlers enrolled for habilitation are grouped by age or communication levels for play/learning activities two or three times a month while the parent group is meeting. Sometimes preschool-age siblings also attend these groups. The activities planned for the child groups incorporate objectives from the following areas of child development: cognition, audition, receptive and expressive language, perceptual and fine motor, self-help, and socialization. Self-help and socialization activities promote the children's development of self-confidence and appropriate assertiveness, acceptance of responsibility, turn-taking, sharing, following directions, and different types of play. Preschool teachers who work with IHR graduates report that this group experience produces children with much higher readiness for preschool learning activities than that of children with no prior group experience.

An older sister and a grandmother assist the parent-infant specialist during the weekly group session for the "younger set" at IHR.

PARENT GROUPS

For the past several years, parent and child groups have met at IHR either two or three mornings each month for an hour and a half. Parent meetings are conducted in the library while the children meet in groups in the three teaching rooms. Because many of the families enrolled at Infant Hearing Resource travel from outlying areas, evening meetings have not proven convenient for families. A decision was made to hold parent meetings during the day, the rationale being that it is better to have one parent attend (if both are not employed outside the home) than to have neither attend. In fact, attendance at the daytime meetings has been consistently better than was attendance at evening meetings. The percentage of families represented at parent meetings varies from year to year. Some years enrollment at IHR consists mainly of families in which both parents are employed outside the home and neither is able to take time off except for regularly scheduled individual sessions with their child. Other years attendance is higher because, in most families enrolled, one parent is not employed outside the home. Parent meetings are planned each year with the needs of enrolled families in mind, so the topics presented from year to year vary.

Parent group meetings have two purposes: 1) to give parents the opportunity to get to know and provide support for each other, and 2) to allow for the presentation of information of interest to all parents. The purpose of each meeting is determined in advance by the IHR staff so that the individual who is leading the meeting is clear as to whether the focus is on providing information or on therapy and support. Information/discussion groups have a defined topic and are generally led by a staff person or a guest speaker. Since conveying information is the main objective, these sessions are not structured to focus on the sharing of experiences and conversational exchange that occurs between parents. The therapeutic/support groups, on the other hand, are designed and conducted so that the parents' thoughts and feelings are the focus. Parents are encouraged to air their experiences and feelings in this environment of acceptance and trust. The group leader comes prepared to facilitate discussion among the parents that provides them with validation and support for their feelings and ideas.

INFORMATION/DISCUSSION GROUPS FOR PARENTS

The IHR staff has experimented with the format and content of informational parent groups. There have been some years when the families enrolled have fallen into two distinct groups: enrolled one year or longer, and newly enrolled. During these years the staff has divided the parents into two groups, with membership in each group dependent on the length of enrollment. The staff was then better able to meet the informational needs of newly enrolled parents and the more advanced needs of parents who had already acquired basic information about hearing loss and how it affects their child and family. Information/discussion groups led by IHR specialists were structured to allow for dissemination of information, parent discussion, signed language practice, and guided observation of the play groups in which their children were participating.

Parent informational meetings address a mixture of topics which have been selected by the parents at the beginning of the year. Topics covered in a typical year are:

- "Behavior Management," led by family counselor.
- "Growing Up with a Hearing-Impaired Sibling," discussion with high school and college-age students who have hearing-impaired siblings.
- "Sibling Relationships and Extended Family Relationships," led by a family counselor.
- "Having A Child with Special Needs — Am I Trying to be a Superparent?", led by a family counselor.
- "Choosing Toys Which Are Appropriate For My Child," led by an early childhood specialist.
- "Child Abuse," led by a psychologist from the Oregon State School for the Deaf.
- "Stages of Child Development and the Impact of Hearing Loss," led by a psychologist from the Oregon State School for the Deaf.
- "Being a Wise Consumer of Psychological Evaluations," led by a psychologist from the Oregon State School for the Deaf.
- "How to Serve as Your Child's Educational Advocate," led by an IHR parent-infant specialist.
- "Overview of Public Law #94-142," led by the area representative from the Coalition in Oregon for Parent Education (COPE).

Promoting communication among the children is a major purpose of the weekly group session for two and three-year-olds.

- Panel of deaf teenagers.
- Panel of deaf adults.
- A special evening meeting held early in the school year to give parents an opportunity to meet some of the members of the IHR Board of Directors. Board members tell parents about their responsibilities for agency direction and management. They discuss the agency budget with parents and tell them about the sources of funding which will be tapped to fund agency activities. They invite parents to participate in fund-raising activities conducted by the Board if parents are able to do so.
- An evening meeting in the spring to discuss the public school program into which most IHR graduates enroll, led by the Director of the Columbia Regional Program for the Hearing Impaired, the Supervisor of the District and Regional Assessment Center, and the Supervisor of the Special Needs Program.
- Visits to local classrooms for the hearing-impaired at several public and private schools, with parents accompanied by IHR staff.

THERAPEUTIC/SUPPORT GROUPS FOR PARENTS

Participation in a regularly scheduled therapy/support group which is led by a skilled counselor is a critical need of most parents of children with handicaps. Each year, many of the parent group meetings are designed to allow parents to address the feelings they have resulting from their child's disability. It is sometimes a challenging task to find a skilled counselor who is knowledgeable about the impact of hearing loss on a family to lead these groups. IHR specialists have not always been able to find such an individual.

Motivating parents to attend a first meeting in which their feelings are the topic can also be a difficult task. During these 15 years of our work with parents at IHR, we have noted that parents seem to give priority to aspects of the habilitation program which meet their child's needs rather than to aspects of the program which address their own needs. This parental perception that their own needs are less deserving of time is directly opposed to the view of specialists at IHR. It is our experience that parents are most effective with their handicapped child when they have skilled assistance in dealing with the feelings that evolve from their child's handicapping condition and the changes the family must make in adapting to the handicap. Once parents have attended a group led by a skilled counselor who creates an environment of safety in which to talk about feelings, motivating parents to attend is no longer an issue. Learning that other parents have the same feelings they do is a powerful and healing experience that most parents are eager to repeat.

When the counselor meets with a group of parents who find it especially difficult to initiate talk about feelings, the counselor may lead successive sessions so that discussion proceeds from issues related to the children, to the children within the family complex, and then to parental issues, concerns, and feelings. The development of a mutual support system among parents is a major purpose of the group. As the parents share their experiences with each other, they create a strong network of support that overflows the limits of the ninety-minute group and continues to exist past the time families graduate from IHR.

SPECIAL GROUPS SESSIONS

SESSIONS FOR FATHERS

In the "ideal" parent-infant program, both parents would be able to attend all the individual and group sessions which are offered to their family. This "ideal" is not reality for most families enrolled at IHR. While each year there are a number of families in which both parents attend or alternate attendance at sessions, there are also families in which one parent is not able to attend any of the sessions. Generally, it has been the father who cannot participate in sessions. Specialists at IHR want to provide some service for these fathers. Again, the ideal would be to hold frequent sessions that address the needs of fathers. At IHR it is not possible to do so. Meetings of this kind generally must be held on Saturday mornings and, for financial and staffing reasons, IHR is able to present just one or two such special meetings each year.

Fathers who are able to attend their child's individual habilitation sessions have the opportunity to discuss their feelings with the parent-infant specialist on an ongoing basis. Fathers who attend signed language classes get to know both the signed language instructor and other class participants with whom they can talk about mutual concerns. Fathers who can attend neither regular habilitation sessions with their child nor signed language classes are usually at a disadvantage in their understanding of their child's handicap and its effect on themselves, their child, and their family. Some fathers are uncertain about what is happening during the habilitation process. If the father and mother have a well-established pattern of clear and frequent communication, this disadvantage may be diminished. However, if communication between the parents is limited, the father can come to feel more and more estranged both from the child and from the mother who may, in turn, grow to resent her unshared responsibility for the child's habilitation.

A group of fathers in attendance at a Saturday morning meeting may be composed of men whose emotional states and intellectual grasps of hearing loss vary widely. For this reason the fathers' meetings that IHR has offered have been led, in the past, by a male psychologist who is familiar with deafness and the effects a deaf child has on the family. A male sign language interpreter is also employed. The objective of these meetings has been to give the fathers an opportunity to talk about the feelings they have related to their child. It is important, therefore, that the individual who leads the fathers' meetings be highly skilled at eliciting discussion and comments from the fathers present. Since many of the fathers in attendance are not familiar with each other, disclosing their feelings can be a scary proposition. The leader works to establish an atmosphere of relaxation, safety, and camaraderie. This has sometimes been done by the counselor recounting a brief personal anecdote in which everyday, colloquial language and humor are used to set the tone of a "man-to-man" exchange as opposed to a "professional-to-client" interaction.

One way in which the leader may elect to set this tone is to share a brief summary of his experience with hearing-impaired individuals. He may also elect to describe his own family, possibly including an anecdote related to a crisis area that the family is presently working on (e.g., "Our older boy has been having a lot of trouble in school lately. He seems to have a problem learning to read. My wife and I haven't figured out if it's embarrassment about that or what, but he has become a real behavior problem for the teachers. Our family is currently putting a lot of energy into this and it has put a strain on us since my wife and I don't always have the same ideas about what we should do.") In this introduction, the leader establishes a pattern for the type of information he would like each father to share with the group, including the possibility of describing current problem spots.

Once the introductions are complete, the leader can use a series of questions to direct the discussion toward the feelings associated with the impact that a hearing-impaired child has on the family. "How has your family life changed since your child's hearing loss was diagnosed?" and "How has your hearing-impaired child affected your marriage?" are excellent questions. The experiences and feelings expressed by one father can be summarized and directed to another father as a way of encouraging other members of the group to talk about their situation. "Bob, John has said that his initial reaction to learning about his daughter's hearing loss was extreme depression and hopelessness. What kinds of feelings have you been dealing with since learning about your boy's hearing loss a few months ago?"

A leader who is helping group members explore feelings must be aware that some participants will feel a need for further discussion and support once the issue of feelings has been broached. If the agency is unable to provide discussion groups on a continuing basis, the leader must be prepared to offer options to those group members who demonstrate an interest in or need for additional help. The leader may provide all group members with a list of local agencies or counselors who could be of help; he may be willing to lead additional group sessions on a private basis with group members underwriting the cost of the sessions themselves. The leader might also suggest to group participants that their wives are likely to be experiencing feelings similar to some of those expressed during the session and that participants might want to use some of the information shared as a springboard for discussion at home.

Crowley, Keane, and Needham (1982) describe the goals and outcomes of a program for fathers of hearing-impaired children conducted at St. Joseph's School for the Deaf.

SESSIONS FOR EXTENDED FAMILY

Members of the extended family are almost always involved to varying degrees in the habilitation process for the child and his parents. The child's grandparents, who may live half-way across the country, may still figure prominently in day-to-day decisions that are made by the child's parents. In some cases the input from extended family members is supportive of and helpful to the parents. In other cases relatives or close friends may contribute to the level of stress the parents are experiencing by offering advice and solutions that are in opposition to what the parents hear from professionals. Diagnosis of hearing loss in a grandchild is devastating for many grandparents who experience pain and sorrow not only for the baby who has impaired hearing, but for their own grown child who is grieving because of the baby's handicap.

Many grandparents and older aunts and uncles have peers who have had a hearing loss that has been surgically treated so that normal hearing has been restored. Unaware of the different causes and types of hearing loss, they assume, when the child's hearing loss is diagnosed, that it too can be restored to normal with surgery. Parents of a child with hearing loss, confronted with their own parents' insistence that they carry out a course of action they have been told by professionals is inappropriate, often feel conflict: should we satisfy our parents at the risk of annoying the professionals, or should we stand by the professionals' advice, thus risking loss of parental support (not to mention hearing, "I told you so," at some future date)? If parents of a child with hearing loss have not established an adult-to-adult relationship with their own parents, it will be very difficult for them to transmit information and to share their concerns without appearing to be seeking advice and direction that is, in fact, unwanted.

Grandparents, aunts and uncles, and close family friends are an important source of support for parents who are raising a child with impaired hearing. Sometimes, feeling inadequate because they lack information about hearing loss and its effect on the child, relatives and friends pull away from parents at the very time parents need support the most. The agency serving hearing-impaired infants and their parents can provide a valuable service to families by offering informational sessions to their extended

The participation of grandparents has benefits for the entire family.

families and close friends. IHR has held two types of Saturday morning meetings — informational and therapeutic — for extended families and friends. The first type incorporates three to four 20 to 30-minute mini-sessions covering topics such as: Types and Causes of Hearing Loss, What Hearing Aids Can and Cannot Do, Services Offered to Families at IHR, The Effect of Hearing Loss on a Child and His Family, and What It's Like to Grow Up Hearing Impaired. The second type of Saturday meeting for extended families has been led by a skilled counselor who is knowledgeable about deafness. The counselor talks about the feelings that members of the extended family may experience when they learn of the child's hearing loss. In the safety of these groups, some family members have voiced for the first time concerns, feelings, and needs which have been too frightening to express within the family unit. They receive answers to their questions, guidance and support from one another, and the affirmation that they are not alone in their feelings.

It has been the experience of the IHR staff that extended family members are extremely grateful to be included in informational and support sessions. Some grandparents have said that they have wanted to learn how to help their grown child and grandchild, but have refrained from asking how they could do so for fear of intruding. The degree to which children's handicaps affect their grandparents was illustrated clearly one year when, following an IHR meeting for extended family members, several sets of grandparents who first met during that meeting formed a support group on their own that evolved, over time, into a signed language practice group and into friendships that endure to this day.

HABILITATION ACTIVITIES IN THE FAMILIES' HOMES

At IHR, habilitation activities are carried out in the family's home as well as at the agency. Some parent-infant programs base all of their habilitation activities, except for audiological and assessment services, in the families' homes. Since IHR was founded, the staff has utilized a number of different schedules in which the ratio of agency to home sessions has varied. The present schedule, which has been employed for the past several years, includes one 50-minute session in each family's home every month.

BENEFITS OF HOME VISITS

Home visits are useful to the specialist and to the family for several reasons.

1. **A major advantage of holding sessions in the family's home is that parents can practice using normal daily activities and play to help their child acquire listening and language skills in the location where most of the child's learning will take place.** All of the resources which the parents will utilize to teach their child listening and language are present. For this reason the IHR specialist rarely brings any play materials to the home visit. The specialist can help the parent see how to use everyday caregiving activities such as feeding, diapering, and bathing as teaching opportunities. She can show the parent how to include the child in appropriate ways in everyday household activities such as doing laundry, vacuuming, and washing dishes. The specialist can demonstrate how to seat the child nearby as the parent does a task so that, without necessarily being directly involved if that is not age-appropriate, the child can hear the parent talking about and making noise with the objects the parent is using. During the home visit, the specialist can see what kinds of toys the family has for the child and, by modeling play interactions with the child using these toys, expand the parents' ideas for ways to use them. The specialist might also give suggestions for toys that would be appropriate for the child as he gets older.

2. **Home visits are useful because the specialist can observe the child's listening and language behaviors in the comfort and familiarity of the child's own home.** Some children behave very differently at home than they do in a new or different place. Parents can be frustrated by their child's "failure to perform" in the clinic setting. Meeting the child on his own turf may allow the specialist to see another side of the child's behavior. The child may be much more vocal or verbally assertive at home than he is in the clinic. It is equally true that he may be a "holy terror" at

home when he behaves like a perfect gentleman in clinic sessions. The specialist is likely to get a more accurate picture of the child's actual behaviors by seeing him at home. Having observed that the child's behaviors at home may be very different from clinic behaviors gives the specialist confidence in the parent's reports of child behaviors that the specialist has not personally observed.

3. **Having the responsibility for planning an activity that will take place during the home visit affirms for many parents that they are truly an equal member of the parent-specialist partnership.** While some parents may be "scared to death" at the thought of having to plan an activity, others are delighted to show the specialist how the child likes to play a special game at home. Parents who express an initial reluctance to plan an activity generally need guidance from the specialist in selecting something to do. In the clinic session prior to the home visit, the specialist and parent can brainstorm some possible activities and may even decide on one together. Specialists need to remember to reinforce parents for their choice of activity and find positive things to say about the activity even when the parent judges that it was a "bomb."

4. **The relaxed atmosphere of a home can often facilitate discussion of the parent's feelings and concerns about his child.** Regardless of how much reassurance they receive, some parents hesitate to bring up personal issues related to their child during clinic sessions for fear of disrupting the activities the specialist has planned. These parents may feel more "in charge" while meeting with the specialist in their own home and thus more likely to give themselves permission to raise their concerns. IHR specialists do not go to the family's home with the same type of lesson plan they have for clinic sessions. Giving the parent responsibility for the agenda of the home visit tells the parent that they can deal with whatever issue is most pressing for them, whether it be figuring out how to involve the child while cooking dinner or talking about an upsetting disagreement with a spouse over child-rearing practices or hearing aid use.

RESOLVING POTENTIAL PROBLEMS
ASSOCIATED WITH HOME VISITS

The home environment is fraught with interruptions. Rarely does a parent who is at home on a regular basis with young children have an hour that, first, starts on schedule and, second, is not interrupted by a phone call, a knock at the door, or a childhood "disaster." The hectic pace at home may be one reason so many parents enjoy the ivory-tower atmosphere of the agency sessions. Though sessions at the clinic are occasionally disrupted by a fire drill, not once has the phone rung with an encyclopedia salesperson on the other end of the line!

The most effective way to deal with interruptions during home visits is to anticipate them beforehand and come to agreement with each parent about how the interruptions will be handled. Some common types of disruptions and suggestions of ways to agree on handling them are discussed below.

One difficulty might occur because the parent is not ready for the specialist when she arrives. Maybe the parent overslept, had to make an emergency trip out of the house, or inadvertently scheduled a conflicting appointment. The specialist's feelings of irritation and disappointment are likely to be in direct proportion to the distance she has traveled to get to the family's home and the frequency with which this lack of readiness has occurred. It is understandable, however, that unexpected situations arise that change a family's schedule at the last minute. The specialist and parents can agree that if the parent knows in advance that the specialist should not come, the parent can call the specialist at home the evening before or morning of the home visit. If something comes up after the specialist has started on her home visits, the family can call the agency and the staff there may be able to reach the specialist at another family's home.

Disruption in the home visit schedule may also occur because something unexpected happens. On some occasions a parent has met the specialist at the door feeling somewhat embarrassed because the hearing-impaired child has just fallen asleep. This seemingly unfortunate circumstance most often turns into a bonus: the parent and specialist have an hour to talk and to plan future activities. Some of the most fruitful interactions can take place when an unscheduled event occurs. Grandma drops in for a surprise visit? Great — get her involved. The neighbor has an emergency and needs to leave her four-year-old with the family who is expecting the specialist to arrive any minute? Fine — let the four-year-old participate in the interactions with the child.

A common interruption occurs when the phone or doorbell rings while the specialist is at the family's home. It is very important to establish beforehand that, except for emergency calls, the parent will say firmly that he is unavailable to talk and will get back to the caller after the session is finished. The parent and specialist should also agree to turn off the television or radio during the visit since they not only serve as distractors but also provide background noise that makes it more difficult for the hearing-impaired child to hear the parents' and specialist's voices.

Other children may disrupt the activities planned for the hearing-impaired child. This situation is discussed in Chapter 15. Parents should agree to take responsibility for either including young siblings in the activities planned for the hearing-impaired child or for providing siblings with play materials that they can use with relatively little supervision. While it is not wise to exclude siblings regularly from sessions, sometimes it will be necessary to do so. The siblings' feelings of importance can be preserved if the parents can provide something special for them to do during that period and can also offer to spend time alone with them later in the day. If sibling behaviors are persistently disruptive, it is appropriate to use home visit time to plan a program of behavior change as described later in this chapter and outlined in detail in Chapter 15.

Finally, the purpose of the home visit is impeded if the home visit evolves into a purely social event. Some parents feel a desire or obligation to feed and entertain the specialist when she comes to their home. While all of us love this tendency in parents and the resulting "goodies" we may be invited to consume, it is necessary to discourage it in the interest of achieving habilitation goals and objectives. There is nothing wrong with having a cup of coffee while talking with parents, but it should not interfere with the activities the parent has planned.

It is natural that a strong parent-specialist partnership may develop into friendship as the family and specialist share feelings and experiences in their work together. These friendships are a benefit of a job well done. The specialist must insure, however, that when she is interacting with the family in a professional capacity, she adheres to the agreement she has made with the parents to work on habilitation goals. If discussion during home visits veers toward social topics the specialist can gently get them back on track with a remark such as, "I would like to hear more about that. Let's have lunch together tomorrow after our session at the agency," or "I can stay a few minutes longer today — tell me about that later!"

Talking about problem situations that occur during the home visit is an important part of the developing parent-specialist partnership. It can feel very awkward for the specialist to bring up issues in which family practices or home routines appear to interfere with effective habilitation. The practice of having the television on during home visits and for most of the day as "company" is a good example of a habit that does not benefit the hearing-impaired child. Even when it is uncomfortable to say something, it is essential that the specialist take a deep breath and address the issue. The fact is that many parents are unaware of the ways in which family habits such as maintaining constant background noise may adversely affect their child's ability to acquire listening and communication skills. Once they acquire new information, they are often eager to make changes that will benefit their child.

HABILITATION ACTIVITIES IN THE AUDIOLOGICAL SUITE

The third site in which IHR habilitation activities occur is the audiological suite. Audiological assessment and hearing aid evaluation are discussed in detail in Chapter 6. These services are an essential part of the habilitation process for the child. There may be periods of time during the habilitation process when obtaining audiological data is the most important activity. Time spent gathering this data should never be regarded as less important than other habilitation activities. The child's ability to develop a well-functioning auditory input and processing system is dependent on his wearing the most appropriate amplification system. If a series of sessions needs to be held in the audiological suite gaining information about the child's auditory abilities, IHR specialists do not feel that "learning time" is being lost. This time spent is an investment which will enable the child to learn about his world through sound.

CHAPTER 3

ASSESSMENT AND RECORD KEEPING

Assessment of the Child
- Audiological Assessment
- Assessment of the Child's Level of Function in Auditory, Language and Vocal/Speech Development
- Assessment of Other Areas of Child Development
- Conditions Necessary to Promote Accurate Assessment of the Child

Assessment of Parent Information and Skills

Record Keeping
- Types of Records Maintained
- Principles Governing Record Keeping at IHR

ASSESSMENT OF THE CHILD

Three types of assessment are done with children enrolled at IHR. These are audiological assessment; assessment of the child's level of function in auditory, language and vocalization/speech development; and assessment of other areas of child development.

AUDIOLOGICAL ASSESSMENT

The goals and procedures of audiological assessment and hearing aid evaluation are described in detail in Part II. Assessment is an ongoing process shared by the audiologist, parent-infant specialist, and parents. The tools used in audiologic assessment are:

1. Audiometric testing using pure tones, voice, and environmental sounds under both unaided (sound-field and earphone) and aided conditions.
2. Tympanometry and acoustic reflex testing.
3. Auditory Brainstem Response Testing.
4. Observation of the child's responsiveness to sound at home, in the clinic, and at large.

Data gathered from the sources listed above are factored into the decision of what amplification systems to select for the child to use for trial periods and eventually for purchase. Other variables that figure in this decision are monaural vs. binaural placement, ear-level vs. body aids, frequency response of aids, maximum power output of aids, determination of amount of appropriate gain, and type of earmold (see Chapter 6).

ASSESSMENT OF THE CHILD'S LEVEL OF FUNCTION
IN AUDITORY, LANGUAGE, AND
VOCAL/SPEECH DEVELOPMENT

Parent-infant specialists at IHR use the following resources for initial and on-going assessment of an infant's level of communication function:

1. The criterion-referenced sequence of infant objectives from the following sections of *Parent-Infant Communication* (Infant Hearing Resource, 1985): Auditory, Presymbolic Communication, and Receptive/Expressive Language.
2. Observation of the child's communication interactions.
3. Parent report.
4. Diagnostic teaching (see Chapter 16).

IHR specialists do not administer a standardized test to determine a child's levels of auditory and language function. Specialists regard assessment as a *process* that takes place over time and involves gathering data about the child's skills as he interacts with his environment. This view is supported by research conducted at the University of Bristol School of Education (1978) in which the investigators set out to learn more about how children learn to communicate through language. The investigators followed for 2½ years two groups of children who were ages 15 and 39 months at the beginning of the study. The investigators compared the information about the children's language acquired from two sources: spontaneous communication at home and tests of linguistic comprehension and imitation. The investigators concluded that:

"1. There is no single measure that serves as a reliable general index of language development over the whole range studied from 15 to 60 months . . .

"2. There is only a weak relationship between measures of children's performance on language tests administered under controlled conditions and developmental measures derived from spontaneous speech.

"3. Taken together, the findings concerning measures of language development derived from spontaneous speech and those derived from tests indicate the inappropriateness of using any single measure as an index of general linguistic development."

At IHR, assessment of child auditory and communication skills is carried out during initial habilitation sessions, at which time baseline, or entering, behaviors observed by the specialist or reported by the parents are recorded on the Infant Curriculum Checksheet and on the appropriate Record Sheets (see the Record Keeping section which follows in this chapter). Assessment continues throughout the child's enrollment and is the basis for selecting appropriate learning objectives for the child. As one objective is achieved, a subsequent objective which builds on the newly acquired skill is selected. The objectives being taught determine the content of the activities presented to the child and the way in which the activities are presented. *The Sequenced Inventory of Communication Development* (Hedrick, Prather, and Tobin, 1984) is a tool which IHR specialists are beginning to use as a cross-check to confirm periodically the receptive and expressive language acquisition of enrolled children.

ASSESSMENT OF OTHER AREAS OF CHILD DEVELOPMENT

Specialists at IHR utilize "The Early Intervention Developmental Profile" from *Developmental Programming for Infants and Young Children* (Schafer, Moersch, and D'Eugenio, 1985-86) to screen an infant's performance in the six areas listed in the profile. These areas are: cognitive, social/emotional, gross motor, perceptual/fine motor, self-help, and language. The information gained from the language development sections is also used as a cross-check on the information gained from this same area in *Parent-Infant Communication*. The information obtained from the profile in the other five areas is used to determine if the child is functioning within normal limits for his age. *Early-LAP: The Early Learning Accomplishment Profile for Developmentally Young Children Birth to 36 Months*, (Glover, Preminger, and Sanford, 1978) is another tool which assesses development between 0-36 months in the six areas of gross motor, fine motor, cognitive, language, self-help and social/emotional. If the child's performance on either of these assessment tools indicates a serious delay in one or more areas tested, a referral is made for further evaluation.

While IHR specialists do not use standardized tests to measure the child's language achievement, we do rely on standardized tools to measure other areas of the child's development. Evaluation is done by having a professional from the discipline in question come to IHR to carry out the assessment or the family is referred to professionals at another agency to obtain the necessary assessment information.

CONDITIONS NECESSARY TO PROMOTE
ACCURATE ASSESSMENT OF THE CHILD

Assessment of young hearing-impaired children is not always easy. To obtain valid and reliable results that accurately reflect the performance of the child, four conditions should be considered. These are:
1. Assure the comfort of the child.
2. Allow sufficient time.

3. Make certain that assessment activities are reinforcing to the child.
4. Have the child's parents present.

   First, the assessment should be done in a place and by an individual with whom the child is comfortable. The child's comfort can be achieved even in a new site with a total stranger if the evaluator allows time for the child to explore the environment and to let the child interact with him as the child is ready. This may mean that the evaluator is seated on the floor with several toys that are age-appropriate for the child scattered near him when the child arrives. As the child begins to investigate and play with the toys, the evaluator can use friendly verbal and non-verbal reinforcers that let the child know that the child is in control. Ten to fifteen minutes spent in establishing a trust relationship with the child can make the difference between a child who willingly engages in assessment activities and thus accurately displays his capabilities, and a child who refuses to participate in any of the interactions required to assess his performance.
Second, it should be acknowledged that assessment requires time. We all know that young children can attend to somewhat structured activities for only a limited amount of time before they lose interest and drift away. The evaluator who is familiar with the evaluation tool will be able to move swiftly from one activity to the next, thus decreasing the likelihood of the child wandering off. As long as the child's interest is piqued by the frequent introduction of new materials he is likely to participate happily. In many instances, the evaluation of a young child requires more than one session. In fairness to the child a second evaluation session should be scheduled if the child begins to fade in the middle of the evaluation. This may be particularly true in the case of multi-handicapped children who may need more time to complete each task. The object of the evaluation is to acquire valid results on which to base habilitation objectives. Evaluation is of questionable benefit if the results do not reflect the child's optimal performance.
   Third, evaluators need to remember that successful assessment activities are reinforcing for the child. In an assessment session the child will be presented with tasks that he cannot perform in order to determine his upper limit of achievement. Perceived "failure" is a strong punisher for a child, just as it is for an adult. The evaluator will want to reinforce the child just as strongly for a good attempt as for successful accomplishment of a task.
   Finally, most assessments carried out with young children will go more smoothly if the child's parents are allowed to sit in on the evaluation. Asking parents to remain in the room usually creates two advantages. First, the child's level of anxiety is not accelerated by being alone in the room with an examiner who may be a stranger. Second, parents are more likely to accept the evaluation results when they can observe the evaluation. When parents have not observed the assessment, they may question the validity of results when an evaluator states that the child was unable to perform a task the

parents had seen him do at another time. If they are present in the room as the child tackles the task, they may see that the criteria for achievement differ from the child's usual performance. If parents do not accept evaluation findings they are unlikely to act on recommendations that result from the evaluation.

As the specialist works with different evaluators she can determine which evaluators follow assessment procedures that coincide most closely with these — and other — criteria that the specialist may feel are important. Specialists at IHR try to determine what procedures are followed at an evaluation site so that they can prepare the family and help them set expectations that correspond to what will happen during the evaluation session (see Chapter 25 for a further discussion of out-of-agency referrals).

ASSESSMENT OF PARENT INFORMATION AND SKILLS

Assessment of parents requires a delicate touch. In Part III we discuss the attitudes and feelings parents may have associated with being students whose assignment is to learn about the effects of their child's hearing loss and their role in the habilitation process. The specialist can gather a great deal of data simply by observing and talking to the parents. It is not necessary to give the parents a test to determine what they know about hearing loss and its remediation. Rather, the specialist can say, "Please let me know if I pass along information that is already familiar to you." While most normally hearing parents have very little knowledge about hearing loss, giving them the benefit of the doubt will always feel better to them than if the specialist assumes they are entirely without knowledge. As a specialist observes a parent demonstrating knowledge or skills that are contained in objectives, she can mark off the objective on the Parent Curriculum Checksheet as "achieved."

RECORD KEEPING

TYPES OF RECORDS MAINTAINED

Records of child and parent participation and achievement are kept in six ways at IHR:
1. Lesson plans.
2. Curriculum checksheets.
3. Record sheets.
4. Written reports.
5. Videotapes and audiotapes.
6. Office files.

The forms used for the first three record keeping methods listed above can be found in the Record Sheets section in *Parent-Infant Communication*. A brief description of how each is used at IHR is provided below.

LESSON PLANS

Prior to each clinic session with a family, the specialist completes the left-hand side of the lesson plan form (Figure 1). She briefly describes the activity and materials to be used and the child and parent objectives the activity is intended to address. Generally, each session includes activities to promote acquisition of objectives from all areas of development: auditory, presymbolic communication, and receptive and expressive language (including vocal/speech).

During the session, as the activity is carried out, the specialist jots down significant adult and child behaviors that are of interest. Rarely does an entire session go as planned. The parent may arrive with a concern to discuss or the child may decline to play with certain materials that are presented. The specialist must be creative, flexible, and open to utilizing the child's interests to teach objectives, even if those interests have no resemblance to the activities on the lesson plan.

At the end of the session (or later in the day) the specialist fills out the "Results" side of the form (Figure 2), then notes other comments, assignments, or reminders to herself for future lessons at the bottom of the form. The specialist keeps track of the dates of each session, the number of each session attended, and the adults who attend at the top of the lesson plan form. This information is used for billing purposes and for end-of-the-year written reports. The completed lesson plan provides the specialist with the data for filling out each child's Curriculum Checksheet and Record Sheets, and the parents' Curriculum Checksheet.

CURRICULUM CHECKSHEETS

The Infant and the Parent Curriculum Checksheets list objective numbers corresponding with the objectives in the sections of the Infant Curriculum and with the objectives in the sections of the Parent Curriculum. As the child or adult achieves an objective (the behavior which describes this achievement is recorded on the Lesson Plan) the date of achievement is written in next to the objective number on the Checksheet. There is also space by each objective number under the title "Description" to record what the child did to indicate achievement of the objective. Up-to-date Checksheets provide the following information to the specialist:

    1. At what developmental level the child is functioning in auditory

LESSON PLAN FORM
(objectives referred to below are in Parent-Infant Communication)

Child D.J. (age 11 mos)   Adult(s) _____   Date 10-17-86   Lesson No. 14 (week 4)

1. Activity: Call "D.J."; reinf. resp. w/ toy
   Child Objectives: Aud # V-2: awareness of voice
   Parent Objectives: Aud #35: factors affecting D.J.'s ability to hear voice (refer to her audiogram)
   Results:

2. Activity: Face-painting, miming in front of mirror
   Child Objectives: Presymb # Sp-34: child imitates adult facial expressions
   Parent Objectives: Model "funny faces". Discuss Presymb # 4: intents of presymb. commun.
   Results:

3. Activity: Observe D.J. during play w/ toy she selects
   Child Objectives: Presymb #37: How is she communicating?
   Parent Objectives: Presymb #3b: look for and record D.J.'s presymb communications
   Results:

4. Activity: Let D.J. play as we discuss last week's parent group in which
   Child Objectives: a parent of an older deaf child talked;
   Parent Objectives: talk about their feelings related to that meeting.

COMMENTS & ASSIGNMENTS:

FIGURE 1. The parent-infant specialist completes the left side of the Lesson Plan Form prior to a session with a family.

FIGURE 1.

LESSON PLAN FORM
(objectives referred to below are in Parent-Infant Communication)

Child DJ. (age 11 mos)   Adult(s) Jack + Marci   Date 10-17-86   Lesson No. 14 (week 4)

1. Activity: Call "D.J."; reinf. resp. w/ toy
Child Objectives: Aud #V-2: awareness of voice
Parent Objectives: Aud #35: Factors affecting DJ's ability to hear voice (refer to her audiogram)
Results: DJ did not turn to Marci's voice until Marci was about 18" away. DJ turned 3 times to Jack's voice at 2-3 feet. She liked getting a little ball to put into a hole in the top of a box. Jack + Marci will play this game w/ DJ at home.

2. Activity: Face-painting; miming in front of mirror
Child Objectives: Presymb# 5-34: child imitates adult facial expressions
Parent Objectives: Model "funny" faces; Discuss Presymb #4: intents of presymb. commun.
Results: DJ did not like having paint put on her face! Parents abandoned that and just made faces into a mirror. DJ imitated opening mouth wide and putting her hands on her cheeks. She vocalized "mmm" in imitation and "a-ya" spontan.

3. Activity: Observe DJ. during play w/ toys she selects
Child Objectives: Presymb #37: How is she communicating?
Parent Objectives: Presymb# 3b: look for and record DJ's presymb. communications
Results: Played w/ doll + cradle. Flopped doll around a lot and poked at face. Looked twice to Marci for help in getting doll out of cradle - vocalized "AAA" in combination w/ worried look as she pulled on doll. (See Presymb. Commun Record sheet)

4. Activity: Let DJ play as we discuss last week's parent group in which a parent of an older deaf child talked.
Child Objectives: (crossed out)
Parent Objectives: talk about their feelings related to that meeting.
Results: Jack was not at meeting-Marci had told him some of what was said. She had felt both hopeful and discouraged as she listened to parent at meeting. Wants DJ to be able to use more speech than other child is using now. We talked more about good speech develop. strategies. Jack wants to listen to audiotape of meeting - took tape home.

COMMENTS & ASSIGNMENTS:
- Gave them Parent Handout PH-89 "Presymbolic Communication: How an Infant Communicates Before He Uses Words"
- Jack will attend session next Thurs.- he will review PH-67 on audiogram at home and will tell me about DJ's latest audiogram, both aided and unaided.
-Reminder: videotape Marci + DJ next session as they play together.

FIGURE 2. The parent-infant specialist completes the right side of the Lesson Plan Form during and after a session with a family.

FIGURE 2.

skills, presymbolic communication, and receptive and expressive language.

2. What infant curriculum objectives should be taught next in each area.
3. The rate at which the child and the parents are achieving curriculum objectives (note dates of achievement of successive objectives in each area).
4. Whether the child is acquiring non-voice and voice auditory objectives at the same rate.
5. Whether the child is acquiring expressive language skills following acquisition of related receptive language skills.
6. In what mode(s), speech or sign or both, the child is acquiring receptive and expressive language.
7. The curriculum areas in which each parent has acquired information and skills.
8. The curriculum objectives which each parent has yet to acquire.

RECORD SHEETS

There are five record sheets in *Parent-Infant Communication* on which to keep data on infant skills:

1. *Auditory Development Record Sheet* on which each sound source is recorded as the child demonstrates awareness, recognition, and then comprehension of the sound.
2. *Presymbolic Communication Record Sheet* on which the child's communication behavior is described and the date the behavior appeared, both in imitation and spontaneously, is recorded. The context or the intent of the child's communication is also noted (Figure 3).
3. *Vocalization Record Sheet* on which the child's lalling, babbling, and jargon are recorded, using a phonetic system such as the International Phonetic Alphabet.
4. *Receptive and Expressive Language Record Sheet* on which words and phrases that the child understands and single words that the child uses expressively are recorded by mode (e.g., auditory only, speech, speech plus sign) and by category (e.g., names of toys, clothing; commands; places).
5. *Connected Expressive Language Record Sheet* on which the child's combinations of words are recorded (e.g., "Daddy bye-bye"). The mode of expression and the context and intent are also noted.

Data from these record sheets are used to determine which objectives the child has achieved, to plan subsequent teaching objectives, to describe progress in written reports, and for research purposes.

PRESYMBOLIC COMMUNICATION RECORD SHEET

NAME **D.J.**

Birthdate: 11-21-85
Enrolled : 9-15-86

I - Imitation
S - Spontaneous

CHILD'S COMMUNICATION BEHAVIOR	DATE ACCOMPLISHED I	S	CONTEXT/INTENT
At Enrollment			
- good eye contact w/ parents		✓	determined through
- smiles, laughs during interactions		✓	parent report,
- vocalizes vowels /ʌ/ and /ɑ/ both sustained + repeated		✓	observation of DJ,
- expresses "no" by crying, turning head away, pushing away w/ hand, crawling away		✓	and by going through Infant
- imitates clapping hands in "pat-a-cake" and banging with hand or spoon on a surface	✓		Objectives in "Presymbolic Commun"
- grabs parents' hands to get food during meals		✓	section of Par-Inf. Commun
During Enrollment			
- pointed to toy	9-23-86	10-11-86	wanted jack-in-the-box, bear
- banged on toy and looked at parent to get toy moving		10-11-86	
- high-pitched "ʌ-ʌ-ʌ"	10-14-86		parent vocalized while moving block, DJ imitated twice
- pointed to own nose, eyes	10-17-86		during play in front of mirror
- vocalized "mmm" w/ descending pitch during play on slide	10-17-86	10-17-86	imitated first, later did spontaneously
- wave bye-bye	10-19-86	10-24-86	when leaving session, imitated parent; did spon. at home while standing by door.

from <u>Parent-Infant Communication</u>
RS-31

FIGURE 3. The parent-infant specialist uses this form to record the way in which the child communicates before he can use symbolic language such as words and signs.

WRITTEN REPORTS

Three types of written reports are commonly produced at IHR: Reports of audiological findings; end-of-the-year, termination, or graduation reports; and special purpose reports.

REPORT OF AUDIOLOGICAL FINDINGS

Each time the child is seen by the audiologist, a report of the findings is written. This report, along with the audiogram generated during the visit, is sent to the child's physician(s), to the parents, and to professionals other than the IHR staff who see the child for evaluation or therapy. A copy of every report goes into the child's office file at Infant Hearing Resource. The specialist may choose to make a copy of the report or audiogram to keep with her lesson plans and record sheets for the child.Parents are encouraged to keep their copy of the child's audiogram and report in their notebook, which also contains written handouts provided to them during lessons.

END-OF-THE-YEAR, TERMINATION, OR GRADUATION REPORTS

At the end of every "school" year (end of July), or at any time during the year that a family terminates enrollment at IHR, specialists write a comprehensive report describing habilitation achievements for each family with whom they work.The format and content of this report is outlined in "Written Report Format" found in the Record Sheets section of *Parent-Infant Communication*. The purpose of this report is to document the child's and parents' achievements during the year in each area of the curriculum; to describe the child's hearing loss, amplification system, and present level of auditory function; to describe family participation in the habilitation process; to list objectives the child is ready to work on next in each curriculum area; to list a representative sample of the child's expressive language at the time of the report; and to make recommendations for action in the next year. If the child and family are graduating from IHR, this report will include a history of the child's achievements during his entire enrollment at IHR. Data from Lesson Plans, Record Sheets, and Curriculum Checksheets are all utilized in writing the End-of-the-Year Report. Copies of this report go to the parents, to the child's physician(s), to other agencies or therapists working with the child, to the school the child will be attending, and to anyone else the parents specify. A copy also remains in the child's office file.

SPECIAL PURPOSE REPORTS

This type of report is written at any time during the year as needed, e.g., referring the child for other services, responding to a request for information from the child's physician, or applying to a service agency or other funding source for a "scholarship" for the child to help meet habilitation costs. This report is generally shorter than the end-of-the-year report and is geared to the specific need it addresses. Copies of these reports are kept in the child's office file and given to the parents.

VIDEOTAPES AND AUDIOTAPES

Videotape is a wonderful medium on which to record the growth and development of the child and the progress that the parents make in interacting with their hearing-impaired infant. Videotape also allows the specialist — and the parents — to scrutinize the child's behaviors in order to detect presymbolic and symbolic communication, responses to sound, and changes in cognitive, social-emotional, and motor functioning. A longitudinal tape is kept on each child/family enrolled. A three to five-minute activity in which the parent and child are playing together is taped sometime during the first sessions following enrollment and at regular intervals throughout the duration of the child's enrollment at IHR. The number of segments taped is determined by the child's rate of progress as the specialist attempts to document new auditory or language achievements on the tape. IHR specialists tape a minimum of three or four segments each year, making sure to get a beginning-of-the-year and end-of-the-year segment. These longitudinal tapes are stored at the agency after the child has graduated. When parental permission is obtained, they are used for demonstration and training purposes. Videotape is also used, as described later in the discussion of the Parent Involvement Method in Chapter 10, to permit parents and specialists to view and evaluate their own interactions with the child. These segments are not necessarily saved.

Audiotape is an excellent means of recording a child's vocal/speech performance. Less intrusive than the videotape camera, audiotape is sometimes considerably more effective in capturing a sample of the child's vocalizations. A longitudinal audiotape can be very revealing as a way of reminding parents of the progress their child has made in his vocal and speech development. Vocalizations can be transcribed from these tapes (and from videotapes) onto the child's Vocalization, Expressive Language, and Connected Expressive Language Record Sheets.

OFFICE FILES

The administrative coordinator at IHR maintains two files on each family enrolled. The first contains copies of all reports and correspondence related to the child and his parents. The second contains confidential financial statements and billing records/history for each family.

PRINCIPLES GOVERNING RECORD KEEPING AT IHR

Three principles govern data collection and production of written reports at IHR. These principles — parent knowledge, parent authorization, and accuracy — are described below.

PARENT KNOWLEDGE

Parents have access to, or receive a copy of, all records of data and written materials regarding them and their child that are produced and maintained by IHR staff. Our staff philosophy is that any information about the child or parents significant enough to be recorded or described in writing should be available first to the parents. There are times when, in an end-of-the-year report on a graduating family, the specialist will want to describe some differences of opinion she may have had with the family. These differences may center around frequency of the child's hearing aid use, use of the auditory-oral versus the auditory-oral with signed English communication methods, or any other area of habilitation. If these differences have been openly aired with the parents and the parents and specialist have agreed to disagree, it is easy for the specialist to briefly describe the different points of view in her report when the issue is pertinent to the subsequent teacher having a better understanding of the child and his rate of development. If, on the other hand, the specialist has disagreed with decisions parents have made regarding their child, but did not discuss this disagreement with the parents at the time it occurred, it is inappropriate to raise the issue in a written report. Nothing that appears in a written report should come as a surprise to parents! This principle is a constant reminder to specialists to keep lines of communication open with parents, even when it means discussing issues that may be difficult for one or both parties.

PARENT AUTHORIZATION

Parents must approve and authorize (usually in writing) the dissemination of any information regarding their family to persons outside the agency. They authorize the use of videotapes and slides which show themselves or their child. And, finally, they authorize their lessons being observed by visitors to the agency. Some of the teaching rooms at IHR have observation windows with one-way mirrors which allow visitors to observe sessions from another room. At any time parents can request that the shades on the observation room windows be pulled down and the intercom turned off so that the session cannot be observed.

ACCURACY

IHR specialists take pride in the procedures they use to determine whether or not a child/parent has achieved an objective. There is no guesswork or inflation of skills involved in the assessment of achievement. Adhering to the sequence of objectives found in each section of the curriculum, *Parent-Infant Communication,* requires that the specialist document infant and parent achievement prior to moving to the next objective. As a result, the data collected on each family in checksheets and record sheets and summarized in written reports are an accurate reflection of the information and skills each child and parent has achieved at the time of the report.

SUMMARY

This chapter has outlined the framework within which habilitation is offered at Infant Hearing Resource. Infant and parent goals, the content of habilitation, the curricula used for assessment and selection of teaching objectives, and the three settings in which habilitation occurs at IHR have been described. Finally, assessment of parent and child achievements and the record-keeping methods used to document these achievements were spelled out. Having laid this groundwork, we will proceed by discussing, in Part II, the identification and auditory assessment of the hearing-impaired infants who are enrolled at IHR.

PART II

IDENTIFICATION AND AUDITORY ASSESSMENT OF HEARING-IMPAIRED INFANTS

CHAPTER 4

RATIONALE FOR EARLY IDENTIFICATION OF HEARING-IMPAIRED INFANTS

Areas of Infant's Development Affected by Hearing Loss

- The Parent-Child Relationship
- Social, Emotional, and Cognitive Development
- Potential for Receiving and Processing Auditory Information
- Acquisition and Use of Language

One of the underlying premises of the IHR model of habilitation is the importance of early identification of infants with impaired hearing. While intuitively it seems essential to begin a program of remediation for any medical or developmental disorder as early as possible, research findings add impetus to common sense. It has not been long since infancy was regarded as a passive state in which the baby could use little of the information in his environment. Research findings in the last decade have shown that nothing could be further from the truth. Babies emerge from the womb with neurosensory systems that have already stored up memories of stimuli that impinged on them prior to birth.

Recent studies by the National Institute of Child Health and Human Development have demonstrated that not only do human fetuses hear during the third trimester, but that neonates recognize stories that were read to them before birth (DeCasper, 1984). From the time of birth babies can detect differences between male and female voices (Kaplan, 1969) and within the second month of life can discriminate between the individual phonemes of speech (Morse, 1972). When the findings from studies of early infant capabilities and function are combined with studies which demonstrate the deleterious effects of sensory deprivation during the first years of life, it is evident that the consequences for the hearing-impaired child who does not get early help are serious.

AREAS OF THE INFANT'S DEVELOPMENT AFFECTED BY HEARING LOSS

Too often professionals working with young hearing-impaired infants attend only to the detrimental effects that hearing loss during infancy has on the child's ability to acquire language. There are, in all, four major areas of development which are strongly affected by the infant's hearing loss:

1. The parent-child relationship.
2. The infant's social, emotional, and cognitive development.
3. The infant's potential for receiving and processing auditory information.
4. The infant's ability to acquire and use language.

THE PARENT-CHILD RELATIONSHIP

The infant's hearing loss can affect the developing relationships between the infant and his parents and other family members. In many cases parents suspect that something is "wrong" with their baby long before the hearing loss is diagnosed. Their concern and anxiety about an unknown condition can radically affect their interaction with their child. Unwittingly, they may convey their growing anxiety and their ambivalence about a potential handicap to the infant by changes in their patterns of holding, touching, smiling, and talking to the infant.

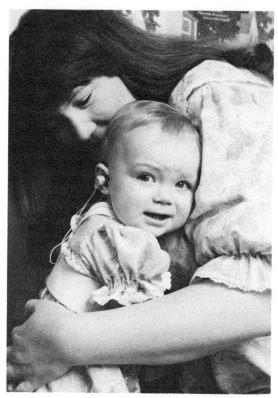

Fostering the attachment between parents and child is a focus of habilitation.

Because the infant does not hear his parents' voices, he may not respond to them with coos and smiles of his own. This diminished responsiveness on the part of the infant means that he is less reinforcing to his parents. As a result, the parents may interact less with the baby and may even attribute the baby's lack of response to resistance, defiance, or dislike. When the parents decrease their interaction with the child, the variety of presymbolic communication that normally develops between parents and infant may fail to materialize (see Chapter 20). The parents may attend only to the child's distress signals and not reinforce or model the other important functions of presymbolic communication. The paucity of presymbolic communication between parents and infant will, in turn, affect the infant's readiness, interest, and motivation in acquiring symbolic language, e.g., spoken or signed language.

The child's hearing loss can have an impact on the parent-child relationship even before it is diagnosed. Once the hearing loss is detected, parents must spend time, money, and energy to meet the needs of this child, frequently at the expense of spouse and siblings. It is difficult for brothers and sisters to understand why their handicapped sibling demands so much of their parents' time and attention. Sometimes parents transfer the responsibility of caring for other children to the eldest so that they have time for the handicapped child. While some of these duties occur in all homes, in families of a handicapped child the other siblings may be expected to do more than they normally would, creating feelings of resentment toward the handicapped child (see Chapter 15).

SOCIAL, EMOTIONAL, AND COGNITIVE DEVELOPMENT

The inability to hear in a world that is filled with sound creates significant difficulties for the hearing-impaired infant. All infants have needs for security, self-identity, connectedness with other people, and a rational, predictable environment. Sound and an adequately functioning auditory system are essential elements in meeting these needs. Information gained through hearing serves many purposes even for the very young infant. First, hearing is used to monitor the environment. We filter out millions of auditory stimuli a day, sounds that tell us that things are normal, are going as expected. When we hear an unusual or unanticipated sound, however, our attention is directed immediately to the source of that sound in order to ascertain whether it signals a "friendly" or "unfriendly" event. The monitoring function of hearing, performing as it does around corners, through walls, at considerable distance, and in the dark, assures us that our environment is safe and gives us a feeling of connection with other people. Both the feelings of safety and of connectedness are important to the infant's sense of well being.

A second way in which hearing contributes to social, emotional, and cognitive development is in helping the infant perceive his environment as predictable, stable, and rational. People change their behavior because of sounds — they leap up from a chair when the phone rings, they grimace when they hear a baby cry loudly, they turn abruptly toward a door at which someone is knocking. To an observer who heard the sound that caused these responses, the responses are predictable and reasonable. The environment feels comfortable and rational because it is not filled with effects that have no apparent cause. Hearing-impaired infants see the effects of auditory stimuli, rarely knowing the cause. Daddy suddenly turns his attention from his game with the baby to the doorway when Mom calls from the kitchen. Sister drops the toy she is dangling in front of baby and dashes off when she hears her friend's voice outside. Sometimes, the world of the hearing-impaired baby doesn't make much sense. Things happen and too frequently he may not know why. This inability to perceive cause and effect relationships cannot help but influence the child's developing trust in the stability and predictability of his environment, his relationships with his caregivers, and his cognitive skills.

Babies with a significant, undetected hearing loss cannot monitor the environment that falls outside their visual range. A parent talking from another room provides no sense of security through continuity of presence. A baby who can hear knows mother still exists when she leaves his visual field because he can hear her talking from a distance. The hearing-impaired baby does not experience this comfort which is provided by the sound of voice. He may feel abandoned and isolated unless he can actually see people who are significant to him.

The effect of hearing loss on the child's cognitive development is discussed more thoroughly in Chapter 19.

POTENTIAL FOR RECEIVING AND PROCESSING AUDITORY INFORMATION

A third area which is adversely affected by an infant's undetected hearing impairment is the development of pathways in the brain which carry auditory stimuli from the ear to the auditory cortex, that part of the brain which processes or makes meaning of sound. Animal studies have clearly defined that there are critical periods during which the organism is programmed to develop the neural pathways and cells in the cortical centers that process input from the sense organs. Studies done by Wiesel and Hubel (1965) demonstrated that visual deprivation in kittens at specific times early in the kittens' lives resulted in greatly reduced sensory-perceptual abilities caused by a severe deterioration of innate cortical connections. Other studies specific to the auditory systems of mammals have shown that when the auditory system is deprived of normal sensory input, retrocochlear signs of the deprivation are apparent. Ruben and Rapin (1980) reviewed the literature reporting studies of auditory deprivation and concluded,

> "Available studies of the impact of auditory deprivation have shown that there is a correlation between the anatomical and physiological effects of deprivation and its behavioral consequences. Behavioral effects of auditory deprivation, whether partial or total, appear to be significant in the species examined. They impair the ability of the organism to make fine

discrimination and, in the case of man, jeopardize the child's linguistic development. The impact of this impairment is not only cognitive, but also social and psychological'' (p. 308).

Implications for the hearing-impaired child are serious: Lack of early amplification may result in the child having significantly diminished capability to process and make use of sound.

ACQUISITION AND USE OF LANGUAGE

Hearing allows us to communicate with others through both vocal and verbal exchange. Feelings, thoughts, ideas, complaints, and questions are all conveyed through words and intonational patterns which are idiosyncratic to every spoken language. Hearing provides us with a rapid and efficient system of receiving this information from another person. The human organism is programmed to attend to speech. Condon and Sander (1974) observed that newborns move in time with the structure of adult speech. Wolff (1963) found that three-week-old infants smiled more in response to human voice than to mechanical noises. McNeill (1966) pointed out that normally hearing children acquire the basis for the use of intricate adult grammatical speech between the ages of 1.5 years to 3.5 or four years of age, a span of only 24 to 30 months.

It has been posited that babbling and cooing are reflexive in nature, especially in response to caregivers' smiles. However, a study by Mavilya (1969) in which the vocalizations of three hearing-impaired infants were compared with the vocalizations of one normally hearing infant showed that by 5½ months of age the number of vocalizations produced by hearing-impaired infants had decreased, and the number of totally silent periods had increased. This study also found that the vocalizations of the hearing-impaired infants contained very little variety, with the neutral vowel the most predominant vocalization. The infant's inability to hear both the language of others and his own vocalizations is reflected in his vocal output very early.

These studies point up the readiness of infants to attend and respond to language from birth. Infants who are deprived of language input by impaired hearing and who do not receive language input through a visual mode experience the negative consequences of this deprivation. Hearing-impaired babies whose hearing-impaired parents communicate with them in signed language do not experience the same early language deprivation (Howell, 1984; Schlesinger and Meadow, 1972; Vernon and Koh, 1970).

A young hearing-impaired child who does not have access to a functional symbolic communication system cannot communicate about anything that is not in the here and now. He misses the essence of his family — values, ideas, and feelings — which is conveyed through spoken or signed words.

Without a symbolic language system the child must continue to rely on non-verbal communication which may be discouraged by some parents who feel he "should be talking by now." As a result, the child's attempts to communicate his wants and needs may be discouraged or ignored and the child may adopt more extreme — and unpopular — behaviors in an effort to make his needs evident.

All four of these areas — family relationships; social, emotional, and cognitive development; critical periods of neurosensory development; and language acquisition — are addressed in a complete parent-infant habilitation program. Many of the problems described above can be substantially diminished if the infant's hearing loss is identified early and the family enrolls in an intensive parent-infant program of habilitation.

CHAPTER 5

IMPLEMENTING EARLY IDENTIFICATION ACTIVITIES

Types of Infant Hearing Screening Procedures

- Hospital High-Risk Questionnaire
- Birth Certificate Data
- In-Hospital Auditory Screening
- Hearing and Communication Screening as Part of the Regular Well-Baby Exam

Public Awareness Activities

TYPES OF INFANT HEARING SCREENING PROCEDURES

Congenital deafness is a low-incidence, non-fatal condition. These two factors have contributed to a general lack of national urgency to implement programs which would identify infants with hearing loss during the first months of life. As of July, 1983, only five states — Utah, Colorado, Oklahoma, New Jersey, and Massachusetts — reported active statewide high-risk screening programs (Mahoney, 1984). At this same time an additional four states reported active regional high-risk screening programs and eight states reported that planning for statewide screening programs was in progress.

Four general types of screening procedures are used to detect newborns and infants who are at-risk for hearing loss: 1) hospital high-risk questionnaires, 2) birth certificate data, 3) in-hospital auditory screening of newborns, and 4) hearing screening during regular pediatric examinations which take place in the first year of the child's life.

HOSPITAL HIGH-RISK QUESTIONNAIRES

The purpose of a high-risk questionnaire is to select out infants whose genetic or medical history contains factors that are identified as causes of, or are highly correlated with, hearing loss. These factors include maternal conditions during pregnancy. Most high-risk questionnaires include risk criteria similar to those established by the Joint Committee on Infant Hearing (consisting of representatives from the American Academy of Pediatrics, the Academy of Otolarnyngology — Head and Neck, and the American Speech-Language-Hearing Association) whose most recent position paper was published in 1982 (Joint Committee on Infant Hearing, 1982).

> "The hearing of infants who manifest any item on the list of risk criteria should be screened, preferably under the supervision of an audiologist, optimally by three months of age but not later than six months of age. The initial screening should

include the observation of behavioral or electrophysiological response to sound (The committee has no recommendations at this time regarding any specific device). If consistent electrophysiological or behavioral responses are detected at appropriate sound levels, then the screening process will be considered complete except in those cases where there is a probability of a progressive hearing loss; e.g., family history of delayed onset or degenerative disease or history of intra-uterine infection. If results of an initial screening of an infant manifesting any risk criteria are equivocal, then the infant should be referred for diagnostic testing'' (p. 496).

The high-risk questionnaire is intended to be completed by the mother prior to discharge from the maternity unit of the hospital. The completed questionnaires are turned over to the individual or group designated as administrators of the high-risk program. In some hospitals, disposition of completed questionnaires is handled by nurses; in other hospitals, paid or volunteer staff may handle the administrative aspects of the high-risk questionnaire. Completed questionnaires must be scanned to find those in which one or more of the mother's responses indicate that the infant is at-risk for hearing loss. Babies who are at-risk for hearing loss should, according to the Joint Committee on Infant Hearing, have their hearing screened, optimally by three months of age and no later than six months of age, preferably under the supervision of an audiologist.

The degree of success which a high-risk questionnaire program achieves in identifying infants with hearing loss may well pivot on who inherits the responsibility for making certain that the hearing of infants designated as "at-risk" by the questionnaire is tested. When audiological testing of at-risk infants is not mandated by law and is left to the discretion of each infant's personal physician, the effectiveness of the questionnaire may be significantly diminished. This was the case in a high-risk identification project conducted in Portland, Oregon.

Between 1981-1986, a coalition of organizations and professionals who work with young hearing-impaired children in Portland carried out a program to identify hearing-impaired newborns through use of a high risk questionnaire. This coalition, called the Registry of Newborns at Risk for Hearing Loss, was organized and administered by volunteers from the Junior League of Portland. Questionnaires were placed in the maternity units of five Portland area hospitals. Junior League members collected and evaluated completed questionnaires, mailing copies of the questionnaires which identified infants as at-risk to each infant's personal physician. These physicians also received a letter explaining the Registry and a postcard which was to be mailed back to the Registry reporting the results of the audiologic screening conducted on the child.

The Registry was terminated in early 1986 because the Junior League administrators determined that the Registry in its present format was not producing credible results. They attributed the Registry's failure to identify hearing-impaired newborns to three factors: non-compliance from physicians, non-compliance from mothers, and inconsistent administrative procedures within the hospitals in which the questionnaires were completed. The Junior League administrators concluded that a state-mandated high-risk registry is essential in order to assure the consistent implementation and physician compliance that will make the Registry effective in identifying infants with hearing loss.

BIRTH CERTIFICATE DATA

Mahoney (1984) reports on three states utilizing a form of birth certificate information to identify hearing-impaired infants. The state of Utah has a section related to health information printed on the official birth record of each infant. Questions related to the medical and genetic factors which put an infant at-risk for hearing loss are included in this section. The completed certificates are computer-screened to identify infants with at-risk factors in their genetic or medical history. The families of these infants are sent information about the screening program, a brochure describing normal infant auditory development, and a postcard on which they can request a free hearing screening appointment for their infant. The Utah Department of Health conducts this program without a legislative mandate. Georgia and Tennessee were other states using birth certificate information with varying degrees of success at the time of Mahoney's report.

IN-HOSPITAL AUDITORY SCREENING

There are several types of tests which can be used to assess the hearing of newborn infants. These include a program in which Auditory Brainstem Response (ABR) screening is conducted on at-risk infants by trained volunteers (Cevette, 1984); the Crib-O-Gram Neonatal Hearing Screening Audiometer (Miller and Simmons, 1984); a high-risk and mass screening project (Feinmesser, Tell, and Levi, 1984); and the use of Visual Reinforcement Audiometry (VRA) and Behavioral Observation Audiometry (BOA) with neonates and infants (Thompson and Wilson, 1984). All of these procedures are effective in identifying infants with impaired hearing. Factors such as cost, equipment, personnel requirements, and access to infants for initial testing and follow-up determine what type of screening/testing method is most appropriate for any given situation.

HEARING AND COMMUNICATION SCREENING
AS PART OF THE REGULAR WELL-BABY EXAM

The final type of screening which is used to identify infants at risk for hearing loss is performed by some pediatricians, pediatric nurses, and pediatric nurse practitioners who have learned to conduct pass/fail noisemaker screening procedures that can be used with infants 0 to 18 months of age. The purpose of conducting noisemaker hearing screening is to determine whether a child gives the types of responses to sound that are normal for a child of his age. Pass/fail hearing screening should always be combined with a brief discussion with parents in which they describe the baby's auditory and communication behaviors at home. When a child does not respond normally to the sounds presented during hearing screening and parents report a similar lack of response to sounds in the home, medical evaluation is necessary and audiological evaluation may be indicated.

It is necessary for medical personnel to put some thought into how best to screen the hearing of an infant or young child at a well-baby examination. The timing of the screening is important since it does not work well to screen the hearing of a chilly baby whose clothing has just been removed for weighing and examination or an angry baby who has just had a shot. Location is equally important. Screening must be conducted in a quiet environment that is free from visual distractions as well as from noise. Working with a relaxed baby in a quiet room, a well-trained screener can conduct a valid and reliable screening of the baby's hearing in two to three minutes. (See Northern and Downs, 1984, Chapter 7, for hearing screening procedures that can be used with infants in a quiet, sound-treated setting. The reader should note that it may be necessary to use louder stimuli than those specified by Northern and Downs to elicit a response from infants 0-4 - months of age when they are being screened in a room, such as a medical office, with substantial ambient noise.)

When results of the screening procedure are interpreted to parents, the parents should be told what the procedure does, and does not, rule out. It is helpful if the parents are also given a copy of a pamphlet that outlines some hearing, language, and speech landmarks that the parent can look for in their child (e.g. Warren and Cunningham, no date).

The nurse or doctor can screen the baby's speech and language development — and indirectly, his hearing — by asking questions about the baby's auditory behaviors at home and about his receptive and expressive language. Samples of questions that the examiner can ask are suggested by Warren and Cunningham (no date):

By 6 months of age:
Does Annie make speech sounds to her toys or to her reflection in a mirror, using sounds like "moo," "ma," "da," "di"?
By 10 months of age:
Does Henry understand "no" and "bye-bye"?

By 18 months of age:
Does Annie definitely use a few single words meaningfully?
Does Henry understand many single words, such as names of foods, toys, and parts of the face?
By 24 months of age:
Does Annie start to use two-word phrases, such as "more juice," "bye-bye Daddy"?

Another scale, the "Early Language Milestone Scale" (ELM) (Coplan, Gleason, Ryan, Burke, and Williams, 1982) was developed by pediatricians for use as a brief language assessment tool. The ELM scale lists 41 language-related milestones that occur in the first 36 months of a child's life. The authors of the ELM scale feel that "delayed achievement of early language milestones strongly suggests the presence of a significant underlying developmental disability" (p. 677).

An infant should be referred for further evaluation if 1) he fails to respond to the hearing screening procedure used, or 2) if questioning the parents about the child's communication suggests that he is unresponsive to sound at home, or that his speech and language are delayed. Even if the parents report a history of hearing responses in the past, the baby who fails a hearing screening should have impedance testing done or should be examined by a physician because he may presently have a middle ear condition that requires medical treatment. If medical examination and impedance testing show that the child's peripheral auditory system is functioning normally and yet the child does not respond normally to the sounds used in screening, a referral for audiological evaluation is indicated.

TRAINING MEDICAL PERSONNEL
TO SCREEN THE HEARING OF INFANTS

Screening the hearing of infants is a difficult task for the inexperienced screener. The problem lies in part with the emotional reaction felt by the screener when the baby does not give the observable response to sound that is expected. When the inexperienced screener does not observe a response, there is often a feeling of, "Oh no! What do I do now?" Without thinking clearly about what she is doing, the screener may make changes in the screening procedure that inadvertently help the baby respond to visual or tactile, rather than to auditory, stimuli. Such changes may include moving the stimulus forward so that it is within the baby's peripheral vision, presenting the stimulus closer to the child's head so that he feels movement of the examiner's arm or of the noisemaker itself, or interpreting a child's actions that are unrelated to the stimulus as responses. The screener is not intentionally invalidating the screening results but is trying to be helpful so that the baby does not "fail" the screening. Two children have enrolled at IHR who had each passed two noisemaker screenings performed in their doctors' offices before their hearing losses were finally diagnosed. In both cases, the parents had serious concerns about their infants' hearing at six months of age, yet the hearing losses went undetected until fifteen months of age because of the incorrect screening techniques used by inadequately trained examiners.

Any program that purports to train personnel to screen the hearing of infants must stress that the screener is *not* responsible for diagnosing hearing impairment. Screeners must learn very clearly what it is that screening does and does not do. If, during a screening session, the infant does not give observable responses to sound, the screener must be entirely comfortable with carrying out the following steps:

1. Telling the parents that, "I am not seeing the responses to these stimuli that I would expect to see in a child of this age."
2. Questioning the parents about the infant's responsiveness to sound and his vocal/verbal behaviors at home.
3. Making recommendations for appropriate follow-up. Depending on the information gained from the parents, that may be immediate medical referral or it may be a repeat screening within one or two weeks.

Hearing screening should be undertaken only when the screener knows how to screen, how to detect and interpret age-appropriate responses, and what to do if the baby does not give observable responses to the sounds presented.

At IHR we have resolved for ourselves the dilemma of "to train or not to train" medical personnel in hearing screening techniques. We have discussed the risk involved in providing short-term training to medical personnel in techniques they can use to identify infants with significant hearing losses early in life. In evaluating some of our first training efforts, we determined that in a workshop setting we are unable to provide the degree of supervised practicum necessary to a complete training program. For this reason, we no longer train medical personnel in techniques of screening the hearing of infants. Instead, IHR offers workshops for medical personnel that focus on the rationale for early identification and on identifying the types and ranges of responses to sound that infants give during the first year of life. We regard the workshop as an introduction that will provide medical personnel with *awareness* of the problems associated with hearing loss in infancy and of the types of tests that will identify those infants whose hearing is impaired.

The workshops are designed so that participants can achieve three objectives:

1. To learn the causes of hearing loss in infancy (high-risk factors) and the importance of early identification of hearing-impaired infants.
2. To observe a number of infants between 0-18 months of age who

exhibit normal responses to sound and some infants who do not give normal responses to sound.

3. To acquire a list of audiologists/agencies to whom medical personnel can refer infants whose hearing status is questioned.

The two-hour workshops are conducted in two parts. The first part consists of presentations on the topics "Causes of Hearing Loss" and "The Importance of Early Detection of Hearing Loss." The second part of the workshop is a practicum in which small groups of participants observe a workshop leader attempt to elicit responses to noisemakers from five to ten infants.

Participants at these workshops who want to incorporate noisemaker hearing screening into their well-baby examinations are encouraged to practice screening techniques on 150-200 presumed normally hearing infants between the ages of 0-18 months in order to observe the wide range of responses infants give to sound. It is essential that screeners have confidence in their ability to present the stimuli correctly and to detect and interpret the responses given by the infant since there are a number of variables in addition to age — e.g., the physical and emotional state of the child — which affect an infant's responsiveness to sound. Screeners need to be aware that there are techniques related to the presentation of the sound stimulus that assure that the infant is responding to an auditory, rather than to a visual or tactile, stimulus. Finally screeners must know what procedures to follow when an infant does not respond appropriately to sound.

PUBLIC AWARENESS ACTIVITIES

Parents and grandparents are the individuals most likely to suspect that a baby may have a problem hearing (Shah, Chandler, and Dale, 1978). For this reason the public awareness activities conducted by IHR are aimed at reaching the populations most likely to encounter young infants: parents, grandparents, expectant parents, pediatricians, family practitioners, ear, nose, and throat physicians, otologists, nurses in hospital maternity departments and physicians' offices, infant day care providers, and professionals in social service agencies dealing with young children. The goals of these activities are to inform these groups about 1) hearing loss in infancy: rate of incidence, causes, and rationale for detection, and 2) child behaviors that signal normal and abnormal responsiveness to sound.

Because hearing loss does not have a visible component, many parents and professionals do not think to question the child's ability to hear. The public, and the medical profession as well, need to be aware that infants, from the time of birth, give predictable and repeatable responses to sound. **It is not true, as some parents are still told by their child's physician, that hearing loss cannot be diagnosed until the child is one, two, or three years**

of age. Should a baby's hearing status be in question at any time, parents and physicians alike need to be aware that there are audiological procedures which can accurately and reliably determine an infant's threshold for sound within the first few months of life.

One of the most potent tools we have used at IHR to spark public awareness is a videotape that shows very young babies responding to sounds. The viewers see that the babies in the tape give a variety of responses to the noisemaker sounds presented. Responses seen in infants two weeks to four months of age are reflexive and include whole body movement, eye blinks, eye widening, cessation of crying, and onset of crying. More mature and learned responses to sound are seen in the 4 to 6-month and older child who has good head and neck control. These responses include a look up in response to sound and head turn in the direction of a sound. When people become aware that most normally hearing infants give easily detected responses to sound, they also understand that absence of observable responses is reason for concern and referral for evaluation.

An effective public awareness campaign utilizes television, radio, and newspapers; periodicals targeted at parents, child care workers and medical professionals; health fairs; and presentations to groups as means of transmitting information. Such a campaign is an excellent ongoing project for a service-oriented club or group which can organize, finance, and carry out the project activities under the guidance of professionals in the audiology community. Local foundations in the Portland area have funded several IHR proposals which promote early identification activities aimed at the medical community and at the community at-large.

CHAPTER 6

AUDIOLOGICAL SERVICES: THE IHR TEAM APPROACH

Skills Required by Parent-Infant Specialists
   on the Team

Goals of Infant Audiology Services at IHR

Steps to Achieving Pediatric Audiology Goals
- Telephone Interview
- Initial Assessment of Hearing Status
- Enrollment in the IHR Program of Parent-Infant Habilitation
- Serial Use of Trial Amplification and Recommendation of Hearing Aids for Purchase
- Ongoing Evaluation of the Infant's Auditory Capabilities

The pediatric audiology program at IHR is a cooperative effort in which the staff pediatric audiologist, the parent-infant specialist, and the parents work as a team throughout the diagnostic, training, and hearing aid evaluation processes. This team approach combines audiological and medical findings with the parent-infant specialist's and parents' observations of the child's auditory behaviors to gain as complete a picture as possible of the child's auditory capabilities. This approach differs from the traditional approach to auditory assessment and hearing aid evaluation in three primary ways: 1) The audiologist shares the problem-solving and decision-making tasks which occur in the diagnostic process; 2) The parent-infant specialist must acquire additional expertise in procedures of auditory assessment and hearing aid evaluation; and 3) The parents must assume responsibility for observing and reporting their child's auditory behaviors, first while the child is unaided and then while he is wearing different amplification systems on a trial basis. (Chapter 13 includes a discussion of techniques for teaching parents observation and reporting skills.) The auditory evaluation process continues throughout the family's enrollment at IHR which ranges from one to four years in duration.

SKILLS REQUIRED BY PARENT-INFANT SPECIALISTS ON THE TEAM

The team approach to audiological services used at IHR requires that teachers of the hearing-impaired acquire and utilize skills from the field of pediatric audiology in addition to those skills acquired in traditional teacher training programs. Specialists at IHR have acquired information and skills related to audiologic assessment and hearing aids from a combination of coursework and extensive experience as a part of the audiologist-specialist-parent team. Participation on this team requires that the parent-infant specialist be knowledgeable on the following topics from the field of audiology:

- maturation of auditory skills in the normal infant
- measurement of hearing in infants and young children including

1) purposes, methods, and limitations of hearing screening; 2) clinical hearing assessment procedures appropriate to infants and young children (visual reinforcement audiometry, play audiometry); and 3) physiological auditory assessment (impedance audiometry and Auditory Brainstem Response testing)
- acoustic parameters of speech
- effects of hearing loss on reception of sound, including speech
- effects of the acoustic environment on speech reception.

Parent-infant specialists are further required to have knowledge of and experience with hearing aids in the following areas:
- electroacoustical characteristics of hearing aids
- hearing aid coupling systems
- relationship of electro- and psycho-acoustical measures
- conventional hearing aid selection procedures and considerations
- hearing aid selection for infants and young children
- hearing aid use, care, and maintenance.

GOALS OF INFANT AUDIOLOGY SERVICES AT IHR

The IHR pediatric audiology program has four goals. They are:
1. Testing the hearing of infants and young children to identify those with hearing loss early in life.
2. Obtaining initial data on the infant's bilateral unaided auditory thresholds within two weeks of referral so that trial use of amplification can begin.
3. Recommending purchase of the amplification system with which the infant has demonstrated maximum use of his residual hearing through trial hearing aid use.
4. Providing parents with knowledge and understanding of audiological testing procedures used with their infant and teaching parents the skills they need to observe and report their child's auditory behaviors, to care for the hearing aids, and to manage and monitor their child's hearing aid use.

STEPS TO ACHIEVING PEDIATRIC AUDIOLOGY GOALS

A five-step process is set into motion as soon as an infant is referred to IHR for assessment of his hearing status. These steps, which will be described in detail below, are:
1. Telephone interview
2. Initial assessments of hearing status

3. Enrollment in a parent-infant habilitation program
4. Serial use of trial amplification and recommendation of aids for purchase
5. Ongoing evaluation of the infant's auditory capabilities and parent education.

TELEPHONE INTERVIEW

Infants are referred to IHR for audiological assessment by parents, physicians, public health personnel, professionals in allied fields, and social service agencies. When the family contacts IHR, usually by telephone, to make an appointment for evaluation of their infant's hearing, the IHR office staff uses the "Hearing Screening Information Form" (Figure 4) to obtain information about the child, including age and presence of high-risk factors, and to learn the concern prompting the request for a hearing test. Unless the referral for evaluation has come from a physician who requests Auditory Brainstem Response testing as the initial test, infants are scheduled for audiological evaluation conducted by the IHR audiologist and a parent-infant specialist.

INITIAL ASSESSMENT OF HEARING STATUS

Depending on the information obtained during the telephone interview with the parent, the infant has been scheduled for auditory brainstem response testing or for audiological assessment.

AUDITORY BRAINSTEM RESPONSE (ABR) TESTING

ABR testing provides information about the child's auditory responsiveness by measuring electrical activity generated by the eighth cranial nerve and the brainstem in response to sound. An ABR test is a good measure of peripheral hearing to use with some infants and difficult-to-test children since it requires no active participation on the part of the child. Though it may be necessary to sedate the child in order to prevent body movement, the sedation does not affect the results.

Infants seen for auditory assessment at IHR are rarely scheduled for ABR as the first test unless the infant's doctor has specifically requested this procedure or the infant is under the age of three months at the time of referral. Some infants who have a hearing loss which was diagnosed through the behavioral test procedures described below are referred for an ABR test as a cross-check on the subjective findings (i.e., findings dependent upon the ex-

HEARING SCREENING INFORMATION

Appointment Scheduled:
Date _____
Time _____

Name _____ Date of Birth _____ Age _____
Parents _____
     Address _____
             _____
     Telephone _____ County _____
Referred by _____

Reason for Concern

	Yes	No
Physician referral	_____	_____
Failed hearing screening in physician's office	_____	_____
Parent reports no observed responses to sound in the home	_____	_____
Child has no words by age 18 months	_____	_____
History of hearing loss in the family	_____	_____
Other _____	_____	_____

Other High Risk Factors

	Yes	No
Jaundice during newborn period (elevated serus bilirubin level)	_____	_____
Maternal rubella	_____	_____
Defects of ear, nose, throat (cleft palate or lip, abnormal pinna, etc.)	_____	_____
Small birth weight (less than 3½ pounds)	_____	_____
Difficulties during labor, or at time of birth	_____	_____
Any serious illnesses since birth	_____	_____
Frequent ear infections	_____	_____
No specific concern, just wants hearing checked	_____	_____

Financial Arrangements for Audiological Services

    Inform family of fee for audiological services and indicate that payment must be made at time of visit unless welfare is to be billed.

    Establishing payment:

_____ Insurance - **Payment must be made by family at time of visit.** We will provide duplicate forms that can then be submitted by the family to their insurance company.

_____ Family will pay full fee.

_____ If family indicates they are unable to pay full fee, ask them what they could pay. Specify that amount on line at left.

_____ If family indicates they are unable to pay at all, check line at left.

_____ Welfare — We will bill welfare.

FIGURE 4.   This form is used when a parent or caretaker, concerned about their baby's hearing, calls Infant Hearing Resource to make an appointment for audiological assessment.

aminer's interpretation of the infant's behaviors) that result from a behavioral test. Because ABR is a test of physiological responses that does not rely on behavioral observations but on electronic recordings of physiological events, some parents find that confirmation of their child's hearing loss through this means facilitates their acceptance of the loss.

    While an ABR test is an important part of the diagnostic test battery, it has several characteristics which limit its use as the sole diagnostic procedure. Obvious drawbacks are the cost of the equipment, the time required for testing, the higher cost of the procedure, and the need to use sedation to insure a readout unpolluted by "noise" caused by body movement. Northern and Downs (1984) describe the main shortcoming of the ABR technique as being the inability of this test to provide information about hearing at specific frequencies. The stimulus that is generally used, a high-frequency click, does not allow frequency specificity in the auditory system. Thus, the click stimulus provides hearing information for the *range* of hearing between 1000-4000 Hz, but not for each of these frequencies, or others, individually. However, some ABR equipment also permits use of 500 Hz tone bursts as a stimulus. When this stimulus is used in combination with the click, information about the child's hearing thresholds at one lower frequency is obtained.

Another drawback of ABR testing is the upper limit of the stimulus intensity at 90 to 100 dB HL. A child whose auditory thresholds fall at 105 dB HL will not respond to the stimulus presented, and the results, therefore, will not present an accurate picture of the child's residual hearing. The audiologist or physician who is interpreting the results of ABR testing to parents must point out this limitation or the parents may be left with the idea that the child has no residual hearing and that amplification, therefore, will not help. Unfortunately, we have interviewed many parents who have been given this incomplete interpretation of ABR test results by physicians who are unfamiliar with the implications of the test.

The issue of which professional interprets the results of ABR tests to parents must be carefully considered. Whether it is the neurologist, the child's personal physician, or the audiologist, this individual must be fully conversant with what the procedure does and does not measure and with the implications of the results. Of equal importance, this individual must be prepared to deal with the parents' emotional responses if the results disclose that their child's hearing is not normal.

AUDIOLOGIC ASSESSMENT

OBTAINING INFORMATION ABOUT THE CHILD'S RESPONSES TO SOUND THROUGH QUESTIONING AND OBSERVATION

Audiological assessment at IHR is done with the audiologist, parent-infant specialist, and parents working together to gain as much information as possible about the infant's auditory thresholds and responsiveness to sound. The initial testing session begins with the specialist reviewing the information that was acquired about the child during the telephone interview and asking the parents to reiterate their concern about their infant's hearing: "Please tell me again your concerns about (child's name) hearing."

The parents' responses generally lead to further questions from the specialist and the audiologist about the child's responses to sounds in the home environment, his understanding of language, and the frequency and variety of his vocalizations and/or words. Questions the audiologist and parent-infant specialist ask include:

> "What sounds are you sure he hears?"
> "What sounds does he seem not to hear?"
> "Does he understand 'No! ' 'Get your shoes.' 'Where's the doggie?'" (depending on child's age).

Parents are asked to describe how the child communicates his wants and needs ("How does he tell you what he wants and doesn't want?") and how his development in other areas (social, motor, cognitive) has proceeded ("When did he sit? stand? walk?" "How does his development compare with that of his siblings?"). The audiologist and parent-infant specialist also ask the parents questions about the pregnancy, perinatal history, and history of hearing loss in either parent's family. Throughout this discussion the audiologist and specialist are observing the child as he is held by his parents or plays on the floor. They look for general responsiveness to visual and tactile stimuli, e.g., does the child look when fingers are moved within his line of peripheral vision or turn if he is tapped on the shoulder? The audiologist and specialist also watch for and record awareness or localizing responses to sounds — including the voices of parents and strangers — and for vocalizations, words, and non-verbal communication.

AUDIOLOGICAL TESTING AND TYMPANOMETRY

When the audiologist and parent-infant specialist have obtained the necessary background information from discussion with the parents and observation of the child, the audiologist describes the audiological testing procedures to the parents. One parent is asked to accompany the child and specialist into the sound-treated room and the second parent, when present, is invited to observe the test procedure through the observation window with the audiologist.

Once inside the sound-treated room the specialist situates the parent and infant in positions appropriate to the child's age and developmental level and to the type of testing procedure to be used. An infant who does not yet have sufficient motor maturity to hold his head up without support is held in a comfortable position in the parent's lap so that his face can be seen by the examiners. An infant with some control of his head and neck is seated, facing forward, on the parent's lap with the parent supporting the child at the waist, thus allowing him maximum head movement. The specialist tells the parent that it is important not to give the baby cues about the presence of the sound by moving when the sound occurs. Older infants are seated in a high chair with a quiet toy on the tray that can be used as a distractor. The specialist points out to the parent the sound field speakers through which the sound stimuli will be delivered. She also points out the lighted toy which is paired with the auditory signal when visual reinforcement audiometry (VRA) is used and briefly describes what the child will be taught to do when the sound is presented.

If the child is two years or older, the specialist introduces a toy appropriate for play audiometry, for example a ring stack toy, and then helps the child learn the task of putting the ring on the stick when the sound stimulus occurs. Some children learn this task rapidly and will stay with it throughout the testing session if a series of different toys is presented to keep their interest. Other children are not ready to learn this task and the evaluation team will revert to using VRA. The parent-infant specialist tells the parent what responses the audiologist will be looking for from the child and how the specialist will help the child learn the task of responding when the sound is presented. The parent-infant specialist is equipped with an earphone which allows her to hear the audiologist's instructions and observations of the child's responses. This system is separate from the audiometric test equipment. Once everyone is situated and the procedures explained, the audiologist begins presenting stimuli.

The first signals are generally presented in the sound-field through wall-mounted speakers so that the audiologist can gain information about the child's awareness responses and the specialist can teach the child to respond to the sound without having the added complication of earphones on the child. When visual reinforcement audiometry is used, the audiologist follows the VRA stimulus protocol outlined by Thompson and Wilson (1984) in combination with standardized clinical pure tone audiometric techniques (ASHA, 1978). The role of the specialist when VRA is used is to initially direct the child's attention to the visual reinforcer as the audiologist presents the signal so that the infant learns to turn to the lighted toy when he hears the auditory stimulus. Between presentations of the stimulus, the specialist draws the child's visual attention back to center.

When information about the child's awareness levels in the sound field to both warbled pure tones across the frequency range and to voice is obtained, the audiologist asks the specialist to put the pediatric earphones on the child. Pediatric earphones are a small pair of earphones that have been calibrated for use with the audiometer. The first information the audiologist obtains is awareness of voice at each ear in order to ascertain if there is a better ear. Some children are extremely resistant to wearing earphones and the audiologist may have a very limited amount of time to gain information while the child can be entertained. Other children do not object to the earphones and will continue to respond to the lighted toy or continue with play audiometry when they hear a signal delivered directly to their ear through earphones so that threshold information for each ear can be obtained.

A study to determine the validity of hearing thresholds obtained on in-

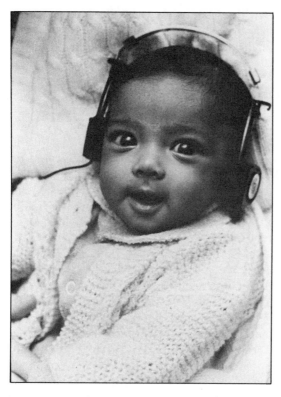

"I just love my
pediatric earphones."

fants using visual reinforcement audiometry was conducted by IHR audiologist, Carolyn Talbott (1984). The study followed seventeen infants whose first audiologic results were obtained between the ages of 6-27 months using VRA and who were later tested between the ages of 25-41 months using play audiometry techniques. Each ear was tested at five frequencies and the scores were compared at all frequencies to which the child responded up to the limits of the audiometer. Twenty-five matched pairs of scores from the seventeen subjects were compared. (Where complete scores for each ear were not available from the early VRA visit, sound field scores from this visit were matched to the better ear responses from later play audiometry results.) The results showed no significant difference in hearing levels obtained using the two techniques. The investigator concluded that VRA test methods can specifically define a hearing-impaired infant's hearing thresholds so that definite recommendations can be made for auditory management.

The duration of the testing session varies widely with children under the age of three. There generally comes a point when the parents, specialist, and audiologist agree either that enough information has been obtained or that the child has "had it" and is not able to participate further. At this point, the parent, child, and specialist rejoin the audiologist (and second parent) outside the sound-treated booth. The child is given a few minutes to relax and adjust to the environment before the audiologist performs tympanometry. The information obtained from tympanometry is recorded on the audiogram form.

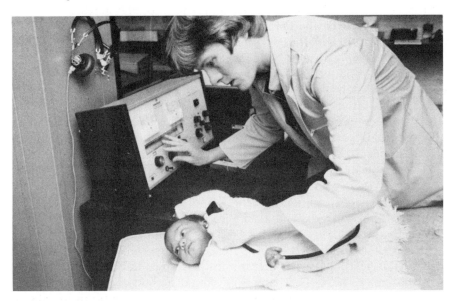

The audiologist performs tympanometry as a part of the audiological assessment procedure.

INTERPRETING TEST RESULTS TO PARENTS AND RESPONDING TO PARENTS' REACTIONS AND QUESTIONS

Because the parents have been present during the entire auditory assessment, they will be aware whether their child has responded to the soft sounds presented, whether the child did not respond until the sounds became loud, or whether their child gave no observable responses except to *very* loud, low-frequency sounds. The audiologist now relates the parents' observations of their child's responsiveness to the information plotted on the audiogram. Holding the audiogram so that the parents can see it, the audiologist briefly describes the parameters of the chart using terms such as "pitch" and "loudness" with which the parents are likely to be familiar. The audiologist's job is easiest and most pleasant when the child's hearing falls within normal range or when the results of tympanometry strongly suggest that the child's hearing loss as plotted on the audiogram is related to malfunctioning middle ear systems. When the latter situation exists, the family is referred back to the child's physician for otological evaluation and possible medical management. A return visit to the audiologist is scheduled once any treatment is completed to ascertain that the child's hearing levels have returned to within normal limits.

When results of testing indicate the strong possibility of a hearing loss that is not medically treatable, the audiologist and specialist are aware that the parents will most likely experience some sharp feelings in reaction to this information. Parents who have suspected that their child has a hearing loss may not be surprised by the confirmation of that fact but may be stunned to hear that the hearing loss is permanent and cannot be cured by medical or surgical intervention. At this point, most parents are likely to be in a state of shock and may not "hear" much of what is said after the initial statement of hearing loss. It is important, therefore, that the information gained from the testing procedures is related to the parents in an uncomplicated but complete way, providing parents with time to think and with ample opportunity to ask questions.

The audiologist and parent-infant specialist must be aware of how parents are reacting to the test results. It may be that acknowledging the parents' fears, concerns, and disbelief is more important than an academic discussion of hearing loss and its implications. Appropriate comments may be an empathetic, "This is very hard for you to hear"; or "It's o.k. to cry." We believe that audiologists and parent-infant specialists who report the diagnosis of hearing loss to parents must be trained in crisis theory and in active listening skills. The parents' eventual acceptance of their child's deafness and of their own feelings related to it is expedited if this initial session is carried out by perceptive, empathetic, and skilled professionals.

Some parents do not want to "feel." They want facts right away. However, they rarely have questions about the audiogram itself. Their immediate concern is usually, "What can be done about the hearing loss?" The audiologist discusses with them the need for repeat hearing testing, for examination by a physician specializing in the ear (if the child has not already been seen for this type of evaluation) and for Auditory Brainstem Response testing, if indicated. When results of tympanometry testing show well-functioning middle ear systems, the audiologist is careful not to imply that there is hope for a medical or surgical solution to the hearing loss. The medical evaluation is seen as the part of the diagnostic process in which any physical or medical cause of the hearing loss is ruled out. The audiologist also conveys to parents the need to test the baby's hearing again within two weeks to repeat the results obtained that day before a firm diagnosis of hearing loss can be made. The audiologist indicates to the parents that the results of the audiological assessment will be transmitted to the infant's physician by written report as well as by telephone if the family will be making an appointment to see the doctor within the next few days.

MAKING RECOMMENDATIONS BASED
ON AUDIOLOGICAL TEST RESULTS

In addition to providing support and understanding, the specialist's role in this part of the hearing assessment is to answer the parents' questions such as, "If he does have a hearing loss, what do we do now?" At this point, the IHR parent-infant specialist describes the services offered by parent-infant habilitation programs and provides the parents with a packet of information about the local parent-infant programs that are available to them. The specialist suggests that if, after medical examination and return audiological testing, diagnosis of a sensorineural hearing loss is confirmed, the parents will want to contact and visit all of the programs available to them in order to select the one that best fits their family's needs.

Keeping in mind that they are most likely dealing with people in a state of shock, the audiologist or parent-infant specialist can mention that it may be difficult for the parents to absorb all the information presented when they are possibly feeling stunned by the test results. They offer to answer any questions the parents may think of later if the parents want to call. Before the parents leave, the audiologist and specialist help them plan a course of action for the next steps to take and indicate that repeat testing should be done very soon. Some parents make appointments for a second audiological evaluation and for a tour of IHR, including an information session with a parent-infant specialist to learn more about the IHR habilitation program.

THE CHILD WITH NORMAL HEARING
AND DELAYED LANGUAGE

Some of the infants and young children who are evaluated have auditory thresholds that fall within normal limits, yet their parents' concern that prompted the evaluation remains. Some of these children have normal receptive language capabilities, but have not developed the expressive language skills expected of children of their age. The specialist generally spends time questioning the parents in more detail about the communication patterns in the home: Are there older children who "talk for" the child? How does the child's language development compare with that of his siblings at the same age? Does the child spend time in a verbally non-stimulating daycare or home environment? How does the child communicate his wants and needs? What kind of communication interactions do the parents have most frequently with the child? What are samples of the child's vocal/verbal expressions? The specialist takes note of the parents' communications directed to the child during the evaluation session: Are the parents providing conversation and descriptive language or are they issuing commands, requests, and prohibitions?

The specialist also observes the child, listening carefully to the child's vocalizations. In many instances the child is using extensive jargon which contains all the suprasegmental aspects of speech, but few, if any, words. Some children are echolalic, imitating many of the words and short phrases they hear adults saying. When the child under the age of eighteen months has good receptive language skills (e.g., understands the names of familiar toys, foods, people, and activities, and can carry out simple commands or requests), is using normal intonational patterns in jargon, and is imitating words, the specialist will generally tell the parents that all of the groundwork for use of expressive symbolic language is laid. The specialist may suggest to parents things they can do that will motivate the child to use symbolic language, most of which center around the parents' use of descriptive language, songs, and fingerplays during play with the child, and reinforcing the child's use of vocalization to communicate.

If the normally hearing child has reached the age of two, has age-appropriate receptive language, is using normal inflectional patterns in jargon, is imitating some words, but has only a few spontaneous words, the specialist can tell the parent that while the child's expressive language falls below the norm, it appears that it is developing in normal sequence. The specialist can use her judgment about making a referral to a language stimulation program for the child, taking into consideration factors such as a history of frequent middle ear effusion and associated transitory conductive hearing loss which may have slowed the child's expressive language development (Gabbard, 1982). All parents are given an information checklist of normal speech and language development so that they can continue to monitor their child's progress at home.

The audiologist and specialist refer normally hearing children to a language evaluation and stimulation program when they fall into the following categories:

1. Children whose receptive language, as well as their expressive language, is delayed by more than six months.
2. Children who have reached the age of two and one-half without acquiring a basic expressive vocabulary of 50-75 words.
3. Children over the age of nine to ten months who are not using any presymbolic communication beyond reflexive utterances or whose presymbolic communication is totally object-oriented (see Chapter 20).

There is one other category of child with auditory thresholds within normal limits whom the audiologist and specialist refer for intervention. These are children for whom auditory stimuli have no meaning. These children are referred to a professional who specializes in auditory processing disorders.

When an infant is diagnosed as hearing-impaired, the family can elect to enroll in the IHR parent-infant habilitation program, the third step in the IHR pediatric audiology program.

ENROLLMENT IN THE IHR PROGRAM
OF PARENT-INFANT HABILITATION

Families whose infant is diagnosed as hearing-impaired are given information about all the parent-infant programs available to them in their locale. The family is invited to set up an appointment at IHR at which time a parent-infant specialist — usually the specialist who will work with the family if they elect to enroll at IHR — describes the services offered to families at IHR. The parents are scheduled to come to IHR at a time when they can observe a habilitation session with a family.

After joining the parents in observing a session which is taking place, the specialist describes the schedule of individual clinic and home visit sessions and of child and parent groups sessions. Parents are shown the curriculum, *Parent Infant Communication* (Infant Hearing Resource, 1985) that is used in habilitation. The process of continued auditory evaluation and hearing aid selection — including the sequential use of loaner hearing aids on a trial basis — is described. The IHR philosophy of offering both auditory-oral and auditory-oral with signed English communication is described and the parameters which are considered as the family makes a decision about which communication system to use are reviewed (see Chapter 18). The specialist also describes the parent-specialist partnership in which enrolled parents are involved and outlines the roles and responsibilities of each member of the partnership.

The parents and specialist discuss the family's schedule and the specialist's schedule and determine when individual sessions could be held. The parents are encouraged to ask any questions they have about their child, their own participation in sessions, and about the agency itself. Prior to departure, parents meet with the administrative coordinator who gives them an estimate, based on their income, of what their fee for service will be if they elect to enroll.

Some families decide on the spot that they want to enroll in the habilitation program. Other families who have not yet visited other programs indicate that they will call IHR with their decision after they have investigated other options. The specialist encourages the family to select the program that will best meet their own family's needs, noting that there are several differences among available programs in number of sessions per week, communication approaches offered, and degree of parent involvement in the habilitation process. IHR specialists feel the habilitation process is most successful when families are fully aware of all their options and have chosen the option that best suits their needs and their family style.

Once the family has enrolled at IHR, the fourth step in the IHR pediatric audiology program is implemented.

SERIAL USE OF TRIAL AMPLIFICATION AND RECOMMENDATION OF HEARING AIDS FOR PURCHASE

RATIONALE FOR TRIAL USE OF SEVERAL SETS OF HEARING AIDS PRIOR TO RECOMMENDATION OF AIDS FOR PURCHASE

At first glance it might appear that the only information the audiologist and parent-infant specialist need in order to recommend appropriate aids for immediate purchase for a young child is an accurate audiogram, medical clearance for hearing aid use, and hearing aids whose specifications appear to match the child's needs for amplification. Many audiologists do recommend hearing aids for purchase for an infant on the basis of this information. Another approach is to utilize a system of trial amplification in which several sets of loaner hearing aids are worn by the child before the most appropriate set is recommended for purchase. Extensive practice with this latter approach has reinforced its use at IHR.

Audiograms give the audiologist and specialist information about the child's hearing thresholds at octave or half-octave intervals. Hearing aid analyzers supply information about the amount of gain provided by the hearing aid at similar intervals. Neither of these sources gives the audiologist information about the child's hearing thresholds or the performance of the hearing aid between these intervals, nor does the audiologist gain any information about the subjective aspects of the sound the child receives.

While infants cannot verbally state their preference for one amplification system over another, they do provide many non-verbal behavioral clues which the careful observer can use to determine which amplification system is providing the infant with the most usable auditory information. Some of the child's behaviors associated with an amplification system that is providing him with effective and useful sound are: increased response to sound, increased amount and variety of vocalization, willingness to wear aids for longer periods of time, protest when aids are removed, and request (non-verbally) for placement of aids. Parents who have been trained to look for these behaviors and who have observed their child demonstrating these behaviors with one set of trial-use aids are very quick to notice if these behaviors are reversed or absent when another set of trial-use aids is placed. Conversely, if the parent has observed few of these behaviors in their child, a marked increase or acquisition of new behaviors when a new set of aids is placed is an exciting development that parents are eager to report.

It may be that the child's acquisition of new auditory skills just happened to coincide with the placement of a different set of trial-use aids. If the question of maturation versus the effects of the new aids is raised, there is no reason not to reinstate use of the first set of aids (after the new auditory skills are established) then observe the child to see if the new behaviors are maintained and acquisition of further skills occurs.

IHR has a stock of over 100 hearing aids which are available for trial use. The stock includes more than 45 models of 15 different brands of aids. Each child is observed and tested with 2-5 different models of aids on the average before a recommendation for purchase is made.

SELECTION OF APPROPRIATE AIDS FOR TRIAL USE: CONSIDERATION OF THREE VARIABLES

The objective in placing amplification is to raise the child's aided auditory thresholds to within a range that he can both perceive and discriminate speech without exceeding his tolerance level. The audiologist and parent-infant specialist must consider variables in three areas when selecting appropriate amplification to meet this objective. These areas are: 1) the child; 2) characteristics of the child's hearing loss and residual hearing; and 3) specifications of hearing aids available for trial use.

In considering the variables in each of these areas, the audiologist and specialist turn to six sources of information that will assist them in making decisions about appropriate amplification. These sources of information are:

1. Auditory data on the child gained from behavioral audiometric assessment, tympanometry, and ABR testing.
2. Results of medical examination of the child's ears.
3. Reports from parents and/or daycare providers and the audiologist's and specialist's observations of the child.
4. Electroacoustical data on hearing aids published by the manufacturers.
5. Electroacoustical data on hearing aids obtained by the audiologist and specialist from use of the hearing aid analyzer.
6. The audiologist's knowledge of and experience with different aids: the accessories that are available, repair frequency, and successful past fittings.

CHILD VARIABLES TO CONSIDER IN SELECTING AMPLIFICATION FOR TRIAL USE

An important aspect of hearing aid usage by infants is the fit of the aid. The aid must be secure and comfortable. If it bounces around on the child or hangs uncomfortably off the ear, the aid will annoy the child and may become a plaything to be removed and disassembled. A body aid that is held securely in place by a comfortable, well-fitted harness or an ear-level aid that fits and stays snugly against the head is likely to be forgotten and ignored by the child once his initial curiosity is satisfied. When two amplification systems appear to be equally beneficial to the child in terms of the quality of sound that they provide, fit, and convenience related to maintenance and repair may be the factors which determine choice of one system over another for purchase.

The child's size, degree of mobility, and predominent posture (e.g., supine, prone, upright) must all be considered in the selection of amplification. Some infant's pinnae are too soft or too small to support an ear-level aid positioned behind the ear. At the same time, if the infant is very small and spends a great deal of time on his stomach, body aids placed on his abdomen will be both uncomfortable and ineffective in picking up sound. One solution for a first set of trial-use aids to be placed on a very small infant may be ear-level aids attached to earmolds with a long enough piece of polyethelene tubing that allows the aids to be put inside lightweight cloth bags (such as a baby sock) and pinned to the infant's shoulders. Though only a few inches of tubing are involved, the gain of the aid, especially in the high frequencies, will be reduced. With the tubing in place, the output of the aid should be measured using the hearing aid analyzer and the output of the aid adjusted, if necessary, to compensate for changes created by the extra tubing. Another solution for infants may be placement of body aids in a harness that can be switched from the infant's abdomen to his back, depending on his position. The back is not the ideal location for body aids, however, because the infant is less likely to hear his own vocalizations.

Children who have limited control of head and neck muscles frequently experience feedback when using ear-level aids if their ear falls against a surface as their head tilts or rolls to one side. This factor in itself may be sufficient to warrent the use of body aids until the child acquires more voluntary control of his head.

CHARACTERISTICS OF THE CHILD'S HEARING LOSS AND RESIDUAL HEARING

Four characteristics of the child's hearing loss and residual hearing must be considered when selecting appropriate aids for trial use: type of hearing loss, degree of hearing loss, configuration of hearing loss, and tolerance limits and recruitment.

1. **Type of Hearing Loss**

   Conductive Hearing Loss: A conductive hearing loss created by a condition such as atresia requires a different type of amplification system than does a sensorineural loss. In the case of atresia, and other kinds of conductive losses that are not amenable to immediate medical or surgical remediation, a bone conduction aid is generally the appropriate type of aid to use. A bone conduction aid utilizes an oscillator, usually worn on a headband, in place of a receiver/earmold. The oscillator carries amplified sounds to the intact inner ear by vibrating the bones of the head.

Sensorineural Hearing Loss: An infant with a unilateral sensorineural hearing loss with normal hearing in the other ear is generally not fitted with amplification during infancy. At some later time the child or young adult may elect to try a CROS system in which a microphone is placed on the poor ear with the sound carried to a receiver at the normally hearing ear.

An infant with a bilateral sensorineural hearing loss is generally fitted with two hearing aids which are worn either at ear-level or on the chest, depending on the type chosen. Bilateral hearing losses vary from similar thresholds and configurations in the two ears to very different thresholds and configurations in the two ears. When fitting binaural losses, the requirements of each ear must be considered separately. What is an appropriate aid for the left ear may not be a proper choice for the right ear.

Mixed Hearing Loss: When the infant has both sensorineural and conductive hearing losses present, his thresholds for sound reflect the combination of the two types of losses. It is very important to try to eliminate the conductive component of the hearing loss through medical or surgical intervention; however, if the conductive component remains, the child's amplification system must reflect the poorer auditory thresholds caused by the addition of the conductive loss. If the child has a history of fluctuating hearing thresholds because of intermittent middle ear effusion (fluid), the audiologist and specialist will want to select adjustable amplification systems for trial use so that the aids can provide the necessary gain for both the sensorineural loss alone and for the greater mixed loss.

2. Degree of the Hearing Loss

A child with a severe-to-profound hearing loss requires a more powerful hearing aid than does a child with a mild loss. The aids selected for trial use should be evaluated for gain and output to ascertain that these specifications meet the child's needs.

3. Configuration of the Hearing Loss

Some infants have what are called "flat" hearing losses: their thresholds across the frequency range tested fall at about the same intensity level. Other infants have "dish-shaped" or "cookie bite" configurations, with poorer thresholds in the mid-frequencies than in the low and high frequencies. A "falling" or "ski-slope" configuration describes a hearing loss in which the thresholds get poorer as the frequencies get higher. A "rising" configuration describes the opposite configuration — thresholds are poorer in the low frequencies than in the high frequencies. An audiogram showing measurable hearing only in the low frequencies (at and below 500-750 Hz) with the thresholds at these low frequencies falling in the severe or profound hearing loss range is frequently called a "left corner" or "corner" audiogram. In selecting amplification for trial use, the audiologist and specialist must be certain that the frequency response characteristics of the aids are suitable for the configurations of the child's hearing losses.

4. Tolerance Limits and Recruitment

All of us experience a point at which sounds become too loud to be comfortable. This point is called the "tolerance level" or "threshold of discomfort." In the normal ear, the threshold of discomfort will generally be reached at approximately 100 dB HL or 120 dB SPL (Alpiner, 1975). There are several ways to determine an infant's threshold of discomfort. One method is to talk to the infant through earphones, slowly increasing the volume level until the loudness level at which the child displays signs of discomfort is reached. The child may frown, blink, turn his head from side to side, cry, or pull at the earphones to show his discomfort. Ling and Ling (1978) describe a procedure for subjectively judging a child's loudness discomfort level while he is wearing aids. They suggest using "noises with sharp onset like a handclap, one castanet struck against another, or a syllable such as [ba] spoken in a loud voice close to the microphone of the aid..." (pg. 93). It is important to know an infant's threshold of discomfort so that the maximum power output of his aid (discussed below) can be set below this level.

Recruitment is a condition in which the hearing-impaired individual perceives an abnormally rapid increase in loudness of a signal as the intensity of the signal is increased. Recruitment is experienced by some individuals whose hearing loss is a result of damage to the hair cells in the cochlea. One way to detect the presence of loudness recruitment is through use of the acoustic reflex test (Jerger, 1975). It is important to test for recruitment so that the amplification system placed on the child does not create discomfort by making sounds too loud.

SPECIFICATIONS OF THE HEARING AIDS
AVAILABLE FOR TRIAL USE

Three categories of variables related to the placement of hearing aids for trial use will be discussed: type and number of aids, electroacoustic parameters of aids, and earmold variables.

TYPE OF AIDS PLACED ON THE CHILD

Ear-level or body aids? Some of the child-related factors affecting this decision have been discussed above. If there are no compelling child-related reasons for selecting one type of amplification system over the other, then other factors can be considered. These factors can be discussed in terms of advantages and disadvantages of each system.

Ear-level Aids: Advantages

1. Because the aids are placed on the ear, the position of the microphone closely approximates the way in which the ears normally collect sound. The ear-mounted position helps the individual to localize the source of sound if his hearing thresholds are reasonably equal bilaterally.
2. There is nothing covering the microphone of the aid (e.g., clothing) that will create a noise.
3. The aids are out of the child's sight which may promote more rapid adaptation to their use, and out of the way for activities that are common to young children.
4. The frequency response characteristics of ear-level aids are more flexible than body aids, especially in obtaining high-frequency emphasis.
5. Ear-level aids can now produce as much gain as most body aids.
6. Ear-level aids are not as visible as body aids. This creates advantages for the child in social situations. As one parent reported (Flexer and Wood, 1984): "One of the greatest advantages we found since our child wore the ear-level aids is that she is treated as a little girl, not a hearing-impaired little girl . . . A body aid is like a flashing announcement to the public that she is hearing-impaired, which in turn hinders normal communication" (p. 358).

Ear-level Aids: Disadvantages

1. FEEDBACK! One of the major problems associated with hearing aid placement on young, therefore small, children is the problem of amplified sound leaking out of the ear canal and being picked up by the microphone of the hearing aid. This process disrupts the normal function of the hearing aid and produces a squealing

sound that can drive a parent and specialist crazy. Worse than the sound is the fact that when a hearing aid is in this state of electronic super-saturation, *it is amplifying sound in a distorted form, if at all* (Ling and Ling, 1978). If the child hears anything at all, it is the squeal. Feedback cannot be tolerated. Unfortunately, the easiest way to eliminate feedback — lowering the gain provided by the hearing aid by turning down the volume wheel — is the least productive solution. Lowering the gain may eliminate the possibility of sound being made loud enough for the child to hear. Effective ways of eliminating feedback will be discussed later in this chapter.

2. Batteries used in ear-level aids must be replaced frequently. Keeping well-functioning batteries in the child's aids requires regular measurement of the voltage of the battery on a battery tester and replacement every 10-20 days when the battery dies. The life of a battery depends on several variables, including the gain setting at which the aid is worn and the number of hours the aid is worn each day.

3. Batteries used in ear-level aids are small and can be easily swallowed by little children. Since batteries contain caustic substances, their ingestion can result in serious problems for the child (Kenna and Stool, 1983). Parents of small children who use ear-level aids must monitor their child as he wears the aids until he can be trusted not to dismantle them.

4. Ear-level aids are small. When they fall off a child's ear they are difficult to spot in some environments. Dogs, however, have no trouble finding and chewing on them. Lawnmowers have also demonstrated an affinity for ear-level aids.

5. Because of the size, shape, or position of some children's ears, aids do not always lie naturally against the child's head. Aids that dangle in mid-air by the child's ear are susceptible to being knocked off or being pulled off by the child and damaged.

Body Aids: Advantages

1. Because body aids are usually worn on the chest in a harness or pocket, the microphone of the aid is separated from the ear canal by a greater distance than is the case with ear-level aids. Thus, if amplified sound leaks out of the ear canal, it is less likely to be picked up by the microphone and re-amplified, producing feedback.

2. Some body aids have built-in batteries that are rechargeable. These batteries must be recharged every night but replaced only every 12 to 18 months as compared with every 10 to 20 days for batteries used in ear-level aids.

3. The batteries used in body aids are larger than those used in ear-

level aids and cannot be easily swallowed by a child.

4. Body aids are larger and more durable than ear-level aids. However, they are not impervious to damage.

5. Some parents prefer the security of being able to fasten body aids into a harness on the child's chest as opposed to dealing with problems that may be associated with keeping the ear-level aid in position behind the child's ear.

6. The controls on body aids are generally more visible and accessible to parents who need to change and check the settings of the aid.

7. Some professionals swear by body aids for children of all ages who have measureable hearing only at 250 and 500 Hz because body aids do not generate the low frequency distortion that is characteristic of ear-level aids.

Body Aids: Disadvantages

1. The microphones of the aids are located at the level of the child's chest, so the origin of all sound the child hears is his chest area. When the microphone is covered by clothing such as a heavy shirt, not only is the effectiveness of the microphone reduced, but the child may hear the amplified sound of cloth rubbing over the microphone.

2. The cord which connects the body containing the microphone and amplifier of the aid to the receiver-earmold of the aid is the weak spot in the system. Young children like to chew on and twist cords. A tiny break in the cord will cause either intermittent transmission or no transmission of amplified auditory signals to the child's ear.

3. Since body aids are generally visible to the child, the instruments and dials are a constant source of temptation as entertainment.

4. Body aids and harnesses are bulky. When worn on the chest, they are susceptible to food being spilled on them, to the child falling on them, and to being situated under a table top when the child is seated at a table so that the microphone does not pick up sound well.

5. Some parents may feel that the more bulky and visible body aids mark their child as handicapped. This is a valid observation. However, if the result of this feeling is that the parents do not put the aids on their child in certain situations, the child's opportunity to acquire listening skills is diminished. When parents' decisions have an adverse affect on their child's opportunity to achieve essential skills, the specialist must give them this information. It may be that the parents' behaviors are symptomatic of their lack of acceptance of their child's hearing loss, a difficult issue but one the specialist must quickly address.

IHR PREFERENCE FOR TYPE OF AIDS AND
APPROACH TO HANDLING PROBLEMS

The audiologists and specialists at IHR regard ear-level aids as the fitting of choice, unless child-related factors or uncontrollable feedback indicate that body aids will work better for the time being. We have learned strategies for dealing with two of the main problems associated with use of ear-level aids on small children: feedback and keeping the aid in place behind the child's ear and against the child's head.

Eliminating Feedback

Specialists and parents take the following steps when a child's aid is producing feedback. If Step 1 does not solve the feedback problem, we move to Step 2, then Step 3, etc.

1. Re-position the earmold in the ear canal. Almost every child experiences feedback when the aid is moved so that the earmold is partially dislodged from its proper place in the ear. This feedback can be eliminated by pushing the earmold back into place in the ear canal. Children who can hear the feedback learn to do this themselves at a young age.
2. Check to make certain that the volume wheel of the aid has not been turned higher than the infant's prescribed setting.
3. Check the hearing aid system for feedback. Remove the squealing aid from the child's ear (do not turn the aid off). Place thumb firmly over the hole in the end of the canal of the earmold. If feedback continues, the problem is in the hearing aid system:
   • Check for holes in the earmold or tubing.
   • Check the connection between the tubing and earhook. The tubing should be pushed up far enough over the earhook to prevent sound from escaping.
   • Check for cracks in the case of the hearing aid.
   • If none of the above problems are evident, the hearing aid is most likely malfunctioning and producing internal feedback. If the aid is malfunctioning, this should be apparent when the aid is tested electroacoustically on a hearing aid analyzer. Send malfunctioning aids in for repair.
4. Check the fit of the child's earmold. A visual examination of the earmold while it is in the child's ear should not show any gaps between the earmold and the child's concha. Rock the earmold gently back and forth in the child's ear and see if gaps appear. If the earmold does not fit properly, it is necessary to have another impression and earmold made.
5. Check the length of the ear canal on the earmold. If the earmold is new and it appears to fit well, yet feedback is still occurring,

compare the length of the ear canal on the new mold with one of the child's outgrown molds or with another child's mold. A canal that is too short can be the cause of feedback.

6. Conduct tympanometry or do a physical examination to check for signs of middle ear effusion. This condition can alter the flexibility of the eardrum and the shape of the ear canal, resulting in an improperly fitting earmold and feedback.

7. Replace the tubing on the earmold with heavy-wall tubing.

8. If none of the procedures listed above eliminates the feedback, the audiologist or specialist can do one of three things: have another impression and earmold made; fit the child with a different brand or model of aid, perhaps trying one with the microphone in a different position on the aid; or switch to the use of body aids (which will also require that another earmold be made).

IHR specialists have, in the past, used a denture adhesive which we molded around the ear canal of the earmold to stop feedback. We abandoned this practice when we found that the substance cracked after a short period of time, leaving sharp edges.

Keeping the Hearing Aid in Place Behind the Child's Ear and Against the Child's Head.

If the child's ear-level aid does not stay in the proper position, the specialist or parent can follow the steps below and make adjustments as necessary:

1. Remove the earmold from the aid and check the angle at which the tubing emerges from the earmold. If the tubing was improperly installed or has rotated inside the earmold, it will not allow the aid to be attached at the proper angle to the earmold. The tubing should come out of the earmold so that it angles up and slightly toward the front of the earmold (the edge closest to the child's face) (Illustration 1a). Earmolds can be retubed in a relatively simple process that requires only a few special tools.

2. The hearing aid can be attached to the tubing so that a slight torque or twist is introduced into the tubing (Illustration 1b). When the earmold is inserted into the child's ear, the slight twist in the tubing pulls the aid against the child's head. This can be an effective way to counteract the tendency of an aid to dangle away from the child's head.

3. With the aid in place on the child's ear, check the length of the tubing. The earhook of the aid should curve right around the top front point at which the pinna meets the head. If the earhook is above this point, the tubing may be too long.

ILLUSTRATION 1.

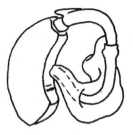

1a. Angle at which tubing should be installed in ear-mold for ear-level aid.

1b. Angle at which hearing aid should be attached to tubing of earmold to introduce a torque that pulls aid against child's head.

---

4. Another cause of improper fit at the junction of pinna and head is having the wrong size earhook attached to the aid. Earhooks come in several sizes commonly called standard, half-round, and quarter-round or "pediatric" earhooks. The half-round and quarter-round bend at sharper angles than does the standard earhook (Illustration 2) and may wrap around the child's ear in a better fit. Local hearing aid dealers will be able to provide you with a supply of all sizes of earhooks that are appropriate for the brands and models of aids being worn by the children you serve.

5. Different brands and models of ear-level aids vary in size and shape. Thickness, length, and curve of the aid are all factors that will affect the way in which the aid fits the infant. The specialist and audiologist may determine that one aid has the correct electroacoustic specifications for the child, yet find, during the trial-use period that the aid simply does not conform to the child's head and ear in a comfortable, secure manner. This would be sufficient reason *not* to recommend the aid for purchase if other aids with equally appropriate electroacoustic properties and behavioral results provide a better fit.

6. Huggie Aids (TM) are a product designed to keep ear-level aids securely fixed on a child's ear (Huggie Aids, 837 N.W. 10th, Oklahoma City, OK 73106).

7. A last resort, and a less than satisfactory solution for the flopping aid syndrome, is the use of some kind of adhesive to hold the aid to the child's head. Double-sided cloth-type tape (not carpet tape!) such as that made by Johnson and Johnson can be used. Hal-Hen Company (Long Island City, New York) sells double-backed round adhesive pads that can be used for this purpose. Parents will need to examine the skin behind the ear after tape has

been used to make certain that the tape is not causing redness or sores.

Parents worry about their young child losing an aid that gets bumped off the child's ear. Some parents have tied dental floss or fishing line from the child's aid to a safety pin which is attached to the child's shirt. It the child removes the aid or if it falls out of the child's ear, the aid will stay connected to the child.

ILLUSTRATION 2

SIZES OF EARHOOKS

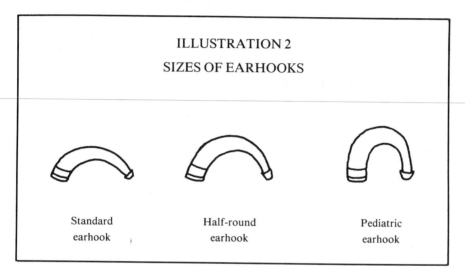

| Standard earhook | Half-round earhook | Pediatric earhook |

NUMBER OF AIDS PLACED ON THE CHILD: ONE OR TWO HEARING AIDS?

The normally hearing person has binaural hearing, that is, he hears with two ears. The information he receives from the opposite sides of his head is blended together and perceived in the brain as one signal. Briskey (1978) discusses the many advantages of binaural hearing. One advantage of binaural hearing is that it allows us to localize sound, that is, tell where sound comes from. When a sound originates on our right side, the waves generated by the sound strike the right ear milliseconds before the sound waves travel around the head and strike the left ear. Our brain is able to make use of this difference to let us know to which side we should look to find the sound source. Another advantage of hearing with two ears is evident in noisy situations, such as at a party. The use of two ears is helpful in hearing a signal such as voice over the noise, partly because we can situate ourselves with one ear directed toward the sound source to which we want to attend. Perhaps the most compelling advantage of binaural hearing is the fact that when listeners are asked for their subjective opinion, they prefer listening with two ears.

The IHR audiologist and specialists choose to fit hearing-impaired infants with two hearing aids unless there is a good reason to fit only one ear. Two factors support this preference for binaural fittings. First, binaural hearing is a natural condition for the normally hearing child. It apparently creates differences in listening that are experienced by the listener as preferable to the monaural condition. The binaural listening condition that most closely approximates normal for the hearing-impaired infant occurs when he is fitted with ear-level aids that provide him with near-equal aided hearing thresholds in both ears.

Second, auditory evaluation with infants does not give us a definitive picture of what and how an infant hears. We know how loud sounds must be in order for the child to hear them at the frequencies that are measured, but we know nothing about the quality of sound that the child receives. While the child may test as having better auditory thresholds in one ear, for example, he may also have a pathological condition in that ear which creates noise or distortion. This noise or distortion, when added to or subtracted from the incoming signal, may render the signal unusable. The child's other ear may test as having poorer thresholds for sound but may be free of distortion. The information the child receives from that ear may be much more useful to him. In addition, placement of amplification binaurally stimulates the development of nerve pathways from both cochleae to the brain so that the child later has the option of choosing to use a hearing aid on only one ear if he finds that he functions better that way.

ELECTROACOUSTIC CHARACTERISTICS OF HEARING AIDS

Hearing aids are built with differing specifications in an effort to meet the broad range of needs found in hearing aid users. Because no two people and hearing loss combinations are alike, no one hearing aid can work for the entire hearing-impaired population. The electroacoustic characteristics of hearing aids can be measured on a hearing aid analyzer in three ways to determine which aids are appropriate for which hearing-impaired person. These three electroacoustic characteristics are: 1) saturation sound pressure level or SSPL (also called Maximum Power Output or MPO), 2) gain, and 3) frequency response. Almost all high gain/output ear-level hearing aids have controls that allow adjustment of these characteristics within the aid itself. Each of these characteristics is discussed below.

DETERMINING APPROPRIATE SATURATION
SOUND PRESSURE LEVEL

SSPL is the maximum level of amplified signal, measured in dB, that the aid will produce at a given SSPL setting. SSPL is measured on a hearing aid analyzer with the gain-control of the aid turned to full-on and with an input to the hearing aid microphone of 90 dB SPL (Kasten, 1978). Hearing aids have this built-in (and adjustable) maximum level of output so that, regardless of the intensity of the signal that enters the microphone of the aid, the intensity level of the signal coming out of the aid will not exceed a certain predetermined level.

SSPL should be set below the user's tolerance level or threshold of discomfort. When properly set, this built-in limit on the output of the signal protects the user from the uncomfortable or damaging effects of excessively loud sounds that occur in the environment. The two most common means of limiting output on a hearing aid are peak clipping and automatic gain control (also called compression amplification or automatic volume control — AVC). See M. Pollack (1975), Kasten (1978), and Ross (1978) for discussion of the differences in these methods of limiting output.

Setting SSPL on an Infant's Hearing Aids

The audiologist can use three kinds of information in making the decision of how to set the SSPL on an infant's aids. Information can be gained from the infant's tolerance level for loud sounds (Ross, 1975), from measurement of the infant's acoustic reflex (McCandless, 1973), and from observation of the infant's behavior while wearing the aids. The most important rule to observe is that the SSPL must be set below the infant's tolerance level or threshold of discomfort. Once the aids are placed on the child, the audiologist can present sounds of increasing intensity to make certain that the child does not show any behaviors such as blinking, crying, rocking, or pulling at his aids that would indicate he is experiencing discomfort as a result of the intensity of the signal that is reaching his ear. Should these behaviors occur in response to signals of increased intensity, the audiologist should immediately decrease the SSPL of the aid.

The audiologist and specialist will also want to assure that the SSPL of an aid is not set so low that the speech signal is clipped off or the aid is driven into compression at an unnecessarily low intensity, thus cutting off the signal the child receives. As a general rule of thumb, the SSPL of hearing aids fitted on young children with mild to moderate losses should not exceed 120 dB SPL; young children with severe or profound losses can probably safely tolerate SSPL's above 120 dB SPL, but SSPL outputs approaching 130 dB SPL should be used only with caution and a good deal of close observation.

DETERMINING THE AMOUNT OF GAIN
AN INFANT'S AIDS SHOULD PROVIDE

There are several methods set forth as guidelines for determining the amount of gain a hearing aid user requires to enable him to make maximum use of his residual hearing. Adults who use hearing aids commonly adjust the volume control on their aid as their environmental conditions change. Infants are not able to do this. Setting the gain on a young child's aids involves, to a certain extent, educated guesswork. The key term is "educated." Prior to the time a hearing aid is fitted on the infant, the prudent audiologist and specialist have accumulated test and observation data that will enable them to establish an initial gain setting for the child that will be both beneficial and safe. Like other decisions that are made in working with infants and young children, decisions regarding gain are not etched in stone.

The most useful pieces of data on which to base the initial amount of gain provided to a child are his unaided audiogram and knowledge of his tolerance limits, variables which are unique to each child. Having acquired this information, the audiologist asks, "What is my objective in placing amplification?" As stated earlier, the IHR objective in placing amplification is to raise the child's auditory thresholds to within a range that he can both perceive and discriminate speech without exceeding his tolerance level. The audiologist, therefore, must know the frequency range and range of intensity of average speech in order to know how much gain an infant will need to meet this objective. Ling and Ling (1978) have produced a very useful chart, affectionately termed the "speech banana" by many users, which provides the audiologist with information on the frequencies and relative intensity levels (HL) of the main components of five low, mid, and high frequency speech sounds [u, a, i, ʃ , s] as spoken by an adult male at two yards (Illustration 3). By superimposing the "speech banana" over a child's unaided audiogram, the audiologist and parent-infant specialist can determine how much gain the child needs to raise his thresholds to within (or above) the audible range for the speech sound that occurs at each of the five measured frequencies. Ling and Ling (1978) report that children whose aided hearing brings these five sounds above threshold will be able to hear all speech sounds.

There are limits to this approach. One problem is immediately apparent for the profoundly deaf child whose thresholds fall at or beyond the limits of the audiometer. There are no hearing aids powerful enough to raise this child's thresholds to the point where conversational speech will be audible. However, the goal is to get as close as possible. A profoundly deaf child who cannot hear a male voice at two yards may only perceive speech delivered 6-8 inches from the microphone of his hearing aid. That is better than not hearing individual speech sounds or the intonational patterns of speech at all. Another problem arises if a child's hearing loss has a

FREQUENCY IN HERTZ (Hz)

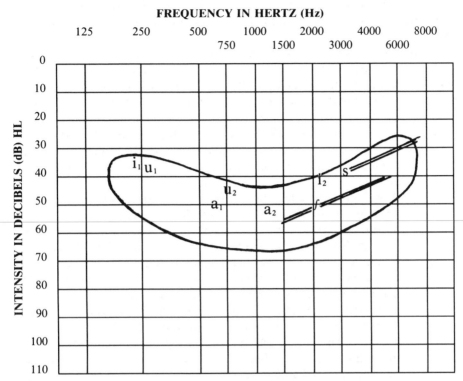

ILLUSTRATION 3. The "speech banana" which shows the relative intensities (hearing level) of the main formants of the five sounds in the Five-Sound Speech Test [u, a, i, ʃ, s] spoken at two yards. [After Ling and Ling (1978), p. 95, with permission.]

precipitously falling or rising configuration. It may not be possible to fit this child with a hearing aid that will amplify all frequencies to the degree necessary to bring all thresholds into the "speech banana." The audiologist will need to make decisions regarding which frequencies will allow the child to best perceive and discriminate speech and which hearing aid will provide amplification in those frequencies.

The aids selected for the child's use should provide the amount of gain the child needs when the volume wheel is *less* than fully rotated. Lotterman and Kasten (1967) report that some hearing aids produce relatively high levels of distortion when the gain control is advanced beyond the one-half to three-quarters position. On the other hand, a hearing aid which meets the child's gain requirements when the volume wheel is rotated only one-quarter on is not an appropriate choice either. A less powerful aid should be selected to prevent the discomfort and/or damage to the ear that may result if the volume wheel is accidently rotated too far.

Once a gain level has been selected and the aid placed on the child, another very significant piece of data can be acquired: an aided sound field audiogram which includes the child's responses to both warbled pure tones and speech. Using this data, the audiologist may decide to raise or lower the gain setting used in generating the audiogram and test the child at the new gain setting.

When an initial gain setting is selected and the child is sent home with his hearing aids, parents are asked to keep track of the infant's use of the aid and to collect additional data about the child's behaviors while wearing the aids (Figure 5). Parents are asked to look for the following child behaviors:

1. Blinks, frowns, grimaces, or crying when loud sounds occur. Parents should be instructed to turn the volume wheel down if they observe these behaviors and to report the behaviors to the audiologist and specialist, who may then reduce the SSPL on the aid.

2. A listening attitude. Some infants who, while wearing aids are hearing for the first time, begin to look up or around, to cease movement, or to smile or frown briefly when sounds occur in their environment. Some infants "freeze" and wait as if trying to figure out what this new phenomenon is. These are all indications of the baby's new awareness of sound — an indication that the hearing aids are doing what they are supposed to do.

3. Increased vocalization. Some infants begin to vocalize more almost immediately after hearing aids are placed. This is a very gratifying signal that the child is hearing — and being reinforced by — his own voice. (See "The Role of the Auditory Feedback Mechanism," Chapter 17).

A listening attitude and increased vocalization provide excellent information about the suitability of the amount of gain that the hearing aids are providing. Conversely, the child's failure to display these types of responses does not necessarily mean that the gain of his aids should be increased, unless the initial setting has been very conservative. Some young children require longer periods of time to adjust to the presence of sound before they give definitive responses. Some profoundly deaf children get very minimal auditory input even with substantial amounts of gain, and it may take them a year or longer to learn to respond to such minimal signals (see Chapter 17).

Audiologists and specialists who have worked with a large number of young hearing-impaired children over several years acquire a feel for how children with varying degrees of hearing loss will respond to amplification. If a child does not respond as anticipated, that information is factored into all the other data that are being collected about the child's auditory behaviors.

BEGINNING HEARING AID USE

Day / Date	Time of Day	Length of Time	Responses Observed to Sounds (look up to speaker's voice? to recorded music at 50dB)	Problems
3/18/86	10:15 (in session)	35 minutes		His hand went up to aids several times.
	2:30 pm	1 hr 15 min	turned to stop clock & watch on TV.	pulled right aid out - I had a hard time getting it back in.
3-19-86	8:30 am	45 min	kept playing with his noisemaker toys	—
	10:30 am	1½ hours	was quite alert a...	some feedback - pushed aid...
	3:00 pm	5 minutes	pulled out - daughter from...	
	6:30 pm	1 hour	dad played with him...	pulled out twice...

Name Philip

Date 3-18-84

Type of Hearing Aid Unitron E1-P

monaural _____   binaural X

Parent-Infant Communication, 1985
Handout — Parent Auditory Development Objectives 14, 40

PH-54

FIGURE 5. The first line of this form is completed by the specialist when hearing aids are first placed on the child in a session. The parents then take several forms home and fill them out for the first week or so that the child is wearing aids. Parents bring the completed forms to sessions to discuss with the specialist the child's responses to sound while wearing the aids and any problems with the hearing aids.

FIGURE 5.

DETERMINING THE APPROPRIATE FREQUENCY
RESPONSE OF A CHILD'S AIDS

Frequency response is a measure of the amount of amplification that a hearing aid provides at different frequencies. Aids can be classified in three groups according to frequency response which can be measured on a hearing aid analyzer:

1. Conventional frequency response: provides the most gain in the frequencies 350 to 3500 Hz.
2. Extended low frequency amplification: provides low frequency energy below 350 Hz in an effort to enable profoundly deaf individuals to make use of low frequency residual hearing.
3. High frequency emphasis: provides more gain in frequencies above 2000 Hz in order to provide more information for understanding speech, particularly the high frequency sibilants [s] and [ʃ]; can also mean "low cut" amplification in which the aid provides little or no gain at 250, 500 and even 1000 Hz for individuals with falling or "ski-slope" configurations of hearing loss.

The child's audiogram gives the audiologist information about the frequency response required in an appropriate hearing aid. The audiologist looks at the configuration of the child's loss to determine which frequencies need to be amplified in order to bring the child's aided thresholds throughout the frequency range up into the "speech banana." If the child has a hearing loss with a relatively flat configuration, an aid with a flat frequency response or one with a gently rising frequency response will be appropriate. Care must be taken not to fit the child with an aid that will amplify the lower frequencies to the extent that, under conditions of low-frequency noise, the high frequencies are masked out (Northern and Downs, 1984). Since it is the higher frequency consonants of speech that carry meaning, the child who hears only the lower frequency vowels will have a difficult time discriminating speech.

A child with a rising configuration — better unaided hearing in the high frequencies than in the low — will require an aid with more gain in the lower frequencies than in the high. A child with a "corner" audiogram (measureable hearing only in the lowest frequencies) may get maximum benefit from an extended low frequency aid, one that provides more gain than usual below 350 Hz.

The frequency response of any given aid can be altered using both the internal controls on the aid (controls other than those the user adjusts such as volume or M-T-O switch) and the earmold which is attached to the aid. The audiologist and specialist need to be aware that the manufacturer's specifications which delineate the frequency response for an aid are measured on the equivalent of an adult ear. The smaller size of the child's ear canal alters the frequency response and gain of the sound reaching the child's eardrum.

To acquire a truer picture of the gain at each frequency delivered to the child's eardrum, it is necessary to measure the output of the aid with the child's earmold attached. To obtain an accurate measure of the amount of gain delivered at each frequency through the earmold while it is in the ear (called insertion gain curve), it is necessary to use a probe microphone. At one time available only for laboratory use, probe microphones are now available for clinical use. Use of the probe microphone may require drilling an extra vent hole in the infant's earmold (the hole is plugged once the insertion gain curve is obtained) and careful and exact placement of the probe in the ear canal, a task that may be difficult to perform on an infant or young child.

It is evident from the discussion of SSPL, gain, and frequency response that these variables are of great importance in selecting aids for trial use and subsequent purchase for an infant and young child. Infants and young children are using their aided residual hearing to acquire a spoken language system. They have a particular need to hear over the widest possible frequency range so that all the individual speech sounds and intonational patterns of speech are available to them.

Use of a Hearing Aid Analyzer

The IHR audiologist and specialists use a hearing aid analyzer to determine the appropriate settings for each aid. The IHR staff regards the hearing aid analyzer as one of the most essential pieces of equipment that the agency owns. The analyzer enables the staff 1) to determine if a hearing aid is performing up to factory specifications, 2) to determine the effects of adjustment of each setting and combinations of settings of controls, 3) to ascertain the amount of gain available at each frequency measured, and 4) to determine the percentage of distortion the aid introduces into a pure tone stimulus at selected frequencies. The use of the hearing aid analyzer makes it possible for the audiologist, specialist, and parents to know most of the parameters of the amplification systems being placed on the child and to monitor the performance of the hearing aids on a weekly basis to determine that the aids are functioning as they should.

It is important to be aware that standard electroacoustic analysis of hearing aids does not provide a complete picture of what the hearing aid will do when an infant's earmold is attached to the aid and the earmold is inserted into the infant's ear. When a hearing aid is placed into a test box for analysis it is attached to a 2cc coupler. The hard metal walls of this coupler are not like the soft wall of the ear canal. This difference means it is not possible to make a direct comparison of the gain of the aid as measured in the test box and at the eardrum of the infant. It is also true that the volume of an infant's ear canal is about one-half that of the volume of the adult ear canal. This smaller volume *increases* the sound pressure level of the signal that reaches the infant's ear drum by about 6 dB relative to the adult ear. These and other factors which create differences between the performance of the aid in the test box and on the infant's ear point out the limits of electroacoustic analysis as the sole source of information used to select personal hearing aids for an infant. However, this information is an excellent starting point when followed by aided audiological evaluation and observation of the infant's performance with hearing aids over time.

EARMOLD VARIABLES

The earmold is an essential part of the hearing aid system. The earmold is the only part of the system that is truly "made to order." While the hearing aid itself is carefully selected and adjusted to match the needs of the hearing aid user, it is not made — as are eyeglasses, for instance — specifically for the user. The earmold is a very important part of the hearing aid system for the infant and young child because a well-fitting earmold can enable many children with severe to profound losses to receive the amount of gain they need to perceive and discriminate speech without experiencing feedback. Earmolds for children should be made out of soft materials such as silicone so that when the child bumps his ear — and they all do — the earmold will be forgiving.

Most children with moderate, severe, or profound losses wear occluding molds as opposed to open molds. It is often necessary to work with the personnel in the laboratory that makes earmolds for children to determine the thickness and shape that works best for small ears. There are instances in which clinicians find it necessary to work with several labs until they find one that can best meet the needs of the pediatric population. In order to have the freedom to do this it may be necessary for the audiologist or specialist to become skilled at making earmold impressions — not an easy task on a squirming, crying baby — so that the impressions can be mailed to the lab from which the best service is available.

As the audiologist gains increasing information about the child's amplification needs he or she may want to use venting, damping (use of filters), or horn coupling to make the amplification system more responsive to the child's needs.

PROCEDURES FOR EVALUATING THE EFFECTIVENESS OF AIDS DURING TRIAL-USE PERIODS

The first set of loaner aids is generally placed for a period of two to six months to give the child a solid foundation of listening experience and to give the audiologist, specialist, and parents the opportunity to assess the child's responsiveness to sound with amplification. During this period the child is seen by the audiologist on several occasions to obtain aided gain scores for both amplified ears together and for each amplified ear separately. The information obtained from formal audiologic assessment is combined with information gained by the parent-infant specialist and parents through observation of the child wearing amplification at home and in habilitation sessions.

The specialist and parents look for changes in the child's behaviors in *two* areas: 1) responsiveness to sound, and 2) production of vocalizations. Using the auditory landmarks and the auditory objectives in *Parent-Infant Communication* (Infant Hearing Resource, 1985), the specialist and parents can determine auditory skills the child has developed prior to the use of amplification and begin the process of teaching subsequent skills as specified in the developmental sequence in the curriculum (see Chapter 17). If the child has achieved several auditory objectives while using one set of trial-use hearing aids, parents and specialist would look for retention of these skills and continued acquisition of additional skills when a second set of loaner aids is placed for a trial-use period.

The series of auditory landmarks listed in the curriculum are particularly useful when the child has first acquired hearing aids. The landmarks are behaviors that cannot be taught to the child, but are behaviors that signal the child's growing awareness of sound as a result of using amplification. As such, they are extremely useful as indicators of the effectiveness of the amplification system being used for a trial period and can serve as one basis for comparison of different amplification systems. Objectives found in the parent curriculum in *Parent-Infant Communication* spell out the skills parents need in order to be good observers of their child's auditory behaviors and information about what kinds of auditory behaviors to look for in their child. This curriculum also contains a list of objectives for parents related to their child's successful use of hearing aids.

The IHR specialist keeps a record of each child's trial hearing aid usage on a form called "Hearing Aid Trial-Use Record" (Illustration 4). She also retains the hearing aid analyzer readout of each aid that the child uses so that there is a record of the actual performance for each aid as the child was using it. As a child is using a set of aids, the readouts for those aids are placed in a notebook next to the test box. When the parents check their child's aids on a weekly basis, they compare the current output and distortion of the aids with the original values that were established for the child's use. If there is a discrepancy, the parents and specialist work together to determine what has caused the change and to make the adjustments necessary to match the original values. If an aid is malfunctioning, it is sent in for repair.

When the child has worn the first set of loaner aids for a period long enough to gather data on his performance with the aids, a second set of aids is placed for trial use. It should be noted that the expectations for each child's performance with amplification are different and decisions related

HEARING AID TRIAL-USE RECORD

Name _Liza_   Birthdate _6/8/78_   Date Enrolled _3/27/79_

Aid: Make _Fonix_
Model _H-1001 (body aids)_
Serial Nos. _2787, 2656_

Settings:	R	L
SSPL*	126 dB	125 dB
Tone	—	—
Gain**	54 dB	55 dB
Other	—	—

(Attach Hearing Aid Analyzer print-out)

Date placed _4/11/79_
Date removed _2/5/80_
Length of time worn _10 months_
Type of earmold worn _occluding_

Child's aided sound-field responses: (dB HL)
250 Hz	50	2000 Hz	70
500 Hz	60	3/4000 Hz	70
1000 Hz	70	6000 Hz	

Speech Awareness _55 dB HL_
Level of Discomfort _—_
Other:

Behavioral responses observed: _Vocalized more with aids on. Responded to loud environmental sounds and inconsistently to voice._
Problems: _Wore during all of her waking hours with no behavioral or technical problems._

Aids recommended for purchase: Makes _Bosch_

* HF Avg. SSPL 90
** HF Avg. Gain at use-level

Aid: Make _Widex_
Model _A 2H (ear-level)_
Serial Nos. _204123, 349689_

Settings:	R	L
SSPL*	128 dB	127 dB
Tone	N	N
Gain**	56 dB	55 dB
Other	—	—

(Attach Hearing Aid Analyzer print-out)

Date placed _2/15/80_
Date removed _4/16/80_
Length of time worn _2 months_
Type of earmold worn _occluding_

Child's aided sound-field responses: (dB HL)
250 Hz	NR	2000 Hz	65
500 Hz	40	3/4000 Hz	NR
1000 Hz	55	6000 Hz	

Speech Awareness _35 dB HL_
Level of Discomfort _—_
Other:

Behavioral responses observed: _Did well with aids; vocalized a lot and became more aware of voice._
Problems: _None_

Models _66 F Super_

Aid: Make _Bosch_
Model _66 F Super (ear-level)_
Serial Nos. _2438111, 2438119_

Settings:	R	L
SSPL*	126 dB	126 dB
Tone	N	N
Gain**	56 dB	57 dB
Other	PC-5	PC-5

(Attach Hearing Aid Analyzer print-out)

Date placed _1/6/81_
Date removed _recommended for purchase_
Length of time worn _occluding_
Type of earmold worn _occluding_

Child's aided sound-field responses: (dB HL)
250 Hz	35	2000 Hz	75
500 Hz	40	3/4000 Hz	NR
1000 Hz	40	6000 Hz	
1500 Hz	60		

Speech Awareness _35 dB HL_
Level of Discomfort _—_
Other:

Behavioral responses observed: _Continued to acquire listening skills and to increase amount and complexity of vocalizations. Alternated trial use period with Widex A2H aids again. Saw slightly better responsiveness with Bosch aids._

Date Obtained _1/82_

ILLUSTRATION 4:   Above are descriptions of three of the five sets of hearing aids placed for trial-use periods with Liza who enrolled at IHR at nine months of age. (See audiogram, p. 526)

ILLUSTRATION 4

to length of trial amplification periods are entirely individual for each infant. Some infants who have sufficient residual hearing exhibit signs of awareness of sound the minute hearing aids are placed. The audiologist and specialist have expected to see these signs of awareness based on the audiological, medical, and parent report information they have gathered. If the child does not evidence responsiveness as expected within a short period of time, another set of loaner aids will be placed. The audiologist and specialist will have a different set of expectations for the infant whose auditory thresholds fall at the output limits of the audiometer. They are aware that, even with the best possible amplification, the infant is receiving faint and less frequent auditory information and his responses are likely to be less immediate and less prominent than those of a moderately or severely hearing-impaired child.

When an infant has handicapping conditions in addition to hearing loss, the process of evaluating auditory responsiveness requires even more detailed observation over time. The multi-handicapped child's responses to sound may be expressed in subtle, seemingly unrelated movements, facial expressions, or vocalizations and may appear some time after the stimulus has occurred. Audiologist, specialist, and parents will need to look for and record behaviors that occur subsequent to a sound in order to determine if they are repeatable and consistently linked to the sound (See Chapter 26).

The process of trial hearing aid use may take up to a year or even two depending on the number of aids tried (generally 2-5 sets) and the amount of information that can be gained from observation of the child's responses to sound. Ear infections, immature behavior, and changing thresholds may complicate the gathering of data from infants and toddlers. During the hearing aid evaluation process the child's auditory perceptual skills continue to develop and the specialist and parents gather additional data about the child's responsiveness to sounds. All of the information that has been gathered on the child during the trial-use periods is used in making a recommendation for purchase of the best available hearing aids for the child. Following purchase of the child's hearing aids, (usually by the parents, though some families need assistance from service clubs to purchase the aids) the final step of the IHR pediatric audiology program is carried out.

ONGOING EVALUATION OF THE INFANT'S AUDITORY CAPABILITIES

When the hearing aid evaluation and recommendation process is completed, the audiologist continues to monitor the child's auditory performance with and without hearing aids at least twice a year for the duration of the child's enrollment at IHR. Evaluation is conducted more frequently if the child's responsiveness to sound appears to be changing or if the child has frequent middle ear problems. Tympanometry is carried out by the specialist during regular habilitation sessions whenever there is concern about the child's middle ear status. The specialist continues to teach parents the information and skills they need to provide their child with developmentally appropriate auditory stimuli. The goals of the IHR audiology program overlap with goals established for both the infant and the parent related to development of auditory perceptual skills. These goals for infants and parents are discussed at greater length in Chapter 17.

COCHLEAR IMPLANTS: A BRIEF DISCUSSION

More than twenty years after the first surgical procedure in the United States to implant a permanent device providing direct electrical stimulation to the eighth cranial nerve via the cochlea, the advisability of cochlear implants for children is still debated. There are several issues involved in the consideration of implants for deaf children. Citing the post-implant data gathered on some of the 1000 adults world-wide who have received cochlear implants, Schein (1984) stated, "There are no reports that, as a result of the cochlear implant, patients have gained or regained the ability to understand speech without visual cues" (p. 329). He described some adult patients' abilities to differentiate male from female voices and to perceive intensity variation and rhythm when listening to speech. Other investigators (Eddington and Orth, 1985; Dowell, Brown, Seligman, and Clark, 1985) report that adults implanted with multi-channel devices do show significant improvement in speech discrimination and understanding.

A major issue regarding implants for children is the question of the amount of cochlear and retrocochlear damage potentially caused by implanting the devices. Since present day technology may not enable the cochlear implant user to discriminate speech, arguments against implanting children center on the concern that damage done as a result of early implants may make it impossible for a child to make use of more effective implanted devices as they become available in the future.

Proponents of cochlear implants for profoundly deaf children such as Dr. William House of the House Ear Institute in Los Angeles, who by 1984 had placed implants in approximately 100 children (Radcliffe, 1984), advocate the use of implants with children who are unable to gain any benefit from hearing aids. Proponents cite the importance of early auditory stimulation and the psychological benefits of bringing the individual into contact with the world of sound and suggest that cochlear implants provide these benefits even if they do not deliver high quality sound or speech information.

The Ad Hoc Committee on Cochlear Implants of the American Speech and Hearing Association (ASHA, 1986) includes in its recommendations the following statement:

"At this time, the risks of neural damage and degeneration associated with the intracochlear device (long-term effects) are not clearly known for the growing child . . . The Committee recommends that further implants in children should be limited to extra cochlear devices *in controlled studies involving small groups of children* (sic) before large-scale implantation begins again" (p. 45).

Families enrolled at IHR generally have questions about cochlear implants and the appropriateness of this procedure for their child. We provide parents with written materials, such as the articles cited in this section. We have also invited Dr. Owen Black, a neuro-otologist from Good Samaritan Hospital and Medical Center who has performed a number of cochlear implants on adults, to speak on the subject of cochlear implants at our parent groups.

The Report of the Ad Hoc Committee on Cochlear Implants (ASHA, 1986) contains a summary of the risks, important considerations and recommendations relative to cochlear implants that is a good handout for parents. *Seminars In Hearing: Cochlear Implants in Children* (Northern and Perkins, 1986) presents discussion of the many issues associated with cochlear implants for children. Sonnenschein (1986) also discusses cochlear implants. Parent-infant specialists are encouraged to study these sources and to survey recent journals for current information and views on the procedure as it applies to young children.

PART III

PARENT INVOLVEMENT IN THE HABILITATION PROCESS: ESTABLISHING THE WORKING ENVIRONMENT

CHAPTER 7

ESTABLISHING THE PARENT-SPECIALIST PARTNERSHIP

Roles and Purposes of the Parent-Specialist Partnership

Inviting Parents into the Partnership

Factors Affecting the Development of the Parent-Specialist Parntership
- The Parents' Feelings About Being Students
- The Parents' Feelings of Competence in the Habilitation Setting
- The Parents' Feelings of Being Valued by the Specialist
- The Parents' Emotional States
- The Specialist's Ability to Create the Conditions That Promote Learning on the Part of Parents
- Frequency of Contact with a Family
- The Effects of Personal Style
- The Element of Fun

The IHR goals for parents who are enrolled in habilitation with their hearing-impaired infant are:

1. That parents experience and accept the feelings associated with the discovery and reality of hearing loss in their child.
2. That parents acquire the information and skills they need to teach their child listening and communication skills.
3. That parents acquire the knowledge they need to participate actively in the management of their child's educational career.
4. That parents interact with their hearing-impaired child in ways that promote the development of the child's feelings of self-esteem and competency.

These goals reflect the IHR specialists' view that parents are the individuals who transmit information, skills, and values to their infants. The major vehicle for accomplishing these goals for parents — and the ones set for the child — is the partnership which is established between the specialist and the parent.

ROLES AND PURPOSES OF THE
PARENT-SPECIALIST PARTNERSHIP

The habilitation process begins in the first meeting with the parents during which the tone of the parent-specialist relationship is set. As the specialist describes how the program operates, it becomes apparent that the specialist and parents are entering into a partnership. The parents have a two-fold role in the partnership: first, teachers who impart communication skills, values, and ideas to their child; and second, experts on their child's interests, developmental levels, and behaviors. The role of the specialist is to help the parents acquire information and skills that enable them to fill these roles effectively, despite the obstacles posed by their child's hearing impairment.

The purpose of the partnership is to accomplish the goals set for the parents and for the child, goals which are defined both by the agency and by the parents. It is essential that there be agreement between partners on what the goals are. If there are misunderstandings or if there is dissent about what the goals are or how the goals will be met, the partners will be working at cross-purposes and the partnership will not succeed. It is critical, therefore, that the specialist is clear about the agency's goals and the format through which the goals can be achieved. It is equally critical that the parents have the opportunity to express their needs and their goals for themselves, their child, and the specialist. While this should happen during the first sessions, the issue of goals and means for achieving these goals will come up time and again in the partnership.

The parents' goals and expectations related to the specialist are very likely to change as parents gain a fuller understanding of what "school" means for them, what it will give them, and how they will be participating. The specialist may have to prompt parents to express what they are expecting from her. Questions such as, "How can I be of help to you this week?", "What do you need for yourself today?", and "Is there anything I've forgotten to do?" will all extract from parents information about their expectations and needs related to the specialist and should be a regular part of the parent-specialist dialogue. **The process of listening, understanding the other's viewpoint, negotiating, and coming to agreement on goals and activities is essential to a compatible, effective partnership.**

INVITING PARENTS INTO THE PARTNERSHIP

Parents of newly diagnosed hearing-impaired infants generally have no idea of what is involved in a parent-infant habilitation program. IHR specialists are aware that as they describe the IHR program to parents, the parents may experience several minor shocks. They may feel alarmed when they find that they are expected to participate actively in sessions, dismayed when they hear the frequency and number of sessions recommended, and disturbed when they realize that their "baby" must go to school in order to learn what a normally hearing baby learns with ease. Parents may also be feeling particularly vulnerable at this point because they are having to rely on professionals who are strangers to them to guide them in making decisions they feel incompetent to make. Some parents will accept whatever it is they are told; some react with resentment or suspicion. Some parents suspend judgement until they can decide whether or not to trust the information they are receiving.

When introducing parents to program content, the IHR specialist involves them in decisions about how the family will participate in habilitation. She does this by presenting information in a non-authoritarian, nondirective manner and by asking parents for their response to what she proposes. Rather than saying, "We require the parents to come in for sessions twice a week with their infant," the specialist might say, "Over the years we've tried several different schedules for families. We've found that parents and children alike make excellent progress with a schedule of two individual sessions and one group session or home visit each week. That is what I would recommend for your family. How does that sound to you?'' This approach gives parents a short rationale for the suggested number of sessions and an invitation to respond to a recommendation rather than to a requirement.

If it is an agency's policy that all enrolled families attend a certain number of sessions a week as a condition of enrollment, the specialist at that agency could explain the policy to the family and let them choose whether or not to participate: ''The agency has established a policy that all families attend three sessions per week. This policy is based on a three-year study we did of parent satisfaction with the program and of parent and child progress during their enrollment. We feel we can be most effective and helpful to you when we meet with this frequency. How will this work out for you?'' Some families may elect to enroll in another program whose requirements better meet their needs if traveling distance or work obligations prevent their attending sessions that frequently.

In areas where there is only one habilitation program available, a family who cannot meet attendance requirements is in a bind. It seems particularly essential that these programs be flexible in their requirements of enrollment. Negotiating the number of sessions a family will attend is an excellent way to convey to parents that their needs are considered and that they have input into the design of the habilitation program for their family.

Families who enroll at IHR have already had the ''ground rules'' for enrollment described to them in their introductory visit. We have few such rules at IHR. At least one parent or primary caregiver is required to attend each session with the child and to be involved in the activities. Parents are requested to notify us in advance when they cannot attend because of illness or an emergency. Families who elect to use signed English in combination with the auditory-oral approach are asked to attend signed language classes. Parents who enroll at IHR have already talked with the administrative coordinator about the fee for habilitation services. They have been given a sheet describing how fees are set and, on enrollment, are prepared to sign an agreement establishing the amount that they will pay for each habilitation session.

In working with each family, the specialist is working with different personalities, life circumstances, dreams, attitudes, and plans. The challenge for the parent-infant specialist is to look at and listen to each parent carefully in order to determine how to be effective in meeting his or her needs. A parent's tone of voice and body language — as well as his words — tell us what he is feeling and how he is reacting to the information the specialist is presenting. Some parents enter the habilitation process ready to get to work and wanting the support of professionals. Some parents come into habilitation feeling overwhelmed, hopeless, and helpless. It is not uncommon for parents to feel anxious about all that they do not know and to fear that they will not be able to learn how best to help their child. Some parents want information right away. Others, caught up in the strong feelings that result from the diagnosis of hearing loss, do not hear much of anything the specialist says at first.

The specialist must listen to the words each parent says, "read" the parent's body language, and check out with the parent her perception of what the parent is conveying in order to understand what the parent's present needs are. By responding to the concerns of each individual rather than following a set format for the first sessions, the specialist sets the stage for the development of the parent-specialist partnership.

FACTORS AFFECTING THE DEVELOPMENT OF THE PARENT-SPECIALIST PARTNERSHIP

There are many factors which affect the development of parent-specialist partnerships. Eight of these factors will be discussed below. They are:
1. The parents' feelings about being a student.
2. The parents' feelings of competence in the habilitation setting.
3. The parents' feelings of being valued by the specialist.
4. The parents' general emotional states.
5. The specialist's ability to create the conditions that promote learning on the part of parents.
6. The frequency of contact with a family.
7. The effects of personal style.
8. The element of fun.

THE PARENTS' FEELINGS ABOUT BEING STUDENTS

Soon after learning about their child's hearing loss, most parents are advised to go to "school" in order to gain skills and information that will help their hearing-impaired infant learn what most normally hearing infants learn with no apparent effort. Most adults who are in school are there to learn information and skills related to a topic they have selected. When parents discover that their child is hearing-impaired, the majority of them enroll in a program that will teach them about deafness, a subject that suddenly becomes important to them because of their child. They did not plan to go back to school, they did not choose the topic, but they enroll because it is what they need to do for their child. It is a courageous and unselfish act.

Parents are in the position of having to learn information and skills at a time when they are, for the most part, experiencing strong emotions. These emotions, resulting from not wanting their child to be deaf and not wanting their lives to change, initially may prevent them from being effective and efficient learners. It is crucial that the specialist consider parents' feelings about being students along with the other things she knows about teaching adults. The specialist can let parents know that she admires them for choosing a path of action when it may have been easier to do nothing at all.

THE PARENTS' FEELINGS OF COMPETENCE IN THE HABILITATION SETTING

Learning theory tells us that people learn best in an environment in which they feel competent, trusting, and secure. The specialist can promote this type of environment by calling attention to the areas in which the parents are experts (e.g., their child) and by frequently acknowledging their importance and their contributions to the habilitation process. Asking the parents for information about their child's schedule, interests, and preferences, asking their opinion on how their child is likely to respond to a toy or activity, and incorporating parent-initiated games and parents' suggestions into sessions are some ways in which parents' expertise can be acknowledged. These approaches are all indicators to parents that they are equals in the parent-specialist partnership. If the specialist can ask for help and advice from parents, parents are more likely to feel safe enough to ask for help as well.

THE PARENTS' FEELINGS OF BEING VALUED BY THE SPECIALIST

It is extremely important that parents sense that the specialist enjoys them and their child. A professional who just plain "likes people" generally has a more effective style of relating to parents than does the more "picky" sort. A specialist who has rigid notions about what people "ought to do" will have greater difficulty feeling a genuine liking for and approval of families whose values fall outside of her limits of tolerance. When parents sense they are enjoyed and appreciated by the specialist, they relax and trust more easily. If they feel they are being judged and found inadequate, they are not likely to feel as if they are partners in their relationship with the specialist.

Families of hearing-impaired infants come from throughout the socioeconomic, educational, and cultural spectra. Some families place a high value on their child's educational achievement. These parents are the most likely to share the specialist's feelings of urgency about making auditory information and communication available to their child, since these are the avenues through which educational gains are made. It may be easier for the specialist to appreciate these parents than those for whom educational achievement, or even communication with their child beyond everyday transmittal of information and direction, is not a high priority. Some parents may have to invest all of their energy into providing for their family's basic needs. Habilitation for a handicapped child may feel like an overwhelming task to them. These parents may be less reinforcing to the specialist. If this is the case, the specialist will want to look at how her need to feel effective is affecting the parent-specialist relationship.

The specialist who gains a high degree of her feelings of competence from the achievement of infants in her caseload will experience a great deal of frustration in working with families whose goals for their child do not match the habilitation goals the specialist has in mind. It is sometimes necessary for the specialist to adjust her expectations regarding the rate at which the child and his parents will achieve habilitation objectives and goals. The need to adjust expectations may occur when there is broad disparity between the values or goals held by the parents and those held by the specialist or when there are differences between what the specialist wants and what the parents are capable of doing.

For some families, regular attendance at habilitation sessions may be as much as they can do. Attending evening signed language classes or parent meetings may be impossible. If the parents or the daycare provider do not give the child much listening and language stimulation, the child's progress will be slower than that of a child who has an optimal learning environment. The specialist must also keep in mind the other conditions that affect the child's rate of progress (intelligence, age of identification of hearing loss, degree of loss, etc.) and factor these in to produce realistic expectations.

Our specialists have found that when we can focus on the positive contributions that parents do make, rather than on "things they should be doing" according to our personal value systems, and when we are able to extend a feeling of acceptance to the parents, they sense our belief in them and are able to be most effective. The fact is, parents want to do their best for their children and most parents of hearing-impaired children do the very best they are able to do given the tremendous pressure their child's disability has introduced into their lives.

The ideal situation exists when the specialist fosters a trust relationship with parents in which they feel free to discuss their life situation and the ways in which they struggle with and/or handle the demands of a child with hearing loss. A specialist is most effective when she approaches each family with an attitude of openness, a willingness to accept differing values, and the desire to negotiate goals and timelines for meeting them. The more willing the specialist is to accommodate the parents' life situation, the more likely parents are to accept habilitation goals suggested by the specialist.

One major purpose of maintaining an ongoing dialogue with parents about their thoughts and feelings related to their child's hearing loss is to make certain that there is congruence between parental and specialist expectations and goals. Out of this mutual agreement emerges an environment of trust that makes further exploration of feelings and alternative approaches possible. As happens in any relationship, getting to know and understand each other promotes the more open communication and effective participation that results from trust.

One parent, who had attended IHR with his son for 16 months until the family moved to another city, described how the element of trust had affected him.

"We have moved twice since participating with our son in the parent-infant program at IHR. From my experiences with Ryan in three different parent-infant programs, I don't think you can emphasize the importance of TRUST enough. Without it, there simply is no way the agency can accomplish its educational mission.

"I have no trust in the educators in Ryan's current program. I don't trust their professional judgement. In analyzing why I don't trust them, I think it's because they never conveyed a concern with 'what's best for Ryan.' Instead, their concern seemed one of bureaucratic issues — numbers of children, programs, requirements.

"This lack of trust has a depressing effect on parents — at least on me. Trusting in IHR was a critical source of support for me in so many ways. I think my lack of trust with the system here has resulted in my being a poorer educator for Ryan. I don't want to get involved. I scorn efforts by the school. Even though the teacher may be well-trained, I doubt her abilities. I dislike this attitude of mine, and I most dislike the negative effect it has on Ryan's development. I'm bitter! What more can I say about the element of trust?"

The specialist who works to understand the dynamics, needs, and goals of each family is likely to convey the type of concern that promotes a trust relationship with parents. When parents trust the specialist, she is a source of support, encouragement, and strength to them rather than a source of one more stress in their lives.

THE PARENTS' EMOTIONAL STATES

The specialist must recognize that a parent's ability to participate in the habilitation process is strongly affected by his or her emotional state. IHR specialists have found that if they are to help parents achieve habilitation goals, they must attend to the parents' feelings that result from their child's handicap, and to the attendant altered family dynamics. Stated in another way, IHR specialists have found that if they fail to recognize and respond to the feelings that parents bring with them into the habilitation setting, these feelings become obstacles which prevent the parents from learning the information and skills they need to help their child, not only in the present but in ensuing years as well. Attending to parents' feelings is discussed in detail in Chapter 9.

Some parent-infant programs draw very rigid lines between the roles and responsibilities of the professionals on their staff. In these programs the specialist may be told to refer the parents to the staff counselor, psychologist, or social worker when the parents have concerns outside the realm of "education." The specialist may be constrained from any discussion with the parents that touches on their emotional state. If the staff works as a team and all members have frequent contact among themselves and with parents, this system can work. When, however, the services of the counselor are not readily available, it is very unfortunate if the specialist is prohibited from utilizing some basic counseling skills in her interaction with parents.

THE SPECIALIST'S ABILITY TO CREATE THE CONDITIONS THAT PROMOTE LEARNING ON THE PART OF PARENTS

Awareness of four conditions which promote child and parent learning can increase the specialist's effectiveness. These conditions are motivation, readiness, interest, and reinforcement. Sometimes parents, not understanding why it might be important for them to acquire a certain skill in order to help their child, are not motivated to learn. Some parents may have a difficult time learning a new skill because it must replace a strongly established habit. It is the job of the specialist to provide the parent with the *motivation* to learn a new skill.

The specialist has training and experience that have convinced her of the importance of a particular skill she is presenting to the parent. Her job is to present the parents with a rationale or reason for the skill in such a way that the parent can see its potential use and feel motivated to acquire it. The following example describes the way in which the specialist, Julia, motivated a parent, Donna, to learn a new skill.

Julia has been watching Donna play with her 12-month-old hearing-impaired daughter, Melissa. Before Melissa acquired hearing aids she was not able to detect voice. Donna had learned to gain Melissa's attention by tapping Melissa or by stamping her foot on the floor. These are still Donna's habitual ways of gaining Melissa's attention even though Melissa is now wearing hearing aids and has demonstrated awareness of her mother's voice during habilitation sessions and at home.

Julia knows that it is now appropriate for Donna to learn to gain Melissa's attention by calling her name. She decides to capitalize on Donna's strong desire that Melissa learn to talk as a part of the rationale she gives Donna for teaching Melissa to respond to her name. Julia knows that the fastest route to good speech is good listening skills, and that one of the most motivating sounds to a child is the sound of his/her name. She gives Donna this information and points out the related objective from the infant auditory curriculum: child responds to own name. She demonstrates to Donna the technique of pairing Melissa's name with a tap on the arm. She shows her how to call Melissa's name once or twice before tapping her, then handing Melissa a toy when she turns. Given the rationale for this objective, Donna expresses a strong interest in working on the skill, even though it means changing a behavior that has worked well for her in the past.

The specialist can help parents in their acquisition of new skills by giving them very specific feedback and *reinforcement* as they practice the skill. "Good, Donna. You called her name twice, waited a bit, then called her name and tapped her at the same time." All of us tend to repeat behaviors that earn us praise. When we are learning a new skill it is helpful to hear in descriptive, behavioral terms, exactly what it was that we did well, as opposed to a general statement such as "good job."

Another part of the specialist's job is to determine when the parent is *ready* to learn a new skill or to acquire additional information. In some instances this determination is easily made when the parent expresses a direct *interest* through asking "how to" or informational questions. In selecting information and skills to teach it is important to consider these four factors — motivation, readiness, interest, and reinforcement — as they relate to parents. However, other clues can come from the child. Specialists often observe that a child is emerging into new skill areas that will require that the parents behave differently. When given this information, parents generally express a readiness and interest in changing their behavior in order to promote their child's acquisition of a new skill. An example of this would be when the child is developmentally ready to learn to understand and use prepositions. The parents need to be made aware of this so that they can begin to observe the child and his/her possessions relative to other objects or people in the environment and begin using language that describes these relationships. They will want to begin using statements such as, "Your shoe is by the bed" instead of "Where's your shoe?," and "Your spoon fell under the high chair" instead of, "Oh-oh, you dropped your spoon."

FREQUENCY OF CONTACT WITH A FAMILY

An effective parent-specialist partnership develops more readily when contact with parents is frequent. It is more difficult to establish mutual understanding and trust and to practice the cooperative work style essential to an effective partnership if contact between parent and specialist is infrequent. When the specialist can spend only an hour to an hour-and-a-half each week — or worse, each month — with a family, the specialist and parent alike experience a need to "get something done" or to spend the time "teaching the child."

In a traditional teaching approach, talking with and developing a relationship with parents is viewed as an "extra," not as the basis for an effective teaching program. The parent-infant teacher who uses a *child-oriented* instructional approach may feel that it is impossible to allocate time to ask the parent the genuine question, "How are you doing (John/Nancy)?" and to feel relaxed enough to really listen to more than a single-word response. The reality of the situation is that, if a program can offer only infrequent visits or if a family attends sessions infrequently, the working partnership between parent and specialist will be different from the partnership in which contact is frequent.

IHR specialists have found that even when contact with parents is very limited, if parents' needs are not attended to, the effectiveness of habilitation sessions is significantly diminished. A parent who is experiencing pain or grief cannot focus on descriptions of the parts of a hearing aid, the stages of auditory development, or how to get their child's visual attention. That parent requires the opportunity to express his or her feelings and to have them acknowledged by the specialist.

An important outcome of frequent sessions with families is motivated parents. During inservice training sessions which IHR specialists have conducted around the United States we have often heard the concern expressed by parent-infant teachers, "But how do we get the parents to do what we want them to do?" Our experience is that parents with whom we meet frequently have the opportunity not only to acquire the information and skills they need but to express their feelings and concerns to an accepting, understanding listener. Having had the time both to deal with their feelings and to attain the skills they need to feel competent, most parents are motivated to do whatever their child needs.

Some program formats make it difficult to work regularly with parents on an individual basis. When infants or toddlers are always seen in groups and most contact between teacher and parents is in a group setting, the teacher has little opportunity to establish partnership relationships. If, however, home visits are added to the group format, gains can be made. The teacher can utilize this period of time to attend to individual family needs.

The parent-infant specialist who works in a program where contact with families is limited to one session every week or every two weeks can use other types of contact that will keep the parent-specialist partnership growing. First, she can explore the possibility of extending the length of time she spends with the family when she does see them. If it is possible to add even a half hour to an hour-long session, the specialist can use that time for talking with the parent about issues that come up during the session or between sessions. It may also be possible for the specialist to agree with the parents on a time when they can talk by telephone in order to cover material they cannot get to in the time allotted for sessions. The specialist can arrange to call during the child's nap time so that they can talk uninterrupted. It is also possible to use the mail to get materials or written thoughts to parents. While the options of telephone calls and mailing information may not feel as satisfying as face-to-face contact, they are certainly better than no additional contact at all.

THE EFFECTS OF PERSONAL STYLE

Another factor which can affect development of a good working partnership is a difference in personal styles between a specialist and a parent. While it is true that individual differences serve as a source of stimulation and growth in most of our relationships, it is also true that "personality conflicts" are a fact of life. There are simply some individuals for whom the specialist may be unable to develop positive and empathetic feelings. If it is possible to assign the family to another specialist, it is important to do so. In the rare instances that this has occurred at IHR, the director has explained the change to the family as necessitated by a shift in staff responsibilities. Since the family will be getting better service from a more compatible specialist, we have felt that such changes are essential.

If it is not possible to make a change in specialists, it is important that the specialist, with assistance from other staff, isolate and define the issues that make it most difficult for her to work comfortably with a family or individual parent. In so doing, the specialist can determine which, if any, issues are possible to discuss with the parent(s).

It is unrealistic for a parent-infant specialist to expect to be compatible and entirely comfortable with every family with whom she works. The practice, mentioned earlier, of acknowledging the differences among families and of accepting individuals as they are will provide the specialist with her most effective tool, a relationship characterized by trust and concern. An individual who is comfortable with herself, who feels competent professionally, and who is at ease with her own feelings is more easily accepting of other people, even if they are very different from herself. A parent-infant specialist who finds that it is difficult to be accepting and supportive of many of the parents with whom she works may want to explore the possibility of counseling for herself with the intent of looking at her own feelings of competence and self-esteem. Counseling can assist those of us who are not as effective as we might be by helping us to acquire a more positive view of our self-worth and competence.

THE ELEMENT OF FUN

Does anyone have fun during habilitation? Sometimes life seems to be a very serious business, especially life that includes a child with hearing loss. But there is still room for fun. When the specialist can laugh at herself, find humor in situations, and promote fun during sessions, everyone relaxes, the parent-specialist relationship is enhanced, and the time spent "working" is more effective. In promoting fun, the specialist is modeling an important attitude: Yes, there is a lot to be learned and there are optimal ways to accomplish our goals, but if we can take ourselves less seriously, we can play and have fun as we do it!

These eight factors, and others that are generated in each parent-specialist pair, will affect the ease with which the parent-specialist partnership is established. Some partnerships are established easily and proceed smoothly and effectively throughout the duration of habilitation. Some partnerships take longer to evolve and require patience and experimentation on the part of the specialist as she works to build an environment in which parents feel secure enough to enter fully into the habilitation process.

In rare but memorable instances, the partnership never does jell. If changing specialists — or changing to another agency — is not an option, parents and specialist will want to continue to explore ways in which they can find common ground that can create the basis for a more comfortable working partnership. Not every partnership can or will be ideal, but in most cases, it is better than nothing if the goal is to promote the child's acquisition of skills. **It is important here for those professionals who are in this business because they like to help people and to "fix" things to realize that we all have our limitations. We cannot solve all the problems. We do our best and sometimes we just have to let go.**

CHAPTER 8

PARENTAL REACTION TO THE DIAGNOSIS OF HEARING LOSS IN THEIR CHILD

Reaction to Crisis

- Shock
- Realization
- Denial
- Acknowledgement
- Adaptation

Parents' Feelings Affect Their Interactions with Their Hearing-Impaired Child

Some excellent descriptions of how the diagnosis of their child's hearing loss affects parents exist in the literature. McCollum (1985) points out that parents grieve not only the loss of their fantasized child, but "grieve for themselves in their state of loss." Part of this loss they feel is a loss of self-esteem for having failed to live up to their own expectation of producing a healthy baby. Moses (1979) describes parents' discovery of their child's impaired hearing as "an elusive loss" since, unlike loss of a limb or of a person through death, there is no tangible evidence of the loss that would immediately validate why a parent is grieving. The loss is experienced by the parents as the loss of their dream about their child, the loss of their ability to predict how their relationship with their child will be, and the loss of a feeling of sameness and identity with their child.

Some parents have described feeling that their baby has become a stranger to them because they cannot imagine how it would be not to hear. This perceived loss of shared experiences creates a gulf between parents and child so that suddenly parents do not know how to interact with their child. They are afraid to hold the baby or talk to him because the estrangement they are experiencing makes them uncertain as to whether they are "doing it right." Along with everything else, they have lost their proud parental feelings that, "I am the one who really knows my baby and can do best for him."

Kubler-Ross (1969) describes a five-stage feeling process common to people who know they are dying. This process, sometimes referred to as the grieving process, has also been used to describe the feelings of parents who have lost not their child's life, but the dream of their "perfect child" upon learning of the child's hearing loss. Kubler-Ross' five stages — denial and isolation, anger, bargaining, depression, and acceptance — are elements in another model described by Shontz (1965) as stages through which individuals pass in reaction to crisis. Schontz' model also incorporates five stages: shock, realization, denial, acknowledgement, and adaptation. These stages will be discussed in detail below.

"Crisis" is defined in part in Webster's New Collegiate Dictionary (1974) as "an emotionally significant event or radical change of status in a person's life." The diagnosis of hearing loss in their child is both an emotionally significant event and produces a radical change of status for parents. It is important for the specialist to understand the feelings that parents experience as they weather the crisis of detection of their child's hearing loss so that the specialist can be helpful and appropriate in her responses as she interacts with parents.

REACTION TO CRISIS

SHOCK

The diagnosis of deafness confirms for some parents a suspicion they have had that something is "wrong" with their child. For parents who regard hearing loss as preferable to other possibilities such as retardation or emotional disturbance, this confirmation may actually produce initial feelings of relief. Their relief may last for several days or weeks, and may prevent them from realistic consideration of the implications of deafness. When the relief fades and the reality of deafness sets in, these parents begin experiencing the feelings associated with reaction to a crisis. The initial feeling of shock may not be so strong, but they may still experience numbness and inertia as they try to sort out what this diagnosis means.

For other parents, hearing the diagnosis of their child's deafness is a tremendous blow. They are totally unprepared for this news and their reaction, like that of persons involved in an unexpected natural disaster or accident, is one of shock, disbelief, horror, and eventual numbness. Parents have reported to us that when the audiologist showed them their child's audiogram and said that he had a hearing loss or was deaf, they did not hear any information past that point and later did not even remember having driven home. They reported that they felt like they were in a fog, yet somehow got through their routines as usual. During the initial period following the diagnosis parents are sometimes not aware of having any feelings about their child's hearing loss or about anything at all. Parents in this stage often say things like, "I don't believe this has happened," "I just can't understand how he could be deaf," or " It can't be true — last month the doctor said he was fine."

Specialists working with parents who are in this initial stage can help by reflecting back the parents' feelings: "It's hard to hear that your child is hearing-impaired." It does *not* help to reassure parents that, "It's not so bad as you may think," or to deny them their feelings with statements such as, "You'll feel better when we get to work here." Parents work through this stage more easily when they are allowed to have the feelings they are experiencing and do not think they have to hide them from the specialist. Specialists can also help by limiting the amount of factual information they present to parents at this point. Frequent repetition of important information and skills will help parents retain what they need to know.

REALIZATION

The second stage in the reaction to crisis as described by Shontz (1965) is a period of realization, during which, slowly but surely, awareness of the facts of the situation creep into the parents' thoughts. This is a period of high stress and anxiety. Parents recognize that the condition is permanent and that they are helpless to change it.

As mentioned before, few parents have any advance warning that their child may be born with or will acquire a hearing loss. Most parents *are* aware of the enormous responsibility they are undertaking in choosing to have a child. They can predict to a certain extent the commitments in time, energy, and financial resources that are necessary to raise a child. When they discover that their child has a handicapping condition, these predictions are no longer entirely adequate or applicable. The parents feel disoriented, confused and, in some cases, cheated out of the picture of happy childhood they had envisioned.

Some parents, in attempting to understand the deafness, formulate dozens of questions, some of which will be directed to the specialist: "What do I do now? How do I know who to believe? How do I know if I am doing the right thing?" The questions reflect the panic that many parents are experiencing. When they are given information in response to these questions it is frequently apparent that parents cannot attend to or organize the facts they are given. The specialist who recognizes these questions as an indicator of the parents' fears will be most helpful by responding to the emotional content of the question with comments such as, "It seems that learning about David's hearing loss has left you feeling disoriented — maybe a little panicky."

During this stage many parents become preoccupied with the cause of the hearing loss, if it is not already known. They appear to think that if they knew what caused the loss of hearing, they would know how to restore it. In the process of sleuthing out the etiology, each parent and his or her family tree becomes suspect. Some spouses cling to each other as support against a common "enemy," the hearing loss. Other spouses turn accusing eyes on each other; the hearing loss serves to increase any anger and divisiveness that may have existed between them over other issues. Guilt and blame are common to this stage.

Guilt is especially potent since a parent, particularly the mother who has borne the child, can generally imagine any number of things she did or did not do that could have caused the hearing loss. Some mothers wonder if it was the wine or marijuana they had during the third month of pregnancy, the cough and "heat rash" they had during the second trimester, the night they went out dancing and got excessively tired. Some parents are certain that the hearing loss is retribution for some offense or indiscretion they committed in their past. Sometimes it seems that the lower the parent's self-esteem, the more willing he or she is to assume that the cause of their child's hearing loss somehow lies within themself, or conversely, the more essential it is to establish the blame outside.

Julia, a parent-infant specialist, was working with Lyle and Lorene and their son, Jody, who has a severe hearing loss. During one of their early sessions the question of the etiology of Jody's hearing loss came up. "Lorene's Uncle Morty has always been strange." Lyle looked accusingly at his wife. "He lived at home with his folks and did odd jobs for the neighbors. He didn't talk right and they always said it was because he fell as a baby. Heck, all babies fall. I think it's bad genes and now here they are again making Jody deaf. What if he's just like Mort? I don't have time to watch out for Jody for the rest of his life."

"Lyle." Julia, the specialist, intervened. "Let's talk about this a minute. I can see that you are really upset about Jody's hearing loss. You may be worried that because of his hearing loss, Jody will be dependent on you for his entire life. Is that one of your concerns?"

"You bet," Lyle agreed. "That boy was meant to go hunting and fishing with me and join my law firm when he grows up. What if that's all ruined by bad genes?"

Julia intervened again. "I'm concerned, Lyle, that you feel so strongly that somehow Lorene is the cause of Jody's hearing loss. The cause of his loss has not yet been established. Would you be willing to hold off on your judgement until you have the opportunity to meet with the genetic counselor? He will want all kinds of detailed information about both your families' histories. I'm sure that Lorene's hurting about this just like you are. Lorene, what's going on with you?"

Lorene was a quiet woman who was obviously in the habit of deferring to her more outspoken husband. "Maybe it is my fault, but it's not what I want anymore than you do, Lyle. I just can't think much about it because I start crying again and then I can't get anything done. "He," nodding toward her husband, "will feel better when he knows what caused Jody's hearing loss. I'll feel better when I know what I should be doing now to help Jody. If I don't stay busy I get depressed and that doesn't help any of us."

"You both have very understandable concerns," Julia said. "We will want to talk more about both of your impressions and feelings related to the cause of the hearing loss. Do you want to talk more now or should we spend the rest of the session working with the first loaner hearing aids that we will be placing on Jody? I want both of you to feel entirely comfortable with managing the aids before you take them home."

When parents are functioning in the realization stage of reaction to crisis, the specialist can be very helpful by maintaining an empathetic, but matter-of-fact, approach. The parents are confused, disorganized, and highly anxious. The specialist can allow them these feelings without getting caught up in the feelings of panic herself. By maintaining an attitude of calmness and purpose, she conveys to the parents that the whole world has not disintegrated forever, just their own world temporarily. Parents in this stage may say things like, "I don't know what to do." "Why did this happen to my baby?" "If I knew why he is deaf, I could handle it better."

DENIAL

The second stage, realization, by no means implies acceptance of the handicapping condition. In fact, following closely on the heels of the stage of recognition or realization may come the third stage, denial or defensive retreat. In this stage parents try to think of the situation in a way that makes it bearable. Some parents, while not denying the hearing loss per se, make the reality of it tolerable by refusing to acknowledge the implications of the hearing loss: "He's deaf, but he won't be any different from the rest of us." "We'll get the best possible treatment and no one will ever know he has a problem." "He can learn to talk — look at Helen Keller."

Because the panic they experienced in the second stage is too frightening to maintain, parents have to deny, rationalize, think wishfully, and sometimes outright run away in order to restore some equilibrium to their life. As Shontz (1965) described it,

> "The individual . . . is in a situation (he) cannot handle. People then do what you would expect under these circumstances; they retreat, they run away. The usual way is to try to go back to the structure that existed before the critical event (in this case, diagnosis of hearing loss) occurred . . . This defensive retreat might take the form of denial expressed in such terms as . . .'Really there is nothing wrong with my child; he is in no way different'"(p. 367).

During the first several stages of reacting to crisis, parents may make decisions or accept any information they are given as fact as a way of restoring some structure. They may cling tenaciously to these decisions or "facts" and express great anger when given conflicting information. Because parents need a structure around which to organize their confusion, they are particularly vulnerable in this stage to one of the "gospel truths" of the communication modes battle that persists in the field of habilitation of the hearing-impaired. **An authoritarian professional who tells parents who are functioning in early stages of reacting to crisis that, "All you have to do is X, Y and Z and your child will be just fine," is tying into and reinforcing the parents' fantasies which deny the seriousness of the situation.**

The responsible professional will instead provide parents with ample opportunity to talk and will assure them that, while parents must make some decisions at this point, none of these decisions is final. It comes as a great relief to parents to hear that if they decide on an audiologist or program or communication approach today, they are not irrevocably bound to that decision. Being given permission to make decisions that are not necessarily final makes it possible for some parents to make a decision at all. It relieves the parents of feeling that they must defend that decision at all costs when they are unprepared to do so.

Some parents have shared with us the intense anger they felt during this stage when their decisions were challenged by well-intentioned friends or relatives. Ted described the phone call he received from his mother. "Mother doesn't live here, and she hasn't talked to the doctor or the audiologist, yet she thinks she knows better than us what we should do. It made me so furious I almost hung up on her. She tells me about a clinic in her area: 'Don't do *anything* for Elizabeth until you have seen these doctors,' she says. Well, we have seen plenty of medical specialists right here and she wouldn't even listen to me when I tried to tell her what they said." Ted admitted later, when he could talk about it, that part of his anger came from his fear that he had not made the right decisions for Elizabeth. "I was an emotional wreck. I really wasn't capable of making well-thought out decisions. And I was unable to tolerate criticism about the decisions I did make. I really just wanted to hide under my bed. My Mom has a way of setting me off. We've both calmed down since and have talked it out."

"I'll tell you what made *me* mad." Jennifer was in the parent group the day Ted described his feelings. "What made me so mad was when we went to visit the programs that were available to help us with Danny. At the first one they said if we used signed language with Danny he would never talk, and at the second place they said that if we didn't use signed language he would learn so slowly he would be educationally retarded. Who am I supposed to believe? I'd never given a moment's thought to how deaf children learn to communicate and I thought the professionals would give me that information. I got information all right, except that all it did was confuse me even more. I just went home and cried. It sounded like anything I did, I had a 50-50 chance of ruining Danny's life. You remember that I cancelled the first appointment I had made to visit here? I was afraid you would tell me about a third option and *that* would have pushed me over the edge. You can't imagine the relief I felt, the day I finally did come to visit, when the parent-infant specialist said that you used both auditory-oral and auditory-oral with signed English here and that we didn't have to make a decision about it until we had more information. That's one of the reasons Dick and I decided to enroll with Danny in this program."

It is important to recognize that while almost all parents eventually pass through this third stage of denial in reacting to crisis, almost all parents (and teachers) continue to practice "selective denial." There is usually at least one aspect or implication of deafness that remains too painful to accept and, thus, learn about or act on. Pockets of denial can be detected when parents faithfully carry out the habilitation plan, yet balk at consideration of some recommendations, refuse to think about the child's future, or express projections of the child's future that contain elements of magic. Teachers demonstrate denial when they fail to encourage parents to interact with, and let their child interact with, hearing-impaired peers and adults.

Parents who are actively engaged in denial of many of the implications of deafness are visible because of their tension and high anxiety levels. They may be very aware of their reasons for being unable to face some of the consequences of deafness. They may be able to articulate clearly the pain they feel when they think about how deafness will affect their child. In some instances the pain is directly related to their fear that their child may experience rejection similar to rejection they themselves experienced as a child because they were perceived as different. Some parents have a strong need for their children to be perfect in order to validate their own worth as people and parents. A "flaw" in their child is perceived as a reflection of their own inadequacy.

Denial can be expressed not only in words, but in actions. Some parents may make certain that their hearing-impaired child wears well-functioning hearing aids during school time and at home, but are unable to put the aids on the child when they go out in public. Some parents will not accept the use of signed language because it is a too visible sign of difference.

IHR specialists become concerned about a parent's denial when it affects the parent's ability to do what needs to be done to help the child and, therefore, impedes the child's progress. It takes a tremendous amount of energy for a parent to maintain attitudes and opinions that fly in the face of the reality they confront daily in their child. The energy it takes to maintain the denial is energy that is not available for positive action. The specialist who has worked to create a relationship with the parent based on trust and support can gently confront the parent with the effect his/her denial is having on the child and propose the possibility of counseling as a way to explore the need for the denial. If this suggestion is rejected, it need not rupture the parent-specialist relationship. The specialist can watch for an opportunity to broach the subject again as it seems appropriate.

ACKNOWLEDGEMENT

It is the very energy required to maintain defensive retreat or denial that causes parents to move slowly into the fourth stage, acknowledgment. Acknowledgment "differs from realization in that it means more than an encounter with reality. It includes the concept that reality, once it has been encountered, must be acknowledged and accepted" (Schonz, 1965, p. 368). During this period parents may experience a genuine sadness or depression related to their recognition of the realness of their child's hearing loss. They mourn the loss of the experience they had anticipated having with their child. They experience renewed anxiety as they try to accommodate thoughts of the unknowns in the future. Parents allow the implications of the hearing loss and its effect on their child and family to enter their consciousness at a rate they can tolerate. This process can often be facilitated by a professional counselor or by an insightful parent-infant specialist who recognizes the parents' feelings and encourages the expression and acceptance of them.

Acknowledgment or acceptance is not the end of the process of reacting to crisis. It is a stage that can be characterized by bitterness and remorse, and by anger about having to do something about the problem. The habilitation process requires that the family expend time and money. Even if the program itself charges no fee, there are expenses related to audiologic evaluation, hearing aid purchase and maintenance, and travel. The parents may focus on the cost of habilitation or the time and effort it requires as an outlet for their anger and bitterness. They may generate a proliferation of ideas about how the process could be accomplished without having to follow the program proposed by the professionals. For some parents, this may be a stage in which they do some private bargaining with God in hope that they can trade off this disaster which has affected their child for some personal affliction so their child will not have to suffer. Mindel and Vernon (1971) and Moses (1985) discuss in detail the feelings of denial, guilt, depression, anger, and anxiety that occur in these first four stages of reacting to crisis.

ADAPTATION

Out of all the options that arise, a plan for action slowly begins to emerge. Parents may have been enrolled in a habilitation program for months — or even years — before they begin to feel direction coming from within themselves. They may have attended habilitation sessions faithfully and carried out assignments because the professionals told them that is what they needed to do for their child. When they have reached the stage where their own plan of action begins to evolve, however, their participation in the habilitation becomes more active and self-directed.

At the point when parents begin to carry out a plan of action which they have formulated, they are entering the final stage of the reaction to crisis, adaptation. Adaptation implies change, an adjustment in attitudes, actions, and dreams which results from the change in reality that has occurred. During this stage the parents experience a gradual decrease in anxiety and begin to experience some satisfaction in carrying out their plans for their child. Parents change their own life plans so that they can accomplish habilitation goals set for themselves and their child. They begin to explore their prejudices and biases about hearing-impaired people. They adjust their dreams to accommodate the new information they acquire about their child.

Acknowledgment and adaptation are life-long processes for parents. In fact, parents may cycle through the entire process of reacting to crisis each time another unanticipated aspect of their child's handicap appears. The beginning of formal school, relationships with hearing peers, and adolescence frequently are times of crisis for parents.

The subject of "cures" for hearing loss is also one that evokes powerful feelings of crisis in parents. Bonnie is the parent of a seven-year-old hearing-impaired daughter, Jill. Jill had graduated from IHR at age four and has since been in the public school program for hearing-impaired children. Jill had acquired a profound hearing loss as a result of meningitis when she was 14 months old. Bonnie called Julia, the specialist, one day to tell her about an article she had seen describing a cochlear implant performed on a three-year-old girl. "I could not believe the intensity of my reaction to that article," Bonnie said to Julia. "I realized what it would mean if Jill could hear even just a few sounds. Thinking about that brought back all those feelings I had when we first learned about Jill's deafness. I thought I'd gotten over those feelings, but I couldn't stop crying when I read that article. It is amazing to me how we go along living with and accepting her hearing loss. But I have realized that I will always feel sad and angry that it happened, and that while those feelings do not surface very frequently, they are still there, deep inside me."

Not all parents will experience the feelings associated with all five stages of this process of reacting to crisis. Nor do these stages necessarily occur in a chronological order. Parents may be experiencing the feelings associated with two or more stages at the same point in time. They may work through some feelings only to have them resurface a week later when they acquire new information about their child's disability. Specialists will want to be alert to the fluctuations in parents' moods and give parents ample opportunity to express and re-express the feelings they are having.

PARENTS' FEELINGS AFFECT THEIR INTERACTIONS WITH THEIR HEARING-IMPAIRED CHILD

The feelings that parents have about their child and his hearing loss have an effect on their interactions with the child throughout his life. Even before the diagnosis of hearing loss is made, many parents suspect that something is different about their baby. This suspicion may be based on unusual aspects of the infant's behavior that the parents observe, but do not know to attribute to hearing loss. Parents may observe, for example, that their infant does not seem particularly responsive to the vocal play that they initiate. Since the infant does not respond, the parents are not reinforced to continue this type of interaction. Since the baby seems to ignore the parents' vocal attempts to engage him in social interaction, the parents may initiate fewer and fewer social interactions with the infant. The parents may then, without being consciously aware, make the assumption that the child does not respond by choice, thus assigning a value judgment to the infant's behavior which in fact he cannot help.

Meadow (1980) points out that the process of diagnosing the child's hearing loss is frequently difficult, prolonged, and fraught with ambiguity so that the process itself is traumatic to parents and "may influence their response to the deaf child for many years" (p. 130).

Once the diagnosis of hearing loss is made and the family is enrolled in a program of habilitation, the parents face two challenges that can affect their feelings about and relationship with their hearing-impaired child. The first challenge is dealing with the feelings of shock, realization, denial, acknowledgement, and adaptation that result from the discovery and reality of their child's disability. The second challenge is making the immediate changes necessitated by the special needs of the child. Parents' plans may be seriously disrupted by the unexpected expenditures of time and money required once the hearing loss is discovered. Parents — and specialists — must acknowledge that having to change plans and even relinquish dreams may result in feelings of anger and resentment that, if not dealt with, may influence the parents' interactions with the child, not only in the child's early years, but as he is older, too.

Parents' feelings about and views of their child's hearing loss and their behaviors based on these views can have an effect on the child's academic achievement. Bodner-Johnson (1985) found that children with higher academic achievement (measured by reading comprehension and mathematics achievement) had parents who had adapted to the child's hearing loss and who had higher expectations about their child's achievement.

> "For parents of proficient readers, the hearing-impaired community was an integral part of their lives, as was the learning and use of sign language. Further, they believed their hearing-impaired child should be subjected to the same supervision as normal-hearing children. Rather than change rules of behavior for their hearing-impaired child, parents made modifications in style due to the child's inability to hear rather than to his or her inability to understand." (Bodner-Johnson, 1985, p. 135).

Parents who learn to accept and deal with their feelings related to their hearing-impaired child will have acquired a valuable life tool. Certain feelings come up time and again as the child grows. If the parent has learned that these feelings are normal, that they are acceptable, and that facing them and *feeling* them helps them pass, they are better able to focus on attitudes and feelings that promote their child's self-esteem and achievement.

IHR specialists are committed to using specific skills that help parents deal with the feelings they have related to their hearing-impaired child. These skills are the subject of the next chapter.

CHAPTER 9

THE ROLE OF THE SPECIALIST IN ATTENDING TO THE FEELINGS AND NEEDS OF PARENTS

Needs of Parents of Young Hearing-Impaired Children

Principles Governing the IHR Specialists' Role

Attending to the Feelings and Needs of Parents: A Three-Step Process
- Listening
- Reacting
- Responding

Resolving Conflicts Between Parents and Specialists

Referring Parents to a Skilled Counselor

IHR specialists believe that addressing the emotional needs of the parents of hearing-impaired infants enrolled is crucial to meeting habilitation goals for parents and child alike. Parents' emotions affect the way they feel about their child, the way they view the child as a person, and the way they interact with the child. All of these factors have a strong influence on the child's self-esteem and on his capacity to learn (see Chapter 11). Parents need a safe environment in which to work through the feelings they have that do not contribute to their child's feelings of well-being and self-esteem. The habilitation partnership with a parent-infant specialist can provide such an environment. However, in order to help parents, specialists must know what kinds of needs parents have related to their child's hearing loss and how to respond to these needs and the associated feelings that parents experience. These topics are discussed in the pages that follow.

NEEDS OF PARENTS OF YOUNG HEARING-IMPAIRED CHILDREN

IHR specialists have identified six needs that parents of hearing-impaired infants have expressed or demonstrated as they learn about their child's handicapping condition(s) and as they begin dealing with the feelings that result from discovery of their child's hearing loss. These six needs are:

1. Parents need to be able to express their feelings in an environment in which these feelings are acknowledged and accepted.
2. Parents need to be able to talk to individuals with whom they have established a relationship of trust so that it is safe to express their strong feelings.
3. Parents need empathic and objective feedback about their "worst fears" related to their child's hearing loss.
4. Parents need a sense of community, a sense that others can understand or have experienced and survived what they are feeling.
5. Parents require information concerning their child's communica-

tion needs and help in establishing an interaction style that will promote their child's desire to learn communication skills.

6. Parents need help in defining and sorting out the options related to their child's needs.

The parent-infant program in which the family is enrolled for habilitation is the logical source of help to parents in meeting these needs when the parent-infant specialists are familiar with the process of reaction to crisis and have acquired the skills of listening and attending to parents' emotional needs. Unfortunately, the vast majority of centers which train educators of the hearing impaired do not include in their curriculum coursework or practicum related to attending to the emotional needs of parents of handicapped children.* IHR parent-infant specialists have acquired the skills of attending to parents' needs through post-graduate coursework and supervised practicum, participation in workshops and seminars, individual personal counseling, and experience in working with parents of hearing-impaired infants.

PRINCIPLES GOVERNING THE IHR SPECIALISTS' ROLE

From their work with parents, IHR specialists have formulated the following principles which govern their interactions as they attend to parents' feelings related to their handicapped child:

1. The specialist is effective in attending to parents' emotional needs only to the extent that he/she accepts and experiences his or her own broad range of feelings.

2. The specialist can learn to use basic counseling techniques that allow and encourage parents to discuss, explore, and accept their feelings about their handicapped child.

3. The parent-specialist partnership, as it exists at Infant Hearing Resource, is effective in working toward achievement of parent and child goals only if a counseling function is inherent in the partnership.

4. The specialist's effectiveness as a counselor is dependent on the degree to which he/she can create an environment in which the parent feels accepted, appreciated, and valued by the specialist.

5. The specialist is not responsible for solving parents' problems or for making parents feel better. The specialist interacts with parents in a way designed to encourage them to explore and accept their own feelings and to make the necessary decisions regarding

---

* *Training the Parent-Infant Specialist: Hearing Impaired,* by Infant Hearing Resource staff (pending publication, summer, 1987) lists more than 185 competencies required by the well-trained parent-infant specialist who may fill up to six roles in performing all the functions required of her/him.

their child.

6. The specialist is responsible for referring parents to a skilled counselor when the parents' needs are more intense than the specialist can deal with or when the parent is having problems that fall outside the realm of their feelings about their handicapped child.

ATTENDING TO THE FEELINGS AND NEEDS OF PARENTS: A THREE-STEP PROCESS OF LISTENING, REACTING, AND RESPONDING

The specialist can generally detect topics that evoke strong feelings from parents by listening to their words and tone of voice, and by observing their body language as various topics related to their child's hearing loss are introduced. Al regularly attended habilitation sessions with his daughter, Sidney. He participated in the games and activities enjoyed by a two and a half-year-old with an enthusiasm that almost equalled Sidney's. During one session, Al mentioned that a change in Sidney's daycare would be necessitated by her babysitter's impending move. As they talked, Julia brought up the option of a combination nursery school/daycare program located in the family's neighborhood. The change in Al was instantaneous. His usual humorous expression was replaced by a frown. He reached out and pulled Sidney onto his lap and stared at the top of her head. Julia noted the change in his mood immediately. "Al, the idea of a nursery school really seemed to affect you when I mentioned it just now. What comes to mind when you think of Sidney in nursery school?"

"I'm not sure," Al said slowly, his eyes still on Sidney. "She's so little . . . but she's smart. I think she'll be able to keep up with the other kids." His voice trailed off and he sat silently, then added, "The other kids — I guess that's what worries me. What if they ignore her because she doesn't say much or, worse yet, make fun of her because of her hearing aids or the sounds she makes? I don't know — it hurts me to think of her being singled out because she's different from the other kids."

"You would like to protect her from being hurt. I can understand that," Julia replied. "Does it seem a little scary to think about her in a group of strangers on her own?"

"Yeah," Al concurred. "Yeah, but you know, when I really think about it, I think those kind of situations don't bother her at all. She loves playing with other kids, even when she's never seen them before. I guess it's really my problem, not hers. But I can see that if I let my fears get in the way of her having the experiences she needs to grow, then she *will* have a problem."

Julia's attention to a change in Al's posture and facial expression was all that was needed to help Al talk about his fears for his daughter. Had Julia ignored Al's non-verbal signals, he may have resisted the option of nursery school for Sidney without ever thinking about the fears that were causing his resistance.

Attention to a parent's emotional status enables a specialist to proceed toward achievement of habilitation goals at a pace the parent can handle. When the specialist is tuned into the feelings the parent is experiencing she can be appropriate in the amount and content of the information she gives to the parent. It may not be appropriate for the specialist to bring up the topic of how friends and relatives are responding to the diagnosis of hearing loss with a parent who is immersed in the realization stage. The parent is trying to cope with his own feelings and cannot effectively get outside himself to worry about how others are responding. It would be inappropriate for the specialist to ask a parent who is operating in the denial stage to accompany her to a meeting of a service club to talk about what it is like to parent a hearing-impaired child.

Many different counseling/interviewing/therapeutic approaches are used by professionals whose clients are reacting to crisis and experiencing the feelings associated with the grieving process. Basic to most of these approaches is a process of attentive listening and empathetic response which encourages the client to explore and experience their thoughts and resultant feelings and to discover solutions to their problems from within their own resources.

Specialists at IHR have found that they can be extremely effective in attending to the emotional needs of parents by following a three-step process:

1. Using good listening skills.
2. Monitoring and evaluating personal reactions to parents' statements.
3. Using responses that promote parents' expression of feelings and needs.

The skills involved in these three steps are described below.

LISTENING

The words fly! Point after point is made. Facts, feelings, plans, dreams all flow out of our mouths every day. What one person says evokes ideas, thoughts, or feelings in someone else. One person, hearing someone else express an idea, responds: "No, you don't say! That reminds me of the time . . ."

During the first year of our lives we are urged and encouraged toward expression of our first word. When it comes, we are encouraged to produce more and more words in longer and longer streams until, finally on one golden day, we are able to hold up our end of the conversation! Thus, we learn one-half of the communication process, the role of talker. It is extremely rare, however, that we experience a similar effort to teach us to fulfill the second half of the communication process, the role of listener.

Our failure to listen well can cause us problems. Sometimes we actually fail to hear what a person is saying because our attention is directed elsewhere. Sometimes we hear a person's words, but not the way in which the words are said so that we miss the intent or real message. Sometimes we hear something that triggers a strong internal reaction and we shut our ears because hearing what is said is painful, scary, or elating. In other instances we may turn our attention inward to focus on our reaction to what we heard and we do not hear what the speaker says next.

Every once in a while, we are reinforced for listening, usually with words such as, "Thanks for listening. I feel so much better." Our tendency may be to discount the praise: "But, I didn't do anything. You figured it out yourself." In reality, we have truly done a most helpful thing: *listen.* We tend to view listening as a passive behavior as reflected in the statement, "I didn't do anything." In fact, a good listener is engaging in an extremely active behavior, a behavior that is exactly what the speaker wants. Through listening well, the listener conveys to the speaker that 1) you are important, and 2) I care about what you say and how you feel.

ELEMENTS OF GOOD LISTENING

Effective listening is the basis of attending well to parents' emotional needs. It is possible to enhance listening skills by practicing several elements of good listening. Three such elements are:

1. Controlling environmental and personal variables.
2. Attending to non-verbal messages.
3. Being aware of the three levels of communication.

These three elements are discussed below.

CONTROLLING ENVIRONMENTAL AND PERSONAL VARIABLES

There are both environmental and personal variables that affect the quality of a listening situation. The specialist who is aware of these variables can control them in order to create an optimal situation in which to listen to parents' concerns and feelings.

Environmental variables include:

1. A quiet, private space in which you will not be interrupted by phone calls or distracted or overheard by other people.
2. Positioning so that the parent and specialist are at a comfortable conversational distance where good eye contact is possible. Posi-

tioning should convey the equality of the partnership by having both individuals seated or standing at equal levels. The specialist should avoid creating barriers by sitting behind a desk or table.
3. Comfortable lighting so that neither individual is having to look into a strong light source.

Personal variables include:
1. Consistent eye contact.
2. Relaxed posture.
3. Pleasant facial expression.
4. No fiddling, doodling, or attention to potential distractions.
5. Use of minimal encouragers such as head nods, smiles, and *short* verbal responses that do not interrupt the speaker.

It is not always easy for the specialist to control all of the environmental variables that create an optimal listening situation, especially since the hearing-impaired infant or child is present during sessions. It is possible, however, to provide the child with an interesting toy or activity with which he can entertain himself while the parent is talking. If the parent brings up an issue he wants to discuss, the specialist may elect to say, "Let's get Tommy entertained with some toys so we can talk without interruption." After attending to the child, the specialist can then signal resumption of the topic by reiterating what the parent had said earlier: "You were feeling some concern about how your older boy is reacting to Tommy's hearing loss. What kinds of reactions are you seeing?"

ATTENDING TO NON-VERBAL MESSAGES

Another critical aspect of being a good listener is attending to the non-verbal messages the speaker is sending. *Between 80-90% of a message is conveyed through body posture, gestures, gaze, facial expression, movement, and tone and quality of voice.* Changes in breathing, speed of talking, sighs, blushes, stammers, and emphasis on words are other non-verbal cues to the speaker's feelings. In most instances, the verbal message and the non-verbal message are congruent. But there are instances in which the speaker is saying one thing verbally and something else non-verbally. The non-verbal message, which the speaker feels either consciously or unconsciously uncomfortable about saying directly, reveals the true feelings the speaker is experiencing. The person who is attending well to the speaker will give importance to how a message is delivered as well as to what is said in order to understand the full message.

The specialist who is just acquiring some basic counseling skills may be confused about what to do when he or she gets a mixed message from verbal and non-verbal information. We need to give ourselves permission to practice detecting these discrepancies while watching and listening to parents.

We can make a mental note of the feeling state that the parent may be expressing through his or her body language: He looked embarrassed, angry, or sad as he said that. Our awareness of this feeling state will help us be more appropriate in our interaction with the parent even if we do not comment on it directly.

Some parents find it difficult or impossible to disagree with a teacher or to express how they feel about a teacher's request. A teacher is an authority figure and most of us probably have a history of complying with teachers' requests. For this reason, specialists need to be particularly alert to nonverbal messages that signal a parent's discomfort or disagreement with our suggestions. When specialists comment on or ask parents about these nonverbal messages the parent learns that their feelings are noticed and that it is acceptable to talk about them.

BEING AWARE OF THE THREE LEVELS OF COMMUNICATION

An important part of attending and listening to a parent is recognition of the three levels on which communication occurs. The first level of communication is the *content,* or the words that are said. The second level is the *feelings* that accompany the words. The third level is the *intent* of the speaker. The intent is the real message the speaker is sending.

Mary is the mother of Beth, who is hearing impaired. During a habilitation session Mary said to the specialist, "I can't get Beth to keep her hearing aids on." The specialist guessed that Mary most likely had some strong feelings associated with this statement and that there were several possible meanings behind the statement. Specialists, when faced with a wide choice of possible intentions, need to probe in order to understand the real message. The specialist might respond to Mary's statement by saying, "How are you feeling about the hearing aids, Mary?" If Mary replies, "I'm not motivated to make Beth keep the hearing aids on because I don't want Beth to look different," the specialist will respond very differently than if Mary replies with a statement such as, "I worry that the hearing aids are hurting her." Listening to the message at all three levels is crucial to understanding the feelings and intent of the speaker. When the specialist truly understands what the parent is saying, she can respond in ways that are helpful to the parent.

WHEN GOOD LISTENING IS DIFFICULT

It is a fact of life that there are times when specialists fail to listen and attend well to parents who are expressing feelings either verbally or nonverbally. There are several reasons specialists may choose not to attend to the feeling content of a message from a parent.

First, hearing and attending to another person's feelings may feel very scary. If a parent is expressing anger, the specialist may feel threatened, even if the anger is directed at someone else. Her fear may paralyze her so that all she can think is, "Oh no, what do I do now?" Second, some specialists have a habit of assuming responsibility for causing the feelings that parents express. This habit may make it uncomfortable for the specialist to hear feelings expressed because he or she feels an obligation to "fix things" so the parent doesn't need to feel that way. Third, some specialists have learned that having and expressing strong feelings is not "genteel" or "polite," especially if those feelings are anger, annoyance, or dislike. Fourth, some specialists have grown up with the "stiff upper lip" school of thought that teaches them that "strong, competent individuals" handle these things themselves, and quietly at that. Fifth, pressures of limited time in sessions sometimes put the specialist in conflict about whether to attend to the parents' concerns or to work on the objectives set forth in the lesson plan. Since the child is present and requires attention, it is sometimes difficult to find the time needed to talk about feelings.

If the specialist experiences any of these feelings in response to a statement made by a parent, it is likely to block her effectiveness as a listener. When a specialist fails or chooses not to respond to the emotional content of a parent's message she must be aware that she is sending the parent the non-verbal message, "I am not responding to your feelings." The parent may interpret that message as, "The teacher does not care about me," or "My feelings are inappropriate or wrong," or "Talking about feelings is not part of habilitation." Whatever the interpretation, the parent may close down and that opportunity for clear communication is lost. Specialists who want to be effective listeners will want to examine their degree of comfort with the expression of feelings and work on overcoming the barriers that stand in their way of listening to understand.

Finally, the specialist's own state of mind may preclude her being a good listener. If she is preoccupied with her own thoughts and concerns and is unable to set these aside for the duration of a session with a family, she will not be an effective listener or an effective participant in habilitation activities. In rare instances, the specialist may need to cancel a session, knowing that because of a personal situation she will not be able to address the objectives of the session and meet the needs of the family.

Good listening entails a strong commitment to hear and understand the intent and feelings of the speaker. Control of environmental and personal variables which affect the quality of the listening situation is important, as is attention to the non-verbal content of the speaker's message.

REACTING

As noted earlier, our ability to listen well can be hampered by our reaction to what we hear. Reacting, the second step in the process of attending to the emotional needs of parents, has an effect on both the first step of the process, listening, and on the third step, responding. Our reactions, like our ability to listen well, are determined by a number of variables.

We have discussed how parents' biases, priorities, and values affect their participation in habilitation and may affect their ability or desire to achieve the goals established for them by the agency. Specialists also bring their own sets of biases, priorities, values, and beliefs into the habilitation setting. When we listen to parents expressing their thoughts and feelings, these biases, priorities, and values are brought actively into play without our being aware of them. As we listen to someone express an idea, opinion, or feeling we have a reaction to what we hear. Much of the time this reaction is an internal event — a comment we make to ourselves — of which we may be completely unaware.

Reacting, the second step in the process of attending to the emotional needs of parents, is a step that is unique for each individual. Specialists who want to know how their reactions affect their ability both to listen and to respond to parents will want to:

1. Identify some of their common reactions to expressions of feelings.
2. Examine what beliefs, biases, experiences, and values go into creating their reactions.
3. Evaluate how their reactions affect their responses to parents.

FACTORS WHICH DETERMINE REACTIONS

Millions of times every day each of us observes events or external stimuli to which we react. This reaction is what we sometimes call our perception of the world. Our reactions to events are determined by a highly personal combination of experiences we have had, values, biases, and beliefs we have been taught or have acquired, and our feeling state at the time.

In order to integrate or make sense of events or external stimuli that impinge on us, we attempt to relate the incoming information to other information we already have. When someone makes a statement containing information new to us, we tend to compare the new information with previously acquired information. We then form an opinion about the validity of the new information. If it agrees with what we already know or think, we are likely to think it is valid. If it is not in agreement, we may reject it as invalid. If we highly respect the knowledge of the person conveying the new information, we may reject our previously held opinion and replace it with the new information. A statement such as: "Teachers generally fail at business ventures'' will elicit a variety of reactions from different people with each reaction being dependent on that person's internal pool of experience, information, and feelings about the speaker and the topic.

Some incoming information tells us how an individual is feeling. Our reaction to this information will be dependent on our own feelings about the person, whether the feeling they are expressing is directed at us or is expressed about something else, our state of mind at the time, and our comfort level with expression of feelings in general. Some information is in the form of a request to which we must respond. For example, if someone asks you to volunteer for a job, your reaction to the request might depend on your experience in helping out in the past, your feelings of competence, your energy level, your perception that you might "earn points" for volunteering, or your biases about people who offer to help.

REACTIONS ARE LIKELY TO DETERMINE RESPONSES

It is important to study our reactions to events because our reactions are very likely to determine our responses. Many times our reaction — based on past experiences, beliefs, or our feeling state at the moment — takes the form of an assumption on which our response is based. In the following dialogues, Arla's different *reaction* to the same statement made by two friends determines that she *responds* differently to each of the friends.

The first friend, Norene, said, "Arla, I'm sorry I won't be able to come to your party next Friday." Arla's internal and unstated reactions are: Norene probably has something better to dc; she doesn't like me; she thinks she's too good for me. These reactions determine Arla's response, a cool, "Oh, well I'm sorry you can't make it."

Arla's less-than-friendly response to Norene was determined by her reactions, which were a series of assumptions that she made as a result of Norene's statement. These assumptions were obviously based on some past experiences or feelings, since there was nothing in what Norene said or in the way that she said it that conveyed the information that Arla assumed.

When a second friend, Cathy, makes the same statement as Norene had, Arla's reaction and response are very different. Cathy said, "Arla, I'm sorry I won't be able to come to your party next Friday." Arla's internal and unstated reactions are: Cathy is so much fun. I know she would come if she could. Too bad she can't. These reactions determine Arla's response, spoken with genuine disappointment: "Oh, I'm so disappointed to hear that. I've been looking forward to your being there."

Arla's reaction to Cathy was based on positive feelings and on her assumptions that Cathy would come if she could. Again these feelings and assumptions were based on past experience with Cathy and feelings about her rather than on anything Cathy had said right at that moment.

JUDGMENTAL VERSUS UNDERSTANDING REACTIONS

Rogers (1951) proposed that a major barrier to good communication is our natural tendency to judge, to evaluate, to approve (or disapprove) statements people make. Our reaction to hearing a statement is to evaluate it from our own point of view: "I feel the same way " or "This person must be real smart " or "That is *not* true." Rogers suggests that our tendencies to react to emotionally meaningful statements by evaluating them from our own point of view is the major barrier to interpersonal communication. His solution to avoiding this barrier parallels the skills of listening and attending that we have been examining. He suggests that real communication occurs when we "listen with understanding," when we "see the expressed idea and attitude from the other person's point of view and sense how it feels to him, to achieve his frame of reference in regard to the thing he is talking about." This means "understanding *with* a person, not *about* him." When a person feels he is being understood and not judged, his statements are likely to become less exaggerated, less defensive, and less distorted.

The difference between reactions which evaluate or judge and reactions which understand is illustrated below:

Parent's statement: "Five o'clock is the hardest time of the day for our family. My kids drive me crazy at that hour and I don't know what to do about it."

Judgmental reactions:

"You chose to have three kids; don't complain to me." "If you had good parenting skills you wouldn't have this problem." "Your kids would drive me crazy any time of the day."

Understanding reactions:

"I know what you mean." "Sounds like you might dread that time of day." "You'd like to be able to change that situation."

Specialists have the opportunity to understand *with* parents when parents say something like, "I'm sure that my baby's hearing is improving. I don't think he'll need hearing aids much longer." The reaction: "You've got to face the music and accept this hearing loss" is judgmental. The reaction: "You are wondering if your baby has a permanent hearing loss" is understanding from the parent's frame of reference.

LEARNING FROM OUR REACTIONS

Paying attention to our own reactions to events, behaviors, and statements can be very revealing. We may learn about biases and prejudices that we hold. We may learn that past experiences, though no longer applicable, color our perception of our present abilities and competence. By attending to our reactions we learn how comfortable we are when others express their feelings to us. We learn how we frequently make assumptions about present circumstances based on past experience — and learn that those assumptions can be incorrect.

By studying our reactions we may learn that there are some things about ourselves that we want to change. We may want to broaden the range of our reactions, reduce the number of reactions based on out-of-date experiences, or decrease the number of reactions resulting from fear or discomfort. We may want to work on increasing the number of reactions that understand *with* a person, that consider the idea or attitude that is expressed from the speaker's point of view.

When we stop evaluating another person's statement of feeling from our own point of view we are more open to hearing what that person is really saying. We become better listeners and are better able to respond to the person in a helpful way. Responding is the last step in the three-step process of attending to the emotional needs of parents.

RESPONDING

As our listening skills increase, and as our reactions become more understanding, most of us find ourselves wanting to respond to parents' expressions of feelings with more than an encouraging, "Uh-huh" or an empathetic, "Boy, I can sure understand your feeling that way." Sometimes we can see that parents get stuck as they start to describe their feelings and we want to say something that will help them better define what feelings they are experiencing. Sometimes parents seem distracted, sad, withdrawn, angry, or upset. We know something is on their mind. We would like to give them an opportunity to express what those feelings are in order to clear the air so they can attend to the activities in the session.

Many parents do not volunteer or talk freely about their feelings because it is not a typical communication pattern for them. Some parents may not even be aware of what they *are* feeling and are not at all able to label or name their emotions. Specialists who respond to these parents' non-verbal expressions of feelings may help them become more aware of and comfortable with the range of emotions that they experience while they participate in habilitation.

TYPES OF RESPONSES

There are a variety of responses a specialist can make when it is evident that parents are experiencing feelings related to their hearing-impaired child. Some of these remarks are helpful in eliciting statements of feelings from parents and some are not. Specialists generally want to respond to parents in a helpful way, conveying that the parents are important to them and that they care about how the parents feel. A helpful response assists parents in dealing with their feelings about their handicapped child. A non-helpful response is one that discourages parents from talking further about their feelings.

NON-HELPFUL RESPONSES

There are several types of responses that are non-helpful because the impact they have on parents is to discourage further expression of feeling. Some examples of these non-helpful responses (adapted from Wallin, 1965) are listed below:

Mary, Johnny's mother, states: "I feel sick whenever I think of Johnny being handicapped."

Non-Helpful Response 1: "You probably always react hard to this kind of thing." With this response the teacher generalizes the parent's feeling, making it sound like a bad habit.

Non-Helpful Response 2: "Oh, Mary, you shouldn't feel that way. Johnny is such a cute a little boy." The teacher is denying Mary the right to her feeling, both by telling her what she shouldn't feel and by suggesting that she should have other feelings.

Non-Helpful Response 3: "What did the pediatrician say about Johnny during your appointment yesterday?" This response changes the subject, effectively shutting down continued discussion of feelings.

Non-Helpful Response 4: "Mary, I feel so badly when you say that. What can I do to make you feel better?" This response reveals that the teacher is distressed by the parent's feelings and has a need to take responsibility for fixing the parent's feelings.

Non-Helpful Response 5: "I think you should do three things to make yourself feel better. First, keep busy; second, read the handouts I send home with you; and third, come to the parent meetings." This response is another "fixer-upper." It says to the parent, "Follow my advice and everything will be o.k."

Non-Helpful Response 6: "It's not nearly so bad as all that, Mary. Most people won't even notice his handicap. And he's much better off than many deaf children." This response minimizes the effect of the handicap and tells Mary that her response to Johnny's handicap is inappropriate.

Non-Helpful Response 7: "I expect you to keep your spirits up, Mary, so you can do your part to help him. I know you will want to do the best possible for him." This response sets up expectations for Mary's behavior and, in effect, says "I'm disappointed in you for having your feelings."

Non-Helpful Response 8: "What is your definition of handicapped, Mary?" This response attends to the verbal content of Mary's message and ignores or discounts the emotional content.

Most, if not all, of the above responses would most likely inhibit Mary from expressing more of her feelings.

TWO CATEGORIES OF HELPFUL RESPONSES

The specialist who considers the parents' exploration of feelings as critical to their ability to be most effective with their child will want to utilize helpful responses that encourage discussion of feelings related to the child. This specialist knows she is not being asked to solve the parents' problems or to "fix" the situation that creates the feelings when she encourages parents to talk. Rather, **the specialist views her role as an enabler, someone who can let parents know their feelings are valid, can help parents define the thoughts behind their feelings, and can assist parents in setting forth all the alternatives in a problem-solving situation.**

Some examples of helpful responses to Mary's statement, "I feel sick whenever I think of Johnny being handicapped," are:

> "Tell me more about how you are feeling, Mary."
>
> "It sounds like it might be hard for you to think of Johnny being deaf."
>
> "What do you think of when you hear the term 'handicapped,' Mary?"

These, and other types of helpful responses, will be discussed below.

Helpful responses have several characteristics:

- A helpful response *stays with the topic* that the parent introduces.
- A helpful response focuses on *exploring the feeling content* of the parent's statement.
- A helpful response conveys the listener's belief that *parents can deal with their feelings* and do something about their problems. A helpful response does not try to protect parents from their feelings or to "fix" the problem.
- A helpful response is *short.*

There are two categories of responses that encourage parents to explore the thoughts behind their feelings. In the first category are **responses that let the parent know that the specialist is hearing what they say.**

CATEGORY I: 3 TYPES OF RESPONSES

There are three types of responses in this category: paraphrasing, summarizing, and asking for clarification. All of these responses let the parent know that they are being heard.

A *paraphrase* is simply a restatement of what has been said. A parent says, "My in-laws have been calling me every day to ask if Kelly's hearing has gotten any better." The specialist can paraphrase this statement by saying, "They want to know if her hearing is improving." When you have paraphrased correctly, you will almost always elicit an affirmative "uh-huh" or "yes," followed by further information, since the parent has been assured by your response that you are listening and that the topic is acceptable to talk about.

A paraphrase does not introduce any new material. It may use words identical to what the parent has used or it may state the same information using synonyms or a different grammatical structure. The potency of using paraphrase is the indication to the parent that you are listening carefully to what they are saying and that they have permission to go on.

The second type of response in the first category is a *summary* of what the parent has been saying. When a parent begins to express feelings, he/she may mention experiencing several feelings and several different situations that elicit those feelings. A specialist may want to summarize what the parent has said both to indicate that she is hearing the parent and to make certain that she is retaining all the information. After a parent has described her experiences of the past week, the specialist might say, "So, when your neighbor made a comment about Jessie's hearing aid it didn't bother you, but when the woman in the store and the pharmacist remarked on it you were irritated."

As in paraphrasing, a summary does not introduce new material. It does not include the specialist's interpretation of what the parent has said or any judgements or advice. A summary tells parents that you are attending to what they have said.

The third type of response in this category *asks for clarification*. Because it is not always easy to express feelings, people are not always clear in saying how they are feeling and why. A careful listener will not want to be confused and can say, "I have to admit I'm a little confused. You said you felt 'put down' when the doctor said what?" If we fail to clarify issues about which we are confused, we may respond inappropriately to the parent's feelings or concerns. Since all of us want to be understood, it feels as if someone really cares when they ask for clarification.

Paraphrasing, summarizing, and asking for clarification are all responses that let parents know that you are hearing what they say.

CATEGORY II: 2 TYPES OF RESPONSES

The second category of helpful responses consists of **responses that not only let parents know that they are being heard, but that also encourage them to explore and think more about their feelings.** The two types of responses in this category are open-ended requests or questions, and perception checks.

The first type of response that encourages parents to explore their feelings is an *open-ended request or question.* An open-ended question or request is one that cannot be answered with "yes" or "no." Open-ended questions are helpful responses if they stay with the content of what the parent has said.

Three different open-ended requests or questions might be used in response to the parent's statement: "I feel sick whenever I think of Johnny being handicapped."

First, the specialist can use an open-ended request to encourage the parent to talk more about the feeling expressed, for example, "Tell me more about how you are feeling, Mary."

Second, the specialist can ask an open-ended question that helps the parent identify the thoughts behind her feeling, such as, "What do you think of when you hear the term, 'handicapped'?" This question is different from the question that was earlier described as a non-helpful response. That question — "What is your *definition* of handicapped, Mary?" — asks for *information.* This question, "What do you *think of* when you hear the word 'handicapped'?" asks for the *thoughts* behind the parent's feelings.

A third open-ended question the specialist can ask helps parents think about their feelings in a different way and may help them explore how they act when they are feeling a certain way: "When you feel sick like you described, Mary, what do you feel most like doing?" Mary's response, which may vary from, "Crawl under the bed" to "Punch the audiologist who told me this" or to "Scream out loud," gives both the specialist and parent better insight into Mary's feelings.

Using open-ended requests or questions helps parents to talk more about their feelings and to discover the thoughts that are associated with the feeling statements they make.

The second type of response which can be helpful in eliciting discussion of feelings from parents is called a *perception check.* A perception check requires that the specialist hears and sees what the parent says and conveys with body language. She can then make a guess about the feeling content of the message. The phrase "makes a guess" is important here. The specialist cannot know how a parent is feeling until the parent expresses how he is feeling. For that reason, when one uses a perception check as a way of eliciting a parent's feelings on a topic, it is important to be tentative. Telling a parent what he feels may create resistance. Suggesting what he *might* be feeling opens up the topic without implying that you know what he is feeling better than he does. In a perception check it is helpful to use words such as "might," "could," "perhaps" and "it seems" as a way of suggesting, rather than telling, a parent what he may be feeling. The response, "It sounds like it might be hard for you to think of Johnny being deaf," is an example of a perception check.

One of the fathers at IHR once remarked, "The other hearing-impaired three-year-olds in his group talk so much more than my son, Bobby." The specialist, recognizing that this topic generally has a lot of emotional content for parents, decided to try a perception check: "It occurs to me that you might be worried about whether Bobby is going to acquire good speech. Is that something you've thought about?"

The specialist introduced the feeling "worry" as a feeling that the father might feel comfortable with. He was free then to confirm or deny the teacher's interpretation. "Yeah, I have been worried," Bobby's father said. "I can't think what it would be like to have a son I can't talk with."

Again, the specialist responded with a perception check. "It seems like you might feel pretty sad about the possibility of not being able to talk to Bobby."

"Sad? Yeah, devastated would be more like it . . ."

The conversation continued with the father expressing not only his concern about his son's speech, but his reluctance to talk over his fears about Bobby's future with his wife for fear of depressing her further. The specialist gained some valuable insights into the family's emotional status, and Bobby's father, upon leaving the session, expressed that he felt much better for having talked about some of the things he had been thinking about.

Helpful responses encourage parents to talk about their feelings by creating an environment in which they feel accepted, nurtured, and understood.

RELATIONSHIPS AFFECT RESPONSES

It sometimes happens that a person's response is identical to his reaction. When told that you have won a hundred dollar prize, your reaction and response might be a simultaneous "Wow! That's great!" When a close friend tells you that she will be late to an engagement, you may feel free to respond with your immediate reaction, "Darn, that's going to be inconvenient for me." If an acquaintance told you the same thing your reaction may be the same, but you may moderate your response to, "Oh, I'm sorry to hear that. I guess I can try to change my schedule to accommodate you." In interpersonal relationships it is generally true that the stronger the trust relationship between two individuals, the safer it feels to express your reaction without censoring it.

In the parent-specialist partnership the trust between parent and specialist frequently develops to a very high level. While this partnership of peers can contain elements of friendship, it differs from a friendship because of the basis on which the relationship is formed. The specialist must remain aware that her role in the partnership is based on provision of a service that the parent needs. For this reason, the specialist must be able to disassociate herself personally from some of the parents' statements and decisions and to respond as a representative of the agency or school.

An instance in which this disassociation process was employed occurred at IHR when a family told the specialist with whom they were working that they felt short-changed and inconvenienced by some changes in their lesson schedule and were, therefore, transferring to another parent-infant program. The specialist's immediate, internal reaction was, "I have gone out of my way time and again to accommodate your changing schedule. Furthermore, you rejected my recommendation that we schedule more frequent sessions so that if we missed a session, the interval until the next would not be so long." The specialist had to censor and repress the feelings of indignation and rejection that were apparent in her reaction and respond in a way that would keep the lines of communication open with the parents. She chose to say, "I'm sorry to hear that you are considering leaving the program here. We've made changes before. Are there changes we could make now that would meet your needs?" While censoring a personal reaction in order to make a professional and helpful response is difficult, it is an essential way in which the specialist can assist the parents of a young hearing-impaired child through a difficult and confusing time.

The parent-infant specialist does not need extensive formal training as a professional counselor in order to help parents deal with their feelings about their child's handicap. One of the greatest needs of individuals in crisis is to feel understood. For many parents, feeling understood may be all that they need. By using good listening skills, monitoring internal reactions, and employing helpful responses, the specialist conveys to the parent the message that their feelings are heard, understood, and accepted. Luterman's book, *Counseling Parents of Hearing Impaired Children* (1979) is another resource for specialists who want to increase their skills in working with parents.

RESOLVING CONFLICTS BETWEEN
PARENTS AND SPECIALISTS

WHAT IS A CONFLICT?

An area of parent-specialist interaction that is deserving of special attention is the area of dealing with conflicts. Conflicts result from the presence of incompatible or opposing needs, ideas, or feelings. There are two types of conflict: internal and external. The first type of conflict, experienced by most people almost every day, is internal conflict which is generated by our own opposing needs, ideas, or feelings: "I need to go to the store to get dinner — I need to be at a meeting in 15 minutes. What will I do?" "I want to say hello to that friendly looking man/woman — I am afraid to approach him/her. What should I do?" We manage to resolve dozens of internal conflicts every day, sometimes without ever consciously verbalizing our ideas or feelings to ourselves. Other internal conflicts stay with us for days, rendering us immobile because we can't make up our minds about what need to meet, what feeling to experience.

The second type of conflict is external — it exists between two or more individuals, each of whom has his own ideas, feelings, and needs. The different ideas, feelings, or needs that two people have become *conflicts* when one or both individuals feel that things should be different from what they are: one or both parties cannot understand or accept the other's action or point of view, or is not willing to compromise to meet the other party's need. A conflict exits between the specialist and parent, for instance, when the specialist has an emergency staff meeting scheduled during her regular session time with a family. The specialist needs to change the session time. If the parents feel inconvenienced by the request to change times or if they feel that their regularly scheduled lesson should take precedence over other events, a conflict exists. The specialist needs to make a change; the parents need to keep the schedule the same. A conflict exists because both parties have different needs.

The state of conflict has some key thoughts and feelings associated with it. Recognition of a few key phrases is often our first indicator that there is a conflict. The word *"should"* is an enormous red flag. Whenever we hear ourselves utter the word "should," we can usually define at least two conflicting issues that apply to the situation. "I should plan my lesson now — but I want to finish reading this article first": two opposing desires. "I should be more friendly to Bill, but I feel hurt when he's so rude to me": two opposing feelings. "They should use signed language with their child; they should buy their child new hearing aids; they should take the baby to the doctor everytime he has ear infections." All these are ideas a specialist might have that do not necessarily coincide with the parents' ideas of what they "should" do.

The phrase, "I wish," can be another indicator of a conflict. Usually we wish things were different from how they are, therefore, we are in conflict. "I wish I weighed 10 lbs. less, but I love to eat." "I wish I could go on vacation but I need to use the money to pay my bills."

Other clues to conflict are thoughts or judgements that we generate:

- He is not cooperating. (He should do things my way)
- She is not following my advice. (I know how it should be done.)
- He is wrong; uninformed; biased; prejudiced; screwball. (My way is right.)
- She won't listen to my point of view. (She should know that my ideas are better than hers.)
- He ignores what I want. (He should pay attention to me.)
- She takes everything (objects, time, love) and leaves nothing for me. (She should give me my share.)

All of these thoughts tell us that we want things to be different from how they are. We want him to cooperate, to agree with our ideas, or attend to our needs. We want her to take our advice, listen to our point of view, share resources with us. As long as others continue to behave as they are and we continue to want them to change, we will be in conflict.

CONFLICT PRODUCES FEELINGS

So, what's wrong with a little conflict? Conflict *feels* bad. If we didn't care about something, it wouldn't matter to us if someone else felt or behaved or thought differently than we did. When we want things our way, it hurts when we can't have them. This hurt is experienced as one of many feelings on a spectrum from mild to intense. Mild irritation to intense anger. Mild misgivings to intense fear. Mild feelings of unimportance to intense feelings of helplessness.

The more the conflict impinges on or threatens our basic needs for survival, love, usefulness, and importance, the more strongly we feel. Conflicts that center around deeply held values evoke strong feelings. Conflicts around issues of competence bring up a very intense feeling response. Conversely, the less we have invested in an idea, thought, or feeling, the less impact conflict will have on our feelings. She wants the walls painted grey, you would prefer beige. You are mildly irritated that you may not get what you want. He thinks he does a better job of organizing tasks than you do. You have always perceived yourself as somewhat disorganized so your feelings of competency are only mildly threatened. The parent wants to come for a lesson at 1:00 p.m. You would prefer 11:00 a.m. so your afternoon is free. You feel mildly annoyed.

When you are experiencing feelings of anger, confusion, frustration, helplessness, unimportance, fear, or inadequacy, if you feel discredited or minimized by someone, it is likely that these feelings have been evoked by a conflict. Someone does not view things the way you do and you want them to change!

It is obvious that conflict is unavoidable. We can't even avoid creating internal conflict for ourselves. Conflict between people is a given. We can't do anything to prevent conflict from arising. We can do a great deal, however, in determining how the conflict is resolved.

CONFLICT RESOLUTION

Conflict resolution requires skill, but even more it requires an attitude or belief that two people can be, think, or feel differently and *neither is wrong.* Effective conflict resolution creates no "winners" or "losers." When there are winners and losers, the original conflict may no longer be at issue, but you can be sure that several other conflicts have been created. Effective conflict resolution requires a desire to negotiate so that some of both persons' needs are met. When conflicts are negotiated skillfully, both persons come away with a better understanding of the other and with feelings of satisfaction that some of their important needs have been acknowledged and met.

The list of potential sources of conflict for the parent-infant specialist is endless:

- Other staff members who need space, materials, equipment at the same time you do.
- Supervisors who give too much/too little "support," who assign too many duties or not enough responsibility.
- Parents who do not carry out assignments, who are late to sessions, who do not participate actively in habilitation, who have different ideas about goals.
- Young children who have their own ideas related to wearing hearing aids, playing with toys, manipulating equipment, sitting still for more than one minute.

INEFFECTUAL STYLES OF "CONFLICT RESOLUTION"

Because the potential for conflict is so great, it is imperative that the parent-infant specialist establish effective techniques for dealing with conflict. There are many styles of dealing with conflict that do not work because they leave one or both parties feeling badly once the conflict is "resolved." Examples of three of these ineffectual styles are:

1. Ava Avoider: Ava hates conflict. She doesn't like to disagree with anyone. Ava always gives in: She agrees with ideas that are in direct opposition to hers, she never speaks up if someone's needs

are in opposition to her own. Ava sometimes wonders why people act like she is invisible. She often feels helpless and even angry, though she knows she shouldn't.

2. Harry Helper: Harry is so anxious to please, he will go to all lengths to meet other peoples' needs. Stay an hour late for lessons so Mrs. Jones doesn't have to ask her boss if she can come on her lunch hour? Sure! Make teaching materials for a co-worker even though it means giving up other plans? Sure! Accept the parents' reasons why their deaf child doesn't need a hearing aid? Fine, if it makes them happy. Harry wonders why he feels used sometimes and why he feels ineffectual as a teacher.

3. Stella Steamroller: Stella has all the answers in her recipe book for success. She is happy to tell people what they must do in order to achieve goals, most of which she has defined for them. Parents must make time to spend two hours per day with their child if they want him to talk. Other staff wouldn't have problems with families if only they would follow Stella's advice. Stella frequently feels annoyed, frustrated, and discredited because people don't carry out her suggestions.

None of these styles results in the resolution of conflict because the style itself creates new conflicts in addition to the original.

AN EFFECTIVE STYLE OF CONFLICT RESOLUTION: NEGOTIATION

The most effective way to resolve conflict is through *negotiation,* a process which ensures that some of the needs of all concerned are met. When a conflict is negotiated successfully, there are no winners or losers. Negotiation is a process in which both parties state their feelings and needs clearly so that solutions can be found which meet some of the needs of everyone concerned.

A good way to approach conflict resolution is with the question, "How can we resolve this issue so that you get most of what you want/need and I get most of what I want/need?" Once each of the persons involved in the conflict has listed what he wants or needs, it is helpful for each to prioritize his list. At the top of the list go the least negotiable wants or needs, the issues that each party feels least able to "give up." Generally, these issues will be defined as "needs" by the person listing them. One such need might be expressed by a parent as, "I need to have our lessons at 5:00 p.m. because that's when I get off work." The specialist may have an equally strong need *not* to have the lesson at 5:00 p.m. since her work day ends at 4:00 p.m. During the process of negotiation the specialist may ask if the parent has asked his boss or supervisor if he might take a lunch hour at 1:00 twice a week in order to attend lessons. The specialist may volunteer to write the parent's boss a letter to describe the importance of the parent's attendance.

Once needs/wants are prioritized, the parent and specialist may see that what is most important to one rates low on the list of the other and resolution of the conflict is easily made by each giving up a low priority item.

Negotiation does not flourish in an authoritarian environment. If the specialist finds herself holding the view that parents should make all the changes necessary to resolve conflicts, she will need to reevaluate her perception of the parent-specialist partnership. If she truly views the parent as a valued partner in the child's habilitation process, then it follows that that partner has a right to have his needs considered and met where possible. It becomes apparent that if one or both parties do not express their needs, then it will be difficult to propose a course of action that will meet their needs. A good indicator that not all the feelings and needs have been laid on the table is given by a parent who rejects all of the solutions that the specialist proposes. In this situation the specialist has two options: ask the parent to express what *would* work for him, or gently state that she is confused — could the parent tell her again what his needs and feelings are regarding this conflict.

REFERRING PARENTS TO A SKILLED COUNSELOR

In addition to having skills of listening, reacting, responding, and conflict resolution, the parent-infant specialist must also know when to refer parents to a skilled counselor. Referral is indicated in the following circumstances:

1. Parents are experiencing such strong feelings as a result of their child's hearing loss that they are severely depressed or locked into an unproductive stage of reacting to crisis. The specialist's use of listening, reacting, and responding are not sufficient to help parents express and get beyond their powerful feelings.
2. The specialist has strong reactions to parents' feelings about their child that make it impossible for her to listen and respond in an effective and helpful manner.
3. The parents present problems, such as marital or other family issues, that are not directly related to their feelings about their hearing-impaired child.

Learning that their child is hearing-impaired may bring up deeply rooted feelings for parents that a specialist is not qualified to deal with. Gently confronting troubled parents with the recommendation that they seek help from a skilled professional is an important part of the habilitation process.

PART IV

HELPING PARENTS ACHIEVE PARENT OBJECTIVES

CHAPTER 10

THE FRAMEWORK FOR PARENT INSTRUCTION: THE PARENT INVOLVEMENT METHOD (PIM)

A Change of Focus

How PIM is Used

The Three Steps in PIM
- Pre-Activity
- During Activity
- Post-Activity

Potential Obstacles to Parental Learning
- Ambivalent Feelings About the Specialist
- Memories of Failure in School
- Biases About Handicapped People
- Values and Priorities
- Cultural Tradition

Information and skill objectives for parents are delineated in the parent curriculum sections of *Parent-Infant Communication* (Infant Hearing Resource, 1985). The four sections are entitled "General Information and Skills," "Development of Auditory Skills," "Development of Presymbolic Communication," and "Development of Receptive and Expressive Language." The parent curriculum contains a total of 325 information and skills objectives for parents. Some parents may enter the habilitation process already possessing some of the skills and information described in the objectives. Through observing the parents' interactions with their child the specialist can note in her lesson plan, record on the Parent Curriculum Checksheet, and reinforce verbally the information and skills that parents bring with them that will promote their child's learning. The specialist can also note parental behaviors or attitudes that will not promote the establishment of a positive learning environment for the child and can include information and skill objectives related to these behaviors and attitudes in her lesson plans for the family.

The habilitation process for each family includes a large number of learning objectives for parents to achieve. It is essential, therefore, that specialists have a well-defined system for assuring that they can convey information and teach skills to parents efficiently and successfully. The IHR staff has developed a three-step process of interacting with parents that provides a systematic and effective means for teaching information and skills to parents. This process is called the Parent Involvement Method (PIM).

The PIM is a process through which the specialist transmits to the parent information and skills that the parent will use in teaching his child listening and language skills. The process requires that the specialist carry on a dialogue with the parents in three steps:

1. Pre-Activity — dialogue that takes place before a learning activity is initiated with the child.
2. During Activity — dialogue that occurs as the parent, specialist, and child are "playing" with the purpose of exposing the child to auditory and language information.
3. Post-Activity — dialogue that takes place after the activity is completed.

Each of these steps is comprised of several specific activities that the specialist carries out (Figure 6).

PARENT INVOLVEMENT METHOD (PIM)
OBSERVATION FORM
Infant Hearing Resource

Name of observer _____ Date _____

Family Observed _____ Specialist _____

Pre-Activity	Yes	No	Comments
Specialist states objective being taught and describes activity	____	____	_____
Parent role described	____	____	_____
Specialist role described	____	____	_____
Expectation of child described	____	____	_____
During Activity			
Parent participates as planned	____	____	_____
Specialist participates as planned	____	____	_____
Child responds to activity as anticipated	____	____	_____
Adaptations made?	____	____	_____
Specialist comments and interprets to parent	____	____	_____
Post-Activity			
Specialist asks parent to evaluate activity	____	____	_____
Parent describes child's performance in activity accurately	____	____	_____
Specialist gives parent feedback on parent's role	____	____	_____
Specialist sums up intent and results of activity	____	____	_____
Parent and specialist generate ideas for home activities	____	____	_____

FIGURE 6.   This form can be used by an observer during a lesson (e.g., one of the parents) or by the specialist and parents as they watch a videotape of an activity they did with the child.

A CHANGE OF FOCUS

Use of the Parent Involvement Method requires that the specialist m a major change in the focus of her instruction, a change that is essent the success of the parent-specialist partnership. In most college or univ programs through which teachers of the hearing impaired are traine emphasis is on providing the prospective teacher with information an to teach children. Her future job or role is that of instructing childr parent-infant specialist must give up the role of being the child's prir structor if she is to function effectively in her partnership with pare must make a mental adjustment so that she no longer perceives h being the person responsible for filling the child with information a but instead, views the parents as having this responsibility. This difficult adjustment to make. Our training almost compels us to direc attention to the child, to feel an intense need to get involved with the child in order to teach him what he is ready to learn. **The successful parent-infant specialist is one who is able to re-direct the focus of her attention to the parents.** She plans her lessons with goals for both parents and infant in mind and plans activities that will give parents the opportunity to put new information to use and to practice new skills. The parent-infant specialist's feelings of competence and accomplishment are derived from parent achievement which results in achievement on the part of the child.

HOW PIM IS USED

The PIM, as outlined in Figure 6, is used in three ways at IHR:
1. As a guideline for how the specialist includes the parent in each activity. By following the steps of PIM, the specialist assures that she is giving parents necessary information, instruction in acquisition of skills, and feedback on their interactions with their child.
2. As a self-check for the specialist. By videotaping an activity and viewing it later, the specialist can use PIM as a check on herself to ascertain that she is following all the steps of involving parents.
3. As a self-check for parents. Through use of videotape, parents have the opportunity to evaluate and critique their own interactions with their child and the specialist's interaction with the child, following the PIM format.

Giving constructive and useful feedback to parents on their interactions with their child is a sensitive area and a skill most teachers do not learn in their teacher training programs. Since "feedback" is often equated with "criticism," the function of providing feedback can be a touchy area for specialists and parents alike. It is essential to be able to give useful and constructive feedback if your objective is to help the individual become a more effective person or to arrive at a more effective working relationship between the two of you (Anderson, 1968). Feedback is useful, according to Anderson, only when it is intended to be helpful to the recipient.

Specialists at IHR have found that *following the PIM format requires them to be very specific with the parent about the purpose of the activity and the parent's role in the activity prior to starting the activity.* Having agreed on the purpose of the activity and the role each adult will play beforehand creates a much more comfortable climate in which to give parents helpful feedback on their participation during and after the activity. In addition, when parents are given the opportunity to discuss their participation in an activity and to observe themselves interacting with their child on videotape, they often note problem areas themselves and comment on their need to make changes. This kind of self-correction is much less threatening than critique from another person.

THE THREE STEPS IN PIM

The sequence of activities and dialogue in the three steps in the Parent Involvement Method — Pre-Activity, During-Activity and Post-Activity — are described in detail below.

PRE-ACTIVITY

SPECIALIST STATES OBJECTIVES BEING TAUGHT AND DESCRIBES ACTIVITY

As the specialist introduces an activity, it is essential that she define the child objective(s) which the activity is designed to teach and the parent objective(s) which the parent will be putting into practice during the activity. In so doing, she describes the purpose of the activity or why it is being presented to the infant and gives the parent the rationale for using the skills specified in the parent objective. This rationale will include the reasons for selecting the particular activity and for asking the parent to practice a specific skill while interacting with the child. Most activities provide the opportunity to work on a number of both infant and parent objectives. Depending on the level of the parent's knowledge and skill, the specialist can specify one child and one parent objective to work on or can select several objectives that can be promoted during the activity.

> **Example:** Julia is working with Anna and her son, ten-month-old Donny, who has a severe bilateral hearing loss. Donny has

been wearing hearing aids for four months. Audiological evaluation, using Visual Reinforcement Audiometry, and observation of Donny at home have shown that when wearing his aids Donny is aware of voice at normal conversational levels within a two to five-foot radius. Donny's vocalizations consist mainly of lalling, though in the past two weeks he has produced the consonant [b] in combination with the vowel sound [ʌ]. Donny has enjoyed reciprocal vocal play in the past, responding to his parents' vocalizations with dissimilar vocalizations of his own.

Julia and Anna have charted Donny's progress in acquisition of presymbolic communication, following the developmental sequence of objectives in the Infant Presymbolic Communication section of *Parent-Infant Communication*. They have determined that Donny has now achieved objective No. Sp-20, "Child vocalizes at least one of the bilabial consonants, p/b/m, in combination with a vowel," but has not achieved No. Sp-22, "Child uses consonant-vowel syllable repetition in self-initiated vocal play, e.g., "ma-ma-ma." This is the objective that Julia and Anna want to work on with Donny.

Julia has also observed that Anna, in her desire to model vocalizations for Donny, tends not to give Donny much opportunity to take his turn in parent-child "conversations." She feels that it is time for Anna to work on the Parent Presymbolic Communication objective No. 9 which reads, "Take turns 'conversing'. Adult pauses to give the child time to respond. Avoid interrupting the child's communication."

Julia has hidden several small stuffed animals in a bag for use in an activity with Donny. Adhering to the first step in PIM, Julia describes to Anna the child and parent objectives she is proposing Anna work on and the activity Anna can use to teach Donny and to practice new skills herself.

Julia: "Anna, last week we determined the next speech-related presymbolic communication objective that Donny is ready to work on. You remember, expanding his new 'buh' into 'buh buh buh.' I thought we could work on that today using some stuffed animals. They are here in the bag. We can take them out one at a time and move them along the floor as we model 'buh buh buh.' One thing I'd like us to practice is giving Donny plenty of time to get in his side of the conversation. One of the objectives for you to work on is No. 9 here (shows Anna the objective in the curriculum)."

Anna: "Oh — I'm not giving him much of a chance to talk, am I? O.k., I'll try to give him more air time!"

PARENT ROLE DESCRIBED/SPECIALIST ROLE DESCRIBED

It is critical that both parent and specialist know clearly what each is expected to do during the activity. The role of both the specialist and the parent in the activity will vary according to the parent's familiarity with how to teach the objective(s) and his/her understanding of the activity.

The roles can encompass the following participation styles:

1. Specialist carries out the entire activity and parent observes.
2. Specialist carries out the activity and parent looks for and records specific specialist or child behaviors.
3. Specialist models behaviors during the beginning of the activity then the parent takes over and completes the activity, using the behaviors modelled.
4. Parent and specialist alternate interacting with the child during the activity.
5. Parent carries out the activity while specialist looks for and records parent or child behaviors.

Videotape can be used to record activities in which any of these participation styles are used so that specialist and parent can review the activity together on tape at a later time.

When a parent or child objective is first being introduced, it is generally best to have the specialist model how the proposed activity can be used to teach the objective and then turn the materials or activity over to the parent and move out of the activity. In this instance the specialist will simply say, "I'll do the first couple rounds (minutes, turns, etc.) so you can see clearly what I meant, then I'll back out and you can take over." It is important that the specialist not carry on her interaction with the child to the point that the child becomes bored with the activity so that the parent must deal with a disinterested child when it's his/her turn to interact with the child.

Example:

Julia: "How about if I do the first round. I'll say 'buh buh' as I move the animal two hops, and repeat it once more, then put the animal in front of you. You do the same thing, then put it in front of Donny, sit back, and look expectantly at him."

If the parent has had experience working on the objective and is familiar with the activity, the parent and specialist may agree that the specialist will sit back to observe, record child and parent behaviors, or videotape the interaction while the parent interacts with the child. The essential element is that the specialist and parent know clearly what each is expected to do during the activity.

EXPECTATIONS OF CHILD DESCRIBED

It is helpful for the parent and specialist to spend a minute or two discussing how they anticipate the child will respond to the activity presented. In so doing, they may realize that they will have to modify their initial approach in order to enhance their chances of working on the objective they have established. When the specialist, for instance, proposes to roll marbles down an incline to model the word "down," the parent may report that the child is likely to hide the marbles in his pockets, since that is a game they play at home. The adults may then decide to use small rubber balls that do not have this association for the child so that they can carry out their original activity without confusing the child.

This discussion also clarifies for the parent what *not* to expect or require from the child. When first introducing a new language concept, the specialist can remind the parent that they will be giving the child the opportunity to hear and see the language several times, but that the child is not required to imitate a word or to use a word spontaneously in order to keep the activity going. As the parent and specialist discuss how they anticipate the child will respond to the activity, they can make certain that their expectations take the child's readiness and interests into consideration.

> **Example:**
> **Julia:** "What do you think Donny will do when you put the animal in front of him?"
> **Anna:** "I think he'll pick it up and look at it. I don't know if he'll make it hop on the ground. Sometimes he waves his toys around in the air."
> **Julia:** "O.K. Well, let's give him a minute to play and we'll watch what he does. If he does move the animal in some way and does not vocalize, why don't you lean toward him and vocalize once or twice, matching the rhythm of 'buh buh' to whatever motion he's making. Then sit back again and watch him. Remember, our goals are to model for him this new type of babbling and also to give him an opportunity to imitate the vocalization if he is ready to do so.

DURING ACTIVITY

This second segment of the PIM observation form is a guideline to keep the adults on track during the activity.

PARENT/SPECIALIST PARTICIPATE AS DESCRIBED

The specialist needs to monitor her own behavior and coach the parent, if necessary, to make certain that each is participating in the activity as planned. The specialist may realize that she is not modelling the agreed-upon vocalization and can note that, mid-activity, by saying, "Oops, I forgot to say 'buh-buh.'" The specialist may need to give the parent feedback, such as the information that while he/she is using the right vocalizations, his/her voice is so soft the child probably cannot hear it: "Real good, Anna. You're remembering to use 'buh-buh' even if I didn't! Try making your voice a little stronger to make sure that Donny can hear you."

Example: Julia demonstrated moving a stuffed pig and vocalizing, then handed the toy to Anna who did the same before giving the pig to Donny.

Julia: "Great Anna — you really got his attention!"

The two women paused to watch Donny, who has picked up the pig to examine it. Donny poked at the pig once, then again, making no sound. He poked again and Anna vocalized, "buh buh buh!" Donny looked up at her and smiled, then poked at the pig again. Anna vocalized again and both she and Donny laughed.

Julia: "That's perfect! Keep it up!"

Donny eventually dropped the pig and turned away. Julia took another stuffed animal from the bag and handed it to Anna who marched it on Donny's arm as she vocalized, "buh buh buh." Donny looked at it, then crawled away. Anna quickly put the animal back in the bag, then made a show of shaking the bag before putting the bag on the floor. Donny crawled to the bag and started hitting at it. Anna vocalized "buh buh" as he hit, and helped Donny open the bag and pull out the animal. He batted at it a few times and Anna vocalized a few more times.

CHILD RESPONDS TO ACTIVITY AS ANTICIPATED

If the answer to this statement is "yes," the parent and specialist can congratulate themselves for their accuracy in having predicted the child's behaviors. When the parent and specialist can present an activity to a child and accurately predict the child's response to it, they are doing a good job of meeting the criteria for a successful learning experience: interest, readiness, motivation, and reinforcement.

If the child does not respond as anticipated, these criteria provide excellent guidelines for indicating what might have gone wrong. Every adult has had the experience of presenting an "exciting" new toy to a child only

Using the Parent-Involvement Method (PIM) format, the parent-infant specialist videotapes the father and child engaged in an activity. Prior to beginning the game, the specialist and father had talked about the language that he could model for his son as they played.

The specialist, father, and child watch the videotape and discuss how the father's use of language matched his intent.

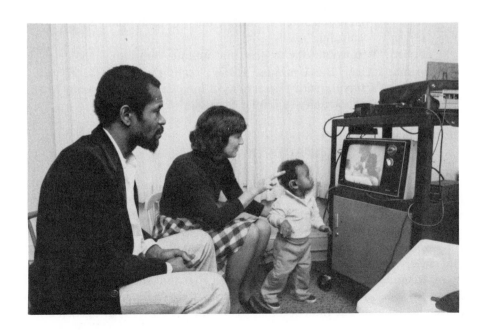

to find that he is more interested in the box. For a young child, there is no such thing as "polite attention." When he is not interested in an activity he simply pushes it away or starts doing something else.

In some instances adults find that they inaccurately predicted the child's readiness for an activity. The child might be unable to participate as anticipated or may be so adept at what is expected that he becomes rapidly disinterested.

The child's motivation to participate in an activity is dependent on many things. The child may be tired or not feeling well and thus unwilling to do much of anything. He may have his own idea about what to do with the materials presented and be unwilling to go along with the adult's plans. He may also have a preference for interacting with either the specialist or the parent and will be more motivated to engage in an activity with his "favorite" of the moment. A parent who is tuned in to his child's state and level of activity can report that, "Donny is droopy today — we'll need to pick quiet activities," or "Get out the trampoline! Donny's got a lot of steam today." A flexible specialist will adjust the activities presented so that they match the child's state.

Finally, if an activity is not intrinsically reinforcing for the child, he is not likely to engage in it for long. Parental and specialist social reinforcers will help maintain interest, but the best reinforcer is the enjoyment and sense of success that a child gains from an activity that is age- and ability-appropriate. These activities provide a challenge that intrigues, but does not discourage, the child.

> **Example:**
> **Anna:** (As she is playing with Donny) "He likes these toys and he seems interested when I vocalize but I'm disappointed that he isn't vocalizing."
> **Julia:** "You would like to hear him imitate 'buh buh.'"
> **Anna:** "Yeah. But I suppose I don't really think he will! At least he's staying with this activity a long time so I'm having plenty of opportunity to model 'buh buh' for him."

ADAPTATIONS MADE?

If the child does not respond as anticipated, the parent and specialist will have several options. The course advocated at IHR is for the **parent and specialist to follow the child's interest in the materials and to work on other objectives if the child's interest does not lend itself to the original objective. It is important to model this flexibility for parents to reinforce the principle that children learn best when they are playing their own game.** Another option is to modify the activity itself so that it better suits the child's readiness, or increases his interest or motivation in the activity yet is still geared to the objective planned. The final option is to abandon the activity altogether and to try something else that would more effectively promote achievement of the objectives (See Chapter 16, Diagnostic Teaching).

Example:

Julia: (Referring to Anna's action of putting the animal in the bag and shaking it) "Putting the animal back in the bag and shaking it was a good idea. That really recaptured Donny's attention. You are so good at keeping his interest by making little changes in the activity!"

At Infant Hearing Resource there is only one activity in which the child is required to participate in a standard way. This activity is learning to give a conditioned response to sound, a skill specialists begin teaching when children are 18-24 months of age (Chapter 17). Specialists reserve specific materials to use in teaching this activity and require the child to respond in a particular way. Specialists do not follow the child's lead in the conditioned response activity since it is important that the child learn the standard procedure of waiting for a stimulus and then giving a response. Once the child has learned this skill, he can participate in play audiometry during hearing evaluations.

In other activities the parent and specialist work hard to keep in mind that learning does not occur in coercive, stressful situations and that if a child chooses to respond to an activity in a way other than that which was anticipated, this interest can be capitalized upon to expose the child to other concepts. If the child responds to an activity with a behavior that is unacceptable, the parent and specialist will handle that behavior in whatever way they have agreed upon (Chapter 14).

SPECIALIST COMMENTS AND INTERPRETS TO PARENT

As the parent interacts with the child the specialist can verbally reinforce the parent for performance that furthers both parent and child objectives. Simple statements such as, "You really have Donny interested, Anna," or "I like the way you look at him when you've finished talking. I can see that you are waiting for him to contribute to the conversation," will tell parents that the specialist is in support of them, not sitting back and finding fault. If the specialist wants to encourage the parent to try another behavior to increase the success of the activity, she needs to be direct and specific, or even step in for a minute to demonstrate. "Anna, try letting Donny play with that one animal for a minute and keep the rest hidden in the bag until he tosses that first one aside. Then hand him another one. Having them all at once may be more than he can handle."

During the course of the activity the specialist can choose to point out and interpret specific child behaviors if this information does not distract the parent from successfully carrying out his/her role. Some activities require the parent's constant attention; in others, the parent and specialist can confer as the child acts on his own. If the child exhibits behaviors that are new or otherwise significant, the specialist can call them to the parent's attention. "Anna, I don't remember ever seeing Donny poking specifically at the eyes of a toy as he is now. I think he's beginning to notice eyes!"

Sometimes the child will alert to a sound that is occurring outside of the room and the parent, intent on the activity, pays no attention to this response. The specialist may want the parent to reinforce the child's awareness of sound and might say, "Anna, I think Donny hears that truck idling in front of the building. He's looked up and around a couple times. Why don't you take him over to the window and show him the truck." The specialist will gauge her interjections according to each parents' tolerance for interruption and suggestions.

Example:

Julia: (As Anna and Donny continue to play with the animal) "Hold on a bit longer before you vocalize at this point, Anna." (Donny continues to manipulate the animal as Julia and Anna watch.) After about ten seconds have passed, Julia cues Anna with a whispered, "O.K. — do it again."

Anna: "Buh buh buh buh!" (Donny looks at her and grins, then drops the animal and turns away.) "Well, looks like he's had enough of this."

Julia: "You're right. Let's let Donny explore and we can talk for a minute."

POST-ACTIVITY

The third part of the Parent Involvement Method is evaluation of the activity. This section is important because it helps the specialist and parent determine if the parent and child met their designated objectives. The parent and specialist can use information gained from the child's participation in the activity and the parent's skill in interacting with the child to plan future objectives and activities. This evaluation also provides an opportunity for both specialist and parent to give each other feedback on their participation in the activity.

SPECIALIST ASKS PARENT TO EVALUATE ACTIVITY

Specialists at IHR had a difficult time with this task until we learned to ask open-ended questions. In response to our questions such as, "How did you feel about that activity?" we got the answers, "Fine" or "O.K." 95% of the time and were frustrated about where to go from there. In contrast, by asking the parent, "Tell me what you felt most comfortable with," or "What was hard for you in that activity?" or "What do you think Donny learned from that activity?," we get useful information on which to build further discussion. If a parent says that it was easy to talk about what the child was doing, but hard to keep her own hands off the materials, then she has defined an area that you can work on in future activities: letting the child control the materials for a significant portion of the activity.

By asking what the parent thinks the child learned from the activity, you help the parent attend to the child's behaviors and responses. Awareness of the child's behaviors is an essential aspect of the parent's learning to follow the child's interest and talk about what the child is doing. Evaluation of the activity can be initiated by the specialist giving a brief assessment of how she felt she filled her role and with a general positive statement about the activity. If it is an activity in which everything seemed to go wrong, a humorous acknowledgment can take the pressure off: "Boy, we really goofed that one up, didn't we!"

Some of the open-ended questions that we have found useful in eliciting the parent's evaluation of the session are:

- What did you feel good about/comfortable with in that activity?
- What was difficult or felt awkward to you in that activity?
- How did this activity go differently from when we did it last week?
- What would you do the same/differently if you did this activity again? (good questions after the parent has viewed a videotape of the activity)
- Why do you think (child's name) did (name behavior) during the activity?
- What did (child's name) do during this activity that impressed you?
- What do you think (child's name) learned during this activity?
- How would you change this activity the next time we do it?
- Pretend you are (child's name). What would you do with these materials the next time you saw them?

Example:

Julia: "Looked like you and Donny were having fun, Anna! How did you feel about the activity?"

Anna: "It was fun. He likes those animals. It seems like it was a good game for him. He *was* listening to me vocalize but, as I said before, I sure wish he would vocalize more himself. Do you think he's ready for that?"

Julia: "You're right, Anna; it is a good game for Donny. I sure think he's taking in the vocalizations you were modeling. Babies need to hear this type of babbling quite a bit before they produce it themselves. Donny has been hearing us vocalize during the past four months as he has been wearing his hearing aids. It's hard to say when he will start this repetitive type of babbling but I do know it is the appropriate vocalization to be modeling for him in play activities like this.''

PARENT DESCRIBES CHILD'S PERFORMANCE IN ACTIVITY ACCURATELY

Some parents see their child's behaviors only in terms of "good" or "bad." These parents need to learn to look at what their child does without attaching a value judgment to it. The request, "Tell me what Ellie did when you handed her the first box," is most likely to elicit the description of an actual behavior. Some parents will not know or remember what the child did and may need to view the videotape if one was made before they can answer the question. These parents need to be exposed to more of the activities designed to help them become accurate observers of their child's behaviors (See Chapter 13).

When parents do describe their child's behaviors accurately, the specialist can commend them for their observations and draw them into speculation about how they might build on the behaviors to encourage achievement of targeted objectives. The specialist can provide the parent with scales of normal child development to help in predicting subsequent behaviors and in planning age- and ability-appropriate activities.

Example:

Julia: "Tell me what Donny did during this activity."

Anna: "Oh, he was real cooperative. I like that!"

Julia: "Yes, it sure makes our job easier when they cooperate! But what specific things did Donny do as you played together?"

Anna: "Let's see . . . He waved the toy, hit at it, crawled away a couple times, then came back."

Julia: "Right! He also looked at you as you vocalized. And what was that one new behavior I commented on?"

Anna: "You mean when he was poking at the pig's eyes? I wonder if that came from playing, 'Where's your eyes?'"

SPECIALIST GIVES PARENT FEEDBACK ON PARENT'S ROLE

This task is not relegated to a specific step in the process, but should be sprinkled throughout the activity. Feedback immediately following a specific behavior is more effective than is feedback related to many behaviors, delivered in a lump at the end. Feedback should include what the parent did well and what the parent needs to do more of. Since the parent has been given the opportunity to critique his own performance, some of the areas in which he feels a need for improvement may have already been mentioned. It is always easier for the specialist to follow up on the parent's own observations related to need for skill improvement than to broach the subject herself. However, there will be several areas in which parents may not be aware of skills they need to acquire. The specialist will want to think of a gentle, but direct, way to start a discussion of parental behaviors that are getting in the way of the child's progress.

Example:

Julia: "You did an excellent job of keeping Donny interested, Anna. You used a good volume level and interesting intonations in your vocalizations. At the beginning of the activity you were giving Donny a lot of time to respond. Later you were giving him less time, but you lengthened it again after I reminded you. It's hard to remember everything, isn't it!"

SPECIALIST SUMS UP INTENT AND RESULTS OF ACTIVITY

Before moving on to the next activity the specialist can briefly relate her perception of how well the execution of the activity matched the intent as described in the pre-activity stage, what she felt was achieved during the activity, and what the parent and specialist will do in subsequent sessions to build on this activity.

Example:

Julia: "I'd like to continue with this sort of activity next session. What kind of changes would you suggest for next time, Anna?"

Anna: "Well, maybe use a different toy but keep the vocalization the same?"

Julia: "Perfect. I'll see what I can dig out of the toy closet."

PARENT AND SPECIALIST GENERATE IDEAS FOR HOME ACTIVITIES

The last step in the process of involving parents is to help them determine how they can continue to utilize the skills they have been practicing and to work on child objectives at home. By talking about how the parent can incorporate specific listening and language stimuli into everyday activities — including the child's play — the specialist can emphasize that the child will learn skills most efficiently when exposed to them over and over in daily routines.

Example:

Julia: "How do you think you might model babbling for Donny at home?"

Anna: "I can probably do it while I'm changing his diaper —
you know, walk my fingers on his tummy as I say 'buh buh'.
Maybe when he is shaking his toys or patting the furniture like
he does."

Julia: "Sounds good. We can see what else might lend itself to
this type of thing when I come for a home visit next
Wednesday."

SUMMARY OF PIM

As parents and specialists work together over time, each pair establishes
their own rhythm and communication system. In some partnerships the
specialist may continue to follow the steps in the three parts of the Parent
Involvement Method fairly explicitly. In other partnerships the parent needs
only a brief introduction to the intent of the activity and to objectives for
the child and for themselves and they have an intuitive grasp of how to proceed. Some parents find it helpful to see and discuss the Parent Involvement
Method Observation Form (Figure 6) as part of the explanation of how they
will be involved in habilitation activities with their child. Other parents
assume an intense involvement in the process and, while they may be interested in seeing the process formalized on paper, do not need it used as an
assist to get them engaged in activities with their child.

The success of the Parent Involvement Method, like any other technique
used at IHR, is dependent on the quality of the parent-specialist relationship. Where trust and openness exist, this method of including parents will
feel natural and relaxed. When the process feels awkward and stressful,
when attempts to get the parent engaged in the activity meet with resistance
or outright refusal, the specialist needs to attend to the feelings behind the
parent's behavior. "I'm concerned about you, Anna. You're not jumping
into these activities like you usually do. What's on your mind?" Or to a new
parent who seems to pull back when asked to play a role in the activity,
"Tim, you seem reluctant to get involved here. Is this feeling awkward for
you?" or "What can we do that would make it easier for you to join in?"

When there is a hitch in the flow of a habilitation session, there is usually
a feeling state associated with it. Sometimes it is the specialist whose feelings
are impeding her performance. Sharing those feelings is one way to
establish an environment of openness. In the course of habilitation,
specialists ask parents to give them a lot of information about themselves
and their family. It is only fair that when specialists are experiencing strong
feelings that affect their work, they share those with the parent. "I'm not as
energetic as I might be," Julia confided to Anna. "My three-year-old has
the flu and I was up with her almost all night. You know how that feels, Anna. I remember when Donny had that serious cold last fall how tired you

got.'' or ''I can't be here on Thursday, Anna. I learned last night that my favorite aunt died and I'm going to her funeral. I'm feeling real sad about it. I will miss her a lot.''

Whether it is a physiological state, emotional response, or just a bad day, we behave differently on different days. Sharing parts of our experiences with our habilitation partners opens up the lines of communication tremendously. The specialist, of course, should also be aware that the habilitation session is not an occasion to unburden herself of personal problems. The focus of the session remains on the family.

POTENTIAL OBSTACLES TO PARENTAL LEARNING

In Chapter 8, the feelings many parents experience in reaction to the crisis of the diagnosis of their baby's hearing loss are discussed. Difficulties the parents may experience as a learner are described relative to each of the five steps in the process of reacting to crisis. In addition to the difficulties experienced as a result of these feelings, parents may experience a number of other feelings that may block their ability to learn during the course of habilitation. Five of these feelings are discussed below.

AMBIVALENT FEELINGS ABOUT THE SPECIALIST

One feeling that specialists may fail to consider is a parent's feeling of dislike, discomfort, or lack of respect for the specialist. None of us learns well from people we dislike or from people whose abilities we do not respect. When a parent is not learning, not cooperating, not following through on assignments, it is important for the specialist to discuss the parent's behaviors with the parent, if possible. If the specialist does not know how to approach the parent, he or she may be able to get some ideas by discussing the situation with a co-worker or supervisor. One approach that can be helpful is the technique of gentle confrontation. Without conveying irritation or anger, the specialist can describe to the parent a specific instance of the parent's behavior and ask how he or she might be contributing to the situation.

Julia had become aware that one of the parents with whom she works, Alice, seemed very detached and made very little eye contact with her as Julia greeted her and talked to her during sessions. Julia noticed that Alice was considerably more animated when she talked with other staff members and parents she encountered at the agency. Julia felt it was important to determine if she was doing something that was causing Alice's discomfort. She thought carefully about how she could bring up the subject with Alice.

At the next home visit, Julia ignored the butterflies in her stomach, took a deep breath, and dove in. "Alice, when you come to IHR you talk with the other parents and staff with so much enthusiasm! I don't see that same spirit as we are working together. I am concerned that I am doing something that causes you to feel uncomfortable. If so, I'd sure want to change that. Tell me about what happens for you when we get together."

Some parents will be able to talk about what is not feeling comfortable to them and discuss changes the specialist might make that would feel better. Some parents may not be able to identify the feelings they have. Other parents may feel too threatened to say what is on their minds. Even when parents cannot describe their feelings, their awareness of the specialist's concern may make them feel better or may make discussion of their feelings possible at a later time.

MEMORIES OF FAILURE IN SCHOOL

Another obstacle to a parent's ability to learn may be the parent's memories of failure as a student during school years. Now, all of a sudden, the parent is placed in the position of being a student again. Parents with anxiety about performance or achievement will find the habilitation setting very threatening if they perceive it as an environment in which they may fail to measure up. Parents who dislike the student role may display that aversion in one of several ways. Some parents are accustomed to being the "expert" at home or at work. Much of their self-esteem is based on feelings of competence. At the beginning of the habilitation process, these parents may fear that their lack of expertise in deafness brands them as being incompetent in general. Since displaying competence is extremely important to these parents (just as it is to specialists!), having to respond to questions to which they do not know the answer (e.g., "What do you remember about Lisa's audiogram?") or practicing new skills (e.g., putting the hearing aid on their child) in front of another adult may feel very threatening.

The specialist may see the parent's discomfort expressed as a brusque, "Is this really necessary?" attitude or as anger when the parent feels put on the spot. These parents need a great deal of reassurance that the specialist can recognize their general level of competence and that she does not have expectations that the parent will know everything about deafness at the outset. The specialist can address the issue, sharing a little of her own competence-related fears.

> "I'm taking a computer class in the evenings. I feel so stupid when I can't remember how to get that darned machine to work. I am sure the instructor thinks I'm a real dud. Being a student again is hard for me. How is it feeling to you, George?"

On the other end of the spectrum is the parent whose self-image includes very few feelings of competence. These parents may fear that they will not be able to do anything right. They may feel certain that the specialist is going to discover very soon how inadequate they are. Quiet and meek appearance and self-effacing remarks may give the specialist notice that she is working with someone whose confidence needs a lot of bolstering. These parents need constant reminders of how well they are doing. "Mary, you always arrive right on time for your sessions. That is a wonderful trait!" or "You have done an excellent job of keeping track of Leo's hearing aid use this week. I wish all parents were this thorough!" Parents need to know that specialists are there to support and nurture them, not to find fault and put them down!

BIASES ABOUT HANDICAPPED PEOPLE

Some parents have strong feelings that come out of biases about handicapped people or from cultural beliefs related to handicapping conditions. Feelings such as fear, distaste, pity, or revulsion for handicapped people as a group or the belief that one is being punished for wrong doing by having been "given" a handicapped child, will affect the parent's ability to relate to their child in a loving, relaxed way. The strain placed on the parent-child interaction by these negative feelings will have an impact on both the infant's and parents' ability to learn. Parents who are experiencing negative feelings about their child because of his handicap need to talk and to be heard. Parents may feel embarrassed about having "bad" feelings about their child; they may feel that their child's handicap is a visible sign of their inadequacy as a parent. These parents need assurance that the handicap is not a reflection on them, and that the handicap is not bigger than the child who has it.

Helping parents discover the ways in which their hearing-impaired child is lovable, cute, and fun and that other people see these qualities in him is essential: "Ron, that kid of yours cracks me up. He has a great sense of humor. Did you see what he did with that ball?" or "Wanda, everytime Jenny comes in the door, holds out her arms, and smiles at me, my heart melts. That girl is irresistible!" It means a lot to parents to hear that specialists, and other people, like their child.

VALUES AND PRIORITIES

Another potential obstacle to learning may be the parent's values or priorities. Some parents may have priorities or values that are not compatible with achievement of the goals set for parents — or infants — by the habilitation agency. Life circumstances may make it impossible for parents to give their hearing-impaired infant the time and attention specialists feel the infant needs in order to learn communication skills. Some parents find it necessary to apply all their energies to providing food and shelter for their family and cannot cope with the requirements of a habilitation program for their hearing-impaired infant. Single parents who must work full-time to support themselves and their children may feel intense conflict about their ability to meet their handicapped child's needs. Specialists must take care not to add a further burden of guilt to these parents' already heavy responsibilities. However, specialists should not make assumptions that these parents "can't possibly do this so I won't tell them about it." All parents need all the information available about their options for their child so that they can make decisions that feel right to them. IHR specialists are continually amazed at the lengths to which parents will go in order to meet their child's needs.

Some parents' values may differ from those inherent in the goals that the agency has established for parents. If parents do not value communication, do not see education as important, or do not value promotion of their child's feelings of self-esteem and competency, they are likely to choose to behave in ways that promote their own values rather than those reflected in the goals of the agency. When working with families whose goals are different, specialists need to accommodate and support those goals unless they are in direct conflict with the purposes of the agency. It does happen that when a specialist acquiesces to the family's goals at the beginning of habilitation, she has the opportunity to open up the lines of communication. Once a trust relationship is established, parents can better hear the rationale behind the agency's goals. Parents are known to change their minds, especially when they find that the specialist is willing to attend to their family's concerns and needs and does not attempt to force changes on them.

CULTURAL TRADITION

In some cultural groups, observing and monitoring the developmental landmarks of infants and young children is not practiced. The specialist's attempts to interpret to the parents results of developmental assessments she has administered to the child and her attempts to encourage parents to acquire behaviors which will help their child "acquire language skills like those of his hearing peers" will not be understood by the parents. In some cultural groups, the view of one's body, traditional medical practices, and the attitude toward child growth and development differ from Western views. It is important that the specialist attempts to understand these differences and develops a high degree of cultural sensitivity in order to approach a common ground with families. Specialists may need to do some research in the library or talk to staff in social service agencies which work with families from other cultures in order to better understand why a family is reacting to the habilitation process as they do.

Potential obstacles to parental learning can often be resolved when the specialist is tuned into the parents' words and actions. It may be difficult to talk about parental behaviors that signal a conflict in values, goals, or ideas. Ignoring these behaviors, however, almost certainly guarantees that the parent-specialist partnership will fail to reach the level of mutual trust critical to its effectiveness in working toward common goals.

CHAPTER 11

HELPING PARENTS LEARN TO PROMOTE THEIR CHILD'S SELF-ESTEEM

Elements that Contribute to Self-Esteem

The Potential Effects of Hearing Loss on the Child's Self-Esteem

Suggestions for Promoting the Child's Acquisition of Positive Self-Esteem

A theme around which most of the chapters in this book cluster is relationships. The previous chapter and those in Part III dealt with the relationship between the parents and the parent-infant specialist. Almost all of the remaining chapters focus on the relationship between the parents and their child who has impaired hearing and, in some cases, other disabilities as well. Chapters 12-26 focus on information and skills related to a number of aspects of this parent-child relationship, among them play and daily activities, observing child behaviors, modifying child behaviors, and teaching children to listen and communicate.

All of the chapters in this book are directed toward a common goal, that of minimizing the effects that hearing loss has on the child's ability to learn about his world. Sometimes we tend to get caught up in the importance of teaching the child individual skills and forget to see the overall picture: that what we really want is to assure that the hearing-impaired child has a chance at having a good life. We would posit that if the hearing-impaired child has acquired the best possible language and speech skills and feels lousy about himself, we have failed in our goal. "Having a good life" is an individual perception that starts with good feelings about ourselves. Our feelings about ourselves evolve from the time of our birth as a result of our interactions with the significant others in our early lives. The result is our self-image, our perception of ourselves which is made up of our feelings about our worth, lovability, and competence.

ELEMENTS THAT CONTRIBUTE TO SELF-ESTEEM

One of the four IHR goals for the parents with whom we work is that parents interact with their hearing-impaired child in ways that promote the development of the child's feelings of self-esteem and competency. Lewis and Harlan (1980) talk about the "emotional well-being" of children, a condition that is strongly related to happiness, love, and trust. These investigators are convinced that "those children who are fortunate enough in early life to have secured the feelings of well-being and happiness are the ones who will progress most rapidly and ultimately with the greatest success in life in general" (p. 24). Self-confidence and self-respect are two other elements that contribute to a child's sense of self-esteem (Frank, 1985).

Underlying all of the individual components that influence a child's sense of self-esteem is his ability to control his environment. Happiness, the sense of well-being, love, trust, self-confidence, and self-respect are all based on being able to convey what your needs are and to get those needs met. The child whose cries are answered with food, dry diapers, or attention begins to gain a sense of control that leads to his feeling good. A baby whose parents respond to his needs acquires a sense of trust that people care about him enough to meet his needs.

As the child grows, his knowledge of the world expands to include the objects he encounters and acts on and the events that involve him. Early in life the child's actions with people and objects begin to resemble the activities that we call play. As the child explores objects he not only learns about their uses, but he incorporates them into imagined uses of his own. Through his manipulation and action on objects and his interactions with people he continues to expand his notion of his control over his environment. As the child plays, he demonstrates to himself his mastery of his environment, and his resultant feelings of pleasure increase his self-confidence and self-respect.

Within the first two years of life the normally hearing child acquires another skill, the understanding and use of language, that also adds to his feelings of well-being and control. People can now tell the child about events in his life; they can use words to label feelings he is experiencing. The child can himself use symbols to express his needs, ideas, and feelings. His sense of competence increases as he can now control his environment with words as well as with his hands.

The child gains information about his competence and control in the world from his own actions and from the effects of his communications with others. He also gains very critical information that contributes to his self-esteem from the significant people in his life. Parents who regard the child as capable, resourceful, and lovable convey this to the child in their actions and their words. Likewise, parents who view their child as always needing help and supervision, as likely to do the wrong thing, and as an annoyance, convey this information to the child.

Babies adopt their parents' attitudes about themselves because they do not have the experience and judgement to determine that their parents may be wrong. If mother thinks I'm helpless or not able to make decisions for myself or not lovable, she must be right. If mother thinks I'm smart or reliable or able to do things for myself she must be right.

Parents are very powerful; what they convey to the young child about "how he is" is likely to be even more potent than what the child experiences in manipulating and interacting with his environment. The toddler wants to try putting his socks on. Mother says, "You can't do that — let me do it." This toddler gets an entirely different picture of his abilities than does the toddler who hears mother say, "You can do it! You got your toe in. Good job!"

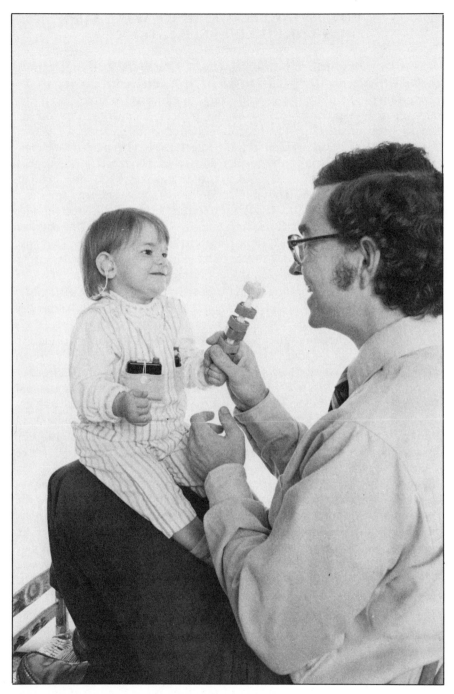

When parents convey to their child, "I like you just the way you are," the child learns to feel good about herself.

THE POTENTIAL EFFECTS OF HEARING LOSS
ON THE CHILD'S SELF-ESTEEM

The child with impaired hearing may have a more difficult time gaining positive self-esteem. Loeb and Sarigiani (1986) conducted a study of 250 hearing-impaired children, ages 8-15 years, in mainstream educational programs. The investigators looked at the impact of hearing loss on the children's self-perception. The hearing-impaired children surveyed viewed themselves as not being popular with their peers, as having a hard time making friends, and as being infrequently chosen as playmates. "Being with friends" was rarely mentioned among those things they liked most. The investigators postulate that "communication deficits pave the way for social isolation and this consequent isolation fosters shyness, often creating a vicious cycle for the child" (Loeb and Sarigiani, 1986, p. 96). The children in this study appeared to lack confidence in their own abilities. They also perceived themselves as being a source of trouble within their families, as being unimportant, and as bringing disappointment to family members.

Three major factors resulting from the hearing loss may create difficulties for the child as he formulates his self-image. The first is the child's inability to hear the positive verbal "strokes" that the majority of parents give their infants. Normally hearing infants get all kinds of good-feeling information from the warmth and tenderness conveyed to them by their parents through words and tone of voice. Hearing-impaired babies miss this input. Secondly, when the hearing loss prevents the child from learning to understand and use language, he may fail to acquire the sense of control that comes with using symbolic language to make sense of and manipulate the environment. In addition, the preschooler who cannot understand and participate in family conversations is likely to feel that he is not important enough to be included.

Finally, when parents learn that their child has a disability, the feelings that result from this diagnosis may impair their ability to give the child the nurturing and support he needs to feel good about himself. Most parents love their children very much. They feel this love as a warm glow of pride, tenderness, and wonder at this small being they have produced. Parents of children with hearing loss also experience this love. Mixed with it, however, may be feelings of guilt, anger, denial, sadness, and inability to cope. The young child senses all of these feelings coming from his parents and sometimes the mixed messages he gets are confusing and upsetting. Why does Mommy look at me so sadly? Why is Daddy mad when we leave the audiologist's office? Long before they have words for feelings, young children read their parents' moods from the way they are held, handled, and looked at. If the baby or toddler experiences a great deal of the parents' ambivalence, he begins to interpret this information as a reflection of his value and worth. Feelings such as "I'm not good enough" or "I'm not lovable" are incorporated into the child's self-identity and can lead to inadequate self-esteem.

Parents who do not acquire realistic and accurate information about how their child's hearing loss will affect his ability to achieve may not be able to formulate realistic goals and expectations for the child. Parental goals that are too high or too low have an adverse affect on the child's ability to form an accurate perception of his competence.

SUGGESTIONS FOR PROMOTING THE CHILD'S ACQUISITION OF POSITIVE SELF-ESTEEM

Since parental attitudes and feelings have such a profound impact on the child's perceptions of his own worth and competence, it is critical that parents are able to interact with the child in ways that tell him he is a valuable, lovable, and capable individual. Parents who are filled with unresolved feelings about hearing loss are not able to extend to their child true acceptance of who he is, to genuinely convey to the child, "You are wonderful just the way you are." Parents have expressed to IHR specialists that while they would choose, if they could, for their child not to have a hearing loss, they also accept that the hearing loss is present and that their child, hearing loss and all, is totally acceptable to them. If the child's hearing loss is not okay with parents at any level of acceptance, the child learns that *he* is not okay.

The parent-infant specialist can help parents deal with their feelings so that they are able to look at their child and see that he is filled with unique potential and that he is lovable just as he is. When they extend these feelings to the child through their words and actions, the child can, in turn, incorporate this positive information into his perception of his value as a person.

A natural extension of the parents' attitude of, "I like you the way you are," is an acknowledgment that the child has impaired hearing. One important way in which parents can help their child to feel good about himself is to provide experiences for the child in which he can meet and choose to get to know other hearing-impaired children and adults. Parents who do not allow their child to know or associate with other children with hearing loss may be conveying to their child that there is something wrong with people who are hearing impaired. A young hearing-impaired child who never knows any older people with hearing loss may assume either that deaf children become hearing or that they die when they grow up. Providing the hearing-impaired child with opportunities to acquire hearing-impaired friends and role models contributes to the child's acceptance of himself and to his understanding of his future.

Just as hearing-impaired children should have the opportunity to form friendships with other children with hearing loss, they should be supported in their efforts to make contacts and friends in the community at large. Parents may need encouragement to expose their child to the normal day-to-day contacts in the community since they may fear that the child will experience unpleasant reactions from people because of his hearing aids or imperfect speech (McElroy and Bernstein, 1976). In fact, when the child is young it is the parents who experience the unpleasantness of another child who, pointing at the hearing aid asks, "Daddy, what's that little boy got in his ear?", or the grandmother who tells the parents about this wonderful surgery which would "cure" the child's hearing loss, just as it did hers.

Parents who model matter-of-fact, informative responses to expressions of curiosity help the child learn that it is all right to talk about his hearing aids or about his less than intelligible speech. Listening to his parents, he can learn responses which he can later use in answer to the questions of his classmates or of strangers. Hearing-impaired children who participate in neighborhood preschools and schools, Sunday school classes, and summer camps along-side their normally hearing peers and who get assistance in this participation when they need it, are likely to feel comfortable operating in the community at large as they grow.

Frank (1985) has spelled out some excellent guidelines for parents and specialists who want to help the child acquire positive self-esteem. He makes the following suggestions for helping the child acquire self-confidence.

1. Do not regard the child as helpless. If you treat him as if everything must be done for him, that is the view he will acquire of himself. Let the child know that you have confidence in his abilities.

2. Allow the child to develop autonomy, independence, and self-reliance. Children need opportunities to play alone, to figure things out for themselves, and to satisfy their own needs for care and self-satisfaction. When children are given opportunities to take responsibility for some of their own needs they learn the connection between their own actions and their own happiness. Children whose parents say, "Go ahead — I know you can handle that," learn that their parents have faith in their ability and adequacy.

3. Help the child experience success. Structure the child's environment so that he can accomplish tasks and achieve skills. Reinforce the child's efforts to achieve whether or not he actually accomplishes what he sets out to do.

4. Promote the child's exploration and sense of curiosity. Permitting him to try new things, with supervision, allows him to learn risk-taking behaviors and to experience his own capabilities at the present time.

5. Permit the child with disabilities to experience some frustration. We all need to experience some frustrations and "failures" in order to learn coping behaviors. Depriving children of opportunities to try something and not succeed also deprives them of the chance to develop coping strategies and the essential

knowledge that they are still okay even if they cannot do everything well.

6. Help the child to acquire assertive behaviors along with respect for others. Children with disabilities may attract people with "helpful" tendencies. Children who can politely and kindly assert their need to act for themselves, validate for themselves their own competencies.

Positive self-esteem is a source of power and confidence. When a child feels good about himself, he is willing to try new things knowing that while he might not succeed at everything, the fun and joy in life come from trying. Parents and specialists can build esteem-promoting elements into all their interactions with the child, no matter whether it be a daily routine or a game geared to an habilitation objective. We all want able, competent, confident children. Treating them as if they have those qualities from the outset will assure that they do!

The book, *Self-Esteem: A Family Affair,* (Clarke, 1978) is written for parents who want to learn more about how to promote self-esteem for all family members.

CHAPTER 12

HELPING PARENTS LEARN TO TEACH INFANT OBJECTIVES THROUGH PLAY AND DAILY ACTIVITIES

The Importance of Play

Types of Adult Interventions in Children's Play

- Positive Adult Interventions During Play
- Negative Adult Interventions During Play

A Problem Associated with Teaching through Play

Some Ideas for Playful Interactions with a Baby/Preschooler

THE IMPORTANCE OF PLAY

The use of play and daily home activities as the major teaching milieu is a key component of IHR's work with families. IHR specialists model auditory and language stimulation techniques in a play setting so parents can practice in that setting and transfer the skills to home interactions with their child. Of course specialists know that there are times when little in the home atmosphere can be called "play" for parents with young children. But "playful" routines and short playful interactions can be incorporated into feeding, dressing, bathing, cooking, trips, and other activities. The challenge to the specialist is to become well-acquainted with the family style and routine so that she can suggest activities to parents that are realistic for their unique situation.

Teaching parents about play and its value to the child is part of the IHR curriculum for parents. The parent section "General Information and Skills" in *Parent-Infant Communication* (Infant Hearing Resource, 1985) includes eleven skills and seven information objectives related to play which are used along with the following information to teach parents about play. The sections below outline why play is important for young children, the effect of hearing loss on a child's play, appropriate and inappropriate forms of adult intervention in a child's play, and problems encountered when using play in the habilitation setting.

Play is the primary occupation of young children. It follows, then, that an eminently reasonable goal of adult intervention with a hearing-impaired child is to utilize the child's play activities as the environment in which to stimulate the child's acquisition of communication skills. Play is a process. It has no inherent end or goal. The most critical element of play is that it must be fun. If it isn't fun, it isn't play. Sometimes adults are amazed to see what very young children consider to be fun. We can tell they think something is fun because they will do the same thing over and over. We've all observed a toddler throwing toys out of a playpen or off a high chair tray, putting blocks in a bucket, or stacking blocks and repeating the same activity for an extended period.

A great deal is known about the play of normally hearing children and the purpose that it serves (see Higginbotham and Baker, 1981, for a brief review of some relevent literature). Play provides the young child with a way to explore the world, to find out what works and what does not work, to act out emotions in a safe environment, and to pretend his dreams can come true. When the child plays with other people, play provides a forum in which to build communication and symbolic language skills, and to develop social and emotional behaviors conducive to interaction with others.

The development of the child's play is closely interrelated with all the areas in which he is developing during his first years of life: cognition, language, social skills, perceptual and motor skills, emotional maturity, and self-concept. A deficit in any one of these areas will have an effect on the development of the others. Sisco, Kranz, Lund, and Schwarz (1979) describe these interrelationships:

> "During the early developmental years, play experiences provide opportunities for the integration of language and personality. Language enables the child to invent and utilize the forms and scenarios of social living through the stages of play crucial to personal and social adaptation. Effective use of language facilitates the child's ability to influence his environment in a meaningful, self-rewarding way. Feelings of competence and self-worth are increased when the child successfully manipulates the environment to achieve personal objectives (p. 852)."

Investigators have also studied the play of hearing-impaired children and have noted differences between their play and that of their hearing counterparts. Sisco et al. (1979) follow their description of the interrelationship between play, language, personality, and self-concept with their observation that, "The linguistic handicap of deafness disrupts the normal process of language acquisition and, consequently, the early developmental play experiences through which language and personality become integrated" (p. 852). Singer and Lenahan (1976) found that the play, fantasy material, and day and night dream content of the deaf adolescents they studied showed a greater concreteness and lack of originality when compared with their hearing peers. These investigators noted that the responses given by the deaf children were similar to those given by hearing children three to five years younger, an observation shared by Sisco et al. (1979).

Darbyshire (1977) found that games involving rules were difficult for hearing-impaired children. Higginbotham and Baker (1981) concur that the communication handicaps of hearing-impaired children interfere with the development of both cognitive and social play skills. Because the hearing-impaired children they studied preferred solitary play to cooperative play, the investigators also noted that the children did not engage in the social interactions critical to communication development. Since even early in the second year of life, other-directed play is associated with higher levels of concurrent and later language usage in hearing toddlers (Ungerer and Sigman, 1984), the preference of some hearing-impaired children for solitary play is a disadvantage to them.

These research findings suggest that the language deficit experienced by many children with hearing loss hinders their gaining the cognitive and social skills from their play at the same rate as do their hearing peers. At the same time, because they shy away from social play interactions, hearing-impaired children miss opportunities for language acquisition. Parents and specialists can break into this cycle of delayed skill development by promoting the child's acquisition of both communication and social skills in their interactions with the young hearing-impaired toddler. Enhancing play opportunities and using play as a learning milieu is a logical and essential goal in our early intervention procedures with hearing-impaired infants and young children.

FUNCTIONS OF PLAY

Play is important to a child's development because of the number of functions it serves:

1. Play fosters creativity, fine and gross motor development, social interaction skills, and problem-solving strategies.
2. The child uses play to express emotions, fulfill wishful thinking, and express aggression safely.
3. Play allows the child to learn many skills in a setting free of fear and consequences. Since play is fun, the child stays with it for a long time, giving him the opportunity to master the skills for which he is developmentally ready.
4. Through play the child develops feelings of competency by learning that he has an impact on and control over his environment.

TYPES OF ADULT INTERVENTIONS IN CHILDREN'S PLAY

One focus of habilitation at IHR is helping parents learn to use adult-child play as one type of interaction through which they can help their child acquire listening, language, and cognitive skills. Specialists begin by telling parents what play is and why it is important to children. For many parents the concept of teaching through play lends a pleasing tone to what at first seems like an insurmountable task. We have found it useful to show videotapes illustrating various helpful ways in which adults can interact with children during play and some ways that are not so helpful. The positive and negative types of adult interventions depicted on videotape are described below.

POSITIVE ADULT INTERVENTIONS DURING PLAY

Adults can join the child in his play with positive results when the adult selects one of more of the following types of interventions.

1. Adult provides support for the child's activities. The adult fills the role of enabler, providing the environment and materials necessary to the child's play.
2. Adult provides positive feedback about the child's play, including reinforcement of self-initiated activity: "You sure know how to build with those blocks!"
3. Adult responds to child's requests and directions and plays the child's game. In this type of game the child learns that he, too, can have some control over what happens in his environment, thus promoting self-confidence and positive self-esteem.
4. Adult talks about what child is interested in or doing: "You see the fish swimming. Those fish are so pretty!"
5. Adult uses orienting comments that assist child in his problem solving: "Think about what you might do next"; or "Do you want to make the front or the back first?"
6. Adult recognizes there are times not to intervene, even by talking. At these times intervention constitutes an interruption of the child's ongoing train of thought and private play.

Before joining in a child's play, it is important that the adult observe the child and determine where his interests lie. The adult can then intervene in ways that promote that interest.

NEGATIVE ADULT INTERVENTIONS DURING PLAY

It is unfortunate that in too many instances in which an adult joins a child in his play, the activity which follows is, in fact, no longer play. We have probably all had the experience of sitting down to "play" with a child only to have the child get up and wander away a few minutes later or to have a peaceful, pleasant play activity turn into a noisy and frustrating battleground. What are we doing wrong when all we want to do is play, and the results are disastrous? Maybe one of the following things!

TYPES OF NEGATIVE ADULT INTERVENTIONS

1. **I have a better idea!** The adult joins the child and tries to change or add on to the child's activity. "Look, Pete, we can take this block from here and this one from here and make a tunnel over the road."

2. **If it's worth doing at all, it's worth doing right.** "Here, fix this, Pete, so the end of that block matches the end of this block exactly right." Adults bring our adult values and skills to the activity, forgetting that we have 20 to 30 years more practice at mastering the art of block play.

3. **Why don't you ever make anything new!** "Pete, you made a road yesterday. Let's make a house today." We ignore the child's need to practice the skills involved in block building at a basic level before he is ready to move to more complex activities. We also fail to see the small differences between yesterday's play and today's play that indicate some new concept has been learned or that some new combination of blocks is being utilized in a creative way.

4. **Finish what you start.** Adults have learned to value a finished product. We have forgotten that play is a *process* and that the learning that takes place is a result of experimentation with different ways of doing things. True play rarely produces a product.

5. **Look, let me show you how to do it.** In this combination of all of the above interventions, the adult ends up controlling all of the materials and relegates the child to the role of passive observer who can learn how it should be done if only he would sit and watch.

CONSEQUENCES OF NEGATIVE INTERVENTIONS IN A CHILD'S PLAY

1. The child may learn that playing with Mom or Dad or the specialist is just no fun. When the child leaves a play environment, the adults' language-building opportunity is lost.

2. The child may avoid the anticipated correction or criticism by refusing to make eye contact or to attend to the adult's communication.

3. The child does not get to tackle problems, thus missing the opportunity to experience failure and success and the learning that takes place through trial and error.

4. The child misses the opportunity to experiment with materials and objects, to discover his effect on them and how they relate to each other.

5. The child misses important opportunities to make something new and to feel the pride of creation.

A PROBLEM ASSOCIATED WITH TEACHING THROUGH PLAY

The specialist or parent who is convinced of the value of play to the child's learning is sometimes faced with a dilemma when learning objectives for the child seem to conflict with the rules of play. "How do I teach the selected language objective when the child is not interested in the materials I present and prefers to play with the drum? Do I follow his interest and scratch the language activity?" There are no clearcut answers to these questions. The creative specialist must make many split-second decisions about which route to take, carefully considering her overall goals and answering the following questions:

- Is the child actually exercising excessive control over the adults? If so, the specialist may want to examine the child's need to control.
- Has the child lost interest in the activity because it's not fun, too easy or too hard, too long?
- Are there materials within the child's visual field that are more interesting than the materials presented by the specialist? Can these materials be used to the same end?

It is a judgement decision whether to try to spark the child's interest in the materials you have presented so that you can work on the objective, whether to switch materials, whether to "manage" the behavior, or whether to forget the selected objective and work on other objectives related to the materials the child has selected to play with. A specialist who knows the child well and has overall teaching goals and behavior management principles well in mind will make the right decisions!

One solution to the proposed dilemma is to keep the materials and input interesting and motivating so that the child's interest is likely to focus on them. Then it's easy to follow his interest; it fits your plan. The following guidelines can be helpful:

1. When the child loses interest in the materials and selects something else, creative specialists and parents can devise ingenious ways to entice, motivate, and interest the child in a specific use of the new materials which allows them to meet their communication objectives.
2. Watch what use the child makes of the materials presented. The specialist or parent may present an activity which is rich with language-learning possibilities only to see the child do something unexpected with the materials. The adults can then fit their communication stimulation to the use the child makes of the materials, perhaps still meeting the stated language objective.
3. Be flexible, changing the activity or objective if necessary to coincide with the child's interest.

In summary, when faced with the dilemma of "play" vs. "objectives," the specialist and parent can change stated objectives in order to adhere to the rules of play, can modify the activity to re-capture the child's interest, can use the new toy/activity selected by the child for working on the original objective, or, if necessary, can attend to modifying an unaccepted behavior that the child is exhibiting.

An important caution is to avoid coercion, directiveness, excessive control, and falling into a "battle of wills" (particularly with two-year-olds). Teachers know that they can mold very young children's behaviors so that they will sit for long periods, follow the teacher's interest, and respond to constant directives. However, not only is it a mistake for specialists to do this, it is a mistake to model this type of interaction for parents. This type of coercive teaching approach is incompatible with a positive parent-child relationship as well as with a positive specialist-child relationship. Teaching through play, attending to the child's interests, managing disruptive behaviors, and still making progress may seem more difficult, but the ultimate pay-off in the quality of the parent-child relationship and in the child's positive self-esteem is well worth the effort.

TIMES NOT TO FOLLOW THE CHILD'S INTEREST

There are a few situations that occur in habilitation sessions during which it is not appropriate to follow the child's interests. Examples of these situations are:

1. During activities when it is important that the child finish a task (e.g., learning to give a conditioned response to sound, during a formal testing procedure, helping the toddler learn to put away toys he has finished playing with).
2. When the child engages in an inappropriate behavior (e.g., throwing toys, emptying Mom's purse).
3. When the child engages in something that is harmful to himself or others (e.g., hitting, damaging toys, banging toy on a window).
4. When the adult anticipates conflict if the child is not distracted from his intent (e.g., child wanting to leave the room when that is not possible).

This chapter concludes with a list of suggestions for adults who want guidelines for defining "play" and for translating the concept of play into behaviors that are comfortable for them.

SOME IDEAS FOR PLAYFUL INTERACTIONS
WITH A BABY/PRESCHOOLER

1. Use a natural tone of voice and colloquial language.
2. Get down on the floor to play with the child.
3. Forget about "teaching" and enjoy the child.
   a. Tune in to the child: watch his facial expression and movement — respond; imagine what he is thinking — respond.
   b. If using both signed and spoken language, you may want to drop your signing or speech occasionally.
   c. Be silly.
   d. Do things that make the child laugh — laugh and smile yourself frequently.
   e. "Talk" to the child with your eyes.
   f. Respond on a non-verbal level to the child's non-verbal behaviors.
   g. Engage in reciprocal play: imitate the child, then expand on the behavior by adding something or altering the movement.
   h. Play "chase" or "peek-a-boo;" "rough house" a little.
4. Use appropriate "teasing." Use suspense and surprise to maintain child's interest.
5. Observe other adults in play. Try behaviors that seem to work for them. Observe the child to get an idea of what he enjoys.
6. Once you feel comfortable with play, add more language to the interaction and begin to think about any teaching goals you might have for the child.
7. Use descriptive language.
8. Let the child explore.
9. Be loving and affectionate toward the child.

CHAPTER 13

HELPING PARENTS BECOME ACCURATE OBSERVERS AND REPORTERS OF THEIR CHILD'S BEHAVIORS

Learning to Describe Child Behaviors
Learning to Report Child Behaviors

The Parent section "General Information and Skills" in *Parent-Infant Communication* (Infant Hearing Resource, 1985) contains a set of objectives designed to help parents become accurate observers and reporters of their child's behaviors. Prerequisite to the process of selecting auditory and language objectives for the infant is determining the infant's current level of function. Because the IHR specialist sees the child only 2-3 hours a week, she relies heavily on the parents to describe the child's listening and communication behaviors as they occur at home.

Some parents have no difficulty with the role of reporter. They are aware of almost everything their infant does and delight in describing his new "tricks." Some parents, however, do not attend to their infant's behaviors except to his gross signals such as crying or smiling or fussing. Other parents tend to attribute to their infant skills and abilities that are well beyond the capacity of an infant of his age. When the specialist is working with parents who are already good observers and reporters, all she must do is ask for specific information such as, "Does Johnny look for you when you start talking to him before he can see you?" These parents will generally reply with very specific information: "Yes, he does if I am within 4-5 feet of his crib, but not if I am at the doorway" or else they will respond with, "I don't remember seeing him do that. I'll check it out before I see you again."

Some parents need specific help in becoming accurate observers and reporters of their child's behaviors; *they need to learn to look at their child to see what he is actually doing.* These parents can tell you when they think their baby is behaving "good" or "bad," but not what the behavior is. They need practice in looking at and describing their child's behaviors.

LEARNING TO DESCRIBE CHILD BEHAVIORS

Specialists can use a three-step sequence to help parents learn to look at and describe their child's behaviors.

1. The specialist and parent observe the child at play and the specialist models what she means when she says, "Describe the child's behaviors."

2a. The parent watches a videotaped segment of a child other than
his/her own at play and describes what that child is doing.

and/or

b. The parent watches a videotaped segment of his/her own child
at play and describes what the child is doing on the tape.

3. The parent sits back while his/her child is playing and describes
what the child is doing at that moment.

The first step is carried out by providing the child with an age- and
interest-appropriate toy with which he can play independently. The parent
(working with one parent at a time usually works best for this activity) and
specialist agree to sit near the child and observe him but not interact with
him. As the child plays, the specialist models for the parent what she means
by describing the child's behavior:

"He's reaching for the rattle. He can't get it. He's fussing.
Now he's rolling over. He touched the rattle — oh, he's
holding it now and he's putting it in his mouth. Now, he's kicking his legs. He let go of the rattle and now he's looking for it."

After she has finished describing the infant's behaviors during a short
period of play, the specialist can ask if the parent has any questions.
Following any discussion to clarify the activity for the parent, the specialist
can move to step 2a. or 2b., depending on the parent's need.

Step 2a — having the parent observe a videotaped segment of a child
other than his/her own — is used when the parent has a strong tendency to
report value judgments about his/her child's behaviors rather than to
describe the behavior itself. An example of this kind of reporting would be
the parent, who, while watching his/her child stack blocks, says, "He's
never been able to stack more than two. I think he's much clumsier than his
sister. Hey — keep that block away from your mouth! He puts everything in
his mouth and I think he's too old for that." As a listener, you have little
idea of what the child is actually doing with the blocks at the moment. This
parent has an equally hard time reporting his child's specific auditory and
language behaviors that occur at home. In response to the question, "What
sounds did you observe Johnny responding to at home?", the parent may
say, "He's getting stubborn; he ignores everything. When I call his name he
runs the other way."

While it is true that the parent may need help in understanding what you
mean by "responding to sound" — a skill we will discuss later — the parent
also needs to learn to look for and describe behaviors rather than interpret
or make value judgments about the behaviors. Watching a videotape of a
child with whom he has no relationship, as specified in step 2a, may free the
parent of the need to evaluate so that he can observe what the child is actually doing.

Step 2b — having the parent watch a videotape of his/her own child playing — can be used with parents who are not necessarily judgmental, but

who may find it difficult to be in the same room with their child and not interact or intervene in the child's activities, or with parents who may just need practice describing their child's behaviors.

The third step, observing the child and describing his actions live, can be done either through a one-way mirror, or with the specialist and parent both in the room. As the child plays with a toy the specialist can introduce the observation period by suggesting that both parent and specialist sit and watch the child for a minute. The specialist may volunteer to describe the child's behavior first.

After she has described the child's behavior for a minute, it is the parent's turn. Parents who have a hard time describing what the child is doing sometimes increase the number of descriptive statements they make if the specialist turns her back so that she cannot see the child. The specialist then asks the parent to tell her what the child is doing. If there is a period of silence the specialist can prompt the parent by asking, "What's Johnny doing now?" The specialist should remember to reinforce the parent for the descriptions they give.

LEARNING TO REPORT CHILD BEHAVIORS

Once the specialist has determined that parents are able to describe their child's behaviors accurately, she can ask the parent to report the child's behaviors specific to the acquisition of listening and communication skills. It is the specialist's responsibility to make certain that parents know exactly what behaviors they are being asked to look for and report. To assure that the specialist and parent are in agreement about what behavior they are looking for in the child, the specialist can use a 4-step process:

1. The specialist defines and demonstrates the child behavior or skill for which the parent will be looking.
2. The specialist defines the criteria for determining that the child has exhibited the behavior or skill.
3. The specialist points out the importance of the behavior by summarizing briefly some of the behaviors that are developmentally prerequisite to the behavior and some of the subsequent behaviors.
4. The specialist sets up a situation in which she and the parent can practice reporting the child's behaviors (either live or on videotape).

Each part of this process will be described below.

STEP 1:   THE SPECIALIST DEFINES AND DEMONSTRATES THE
          BEHAVIOR OR SKILL AND THE ASSOCIATED
          TERMINOLOGY.

Because of the fine lines between some of the stages in the child's
development of listening and language skills, there are many opportunities
for parents to be confused about what the specialist is asking them to look
for. Terminology that is used by professionals in our field is meaningless to
parents of newly identified hearing-impaired infants. Parents cannot
understand what we want them to do when they cannot understand the
vocabulary we use. The specialist must pair unfamiliar or technical words
with terms or behaviors that are familiar to parents so that parents can comply with the specialist's request to report on their child's behaviors.

Parents learn how we use terms such as "awareness" related to listening
only by hearing us use the term over and over as the child demonstrates
awareness of sound, and as we demonstrate our awareness and the parents'
awareness of sound. Written materials are helpful, but specialists cannot
assume that a parent, having read a handout on the developmental stages of
listening, understands what each stage is and how the stages differ. We can
all remember how baffling new vocabulary was to us when we first started
training as teachers. Like us, **parents need to have new vocabulary and concepts demonstrated repeatedly in order to understand what the concepts
mean and what child behaviors to look for.**

STEP 2:   THE SPECIALIST DEFINES THE CRITERIA FOR DETER-
          MINING THAT THE CHILD HAS EXHIBITED THE
          BEHAVIOR OR SKILL.

After defining the child behavior that the parent is to look for, the
specialist needs to tell the parent what the child must do in order to exhibit
the behavior. Criteria will change as the child's developmental level
changes. For example, when first observing and recording the child's oral
communication, the parent may be told to record and reinforce all of the
child's vocalizations. If the child points to a toy and says "uh" the parent
will give the child the toy and record and report the "uh." As the number of
the child's speech utterances increases to include the diphthong [ɔɪ] the
parent may be told to reinforce only the utterance [ɔɪ] when the child asks
for a toy and to record and report the number of times the child uses [ɔɪ]
appropriately. As the child's skill level increases, the criteria for what the
parent reinforces and reports changes.

A common area of confusion for parents is the difference between imitation and spontaneous usage of a spoken or signed word. Initially, parents
will be asked to record and report the child's imitations. As the child begins
to use spoken and signed words spontaneously — that is, without their having been modelled prior to the child's use — parents may be asked to report
spontaneous usage only. This difference may need to be demonstrated and
discussed several times so that parents are clear on what they are looking
for.

STEP 3: THE SPECIALIST SUMMARIZES PREREQUISITE BEHAVIORS AND SUBSEQUENT BEHAVIORS.

It can be helpful to parents who are looking for newly learned behaviors in their child to see these behaviors as part of a sequence. When the specialist spells out for them the developmental steps in learning a skill, the parents frequently gain a better perspective on what behaviors to look for and their importance as an indicator of the child's progress. Specialists are trained to see the small changes in behavior that indicate that the child is making headway toward achievement of a larger, more commonly recognized goal. Parents, who may be unaware of these subskills, may not feel that anything is happening because the child has not yet achieved the end goal.

Parents can easily become discouraged while waiting for the child to utter a first word or use a first sign. But if they are aware of the myriad of subskills that must be acquired before that word/sign comes out, they can work on helping their child achieve these subskills and mark the child's progress toward that goal. Breaking a skill down into a series of subskills is of particular value when the child, for whatever reasons, learns major skills at a very slow rate. Looking for very minimal changes in behavior is an excellent way to help parents focus on the gains their child is making at the present time so that they can feel pride in their child and in their effectiveness in helping their child learn.

STEP 4: THE SPECIALIST AND PARENT PRACTICE REPORTING THE CHILD'S BEHAVIORS.

Practice, the final step in helping parents become good observers and reporters of their child's behavior, is crucial. As the parents and specialist practice these skills, the specialist can ascertain whether she has made the task clear to the parents and whether she and the parents are in agreement about what it is they are looking for. When IHR specialists ask parents to look for behaviors at home we have found it helpful to provide the parents with a sheet (usually created on the spot) with the appropriate columns or spaces in which they can record the data we are asking them to collect (Figure 7). In the first few assignments we specify a short period of time (2-3 days) over which we ask them to observe the child and record a specific behavior. As parents become accustomed to looking for behaviors and become familiar with the terminology that describes the behaviors, many of them will volunteer their observations on a regular basis and will need only a request to look for and report a behavior rather than a formal assignment and record sheet.

The importance of helping parents learn to observe and report their child's behaviors accurately cannot be overemphasized. Having a realistic picture of their child's skills and abilities motivates parents to work on appropriate learning objectives for their child. If parents either overestimate or underestimate the level at which their child is functioning, it will be difficult for the parents and specialist to agree on objectives and goals for the child. Learning to describe rather than judge behaviors and learning the criteria for determining when a behavior is acquired by their child are invaluable skills for parents.

Recording Chuck's Receptive Language

Tally the number of times you say the word and the number of times Chuck responds correctly by looking at, going to get, or pointing to the animal or object.

	DOG		SHOE	
	You say	He responds	You say	He responds
Monday (in session)	///	/	////	/ ?
Tuesday (at home)				
Wed. (at home)				

FIGURE 7. The parent-infant specialist creates forms like this one to send home with a parent so that the parent can record some aspect of the child's behavior.

CHAPTER 14

HELPING PARENTS LEARN TO MODIFY THEIR CHILD'S BEHAVIOR

"The life of a happy home can revolve around a child without spoiling the child — if he knows exactly what he can do and what he cannot do. When he knows that he must be polite, respectful of elders and cheerfully obedient without tantrums, then *he's* happier, and so are his parents. So long as it is a battle to find out how much more he can get away with, a child is actually a miserable little animal. Real authority, with well defined limits, gives him peace of mind and security" (Linkletter, 1978, p. 200).

When hearing-impaired toddlers reach the ages of 15-20 months we often begin to hear increased parental expression of concern about behavior:

"She's doing more hitting than her brother ever did."

"He's into everything and is so stubborn. He pays no attention when I say no!"

"He won't stay in his room at night."

"She throws everything and the more I yell the more she seems to throw."

There is often an accompanying uncertainty about how to manage a hearing-impaired child: "But I can't discipline her like I do the twins. She wouldn't understand and that would break my heart." The task of the specialist is to convey to parents the importance of having behavioral limits and consistent expectations for their child with hearing loss just as they do for their hearing children. Hearing-impaired children can learn to understand and respect appropriate and consistent consequences to their behavior. What follows are guidelines for teaching parents how to extinguish child behaviors they do not accept and to promote child behaviors they want.

FACTORS TO CONSIDER BEFORE INTRODUCING
A BEHAVIOR CHANGE PROGRAM TO PARENTS

THE CHILD

In order to determine the appropriateness or inappropriateness of a child's behavior the specialist must possess a sound knowledge of child development. What are typical activities for children at particular ages? Which behaviors are essential to the child as he tests out theories of how the world works? What is happening to his self-perception and his view of adults around him at his current age?

When contemplating a behavior change program for children it is also essential to consider the child's needs for love, attention, competence, reassurance, a sense of importance, opportunities to explore, and the freedom to fail. Are these needs being met and, if not, what changes can be made in the way adults interact with the child to assure that they will be met? It may be that events in the child's environment are causing him to feel confused, frustrated, misunderstood and, as a result, he is acting in inappropriate ways. Some parent education and a few environmental changes may be all that are needed to extinguish the inappropriate behaviors.

THE PARENT

In addition to characteristics of the child which must be considered prior to implementing a behavior change program, the specialist must also consider parental feelings, values, and beliefs. We have already discussed (Chapters 7-9) the broad range of feelings that parents may experience related to having a handicapped child. It is likely that the child's deafness will add a complicating element to already established discipline practices in the home. Because of the parents' feelings and because verbal messages which had been effective with other children may not work with the deaf child, parents may find that their "usual" discipline practices are inadequate when applied to their child with hearing loss.

Parental values regarding appropriate and inappropriate child behaviors and child behavior management procedures may be in conflict with those held by the specialist. Some families are strongly opposed to formal behavior change programs. They may have a behavior management procedure that they feel works just fine for them. It is important to respect the parents' choice for how they interact with their child at home. If, however, the specialist feels that the behavior management procedures the parents use with the child are damaging to the child's self-esteem or are confusing to the child (e.g., parents who spank a child who hits another child, saying, "You can't hit!"), she can present parents with her point of view. Some parents choose not to change their disciplinary measures and specialists have to accept that fact unless the practice is abusive and should be reported to local authorities.

IHR specialists convey to parents who use their own system of discipline at home that in order to promote learning during sessions we prefer to "manage" the child while we are interacting with him by using consequences to his unacceptable behaviors and rewarding his acceptable behaviors. A major benefit of this approach is that the specialist has an opportunity to model an effective system of behavioral consequences that the parent may not have previously thought useful.

If parents request help in managing their child's unacceptable behaviors we are happy to offer assistance. However, we have learned that there are no gains to be made by applying pressure if the idea of a behavior change program is intolerable to parents. Many families do just fine with their own child-rearing methods. Others are delighted to learn an effective new approach. Some parents never are able to utilize a consistent program of child management. If this is the case and if the specialist has offered assistance in the best way she knows, it is at this point that the specialist must withdraw and let go of any need to "fix" things. We feel it is important, however, to honestly convey to parents our concerns about the long-term effects of the unmanaged behavior on the child's ability to learn, and to express our concerns about behavior management techniques that parents are using (e.g., frequent hitting) that we feel do not produce desirable results in the child. Having acquired this information, parents may choose to use it at a later date.

PROBLEM BEHAVIORS COMMONLY REPORTED
BY PARENTS OF YOUNG HEARING-IMPAIRED CHILDREN

It is not uncommon for parents of hearing-impaired toddlers to report that they are beginning to have difficulty with some of the child's behaviors. Problem behaviors generally fit into three categories: non-compliant behaviors, attention-getting behaviors, and aggressive or destructive behaviors. Each of these is discussed below.

NON-COMPLIANT BEHAVIORS

Young children express non-compliance mainly through refusal to participate in an adult-initiated activity. The goal of non-compliance is control. Small children desire control, probably because they feel overwhelmed by the powerful people around them. The less powerful a child feels, the more things he may try in order to gain control. A child who experiences a lot of frustration during the day because he does not understand what is going on and who has few experiences in which he feels competent is likely to exhibit non-compliant behavior.

Six examples of non-compliant behaviors are:

- Refusal to go to bed and stay in bed.
- Refusal to wear a coat.
- Refusal to stop and wait for an adult before crossing the street.
- Resistance to getting into the bathtub.
- Refusal to wear hearing aids or glasses.
- Refusal to eat at mealtimes.

Having too much autonomy and being in control when it is not age- or ability-appropriate is harmful to children for several reasons. People around the child will resent the child's inappropriate expressions of autonomy or control (e.g., refusal, tantrums) and will become increasingly upset with the child. The child will not understand this negative reaction and will feel rejected. Being allowed to have more control than is age- or ability-appropriate robs the child of the security and important social learning provided by consistent and appropriate behavioral limits established by adults. Limits help the child structure his world and tell him that he is not all-powerful in society. Limits tell him about social reality in which people behave responsibly within a system of rules and expectations.

ATTENTION-GETTING BEHAVIORS

Children may solicit attention out of boredom or because they feel they are important only when they are receiving attention. Some examples of attention-getting behaviors are:

- Whining
- Screaming
- Messing with food
- Grabbing
- Throwing objects
- Loud, high-pitched vocalizations
- Crying
- Tugging and pulling at people

AGGRESSIVE OR DESTRUCTIVE BEHAVIORS

The goal of aggressive or destructive behavior may be an attempt to gain power over adults. It may be the result of frustration or it may be an act of revenge against adults. It may also occur after over-stimulation and when the child is very tired.

Some types of aggressive or destructive behaviors demonstrated by young children are:

- Hitting, kicking, biting people
- Tormenting animals
- Throwing toys, food
- Damaging or breaking objects
- Tearing books or magazines

TWO METHODS OF DEALING WITH PROBLEM BEHAVIORS

Social learning theory says that we *learn* to behave in the way we do through hours of interaction with people and events in our lives. Therefore, by putting thought and care into monitoring children's interactions and environments, we can help children acquire behaviors that are acceptable to us. Learning theory also says that society is based on a reward and punishment contingency system. Work, for example, is rewarded by money. Traffic violations are punished by fines. At Infant Hearing Resource we have found the application of social learning theory to be very useful in helping parents learn techniques of dealing with their children that help youngsters cease using unacceptable behaviors and increase their use of desirable behaviors.

Eliminating problem behaviors is done most effectively through a two-pronged approach: extinguishing the occurrence of undesirable behaviors and increasing the occurrence of desirable behaviors.

EXTINGUISHING THE OCCURRENCE
OF UNDESIRABLE BEHAVIORS

The goal of the parents' behavior is to regain control in situations in which the child is exhibiting problem behaviors and to teach the child acceptable ways of gaining appropriate power and attention. Crary (1979) described several methods for decreasing the occurrence of a child's inappropriate behaviors. Some of these are: ignoring, substitution, natural consequences, logical consequences, and time out.

IGNORING

Ignoring is an excellent technique for use with behaviors which are not dangerous or destructive, but are annoying. Ignoring a behavior can be a very powerful consequence because, by not attending to a behavior, the adult is not reinforcing it. Ignoring is only effective if used *every* time the behavior occurs. So, if the behavior cannot be ignored 100% of the time, even when the child accelerates it in order to gain attention, another consequence must be used. If the behavior cannot be ignored 100% of the time and is attended to occasionally by adults, that intermittent adult attention will actually strengthen the behavior. An example is a parent's decision to ignore whining in an attempt to decrease its occurrence. When the whining child is ignored, he may increase the intensity of his whining until the parent can no longer bear to ignore it. The parent yells, "Stop that whining!" thereby giving the child the attention he desires and increasing the probability that the whining will occur again. The child has learned that if he persists long enough, he does get attention.

Another type of situation in which ignoring does not work to extinguish the behavior occurs when, for example, a child lightly tosses a toy in the air in order to elicit a reaction. The parent decides to ignore this bid for attention. The child accelerates the rate of throwing until it has destructive possibilities. The parent then reacts to protect people or objects and the child has received the desired attention. This attention serves to strengthen the liklihood that the child will use this behavior again to get attention. When parents *are* able to ignore an annoying but harmless behavior the child uses, the child will eventually abandon it as an unsuccessful way of drawing attention to himself. Fair warning: ignoring is more difficult than it seems!

Parents who decide that they will not be able to ignore attention-getting behaviors such as whining and throwing 100% of the time have several options: altering the environment to eliminate situations which provoke or permit the behavior; attending to the child's unmet needs which are inducing the behavior; designing a behavior change program with consequences for the undesireable behavior; and using substitution, a technique that is discussed below.

SUBSTITUTION

In this technique, an inappropriate behavior is replaced with an appropriate behavior. In the example of the child whose accelerated throwing is unacceptable, the parents may want to teach the child that throwing is an outdoor activity which cannot occur in the house. When throwing first occurs, parents may state to the child: "You can throw outside, but not in the house" and then take the child outside to throw. Substitution is useful for the banging on objects that hearing-impaired children especially enjoy. When the child is banging on furniture with his toy drum stick, a drum or a cardboard box can be substituted if the parents can tolerate the sound of banging.

NATURAL CONSEQUENCES

Dreikers (1964) advocates the use of two types of consequences to a child's inappropriate behaviors as a means of decreasing these behaviors. He refers to the two types of consequences as *natural consequences* and *logical consequences*. Natural consequences are those conditions or events that naturally result from the child's behavior. The use of natural consequences is an excellent technique for teaching children responsibility for their own behavior because they experience the effects of what they do. The frustrated child who throws his favorite truck down the stairs is left with a broken truck and does not receive a replacement. The child who drops lunch on the floor for attention receives no more lunch. The beauty of natural consequences is the absence of adult intervention.

LOGICAL CONSEQUENCES

With this technique the adult intervenes, using a consequence that logically relates to the inappropriate behavior. A logical consequence of running into the street is being confined to the house. By ignoring the rule, "stay out of the street," the child has forfeited the privilege of being outside. A logical consequence of not eating dinner is that dessert is not served.

TIME-OUT AND ISOLATION

A very powerful technique for decreasing inappropriate behavior is the use of time-out. Time-out works because the child is removed from a situation which is reinforcing to him. The child forfeits the privilege of enjoying social interaction when he engages in unacceptable behavior. According to Crary (1979), the function of time-out is to interrupt the unacceptable behavior. For young children, time-outs need to be short and may consist of removing the child from the room or of placing him in a chair next to, but not facing, a wall. Once the child is situated, the adult briefly describes what was unacceptable about his behavior, e.g., "No hitting." When parents and specialists first use a time-out procedure with a young hearing-impaired child, the child may not be developmentally ready or may not have the receptive vocabulary to understand a long, detailed explanation of why he must leave the room or sit in a chair. Adults should use pantomine and gesture along with speech and sign to tell the child, "You can't hit."

Taking the child from the room to sit quietly in the empty hall with an adult may be all that is needed to interrupt the behavior and to communicate the rule, "No hitting." When leaving the room is not an option, a time-out chair can be effective. When the child is first placed on a chair and told, "No hitting," he may try to get up after a few seconds since he has no idea of what is going on. Now the adult handling the discipline must show the child what time-out is: "You stay in the chair until I say it is okay to get up." Many children will cooperate with being returned to the time-out chair a couple times. Occasionally, an older preschooler may resist staying in the chair. In these instances, it may be necessary to restrain the child in the chair so that he understands that he is not the one to make the decision as to when time-out is over. Restraining the child in a chair works best when the adult kneels behind the chair and places an arm around and across the child's chest. When this is done, the adult should be very matter-of-fact and take care not to express anger. It is important to remember that this is teaching, not punishment. The arm holding the child should be a restraint, not a punishing, rigid squeeze.

Once the child has remained quiet for 15-20 seconds (this may not occur until after he has protested for a few minutes as the adult holds him in the chair), the adult can release his arm, and, facing the child, tell him, "Okay — you can go play now." It generally requires only one or two trials of being restrained in the chair for children to learn that they are to sit there following interruption of their unacceptable behavior.

As embarrassing as it may be, parents should be prepared to conduct time-out whenever the behavior for which time-out is the consequence occurs. If the child begins screaming for candy in the grocery store or for toys in the variety store, remove him from the cart and take him to the car. The shock value of abandoning the cart in the aisle and of placing the child in his car seat until he calms down is powerful. With the child safely in his car seat, the parent can ignore any protest by remaining outside the car, declining to attend to the child. Driving home immediately is also an effective teaching consequence and one we recommend if the family's schedule can accommodate it. The "price" paid in time spent now will be well worth the many pleasant shopping trips to follow once the child learns appropriate supermarket behaviors.

Once the child has learned what the time-out procedure is and sits quietly during time-out, the length of time he is required to stay in the time-out setting can be as short as one to two minutes. This will be sufficient time to interrupt the unacceptable behavior. A rule of thumb for length of time-out is one minute for each year of the child's age. Three-year-olds can handle three minutes in time-out. Once the time-out period is over the child is permitted to return to his play.

A more potent consequence which should be used with caution and only for very difficult behaviors is isolation. The child can be isolated in a stimulation-free room or corner for two or three minutes as a consequence to highly disruptive behavior. This consequence is sometimes selected for very aggressive, destructive behaviors for which no other solution has been found. In order to be effective, the isolation site must be devoid of any entertainment value. For this reason, sending a two to three-year-old child to his room is usually not effective since he can find toys to play with there.

For the four-year-old, however, who may experience a stronger sense of social isolation when separated from family or friends, having to spend time alone in his room may be an effective consequence to unacceptable behavior.

Parents have sometimes expressed concern that their children would be frightened if confined in a room. With toddlers, an empty play pen can be used so the child can see that he is not being abandoned. A screen door can be used in the isolation room, enabling the child to see that he is not alone in the house. It is important for all individuals to ignore the child during isolation and offer no interaction. Once the isolation period is over the child must not receive continued punishment, reprimands, or reminders of his "misdeed." When isolation is finished, the parent can say to the child, "Okay, time to play again."

Adults may have conflicting feelings about "time-out." They know it is important to interrupt the child's unacceptable behavior yet they may fear the child's reaction, which the parents may project as being one of fear or, worse, one of disliking them. It is important, however, that adults not lavish attention on the child following the time-out as a result of their conflicting feelings. This type of excessive attention could actually reinforce the inappropriate behavior: The child may endure the time-out or isolation period in order to get the attention following it.

Sometimes, parents wonder what people will think when they carry a screaming child from the store or restaurant and put him in the car or when they conduct time-out in a neighbor's or relative's home. However, most people respect parents who will not tolerate children's inappropriate attempts to gain control. When the consequence to unacceptable behaviors is carried out in a matter-of-fact, non-emotional way, it conveys to other people and to the child, "Mommy/Daddy means business!"

Having limits set on his behaviors makes the child more pleasant to be around. People respond positively to children who do not scream, whine, hit, bite, and make constant demands for attention. When people respond favorably to a child, he feels good about himself, and his self-esteem is enhanced. Adults are not doing a child any favors when they let him run the show. He does not have the experience and judgement to make good decisions about all of his actions. Adults who take the time to help define for the child what are acceptable behaviors provide the child with the feeling that he is cared for, secure, and lovable.

INCREASING DESIRABLE BEHAVIORS

The parents' goal in increasing desirable behaviors is to let the child know what he is doing that his parents like. Four techniques parents and specialists can use to increase the occurrence of desirable behaviors in a child are: avoiding problems, positive reinforcement, modeling, and shaping.

AVOIDING PROBLEMS

Adults who know and understand a child can prevent many occurrences of undesirable behavior by altering the child's environment in effective ways, such as alleviating boredom and preparing the child for change (Crary, 1979).

ALLEVIATING BOREDOM

Boredom can be a major cause of inappropriate behavior. Children vary in attention span and in their need for stimulating activities. By knowing the child, his interests, and developmental levels, adults can make available a variety of activities. They can circulate toys, keeping some hidden and bringing them out at intervals to rekindle the child's interest in them, and they can avoid leaving the child for long periods with nothing to interact with. Adults need to strike a balance between ignoring the child's need for appropriate stimulation and providing constant entertainment so that the child never learns to entertain himself. The child who has great difficulty entertaining himself for even short periods presents a different issue. He may need a program to increase his attention span and his ability to play alone for longer periods.

PREPARING THE CHILD FOR CHANGE

A frequently reported example of resistance and resultant tantrums in hearing-impaired children occurs during major activity changes: leaving the house, leaving school, bed time, getting ready for school. Some hearing-impaired toddlers have great difficulty with the unpredictable nature of change, particularly if everyone in the household but them has a clear idea of where they are going and what will happen next. The hearing-impaired child needs to be given language describing the perceived change in family members' behaviors so that he can share in the anticipation of the event or activity. Families have found that a poster with snapshots of frequent destinations, commonly visited relatives, and daily home activities is a great aid in communicating what will be happening. Anticipating events provides rich language opportunities which allow the adult to stretch the child's thinking, his ability to contemplate the abstract, and his understanding of temporal concepts by talking about things not presently in view, or about things that *will happen.*

Another helpful tip is to give the child time to adjust to the change. Begin to prepare him for the termination of his present activity several minutes before he is required to stop. Build anticipation of the next activity giving him sufficient time to adjust to the idea of change. By knowing the times during the day that are difficult for the child and knowing those situations which frustrate him, parents can avoid many problem behaviors by restructuring the environment and how they interact with their child.

POSITIVE REINFORCEMENT

A second technique for increasing or teaching desired behavior is the use of positive reinforcement. **Positive reinforcement is the use of consequences which increase or strengthen a behavior.** These consequences are called *reinforcers*. It is human nature to repeat a behavior that brings us smiles, verbal praise, a pat on the back. Many parents operate on the principle, "If I don't say anything my child will understand that his behavior is acceptable." These parents fail to understand that, to a child, parental silence may mean indifference or failure to notice a positive behavior. **It is as important for parents to positively reinforce their children's desired behaviors as it is for them to select ways to let their child know that some behaviors are not acceptable.** Positive reinforcement is an effective method for teaching new behavior. The reinforcers are usually social or tangible (Figure 8).

Reinforcement is a "When . . . then" occurrence. The parent who says to the child who has behaved well for the first five minutes of the shopping trip, "I sure appreciate your cooperation while we shop. Let's get you a new coloring book while we're here," is reinforcing desirable behavior on the part of the child. The parent who notices the child putting his toys away and says, "Great! I'll put a star on your chart!" is reinforcing the child's desirable behavior.

Effective reinforcement follows several rules:
1. The reinforcer must follow the desired behavior **immediately.**
2. Reinforcement must be used **100% of the time** following occurrence of the desired behavior at the outset of the training.
3. **Pairing tangible and social reinforcements** is effective with young children.
4. **Decreasing the rate of reinforcement** must be done gradually and with a definite plan.
5. **Tangible reinforcers** can be **dropped** after a period of time.
6. Social reinforcement can be utilized at a **decreasing rate,** continuing past the time the tangible reinforcers are dropped.
7. Social reinforcement must be used periodically to **maintain** the behavior.

Positive reinforcement is sometimes thought to be a form of bribery. It is not. When a parent says, "If you put your toys in the box, I'll give you a star," that is a bribe. A bribe is an "If . . . then" proposition. Parents may be tempted to use bribes during the occurrence of an inappropriate behavior in an effort to stop the behavior (Brockway, 1974): "If you stop whining then you can have a candy bar as we leave the store." It is easy to see how the child learns to whine in order to obtain something he wants!

Training in Child Management, A Family Approach (Brockway, 1974) is an excellent source for specialists and parents who want more information about utilizing the concepts described above in their child management programs.

FIGURE 8

Brockway (1974) describes reinforcers as both social and tangible.

Social Reinforcers come in several forms:

Physical Praise	Verbal Praise
pats on the head	"Show me your picture."
hugs	"That tower is so tall!"
clapping	"You run fast."
hand holding	"That's neat."
kisses	"Wow!"
smiles	"You ate all your dinner."
listening to child	"I like the way you are cooperating."
looking at child	
attention	

Tangible Reinforcers can be objects or activities. With young children who may not understand the delay inherent in a reward that comes later, such as participation in a favorite activity, objects may be preferred.

Objects	Activities
toys	going outside
stickers	cooking
prizes	playing a game
pennies	trip to a special place
treats	watching T.V.
	reading a book

MODELING

A third and very effective method of increasing or teaching desired behavior is modeling. Modeling is the one undisputable training technique which parents — and specialists — implement whether or not they are aware of it. Young children learn from watching and will imitate what they see. This most natural learning process can be cultivated in order to reach specific goals. In a modeling situation the child observes another person engage in a behavior that he desires to imitate. The desire to imitate may be motivated by identification with the other, e.g., the child wants to be like Dad or wants Dad's approval so he crosses his arms while watching T.V. like Dad does. Or the child may observe another person get a reward for a behavior so he imitates the behavior in order to receive the same reward, e.g., older sister gets smiles and a hug as she helps unload groceries. The toddler reaches into the grocery bag to get food with the expectation of receiving the same positive attention. Parents can set up modeling situations designed to teach young children desired behaviors. When a desired behavior is matched by the child it should be reinforced.

SHAPING

A fourth technique for teaching desired behavior is a step-by-step process called shaping. This technique can be used to teach the child a new or complex skill. When shaping the child's behavior, the skill is broken down into component skills. The first component is demonstrated, practiced, and reinforced. Components are added one by one until the whole task is learned. An example would be teaching a child to remove and hang up his coat. The parent might shape the child's behavior by helping him acquire the following sequence of skills:

1. Child can remove coat and hand it to parent to hang up.
2. Child can remove coat, push stool over to closet, climb on stool, and hand coat to parent.
3. Child can remove coat, push stool to closet, climb up, and hang coat on hook.
4. Child can remove coat, arrange stool, climb up, hang coat on hook, and replace stool.

Tasks can be shaped over varying lengths of time depending upon the child's age, cognitive abilities, and motor skills.

USING A BEHAVIOR CHANGE PROGRAM

A behavior change program is a formalized approach to modifying a child's behavior. Behavior change programs generally are intended to eliminate a problem behavior and replace it with an acceptable behavior. A behavior change program has specific and sequential steps that guide an adult in knowing when and how to apply the approaches they select for decreasing the occurrence of undesirable behaviors and increasing the occurrence of desired behaviors.

The following "Steps in A Behavior Change Program" and the associated record sheets referred to in these steps can be found in the Parent Handout section of *Parent-Infant Communication* (Infant Hearing Resource, 1985).

STEPS IN A BEHAVIOR CHANGE PROGRAM

WEEK ONE — Establishing Baseline
   1a. Select one of your child's inappropriate behaviors that you want to extinguish.
    b. Select a desired behavior to replace the inappropriate behavior, if applicable.
   2a. Record on Section A of the Behavior Change Record Sheet each incidence of the inappropriate behavior during this one-week period. Record what happened before and after each incidence of the behavior.
    b. Record on Section B of the Behavior Change Record Sheet each incidence of the desired behavior (there may be none). Record what happened before and after each incidence of the behavior.

WEEK TWO — Starting Behavior Change Procedures
   3a. Select a consequence that you will use following each incidence of the inappropriate behavior. Make sure the consequence is one you feel comfortable with and that it will be possible for you to use this consequence whenever the child uses the inappropriate behavior (in public as well as at home).
    b. Select a reinforcer for the desired behavior.
   4a. Whenever the child uses the inappropriate behavior, immediately respond with the consequence you selected.
    b. Help the child use the desired behavior if applicable (model it, physically move him through it) and immediately reinforce it.
   5a. Record on Section C of the Behavior Change Record Sheet each inappropriate behavior during this one-week period. Record what happened before and what happened after (should be the consequence you selected!!) each occurrence of the behavior.

WARNING: When you start responding to the inappropriate behavior with a consequence that is unpleasant to the child, the incidence of the inappropriate behavior will most likely increase, believe it or not! THIS IS NORMAL — DO NOT GIVE UP! The inappropriate behavior will soon decrease if the program is well-designed and properly carried out.

b. Record on Section D of the Behavior Change Record Sheet each spontaneous incidence (no help from adult) of the desired behavior. Record what happened before and what happened after (should be the reinforcer you selected!) each occurrence of the behavior.

WEEK THREE PLUS — Continuing Behavior Change Procedures

6. Continue as in Week Two until the inappropriate behavior is gone and the desired behavior is well-established.

7. Continue to respond to isolated instances of the inappropriate behavior with the consequence you have chosen.

8. Reinforce the desired behavior intermittently (not every time) in order to maintain it.

RULES FOR IMPLEMENTING A BEHAVIOR CHANGE PROGRAM

1. **Be free of anger.** A behavior change program is most effective if implemented in a matter-of-fact way without anger. If anger is introduced then the consequences can take on qualities of punishment rather than teaching. Simply state: "The rule is, we don't tear books; I must take the book away." Or, "The rule is, we don't bite people; I must put you in your playpen for a minute."

2. **Be consistent.** Limits that are consistently spelled out and enforced are understandable and predictable to the child. They help to provide that order to life which is so important for the deaf child.

3. **Always replace an unacceptable behavior with an acceptable one.** Any behavior change program which spells out a negative consequence to disruptive behavior *must* include a definition of what the acceptable behavior is along with a high rate of reinforcement for the occurrence of that behavior. If tearing books is not allowed, then appropriate handling of books must be noticed and commented on. "I am really pleased to see how careful you are with that book." A child who only experiences negative consequences to disruptive behavior and never hears that he does things well will develop a negative view of himself and is likely to increase his use of disruptive behaviors.

4. **Work on changing only one behavior at a time.** It is too confusing to adults and children to try to change a number of behaviors simultaneously. There is plenty of time to take them one at a time.

DESIGNING THE BEHAVIOR CHANGE PROGRAM

Specialist and parents together can design a behavior change program utilizing the techniques and principles described above in combination with their own judgment and understanding of the child. (The rationale and techniques for implementing a behavior change program can also be found in Parent Handouts, pp. 21-31, of *Parent-Infant Communication.*) The steps in a behavior change program are illustrated in the following example of one family's approach to their 17-month-old daughter, Tessa's, newly acquired behavior of throwing toys and objects.

Tessa is the third of the Morgan's four children, who range in age from four months to eight years. Tessa acquired a hearing loss as a result of bacterial meningitis at nine months of age. Having tried various disciplinary measures ranging from reprimands to spanking to stop Tessa's throwing, her parents responded positively to the specialist's offer to help with the behavior. In fact, discussion revealed a number of management problems Tessa's parents were having. They went through the following process with the specialist acting as consultant:

1. They made a list of behavioral excesses and deficits in their child. Tessa's throwing of toys and hitting were their primary concerns. Positive behaviors they wanted to teach Tessa were saying "please" and "thank you" and handing things to people in a gentle fashion.

2. Tessa's parents were advised to select one unacceptable behavior to change and the throwing of objects, toys, and food won, hands down. For one week the Morgans counted the number of times throwing occurred, using a chart on which each day was marked in hourly intervals. The chart allowed for a notation of what happened before and after each throwing incident. In examining the chart at week's end, Tessa's parents observed that the throwing occurred primarily in four situations: 1) during play with several other children; 2) when she had played with the same object for a long time; 3) when she was told it was time for bed; and 4) at mealtimes.

3. Tessa's parents then worked on selecting a replacement behavior, a reinforcer for the replacement behavior, and negative consequences to throwing. With the specialist's help they decided to respond to throwing by stopping the behavior, kneeling close to Tessa and saying, "We don't throw things in the house" (with an accompanying headshake) followed by swiftly placing her in an empty playpen. She would stay there for two minutes. If she cried she would be removed from the playpen as soon as the crying stopped.

   The Morgans decided to significantly increase their positive attention to Tessa when she was playing constructively and when she refrained from throwing food during meals. They would frequently tell her, "I like the way you are playing/eating so nicely," with accompanying smiles and hugs.

4. For one week the parents implemented their new consequence and reinforcers. During this week they charted the occurrence of Tessa's throwing and noted the preceding and following events. The Morgans felt very good about their ability to be consistent in their use of new behaviors and it helped to enlist the cooperation of their eight-year-old, Jimmy. They were disturbed, however, to observe an increase in the amount of Tessa's throwing during the first week. The specialist advised the Morgans that inappropriate behaviors often accelerate when we first implement new consequences to them. This phenomenon occurs because the child is trying to regain control and to test out whether these new consequences will be maintained.

5. During the second and third weeks, Tessa's parents noted a significant decrease in her throwing. They were able to support each other in remaining consistent with Tessa and in giving her a great deal of positive attention for acceptable mealtime behavior and appropriate play with toys.

The Morgans' program worked well because they concentrated their energies on one behavior, were diligently consistent both in providing a consequence to Tessa's throwing and in reinforcing her appropriate behaviors, and were supportive of each other.

SUMMARY

Non-compliance, attention-getting behaviors, and aggressive/destructive behaviors are three types of child behaviors that parents find unacceptable. Parents can select one or more techniques — such as ignoring, substitution, natural consequences, logical consequences, and time-out — to decrease the occurrence of their child's undesirable behaviors. At the same time, parents will want to use reinforcement to increase the occurrence of desired behaviors that enable the child to achieve the power and attention he needs to feel good about himself. Techniques such as alleviating boredom, preparing the child for change, social and tangible reinforcers, modeling, and shaping are ways to help a child increase the occurrence of desired behaviors.

A behavior change program is an organized way of eliminating undesired behaviors and replacing them with desired behaviors. Behavior change programs will work if: 1) the behaviors to be eliminated and increased are clearly defined; 2) effective consequences for undesired behaviors are selected and *used consistently*; 3) effective reinforcers for desired behaviors are selected and used consistently; and 4) the program is carried out consistently over an adequate period of time.

CHAPTER 15

SIBLINGS OF THE HEARING-IMPAIRED CHILD

Including Siblings in the Habilitation Process
- Characteristics of Siblings Who Fit Into Sessions Well
- Problems With A Sibling

Guidelines for Changing Siblings' Behaviors

Helping Parents Address Siblings' Feelings and Concerns

"How many of us heard the news about (our child's) deafness, reacted emotionally, piled the children in the car and went home, again to cry over the phone or in someone's arms? How many of our children watched and listened in wonder and bewilderment at the emotions shown by parents, grandparents, and friends? How many of us stopped to explain to our children what was happening . . .

"From the time of diagnosis of a deaf child in the family, we, as parents are reminded about the tasks that we need to do to help our 'deaf child' become a success — very little is said about making 'the family' a success" (Mendelsohn, 1984, p. 5).

A large majority of the hearing-impaired children who have attended IHR have had either older or younger siblings. Sibling relationships are some of the most potent relationships that young children experience. When one child in the family is handicapped, the relationships between siblings and the way in which siblings experience their childhood is changed. McKeever (1983) reviews the sparse literature concerned with siblings of children with a chronic disability or health problem. She reports studies which identify changes in interpersonal relationships, communication patterns, and family goals, routines, and resources resulting from the presence of a health-handicapped child. It is safe to say that siblings of handicapped youngsters have feelings and needs that are a direct result of this experience.

There are at least two ways in which the parent-infant specialist can help parents address the special needs of siblings of the hearing-impaired child. First, specialists can model for parents how siblings can be incorporated into habilitation activities in a way that promotes fun and learning for all. Second, specialists can provide parents with information about how children may be reacting to their brother or sister's handicapping condition and suggest how parents might get siblings' feelings and concerns out into the open.

INCLUDING SIBLINGS IN THE HABILITATION PROCESS

The successful inclusion of siblings in habilitation has long been a goal of the IHR staff, one that we admittedly do not always reach. Parents and specialists feel an urgency to use their time together to work on acquiring information and skills that will boost the hearing-impaired child's level of achievement. However, it is neither desirable nor possible to ignore young siblings who also attend sessions. One way in which parents and IHR specialists have dealt with this issue is to reach a compromise: The siblings attend one session each week but stay with a grandparent or sitter during the family's second individual weekly session. This schedule gives the siblings a sense of their importance to the habilitation process and allows the specialist and parents to practice incorporating siblings into habilitation activities. The sessions held without the siblings give the adults time to focus solely on the needs of the parents and the hearing-impaired child.

Some of the most gratifying families and some of the most difficult families that IHR specialists have worked with over the years achieved this status because of the presence of other children in the family who regularly attended habilitation sessions. In some families, siblings who were within a year or two of age of the child with hearing loss blended right into habilitation sessions and their presence enhanced the effectiveness of the learning activities in which the child with hearing loss was engaged. In other families, siblings were consistently disruptive during sessions, creating frustration for specialist and parents alike.

CHARACTERISTICS OF SIBLINGS WHO FIT INTO SESSIONS WELL

In analyzing the families in which siblings attended sessions, the IHR staff has identified three characteristics which divide the siblings who were successfully integrated into sessions from the siblings who were not. The characteristics of siblings who can work cooperatively in sessions are:

- They feel good about themselves. They feel lovable and competent.
- They have a strong sense of their importance in the family. Their needs for attention and for acknowledgement of their achievements are met by their parents and extended family.
- The parents' expectations for the child's behavior and for his/her responsibilities in the family are clearly defined, and are age- and ability-appropriate.

It is evident that it is a child's relationship with his/her parents that determine all of the above characteristics. When a specialist encounters a family in which a sibling is disruptive in sessions, an analysis of the child's behaviors will generally uncover the need that the child is trying to get met through use of an unacceptable behavior. Having defined the unacceptable behavior and made an educated guess as to what the child is trying to achieve through use of the behavior, the specialist can talk with the parents about the problem.

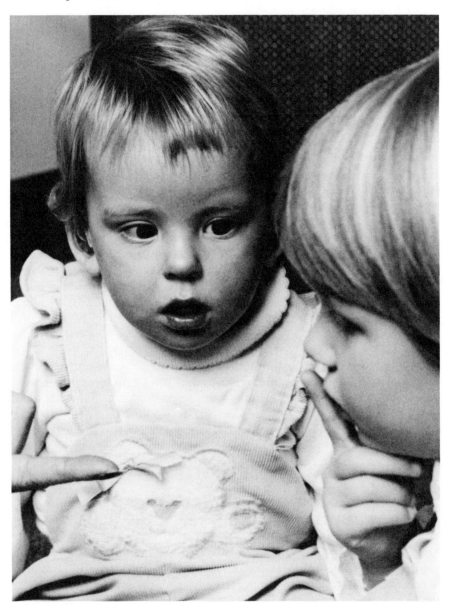

Older sisters are the most fascinating conversationalists!

PROBLEMS WITH A SIBLING

Audrey was a four-year-old who attended habilitation sessions with her mother, JoAnn, and her 18-month-old brother, Peter, who had a severe, bilateral hearing loss. JoAnn expressed apprehension from the beginning about bringing Audrey to sessions: "Audrey will be into everything. She doesn't like to be left out." Julia, the specialist working with the family, pointed out to JoAnn that Audrey was a part of Peter's everyday life. Julia told JoAnn, "To exclude Audrey from all the sessions would create an environment that is not like the natural learning environment you will be using everyday, to help Peter learn listening, language, and speech skills. By including Audrey in sessions we can devise ways to make her participation a positive situation for her and Peter alike."

During the next two sessions with the family, Julia observed Audrey's interactions with Peter and with her mother. Early on it became apparent that two of Audrey's behaviors were going to create problems during the sessions. The first was Audrey's need to control all of the play materials that were presented. Even when it was Peter's turn to handle the materials, Audrey would take the beanbag from his hands to "show" him how to put it in the box. The second behavior was Audrey's need for almost constant attention from JoAnn, signaled by her frequent use of phrases such as, "Mommy, look," "Mommy, watch me do it," "It's my turn, Mommy," or "Let me do it." Julia tallied 13 such entreaties during one ten-minute segment in the second session. Julia also noted that JoAnn most frequently responded to Audrey's requests with phrases such as, "Not now, Audrey. You have to let Peter do it " or "Sit over there, Audrey. This is Peter's time to learn."

Julia's past experience with families alerted her to increasing difficulties with Audrey if these interactions continued. It was her judgment that, along with initial activities such as hearing aid placement and talking with JoAnn about her feelings about Peter's recently acquired loss, it was extremely important to come to agreement with JoAnn on how to handle Audrey's disruptive behaviors and how to better meet Audrey's needs during the sessions and at home.

GUIDELINES FOR CHANGING SIBLINGS' BEHAVIORS

Prior to her next session with JoAnn, Peter, and Audrey, Julia reviewed the format the IHR staff had devised to use when working with a family in which sibling behaviors were interfering with working on the goals set for the child with hearing loss. This format has five steps which the specialist follows:

    1. Describe the unacceptable behavior(s).

2. Count occurrence of the behavior(s).

3. Determine the purpose of the child's behavior, e.g., to gain attention, to express anger, to gain a desired object.

4. Talk with the parents about your observations and the data you collected. Ask for their perceptions of the child's behavior(s), and purpose of the behaviors. **It is essential to reach consensus on these points before proceeding!** If a behavior is not perceived as a problem by the parent(s) (or specialist) or if the parents/specialist do not think that the child is using the behavior as a way of meeting a need, the parents/specialist will not be motivated to initiate action to change the child's behavior.

5. Brainstorm with the parents on ways that the sibling can get his need met without utilizing the undesired behavior.

6. Introduce the steps used in a program of behavior change and agree on the procedures that will be used during sessions and in the home to eliminate undesired behaviors and promote desired behaviors (Chapter 14). Provide parents with the forms they will need to chart the sibling's behaviors.

When JoAnn and the children came for their next session, Julia went over the five-step process with JoAnn. JoAnn agreed to the use of this format to modify Audrey's disruptive behaviors during sessions and at home. JoAnn and Julia decided to focus on one behavior at a time, so they selected Audrey's penchant for taking toys from Peter to "show" him how something should be done. JoAnn agreed to count the occurrence of this behavior for the next five days at home. Julia was extremely pleased when JoAnn mentioned that she also planned to start spending a half-hour each day with Audrey alone so that Audrey would have her full attention to do what Audrey wanted to do around the house. JoAnn felt they could have this time together during Peter's regular mid-day nap.

The behavior change program proceeded well, and by the time Audrey's grabbing behavior had been extinguished, her calls for attention had also diminished noticeably. Audrey frequently came into sessions eager to tell Julia what she and her mother had done the day before and sometimes brought projects they had started that she continued to work on alone during part of the session. By giving Audrey special, individual attention at least once a day, JoAnn successfully met Audrey's needs for attention and Audrey's problem behaviors during habilitation sessions ceased almost entirely.

There are times, especially during the summer months, when families may bring two, three, or even four siblings or neighborhood children to habilitation sessions. Sometimes, parents are caught in a bind of needing to care for a neighbor child at the same time habilitation sessions are scheduled. When there are a number of children attending sessions, IHR specialists have no problem in changing the first activity to a group game, then setting up the siblings in a hallway or room next door with tinkertoys, clay, or some other games with which they can entertain themselves. If the children cannot play unsupervised, it is necessary to modify the plan for the entire session to incorporate all the children. Games such as musical chairs and ring-around-the-rosy, and flannel board stories or a group activity with play dough can all be used successfully to further the hearing-impaired child's listening and language skills, even if it is not possible to work on specific objectives that were planned. Parents often feel guilty about having to bring a number of children to sessions. When the specialist can take the onslaught in stride, she conveys to the parents that she understands and appreciates the reality of their lives.

HELPING PARENTS ADDRESS SIBLINGS' FEELINGS AND CONCERNS

It is important that parents and specialists recognize that the handicapping condition of a brother or sister is likely to be a source of anxiety and concern for siblings. Atkins (1984) suggests that parents talk with siblings of hearing-impaired children about characteristics of each child in the family that have nothing to do with hearing loss so that all the children are encouraged to appreciate each child's unique characteristics. Powell and Ogle (1985) list questions which fall into seven major areas of concern that siblings may feel. These areas are:

1. Questions related to the cause of the handicap: What made him deaf? Will our new baby be deaf?
2. Questions related to the handicapped child's feelings: Does he hurt? Is he happy and sad like me? Why does he act like that? Does he like it when I do this?
3. Questions related to prognosis: Will he always be like this? Can the doctor fix him?
4. Questions about needed services: Why does she go to school? What does that hearing aid do? Why do they make him do _____ at school?
5. Questions about how the sibling himself can help: Can I teach him to talk? Can he play with my friends?
6. Questions about where the child lives: Why does he/doesn't he live in an institution?
7. Questions about the future: When he's four will he be able to talk? When will he learn to hear?

One additional concern that young children have is whether or not they will acquire the handicap of their sibling, especially if the sibling is older. They may ask questions such as, "When I'm five years old, will I wear hearing aids?" Siblings need to have their questions answered seriously since, no matter how silly or cute the questions may seem to adults, the concerns are real for the child.

Talking about a family member's handicapping condition must be an on-going process. As siblings get older they are able to understand more detail-ed information about the condition. Siblings can participate in audiological testing so that they have an opportunity to hear the sounds that come through the earphones their brother or sister wears in habilitation sessions and in the audiological test suite. They can experience how difficult it is to listen to sounds near their own normal threshold for sound, then hear a louder sound that is at the threshold of their hearing-impaired sibling. The audiologist can explain, "This (louder) sound is soft to John just like this (softer) sound is soft to you." Siblings can be supervised as they try hearing aids on to see what they feel and sound like.

It is not uncommon for a child, having seen the hearing-impaired sibling get special time and attention, to say wistfully, "I wish I were deaf!" What the child means is, "I wish I got all that attention!" Parents and specialists need to give siblings, especially those present during habilitation sessions, the feeling that they are important in their own right, not just as a helper for the handicapped child. The specialist can do that by taking a moment to hold the sibling on her lap and ask, "What did you do last night?" or by providing a special activity for the sibling to do during sessions when he/she is not participating in habilitation activities. All of us want to feel special and noticed and important. Siblings are no different.

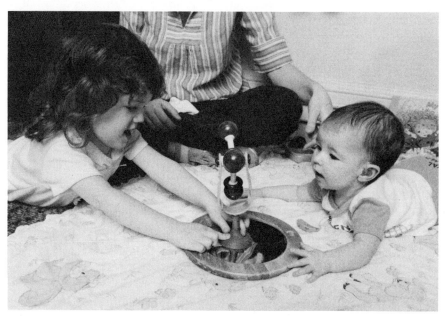

Siblings who feel good about themselves make a positive contribution during habilitation sessions.

Silent Dancer (Hlibok, 1981), *I Have a Sister, My Sister is Deaf* (Peterson, 1977), *Lisa and Her Soundless World* (Levine, 1976), and *A Button In Her Ear* (Litchfield, 1976) are books that can be used to open up lines of communication with siblings.

A great deal more attention is being focused on siblings of handicapped children now than in the past. Reading some of the recently published books and articles has made IHR specialists aware that we need to find ways to do more for siblings in our program. The poignant remarks which follow of two women with handicapped siblings remind us that just as parents need help with their feelings that result from having a handicapped family member, so do siblings.

> "My feelings on this are somewhat kept inside. I've never really come to terms in accepting the dystonia (her brother's illness in which involuntary spasms of muscle contraction induce abnormal movements and postures). I remember going on vacation and expecting that the dystonia would be gone when I returned. For many years, I never believed he would always have it . . . I have felt a lot of jealousy for all the attention Tony has gotten, but it's different now. Oh, I still feel frustration, anger, and sadness, but my *main* purpose for Tony is to be his sister" (Engelhart, 1985).

Miller (1985) describes how important it has been to her as an adult to meet and talk regularly with a group of women who also have handicapped siblings:

> "We had so much to say to one another. So many years of feelings that had been kept inside. Sometimes, because we were afraid that what we had to say would be hurtful to our parents, we did not express or talk about what we were thinking because our thoughts did not seem very nice. We were concerned about what others would think of us. Other times we did not understand what was happening ourselves and it was impossible to find the right words for our feelings. Then there were all those many other times when it seemed selfish and self-centered to take our parents' time when they were already overworked and had so many things to think about. Now finally this (group) was a time that was just for us."

The Siblings Information Network Newsletter (School of Education, Box U-64, Room 227, University of Connecticut, Storrs, Conn. 06268) is an excellent source of materials on siblings. It lists new books and articles and research that is being conducted on siblings. Other excellent resources for families and specialists are the booklet, *For the Love of Siblings* (Therrien, 1984), the book, *Brothers and Sisters — A Special Part of Exceptional Families* (Powell and Ogle, 1985), and the article "Brothers and Sisters of Special Children" (Moses, 1982).

SUMMARY

IHR specialists have worked with a number of families in which the parents' relationships with all their children have promoted the children's feelings of positive self-esteem, lovability, competence, and importance in the family. These children interact with their sibling who has a hearing loss in ways that provide companionship, support, and stimulation both at home and in habilitation sessions. If a specialist finds, in her work with some families, that the siblings and parents need help in establishing a more positive environment in which all the children can grow and learn, she can help the parents learn the skills to make the necessary changes. The specialist must convey to parents her convictions that siblings can be an asset in the process of helping the child with hearing loss acquire communication skills and that to think otherwise is to create problems for siblings that may be as complex to deal with as is hearing loss. Specialists can also help provide siblings with the special attention they need to feel important and valued, even though they do not have a handicapping condition.

PART V

TEACHING PARENTS TO TEACH INFANT OBJECTIVES

CHAPTER 16

DIAGNOSTIC TEACHING VERSUS TESTING

What is Diagnostic Teaching?
- A Definition
- Rationale For the Use of Diagnostic Teaching

Steps in the Diagnostic Teaching Process

Diagnostic Teaching Versus Testing
- How Testing Differs From Diagnostic Teaching

Guidelines for Testing a Child's Abilities

The Infant Hearing Resource habilitation program for hearing-impaired infants is based upon a diagnostic teaching approach. Specialists model this approach for parents during activities presented to the hearing-impaired child. They discuss with parents the principles of the diagnostic teaching approach, the rationale for using this approach, the steps in diagnostic teaching, and how diagnostic teaching differs from testing. Each of these topics is discussed below.

WHAT IS DIAGNOSTIC TEACHING?

A DEFINITION

Diagnostic teaching is a way of working with a child in which questions about the child's abilities and the meaning of his behaviors are posed and tested out during virtually every interaction with that child. Diagnostic teaching is based on an attitude of discovery. Materials are presented to the child in a way that says, "Here is some information — what will you do with it? What can we learn about you from the way you approach this task and interact with these materials? What do your behaviors tell us about you?"

Diagnostic teaching means that though the parents and specialist may have a "best guess" or preconceived notion about how the child will behave under given circumstances, their minds are open to the very good possibility that the child may surprise them with his response. In a diagnostic teaching mode the specialist and parents are not looking for "right" or "wrong" responses. They are simply looking at the child's responses.

Diagnostic teaching is based on three principles:

1. Learning occurs when the environment in which the child finds himself is compatible with his interests and readiness levels so that he is motivated to engage in learning activities and is reinforced by his own participation.

2. There are many variables which affect the child's interests and levels of readiness. These variables are constantly changing as the child's neurological development — including cognitive and motor development — proceeds, as the child's social skills and emotional needs change, and as the child's auditory and language skills increase.

3. The only way adults can be aware of the child's ever-changing interests, levels of readiness, needs, and skills is through continual observation of the way in which the child interacts with objects, people, and events in his environment.

Diagnostic teaching is a very active approach to the child's process of learning. It requires that the adults who are interacting with the child be acutely aware of the elements involved in a task that is presented to a child so that they can analyze the child's responses in view of these elements and formulate their next action based on the child's response.

We can look at a description of how the diagnostic teaching process might work in an activity presented to Eddie, a two-year-old hearing-impaired child. Julia, the specialist, and Kate, Eddie's mother, have decided to use a puzzle that has six individual pieces, with a picture of a vehicle on each, as an activity in which they can model the language concept "in" as Eddie plays with the puzzle. In selecting this activity, Julia and Kate have made several *assumptions* about Eddie's interests, motivation, and readiness related to puzzles. It is also likely that they have some *expectations* or predictions about what Eddie will do with the puzzle. As they talked about how they expected Eddie to play with the puzzle, it was apparent that Julia and Kate made the following assumptions and predictions about Eddie and the puzzle:

1. Eddie will be interested in this puzzle and motivated to play with it.

2. Eddie will understand that the purpose of the puzzle is to take pieces out and then replace them — that being the "right way" to interact with these particular materials.

3. Eddie will know how to remove the pieces and replace them in the correct holes or will use trial and error to find the right hole (an assumption about his readiness).

4. Eddie will be motivated to remove and replace all the pieces, thus completing the task.

The puzzle is presented to Eddie. He removes one piece — a car — and proceeds to "drive" it along the edge of table, down the table leg, and across the floor, humming "mmmmm" as he moves the car.

The response from an adult who is *not* using a diagnostic teaching approach might be: "Eddie, hey, come back here! Look, that car goes in here. Come here, Eddie, Mommy will show you how to do this puzzle. Eddie, I want you over here right now. Julia wants you to put this puzzle together!"

The response from Eddie's mother, Kate, who *is* employing a diagnostic teaching approach, is: "Well, I'll be darned. He recognized that little piece as a car and remembered that we made that noise as we pushed cars together two weeks ago. Hey, Eddie! Here comes a truck — across the table — mm-mmmmmmm — down the leg — mmmmmmmm — Mommy's following your car. Your car went in the box. Here comes my truck — going in the box, too!"

As Eddie approached the table again, Julia lifted a motorcycle piece out of the puzzle and said, "Vroom-vroom! Put it in." She placed the motorcycle piece back in the puzzle. Eddie watched intently, then took off across the floor again with his car. When he returned to the table, he placed his car on top of the puzzle, grinned broadly, and went to collect the truck piece that his mother was holding. When Eddie returned to the table Julia held up the car, saying, "Put the car in," as she placed it in the hole. Eddie smiled and handed the truck to Julia. "Put the truck in," Julia said as she put it in the hole. Eddie stared at the completed puzzle, reached over, picked it up, and carried it to the shelf.

"Eddie loves cars," Kate said somewhat sheepishly. "I should have guessed that he would want to 'drive' it."

"We weren't very accurate in our predictions about Eddie's play with the puzzle, were we," Julia agreed. "But that's not important as long as we do not hold Eddie to our mistaken assumptions. What you did, taking the truck and following Eddie, talking as you went, was perfect. And, your comment relating Eddie's behavior to an earlier activity was excellent. What else did you notice about Eddie's behavior during this activity, Kate?"

During the discussion that followed, the parent and specialist identified three additional behaviors that gave them insight into Eddie's developing skills:

1. He was looking at the adults more frequently for communication than he had during previous sessions.
2. He was aware that one piece was missing after he returned the car piece to the puzzle and knew that his mother had that missing piece.
3. He had used the behavior of putting the puzzle on the shelf for the first time to say that he was finished with the game.

Kate and Julia now have several new pieces of information about Eddie that they can use to plan subsequent activities. Eddie's smile and strut as he replaced the puzzle on the shelf indicated that he had felt competent about the way he had participated in the activity. It is not possible to know exactly what Eddie learned about the concept "in" (the original goal of the activity) but he had been exposed to its use five times during the activity. However, it is clear that Eddie's mother and the specialist were able to learn several things about Eddie's development through their use of the diagnostic teaching approach with Eddie.

RATIONALE FOR THE USE OF DIAGNOSTIC TEACHING

The use of a diagnostic teaching approach is a natural complement to the philosophy of teaching through play and daily activities (Chapter 12). The use of these combined approaches is an acknowledgement of the truth of Galileo's statement: "You cannot teach a man anything; you can only help him to discover what is within himself." The child's most efficient and effective learning will take place when his environment is filled with challenges that he is ready to tackle. Parents and specialists who observe the child carefully will be able to provide him with appropriate opportunities during which he can manipulate materials and interact with people in an experimental way, learning what works and what doesn't work. He will gain confidence in his own abilities as he operates in an environment where there are few "right" and "wrong" ways to do things except where safety for himself and others is involved. The diagnostic teaching approach acknowledges that for children, learning is taking place all the time. The challenge is for the adult to interpret the child's responses in ways that identify the learning that is occurring.

STEPS IN THE DIAGNOSTIC TEACHING PROCESS

Diagnostic teaching does not ignore the fact that the purpose of habilitation sessions is to promote the hearing-impaired child's acquisition of communication skills. Advocacy of a diagnostic teaching approach is not advocacy of an "anything goes" approach to habilitation. There is an underlying structure to diagnostic teaching that keeps adults focused on the objectives at hand, and helps them incorporate and direct whatever responses the child gives into achievement of objectives. It might not be the objective or skill the specialist had in mind, but it may well be an equally important one that, by capitalizing on the moment, the adult can help the child achieve.

There are five steps in the diagnostic teaching process. In keeping with the spirit of technology, the first three steps can be related to the cycle which describes how a computer works: input, process, output. The fourth step is analysis of output. The fifth step is dependent on the outcome of Step 4: either proceed with the activity as planned or change your strategy.

We will use our earlier example of Eddie and the puzzle to discuss each of these steps.

Step 1: Input. Input is determined by the objective selected to work on, and by the materials or activities that are used to give the child the opportunity to achieve the objective. In Eddie's case, the objective selected was a receptive language objective, understanding the concept and word "in." The material selected was a puzzle and the activity was to have Eddie remove and then replace puzzle pieces as the adults modeled the language "in" in short sentences.

Step 2: Processing. Processing is what takes place in the child's mind when he is confronted with the input. We cannot see or know exactly what these mental processes are. Sometimes the child's behaviors, or output (Step 3), give us a good guess at what the child is thinking. Eddie's mother was guessing when she said that Eddie had associated the puzzle piece with the toy car he had played with another time. However, the child's mental processes are not always easy to discern. Had Eddie taken one look at the puzzle and started to cry, the parent and specialist may have been unable to determine what Eddie thought when he saw the puzzle.

Step 3: Output. Output is what the child does with the materials or activities. Output is a behavior, an action. Output results from the processing that takes place in the child's mind, processing that may be 180 degrees from what the parent and specialist predict the child will think and thus do in the circumstances presented.

An excellent example of some original processing and output occurred during a habilitation session at IHR in which a young hearing-impaired child's motor function was being screened. The specialist was modeling movements and positions that the child was supposed to imitate in order to demonstrate his prowess. All went well until the specialist stood on one foot, then looked expectantly at the child to see if he could perform the same act. The child did not even try. Instead, he walked over to the specialist and, linking his hands together, placed them under her dangling foot to help her hold it in the air! A child's behavior, or output, is a direct result of the mental processing that takes place when he encounters the input.

Step 4: Analysis of Output. Analysis of the child's output or behavior starts with the parent and specialist determining whether the child is thinking along lines conducive to accomplishment of the particular objective on which they are working. In Eddie's case, though he did not respond to the puzzle in the way the adults had anticipated he would, his mother determined that Eddie's behavior (or output) was still compatible with her modeling the language "in," which she did when he put the puzzle piece in the box. Had Eddie started to cry upon seeing the puzzle or had he walked away and refused to be enticed back, an analysis of his behavior would most likely have determined that Eddie's behavior was not conducive to modeling the language "in." When the child has not performed as expected, analysis of his behavior, combined with a best guess about his processing of the input, will enable the specialist and parent to speculate why the child performed as he did. When the adults have an idea of why the child did what he did they can then determine a way in which they might change their strategy in order to direct the child toward achievement of the objective.

Parents can be wizards at analyzing their child's output. During sessions at IHR, specialists frequently express confusion about the meaning or intent of one of the child's behaviors. When the parent sees the behavior, he or she is instantly able to interpret the behavior correctly. In one instance, the specialist, parent, and child were reading a story book when the child jumped up from his father's lap and left the room. His father responded to the quizzical look on the specialist's face by saying, "Oh, he's going to the toy room to get the giraffe." Sure enough, the child returned with the giraffe and held it up next to the giraffe pictured in the book.

Step 5: Proceed with the Activity as Planned or Change Your Strategy.

Proceed with the Activity as Planned. If the child has responded to the input with predictable processing and output, i.e., done what the adults thought/hoped he would do with the materials, then the activity can proceed as planned. In the example of Eddie, had he removed the puzzle pieces and attempted to reinsert them in the holes, the parent and specialist could have modeled the language "in" as they had planned to do: "You're putting the car in. Put it in the hole. You put it in, Eddie!"

OR

Change Your Strategy. There are three strategies (well, four if throwing up your hands in despair is included!) that can be used when the child does not behave as expected. Each strategy is designed to allow the specialist and parent to continue to promote the child's acquisition of skills, even if not in the area originally intended. The strategy chosen is dictated by the analysis of the child's output (completed in Step 4).

1. *Modify the adults' roles* in the activity to conform to the child's behavior. Eddie's mother used this strategy when she took a puzzle piece and, imitating Eddie's behavior, followed him around the room. Because she was down by Eddie at the time when he moved his car into a box, she was able to continue with the planned objective of modeling the language "in." The specialist also changed the way in which she participated in the activity, removing a puzzle piece herself so she could put it in and say "put it in" when Eddie returned to the table. She also accepted puzzle pieces as Eddie handed them to her and put them in herself, talking as she did so.

Having determined, in analyzing Eddie's behavior (Step 4), that it was conducive to continuing with the objective, the adults modified their behaviors to accomplish what they had planned.

2. *Modify the input.* Modifying the input can be done by using the same materials but changing the way in which they are presented. Eddie's mother and the specialist may have decided that showing Eddie the puzzle with all six pieces in it was too much input. They may decide to bring the puzzle back again with only one piece in it and see if Eddie would be likely to take it out and put it in. They may decide to give Eddie the puzzle empty with the pieces in a bag and let him take out one piece at a time. They may decide to hide two or three of the puzzle pieces around the room and let Eddie find them and put them in the puzzle.

Modifying the input may also be accomplished by changing the materials or the environment or both. In analyzing Eddie's behavior in response to the puzzle, the adults may realize that Eddie had never played with a puzzle before. He did not know that all the pieces came out and could be replaced. They may decide to select another puzzle with only two pieces and to present it to Eddie while he was seated on his mother's lap so that she could help him remove one piece at a time and replace it. They might deliberately select a puzzle that did not have a picture of a car so that Eddie would not be tempted to "drive" the car.

3. *Change the objective.* Suppose that, in analyzing Eddie's behavior, the specialist and parent had realized that in vocalizing as he moved the car, Eddie was producing a consonant and vowel combination (e.g., "mum-mum-mum") that he had never used before. The adults may immediately decide to reinforce that vocal production by imitating it as they move puzzle pieces around on the floor. They might make a rapid choice to work on one of Eddie's speech objectives that required him to produce consonant-vowel combinations with varying duration, pitch, and loudness levels. Their decision to capitalize on Eddie's spontaneous production of a new vocalization is a valid and intelligent way to change their strategy in the middle of the activity.

Once the strategy has been changed, the adults are, in essence, presenting new input and the five steps in the diagnostic teaching process start again. After new input is presented — whether it be the same materials in a different format, or a change in objective which requires that the adults are now down on the floor imitating vocalizations — the child will process that input and react or behave in some way that must then be analyzed so that a decision can be made as to proceeding with the activity or making further changes in strategy.

DIAGNOSTIC TEACHING VERSUS TESTING

Scenario: Lily, an eighteen-month-old hearing-impaired child and her father, Evan, are sitting on one side of the table. The specialist is seated on the other side. Lying on the table between them are four toys: a ball, a truck, a small doll, and a book.

> **Specialist:** "Wait, Lily. Don't touch them yet. Evan, will you help Lily keep her hands in her lap until I ask her for something? O.K., Lily, give me the ball. Where's the ball? Which one is the ball? Give me the ball, Lily."
>
> **Lily:** (reaches for the doll when Evan releases her hands).
>
> **Specialist:** "No, Lily. (Frowns). That's the doll. I want the ball. Evan, help her pick up the ball. Lily, put the doll down. Where's the ball?"
>
> **Lily:** (squirming and beginning to cry as her father takes the doll away and places her hand on the ball).
>
> **Specialist:** "That's right! (Big smiles). You have the ball. Look at me, Lily. That's the ball. Ball. Can you say 'ball'?"

This technique, which the authors call "teaching through testing," is diametrically opposed to a diagnostic teaching approach. Because the adult is attempting to test the child's acquisition of a concept before she has the opportunity to learn it, the use of this very directive technique is extremely punishing to the child. Yet some adults who work with young hearing-impaired children use the "teaching through testing" technique on a daily basis. What is wrong with this technique in this situation? Several things.

- It is unrealistic to expect an eighteen-month-old child to sit at a table with toys in front of her and not reach for them.
- If she *is* sitting at the table and *does* reach for a toy, she has clearly told the adults where her interest lies. The name of the toy she has selected is the word that should be modeled for her.
- The specialist asks for the ball; Lily picks up the doll. Lily may have heard only the vowel "a" and thought the specialist had said "doll." But, now the specialist says "No! That's the 'a.' I want the 'a.'" Lily is confused.
- When a toy is removed from a child's hand and the child is forced to select another, it is hard to believe that the child will be interested in the second toy and motivated to learn its name.
- Lily is confused and frustrated. She knows she's done something wrong because she saw the specialist frown and say "no." Then while she was squirming and starting to cry because her father took the doll away, she sees the specialist nod and smile and say "right!" Does the specialist like it when she cries? Lily has had it with this situation. She gets down on the floor and cries in earnest.

HOW TESTING DIFFERS FROM DIAGNOSTIC TEACHING

"Teaching through testing" may be a contradiction in terms. Clearly it is not an effective way to capitalize on the interests, motivation, and readiness levels of a young child. Testing is, however, a valid activity with a child of any age. Test, evaluate, assess — we use several different terms for whatever procedure we employ to gain information about a child's skill levels. We have discussed how the diagnostic teaching approach is used to gain information about the child's skill levels. Testing is a faster way to acquire some of the same information that we may gain through extended observation of the child. Testing differs from the extended observation that occurs during diagnostic teaching in at least three ways:

1. In the test situation there *is* a right response. Whatever response the child gives that is not the "right" response is generally disregarded. For test purposes, it is wrong.
2. Testing situations present a specific and limited number of stimuli to which the child responds. The test seeks to determine the child's performance in response to the stimuli. Other skills demonstrated, no matter how closely related to the test item, do not generally count. During the test the child might recite the Gettysburg Address, but there is no way to give him credit for this amazing feat on the test form.
3. Testing is designed to measure a child's performance against some standard. That standard might be as unscientific as the performance of two peers in his play group, or it might be as scientific as a norm-referenced scale of development. The point is that in a test the child's behavior is being compared with the behavior of other children or with his own earlier performance in order to determine how closely his behavior matches up or has changed.

GUIDELINES FOR TESTING A CHILD'S ABILITIES

The characteristics of testing described above apply more to a formal standardized test — one which contains a specified number of items that must be administered and scored in a specific way — than to the informal testing that a specialist might conduct to determine whether or not a child has achieved an auditory, language, or speech objective. Regardless of the "formality" of the test, following the guidelines below will assure that the child has an optimal opportunity to display his skills related to the area being evaluated.

1. Be very clear about what you are testing and what response is required from the child for him to "pass" the test. Example: the specialist wants to know if three-year-old Mickey can associate a

cat meow on audiotape with a cat, and a taped dog bark with a dog. She plays the tape of the cat meow and says, "What's that, Mickey?" Mickey does nothing.

Does Mickey associate the "meow" with a cat? Maybe he does; however, he may not have the word "cat" in his expressive vocabulary. He has no way to demonstrate his recognition of the sound. Since this is not a test of expressive language but of auditory recognition, the specialist must provide Mickey with some way to demonstrate his knowledge. Pictures of the cat and dog that have previously been associated with the taped sounds can be provided so that Mickey can point to the picture of the animal he hears.

2. Teach the child the required test behavior. If he is to point to a picture, show him how you, upon hearing the dog bark, point to the picture of the dog. Play the sound again, guide his finger to the picture of the dog and reinforce him for his correct response. If the child is to hand you an object, find an object, or place an object somewhere, it is necessary for the specialist or parent to model the required response for him. This step is particularly important when testing a young child who may not understand words used in testing such as "show," "put," "hand," "point to," "find."

3. Structure first test situations in such a way to ensure that the child will achieve 100% success.

   Practice: Give the stimulus (e.g., "Where's the ball?") and guide the child's hand to it.

   Limit the choices: Start with two very different stimuli. Add to or change the stimuli when the child is ready.

   Provide clues: When testing begins, present the stimulus, pause and look expectant, present the stimulus again, pause. If the child does not respond, or moves his hand to an incorrect item, guide his hand to the correct item and say "Yes, that's the_____. You have the_____." Replace the item and have the child retract his hand. Present the same stimulus again, pause, repeat, pause. Assist the child again if he does not initiate a response or reaches toward the incorrect item. If, after two cycles of stimulus, pause, stimulus, pause, assist, the child still needs assistance, the test is complete. The child has not yet acquired the skill being tested. *It is time to switch into a teaching mode.*

   Praise correct responses: Use cheerful words, smiles, clapping hands — whatever is reinforcing for the child. Try to avoid tangible reinforcers such as toys or tokens to avoid the risk that the child will be more interested in the reinforcer than he is in the test.

   When the child makes a response we do not want:

   • Do not say "no" or "wrong." If the child is about to select the "wrong" object, guide his hand to the correct object.

• Do not use the name of the incorrect item the child has selected as in, "No, that's a bird. I wanted the airplane." It is confusing to the child who, holding the bird, sees you shaking your head saying "No, . . . bird." Instead, repeat the request, "Where's the airplane?", pick it up and exclaim, "Here's the airplane. I have the airplane."

Stop the test: If the task is ambiguous or too complex for the child, stop. If the child is confused about what to do, simplify the test procedure. If the concept being tested is too complex or beyond the child's skill level, break the task down into its component parts and test at the simpler levels. For example, if the child has not responded correctly in a test situation in which pictures of objects have been used, repeat the test at a subsequent session using actual objects or realistic toys. The child may not have made the cognitive step of associating pictures with objects whose names he knows.

When testing for achievement of objectives with an auditory component, the tester must be certain that the stimuli given as choices are all audible to the child. If, for example, the specialist is attempting to determine if the child can identify sounds as "loud" or "soft," she must be sure that the child can hear the "soft" sounds.

When the child knows the test procedure: When the child has learned the test procedure and has, with assistance, responded correctly in several different test situations, he is likely to have enough self-confidence to be allowed to make incorrect responses *if* the response to his errors is carefully considered. If the child, upon hearing the request, "Put the doll in bed," places the doll on the chair, the specialist might respond with, "Listen again, Mickey. Put the doll in bed." If, after this repetition, the child still does not make the correct response, the specialist would make a note of this and move to the next test item or next activity, planning to come back and work on this concept at a later time.

Children who are reprimanded and made to feel wrong during testing will begin very early to protect themselves from future failure by refusing to participate in any activity that looks suspiciously like a test. They may also become very hesitant and fearful about making a response when asked to do so in any situation, even if it is only a game. Because there are so many areas of life in which children with hearing loss feel confused or make mistakes, they can easily become very sensitive to potential failure. The specialist who alerts parents to this possibility early on and who models techniques that prevent the child from experiencing the negative consequences of "failure" is making a substantial contribution to the child's self-esteem and acquisition of risk-taking behaviors in the learning setting.

Many of us may remember tests as punishment designed to show us and our classmates how incompetent we were. It is unfortunate that testing can indeed be used in that way. Perhaps that is reason enough to use terms such as "evaluate" or "assess" in place of the term "test." Whatever word is used, the fact remains that testing, when done properly, provides parents and specialists with valuable information about what the child knows and what he is ready to learn next. A good test leaves the child feeling proud of his accomplishments and curious about some of the tasks at which he was not yet adept.

SUMMARY

Diagnostic teaching is a dynamic approach to providing an environment in which the child's learning evolves out of his interests, readiness, motivation, and internal reinforcement. The parent and specialist plan objectives to teach and select materials that, based on their knowledge of the child, will provide the child with the opportunity to acquire the skills specified in the objective. **In diagnostic teaching the adults approach the activity with an attitude of investigating the child's response to the input and an attitude of flexibility about modifying the activity or the stated objective if the child's behavior dictates.** An important tenet of the diagnostic teaching approach is that there are no right or wrong ways of doing things; thus, the child is not put in the position of failing. It is the adults' responsibility to analyze the child's behaviors in an activity and to make the changes necessary to assure the child's successful acquisition of skills.

Testing is a shortcut to assessing a child's abilities. If done properly, testing can provide adults with good information about the child's skills and provide the child with a sense of pride in his accomplishments.

CHAPTER 17

TEACHING INFANT AUDITORY OBJECTIVES: AN ORIENTATION TOWARD HEARING

Helping Children Learn to Hear
- Asking the Right Questions
- Establishing an Environment Conducive to Listening
- Teaching Sequential Auditory Skills

The Role of the Auditory Feedback Mechanism in the Infant's Development of Spoken Language

Learning to Listen Takes Time
- Chris: A Profound Loss and Slow Development
- Delilah: Her Parents Thought She Could Not Hear

Auditory development in hearing-impaired infants and toddlers, including rationale, research, and intervention techniques, has been described in detail in the literature (Bess and McConnell, 1981; Clark School for the Deaf, 1971; Clark and Watkins, 1978; Eisenberg, 1976; Griffiths, 1967, 1974; Ling, 1984; Ling and Ling, 1978; Northern and Downs, 1984; Northcott, 1977; D. Pollack, 1985; Simmons-Martin, 1978; Whetnall and Fry, 1966). These sources are excellent and essential references for specialists and parents as they prepare for the critical task of teaching infants to make optimal use of their residual hearing. The materials cited can be used in conjunction with *Parent-Infant Communication* (Infant Hearing Resource, 1985) and this text in planning and implementing a program of auditory development for the hearing-impaired infant. The more parents and specialists know about audition, the more effective they will be in setting "traps" that will catch the child in the act of hearing!

The goal of the IHR auditory habilitation program is to help infants make optimal use of their residual hearing so that they can gain meaning from the sounds in their environment, including speech. Early identification of hearing loss, early placement of appropriate amplification, accurate assessment of auditory abilities, and well-informed parents facilitate attainment of this goal. Parts of each habilitation session with a family are devoted to ongoing auditory assessment and stimulation and to the education of the parents. The auditory objectives for infants in the curriculum *Parent-Infant Communication* are used as the assessment and planning guide. The parent section of this same curriculum provides the specialist with a guide for transmitting information and skills to parents.

HELPING CHILDREN LEARN TO HEAR

In the area of audition, specialists and parents who view the container as half-full rather than half-empty will find a great deal of satisfaction in promoting acquisition of listening skills in hearing-impaired infants. The hearing-impaired child — like any child — is filled with invisible resources, one of which is hearing. Because the characteristics of a newly diagnosed hearing-impaired infant's auditory capabilities are an unknown, the specialist and parents are faced with a mystery to unravel. Fortunately, the path leading to the solution of the mystery is lined with clues. If specialists and parents ask themselves the right questions, establish an environment conducive to listening, provide the appropriate props, and present a sequential series of auditory stimuli, they can start filling their record sheets with data collected from their observations of the child's auditory behaviors.

ASKING THE RIGHT QUESTIONS

A common question asked about a hearing-impaired child is, "What *can* he hear?" It is particularly frustrating to parents of a newly-identified hearing-impaired infant to be told that the answer to that question is mostly unknown and that only time will tell. Even when an audiogram has been obtained for the child, the answer to this question is only a best guess based on the audiologist's and specialist's experiences with other children with similar audiograms. It is important to note that while the majority of first audiograms of very young children obtained using visual reinforcement audiometry (VRA) compare very closely with audiograms obtained when the child is older (see Chapter 6), first responses obtained from young children with profound hearing losses may not represent their true hearing thresholds. For example, when Leah was first tested at IHR at age nine months, she gave no responses to stimuli presented at the limits of the audiometer. Unaided thresholds obtained when Leah was 18 months of age — after she had been wearing hearing aids for nine months — were recorded as follows:

	250 Hz	**500 Hz**	**750 Hz**
Right ear	80 dB	95 dB	105 dB
Left ear	80 dB	105 dB	no response

Leah had learned to *listen* for sound, even sounds that were very soft for her.

At IHR, parents are encouraged to ask questions, the answers to which will guide them in helping their child acquire auditory skills. Three such questions are: 1) What do we need to know in order to help our child develop listening skills? 2) Why does my child respond to some sounds and not to others? 3) How will I know if my child is hearing a sound?

WHAT DO WE NEED TO KNOW IN ORDER TO
HELP OUR CHILD DEVELOP LISTENING SKILLS?

This is an extremely important question for parents — and specialists — to ask. The better they understand the many ways in which human beings use hearing, the more likely they are to be motivated to make auditory development an integral part of their interactions with the child. Likewise, if parents and specialists understand all the subskills that enable a person to make use of sound, they can develop activities to promote acquisition of these subskills. We can look at two complex areas, functions of hearing, and elements involved in listening, to get the information parents need to answer this question.

FUNCTIONS OF HEARING

The importance of hearing as it relates to the child's sense of security, developing self-identity, and connectedness to family and friends was discussed in Chapter 4. These personal aspects of hearing are interconnected with the functions that hearing serves for us. The staff of the Clark School for the Deaf (1971) delineated five major ways in which we use our hearing: arousal, space perception, comprehension, voice control, and acquisition of speech and language.

1. **Arousal:** Hearing serves as an unceasing monitor of conditions in our environment. We hear people approaching before they come into view, we hear sounds that signal emergencies, sounds that signal the passage of time, sounds that alert us to the presence of some change in our environment. Even while we sleep our hearing continues to function and we sleep through the common sounds of our neighborhood and household. But when a sound "doesn't compute" we are roused to attend to a potential danger.

   Because our hearing provides this monitoring function for us, we are freed to direct our attention to other tasks without needing to interrupt ourselves mid-task to check out the continuity of our environment. Studies have demonstrated that working in a noisy environment is stressful. It may be not only the constancy of loud noise that causes stress, but the masking effect that noise has on our ability to monitor our environment that creates a feeling of tension.

2. **Space Perception:** Binaural hearing provides us with a means to localize the sources of sounds in our environment, both in terms of direction and distance. It provides us with a way to gauge distance and direction relationships between ourselves and other entities. A cough from the direction of our office-mate does not disturb us; a cough from the direction of the doorway signals the

presence of a visitor. Even as children, we used the information about distance that we gained from hearing — how many times did we cease a "forbidden" activity and replace it with an angelic smile just as a parent walked into the room?

3. **Comprehension:** Sounds help us make sense of events in our environment and help us perceive our world as a logical, predictable place. We know and understand what is happening in the environment (and actually in the world, by way of radio and television) because of the sounds we hear. Hearing gives us clues about events. We see friends pull up in their car, stop in front of our house, get out, and come up the path to the door. We know it's going to be a short visit. How do we we know this? We can hear that the car engine is still running. A baby knows he'll get a bottle soon. How? He hears the familiar rattle of the bottle warming up in a pan of boiling water or the "beep-beep" signal from the microwave oven.

   Obviously, we use our hearing to comprehend communication from others. We gain understanding not only from the words we hear but from the way in which the words are uttered. Is the speaker relaxed? anxious? hesitant? happy? angry? embarrassed? indignant? The pitch, loudness, and rate of speech convey the emotional content of the message, sometimes even when the speaker is trying to disguise his/her feelings. The information we get from voice, when combined with information from verbal content and body language, helps us to comprehend the intent and meaning of the communication.

4. **Voice Control:** We use our hearing to monitor the pitch, loudness, and rate of our own voices. Sometimes we get an idea of the intensity of our feelings about an issue only as we suddenly listen to ourselves mid-stream in a discourse. It's not uncommon to hear someone abruptly stop talking, then say sheepishly, "I guess I have some pretty strong feelings about this issue." We also use our hearing to self-correct, either mispronunciation of a word or a meaning that was inadvertently conveyed through tone of voice or misplaced emphasis. This ability to hear our own message gives us the opportunity to compare our delivery to our intent to make sure that the two are congruent.

5. **Acquisition of Speech and Language:** While this function is obviously interrelated with the functions of comprehension and voice control, it focuses specifically on the actual process of hearing what others say, learning to recognize words, ascribing meaning to words, and then producing combinations of speech sounds that match the spoken words of others. Since speech is an auditory phenomenon, it is most easily and efficiently learned when received through the auditory channel. Even imperfect

hearing provides the listener with clues to meaning and intent that are not discernible through other sensory input systems.

Most hearing-impaired children can learn to use hearing for these five functions. Their access to the necessary auditory information depends on the interplay of several factors: auditory thresholds, the age at which amplification is placed, the appropriateness of the amplification, intactness of the auditory perceptual centers of the brain, and the quality of listening training. These variables, some of which are within the control of parents and specialists, give the child optimal access to sound.

ELEMENTS INVOLVED IN LISTENING

Having discussed the functions of hearing with parents, it is helpful then to look at what is involved in the act of listening. *While hearing is a sense, listening is a skill.* With present technology there are a finite or limited number of things we can do to improve the *hearing* of a child with a hearing deficit. There are, however, an infinite number of things parents and specialists can do to help a young child increase his *listening* skills. In order to help a child increase his listening abilities, it is necessary to understand the elements that affect the act of listening. These elements are threshold, attention, quality of sound received, and auditory perceptual skills.

1. **Threshold:** Threshold is the point at which a stimulus is just strong enough to be perceived (Webster, 1974). Sounds must occur at or above our auditory thresholds before we can hear them. Listening to sounds that occur just at or just above our thresholds requires a great deal of effort. We are much more comfortable listening to sounds that occur well above our thresholds. In fact, most conversational speech occurs 40-60 dB above normal thresholds in the speech range, which is defined by Ling and Ling (1978) as 80-8000 Hz. It is clear that to implement an effective auditory intervention program with a hearing-impaired infant, we need to know the child's auditory thresholds so that we can determine how intense sounds must be in order for the child to hear them.

There are several things parents and specialists can do to make certain that the child is stimulated with sounds that fall above his auditory thresholds. First, they can make sure that the child's amplification system is functioning as intended and that the child is wearing his aids during all his waking hours so that his thresholds for sound remain consistant. (See Chapter 6 for a discussion of hearing aids.)

Second, parents and specialists can assure that the child with a sensorineural hearing loss does not have the additional handicap of a conductive hearing loss caused by a medically treatable middle ear condition. Frequent tympanograms and *prompt medical attention to middle ear effusion or infections* can prevent the child from having to operate with a mixed hearing loss and the resultant higher thresholds for sound.

Third, parents and specialists need to be constantly aware of the effect that distance has on the child's ability to hear sound. As Ling (1981) states: "Most children with measurable hearing can be aided so that at least some speech sounds are within earshot at or beyond a distance of two meters . . . When a speaker is at half that distance, sound is heard about 6dB louder, and at twice that difference, 6dB quieter." Assuming, therefore, that the loudness of your voice remains constant, your voice will be 12dB louder when you talk to the child at 1 meter rather than at 4 meters. This 12dB can make a considerable difference in whether your voice is audible at all to the child. Ling recommends talking to the child within a yard or less for optimal one-on-one teaching conditions.

Finally, parents and specialists can work to keep background noise that may mask speech to a minimum when interacting with the child. Many families leave the television or radio on for "company" while someone is at home. Parents need to be aware that the television or radio will be a constant sound source which may mask out their conversation with the child.

> "The number of decibels by which speech is more intense than noise is called the speech-to-noise (or signal-to-noise) ratio. A speech/noise ratio of 30 dB permits the quietest sounds of speech to be heard without interference by noise. As the speech/noise ratio decreases, more and more of the speech signal becomes masked by noise and thus is less intelligible" (Ling and Ling, 1978, p. 121).

While adults can learn to ignore "background noise" and attend to a more important signal, the hearing-impaired child who is just learning to listen does not yet have the ability to listen selectively to a more important signal. When presented with competing signals he is most likely to ignore both of them. Adults must assure that their spoken signals directed to the child are at least 30 dB louder than the ambient noise.

2. **Attention:** Attending to a stimulus means that an individual is actively taking notice of it. Parents and teachers can work to structure the environment of the young hearing-impaired child so that he learns to pay attention to auditory stimuli. Attention to auditory events can be encouraged by creating an atmosphere of curiosity about sounds, those that occur naturally during the child's everyday routine, and those that can be planned as part of a game to pique the child's interest in auditory events. Parents and teachers must always keep in mind that the more attention they pay to the everyday sounds that occur in the child's environment, the more attention the child will learn to pay to these sounds. Adults can afford to ignore the roar of a truck passing on the street, the mumble of clothes in the dryer, the sharp bark of the neighbor's dog, because we know what makes these sounds and what they mean. The child will ignore these sounds for the exact opposite reason — he has no idea of what makes these sounds or what they

mean. By attending to a sound ourselves, calling the child's attention to the sound, showing him what makes the sound, and describing the meaning of the sound, we can help the child learn that sounds give him information about his world, and that sounds are interesting and meaningful.

The issue of whether the use of signed language in conjunction with speech diverts the child's attention from the auditory signal cannot be brushed aside. There are advantages to the combined use of spoken and signed communication and there are disadvantages. Using a communication system that requires the child to split his attention between the auditory (spoken) words and the visual (signed) words of a message may have implications for the quality of his attention to both. Fortunately, the issue is not an either/or proposition. Commitment to an approach in which both spoken and signed language are used means commitment to helping the child learn to communicate through *all* the modalities that work for him. For many hearing-impaired children this includes an auditory-verbal system. Parents and specialists who are using both spoken and signed language need to provide the child with regular and frequent opportunities to listen to speech without the use of signs so that the child can focus his undivided attention on decoding the auditory signal.

3. **Quality of Sound Received:** The hearing-impaired child may be subjected to listening to sound that is unlike what you and I hear. The auditory signal that he receives may be distorted, that is, changed, by his own damaged auditory system, by a malfunctioning hearing aid, or both. If the child's auditory system or amplification system changes the wave form of the auditory signal or if either of these systems adds noise to the original signal, the child is experiencing distortion and the quality of the signal he receives is reduced. Unfortunately, there is nothing that can be done to eliminate distortion caused by a damaged cochlea or auditory nerve. However, we do have control over distortion that is introduced by the child's hearing aids. Hearing aid analyzers give us information both about the output of a hearing aid and the distortion produced by the hearing aid. (See Chapter 6 for a discussion of the importance of the use of hearing aid analyzers.) The distortion figure provided by the hearing aid analyzer is presented as a percentage which tells us how much noise the hearing aid is adding to the pure tone signal that is going into the microphone of the aid, or put another way, how much the internal parts of the hearing aid are changing the wave form of the pure tone signal. Most hearing aid specification sheets list "typical" harmonic distortion percentages at selected frequencies. These percentages may be different for different tone settings of the same aid. These typical or acceptable levels of distortion generally fall between 0 to 5-7%. At IHR we send a hearing aid in for repair when distortion levels consistently register more than 3-5 percentage points above the specified levels of distortion.

It is extremely difficult to detect distortion in a hearing aid by listening to it unless the problem is flagrant. Since the quantity and quality of sound a hearing-impaired child receives through a hearing aid are major factors affecting his ability to recognize and comprehend sound, it is imperative that parents and specialists have regular and frequent access to a hearing aid analyzer.

4. **Auditory Perceptual Skills:** The purpose of listening is to gain meaning from what is heard. In order for an individual to gain meaning from auditory stimuli, the center of the brain that processes auditory information must be able to perform several complex tasks rapidly and simultaneously. These tasks are selecting, synthesizing, discriminating, remembering, and sequencing auditory information.

   a. **Selecting.** Listening experience and cognitive abilities enable a child to pick out the most important or meaningful sounds from a number of competing auditory stimuli. In the home we may be asking the child to pick out our voice from an environment of sounds which also includes water running in the sink, the dishwasher motor, the stove timer, a sister talking and laughing in the next room, cars passing outside, and the radio playing. To a child who is just learning to listen, none of these sounds is any more meaningful or important than the others. Parents and specialists need to help the child learn to select which of the sounds is important to attend to by calling attention to significant sounds, making them occur closer to the child, and making them louder than the competing signals, if possible. If the child appears to have difficulty attending to one signal out of many, it is our job to structure his environment so that unnecessary sounds are eliminated as much as is possible.

   b. **Synthesizing.** We gain meaning from much of what we hear by putting together a series of sounds. This is particularly true of speech, in which a limited number of speech sounds can be combined in millions of different ways to convey millions of different meanings. The auditory center of our brain must be able to synthesize, or put together, the individual speech sounds to create a word, and to put together words to gain meaning from a sentence. A hearing-impaired child needs endless opportunities to hear words and environmental sounds so that he can learn to synthesize individual units into meaningful wholes.

   c. **Discriminating.** Auditory discrimination is the ability to tell the difference between sounds. The more disparate two sounds are, the easier it is to discriminate between them. Speech discrimination can be difficult for the hearing-impaired child since he must be able to hear all parts of similar-sounding words in order to hear the difference between the words. As he gains listening experience he will learn to use visual clues, such as speechreading, and contextual clues, such as other words in the sentence and the topic being discussed, to supplement the auditory clues he receives.

d. **Remembering.** It is apparent that if a child is to learn to recognize and comprehend sounds, he must be able to remember them between occurrences. This requires long-term memory for infrequently heard words and sounds. The child must also have short-term memory in order to gain meaning from sentences and paragraphs. The ability to hear, synthesize, and discriminate all the words in a sentence will be of no use to him if he has forgotten the first words by the time the end of the sentence has been uttered.

e. **Sequencing.** Many times different meanings are conveyed simply by changing the order of words in a sentence or the order of occurrence of sounds in the environment. If you hear a baby crying, then hear a thump you are likely to think something different has occurred than when you hear a thump, then a baby's cry. Likewise the difference in the sequence of the words, "There's the lamb for the dinner" and "There's the dinner for the lamb" changes the meaning entirely. The child must be able to retain the *sequence* in which the words or sounds occur, not only the words or sounds themselves, if he is to gain correct understanding from them.

These five auditory perceptual skills contribute to the usefulness of auditory information for all of us. A hearing-impaired child may have difficulty with one or more of these processing skills, thus compounding the handicap of a peripheral hearing loss. The information we gain from an audiogram reflects the child's ability to hear a discrete, non-complex signal at one given moment of time. Using hearing to comprehend and interpret our environment requires that our auditory system captures invisible stimuli, sounds, that occur in the invisible medium of time. An audiogram does not tell us how well a child can perform this act, nor does it give us any information about a child's ability to select, synthesize, discriminate, remember, or sequence sounds. *For these reasons, we cannot look at a child's audiogram and accurately predict how the child will be able to use his hearing.*

It is evident that parents, like teachers, need to know quite a bit about hearing and about the acquisition of listening skills in order to help their child. This information is a part of the parent curriculum in *Parent-Infant Communication* and is taught to parents during the regularly scheduled sessions at IHR. Specialists come back to this information time and again. As the specialist and parent observe the child's responses to sound, factors such as loudness of the sound, distance from the sound source, gain provided by the child's hearing aids, the ways in which the child is using his hearing, and evidence of the emergence of auditory perceptual skills are noted and discussed. As the child becomes a more adept listener, his responses to sounds will change. Reasons for his changing responses are important topics of discussion since they may point to the child's developing listening and auditory perceptual skills or they may point to a change in the child's ability to hear that needs to be checked out both audiologically and on the hearing aid analyzer.

HOW DO WE KNOW IF A CHILD IS HEARING A SOUND?

From the time of birth, infants give predictable responses to sounds that occur above their hearing thresholds (see Chapter 5). Hearing-impaired infants are no different. Parents of hearing-impaired infants need to be aware of the reflexive responses that hearing infants 0-5 months of age give to loud sounds and the learned responses that infants 6 months and older give to softer sounds. Parents can learn to keep tallies of responses until they feel comfortable differentiating between their child's chance turns to check out the environment that coincide with a sound, and his repeated glances up or head turns that are triggered by a sound. A child's response repertoire can be extensive and will change as he develops and as his listening skills increase. His responses to sound may include:

1. A change in ongoing behavior
   a. Cessation of vocalization
   b. Smiling
   c. Eye or head turns
   d. Crying
   e. Cessation of activity
2. Looking at the sound source
3. Reciprocity in babbling (babbling back and forth with an adult)
4. Rhythmic body movement in response to music
5. Pointing to ear
6. Imitation of sounds
7. Identification (point to, name)
   a. Of sound source
   b. Of speaker
   c. Of object named
8. Waiting for sound then acting on it, including conditioned response to sound (specifically taught)
9. Correct behavioral response to verbal stimulus
10. Spontaneous verbal response

As parents become more intrigued by the idea of detecting their child's responses to sound and as they grow more comfortable with their knowledge of their child's hearing loss, they become very sophisticated observers. Many times parents will report that they saw their child give a possible response to a sound, but indicate that they will need to see a response to that sound again before they write it down on their child's auditory record sheet.

When a newly identified hearing-impaired child has just started using hearing aids, IHR specialists spend time each session playing with vocalizations and with noisemaking toys and pointing out to the parents the types of responses their child is making to sound. Profoundly deaf children may respond only to a drum, to low frequency pure tones delivered through a stereo speaker in the room, and to speech delivered close to their hearing aids. Specialists show the parents how to reinforce the child's responses to environmental sounds and to voice with clapping, smiling, and touching. They demonstrate how noisemaking toys — and people — can be moved further away to check for the child's response to a somewhat softer sound. The specialist can show parents how they can lie on their stomachs on the floor, propped on their elbows, facing their child as he sits on the floor. In this position, parents are talking within two feet of the microphones of their child's hearing aids, an optimal distance for their child to hear their voices.

WHY DOES THE CHILD RESPOND TO SOME SOUNDS AND NOT TO OTHERS?

The data that parents and specialists need in order to answer this question can be found through a thorough understanding of a child's audiogram and of the acoustic properties of speech and environmental sounds. Excellent information about the intensity and frequency of speech and environmental sounds can be found in Ling and Ling (1978), Northern and Downs (1984), Calvert and Silverman (1975) and Boothroyd (1971). By relating the frequencies and intensities of a given sound to the child's audiogram, the specialist and parents will be able to see why a child responds to one sound and not another, why the child can tell the difference between some sounds and words and not others, or why the child can hear an /s/ at a distance of 1 foot, but cannot hear it at 3 feet. This information is essential to the specialist as she plans the stimuli, techniques, and environment to be used in activities promoting the child's auditory perceptual development.

Helping parents acquire the information they need to answer the three questions discussed above will prepare them to detect their child's auditory responses as these responses develop and increase. In acquiring this information, parents will also become better equipped to work on the next essential element of helping their child learn to hear, that of establishing an environment in which listening is possible and expected.

ESTABLISHING AN ENVIRONMENT
CONDUCIVE TO LISTENING

As parents acquire answers to the questions they have learned to ask, they will gain a great deal of information about creating a listening environment for their child. **Parents will learn that creating a listening environment has as much to do with their attitude about their child's ability to hear as it does with physical factors such as loudness, distance, and competing noise.** While it is important that specialists not promote unrealistic parental expectations regarding their child's hearing, it is also important that they instill the expectation that the child will be able to hear some sounds. One of the most unfortunate attitudes that we have observed in some teachers of the hearing impaired, an attitude that is passed along to parents, is that hearing-impaired children cannot hear.

Parent-infant specialists at IHR try instead to inculcate parents with the attitude of expecting that their child can hear a sound until proven otherwise. This is not to say that specialists promise parents that their child will learn to hear if only the parents will do X, Y, and Z. Instead, the specialists give parents information about the whole range of possibilities for their child's future use of his hearing, including the fact that there is a small percentage of children whose hearing loss is so profound that they hear very little even with powerful amplification.

IHR specialists have observed and recorded the auditory behaviors of many hearing-impaired infants during the first 2 to 3 years of their lives. We have learned that some children do not respond to sounds during their first year of hearing aid use, yet later are able to respond to and gain meaning from many sounds in their environment. We feel that, until complete information on the child's auditory abilities is obtained, it is wise to call the child's attention to all sounds that occur in his environment.

If, over time, repeated aided and unaided audiological evaluations and continuous observations of the child's lack of response even to loud sounds confirms that a child does not have useable hearing, this fact must be faced. The specialist who is working with the family of a profoundly deaf child will not want to promote false hopes for the parents once a sufficient amount of testing and observation have taken place to ascertain that the child does not hear. False hopes may include the desire for the child to acquire symbolic language through hearing alone. For that small percentage of children who cannot hear speech even with powerful amplification, expecting them to acquire symbolic language through hearing alone may preclude them from acquiring language at all.

When parents believe that it is possible for their hearing-impaired child to learn to listen to sound, they are motivated to use techniques that promote their child's acquisition of listening skills. These techniques, listed in the parent auditory section of *Parent-Infant Communication,* include gaining the child's auditory attention, limiting visual clues, placing the child in optimal positions relative to different sound sources, and introducing novel and interesting sounds into the child's play.

WHAT CAN A YOUNG CHILD LEARN TO LISTEN TO?

Essential to establishing an environment that is conducive to listening is the parents' awareness of the limitless number of auditory stimuli present in a child's environment which can be used to stimulate a child's interest in listening. Sources of auditory stimuli are listed below under two categories: vocal/verbal stimuli and non-vocal/non-verbal stimuli:

1. Vocal/Verbal Stimuli:
   a. Voice
   b. Male vs. female voice
   c. Child's own vocalizations
   d. Angry and cheerful voice
   e. Suprasegmentals of speech (intensity, pitch, duration, rate)
   f. Adult-produced animal and vehicle sounds and nonsense sounds
   g. Words
   h. Phrases
   i. Fingerplays, songs, rhymes
   j. Sentence patterns
   k. Experience stories
   l. Sequence of verbally described events
2. Non-Vocal/Non-Verbal Stimuli:
   a. Louder environmental sounds
   b. Noisemaking toys
   c. Sounds associated with basic needs
   d. Softer environmental sounds

As the child demonstrates first *awareness* and then *recognition* of sounds, parents can begin to vary environmental conditions to challenge the child with more difficult listening situations and, in so doing, gain valuable information about the child's hearing and listening capabilities. If the child is aware of a sound presented within three feet of him, is he aware of that sound presented at eight feet? at 15 feet? from the next room? from outside the house? Can the child still detect the sound with soft background noise (e.g., quiet conversation)? with louder background noise (e.g., television on)?

MAKING LISTENING FUN AND WORTHWHILE

Parents and specialists must keep in mind that young children with profound hearing losses, even when wearing amplification, have to work hard to attend to sound. While conversational speech falls well above auditory threshold for normally hearing children, it may occur at or just above the aided threshold of a child with a profound hearing loss. The deaf child has to attend to an extremely minimal signal, a difficult and tiring task. Some hearing-impaired children may hear some phonemes of speech quite well and other phonemes not at all with the result that they receive only a partial message through audition. These children need to expend considerable energy supplementing auditory information with visual information gained through speechreading in an attempt to get the whole verbal message.

The more adults can do to make listening an enticing, fun, and rewarding process, the more likely a child is to make the effort to make sense out of the whisper of sound that he is receiving. It will, for example, be extremely important not only that parents talk to their child, but that they say things the child is interested in and motivated to hear. None of us likes to hear nagging or commands. A young child is no different. He will be motivated to listen when parents talk to him about *him,* about his body parts, his toys, his world. He will be motivated to listen when parents express love, enjoyment, teasing; when they sing to him, play peek-a-boo, and "I'm gonna get-cha!" He is motivated to listen when he sees that his parents listen to his vocalizations, reinforce them with smiles, imitate what he says. Make it worth his while to concentrate on sound and he will!

PROVIDING APPROPRIATE PROPS

Along with acquiring information about hearing and the essential elements of an environment conducive to listening, parents need to make available to their child the props that will support his listening efforts. The most important of these props are properly fitted, well-functioning hearing aids which are on the child during all his waking hours. **Parents determine whether or not their child will develop his full listening potential in their decisions about when and how long their child wears his hearing aids.** Even while wearing aids, the information the child receives may be incomplete, muffled, and faint, especially for the profoundly impaired child. The "now I hear, now I don't" situation created when a young hearing-impaired child is wearing hearing aids only part of the time makes auditory learning even more difficult for the child. Hearing-impaired children require as much listening time as they can get in order to learn to make use of the reduced information they receive through audition.

Parents who decide that Johnny really doesn't need his hearing aids on while he's eating breakfast, after his afternoon nap, or during evening playtime are missing the point badly. **Johnny needs to hear all day long.** The inconvenience of taking 30 seconds to insert a hearing aid is nothing compared to the "inconvenience" their child will experience as a result of being unable to develop his full listening potential.

Other appropriate props that can be used in helping the child learn to listen include toys and play materials that produce sound, children and adults who babble and talk to the child, children's records, and children's television shows such as Sesame Street.

TEACHING SEQUENTIAL AUDITORY SKILLS

FOUR SEQUENTIAL STAGES OF AUDITORY PERCEPTION

It is helpful to think of the development of auditory skills as having two dimensions, breadth and depth. The hearing-impaired child not only learns to respond to a wider and wider range of sounds, but he also develops increasingly complex levels of response to each sound. D. Pollack (1985), Northcott (1977), A. Ling, (1977), Clark School for the Deaf (1971) and others have described these levels in a variety of ways, using a hierarchy of terms encompassing the following: awareness, detection, attention, discrimination, localization, recognition, reaction, imitation, attachment of meaning, and comprehension.

IHR specialists utilize the four-level hierarchy of auditory perception described by Clark School for the Deaf (1971). These steps are awareness (or detection), discrimination, recognition, and comprehension.

Auditory Awareness is the first level of auditory perception achieved by the infant. *Awareness means that the infant hears that a sound has occurred*; he detects or discovers the presence of a sound. Infants and young children demonstrate awareness of sound in a variety of ways. They may startle, blink their eyes, start crying, stop crying, move their limbs, still, turn their eyes or head, look in the direction from which the sound originated, point to their ear, or perform a learned task such as putting a piece on a stacking toy.

Auditory Discrimination, the second level in the hierarchy of auditory perception, *is the ability to determine whether or not one sound is different from another*. The child discriminates between sounds on the basis of rate, pitch, duration, intensity and, in the case of speech, individual phonemes. Young children demonstrate discrimination by selectively attending to the characteristic adult vocal patterns called "motherese" or "fatherese" but not attending to normal adult conversation. They also demonstrate auditory discrimination skills by starting to cry when an adult uses angry tones, but not when the adult speaks in pleasant tones.

Several investigators (DeCasper and Fifer, 1980; Condon and Sander, 1974; Demany, McKenzie, and Vurpillot, 1977; Spring and Dale, 1977) have demonstrated that neonates have the ability to discriminate several aspects of sound. DeCasper and Fifer (1980) demonstrated that at birth infants are able to discriminate the voice of their mother from other female voices. DeCasper (1984) conducted another study which suggested that newborns could identify the stories read to them before birth. The newborns whose mothers had repeatedly read them a Dr. Seuss story during the six weeks prior to their birth showed a preference for tapes of their mother reading the story they had heard before birth. DeCasper reported that "women who had never recited a story (to their unborn babies) delivered infants who had no preference for the Dr. Seuss stories."

Like normally hearing infants, the hearing-impaired infant or toddler who is wearing appropriate amplification can also learn to discriminate between many sounds during his first years of life even though he may not have access to the entire spectrum of sounds heard by the normally hearing child. The challenge posed for the specialist and parents is to observe carefully in order to detect behaviors which are indicative of the child's discrimination abilities.

The ability to discriminate between many sounds is dependent on having sufficient residual hearing across the frequency range. This is particularly true of the sounds of speech. Let's look, for example, at a child who has no hearing above 1000 Hz. This child will hear the first and second formants (peaks of energy) of the vowel /u/, which are centered around 300 Hz and 800 Hz, respectively. However, though he is able to hear the first formant of the vowel /i/, which is centered around 250 Hz, he cannot hear the second formant, centered around 2500 Hz. Since the first formant frequencies of /u/ and /i/ are similar, these two vowels may sound alike to the child. So, while *aware* of both vowels, the child does not have enough frequency-specific information to be able to *discriminate* one from the other. Ling and Ling (1978) state that, "Positive identification of all vowels demands hearing up to at least 2500-3000 Hz" (p. 74).

Discrimination can be a difficult level to observe or test for since it is demonstrated by the child responding to one sound or word and not responding to another, or by the child responding differently to two sounds. The child's ability to tell us that one environmental sound is different from another can be seen most easily when the child has achieved the next level in the hierarchy, recognition. However, a child who cannot discriminate between two sounds or words will not be able to recognize them correctly.

Auditory Recognition of sound is the third level of auditory perceptual development which parents work to teach their child. *Auditory recognition is the ability to identify the source of the sound, to point out or name what made the sound, or, in the case of speech, to attach the spoken message to the object or action it represents.* Recognition is an association of an environmental sound with its source or of a word with the object or event it represents. Auditory recognition requires that the child be able to discriminate or tell the difference among sounds.

Most hearing-impaired children have begun to recognize many sounds before they have the language facility to tell us if sounds are the same or not. Recognition, therefore, is easier for parents to teach than is discrimination. While parents learn that discrimination abilities are a prerequisite to recognition of sounds, recognition is the level they work on with their child.

Comprehension is the last level in the hierarchy of auditory perception. Comprehension means that *the child has attached meaning to the sounds or words heard.* The child not only recognizes words but understands what they mean. He not only knows the source of a sound but also knows the significance or meaning of the sound.

The two examples below describe how the child is likely to function at each of the levels of awareness, recognition, and comprehension.

Example 1: Environmental sound: telephone ring

Awareness: When the phone rings the child may cease play momentarily, look up, wrinkle his brow, then return to play.

Recognition: When the phone rings the child may point to the phone, thus *identifying* the source of the sound, or he may say/sign "telephone," thus *labelling* the source of the sound. (Note: We have found that in order to test for *discrimination* it is necessary that the child *recognize* at least one sound associated with one of two objects presented to him. For example, if he recognizes the ring of a telephone but has not learned that a toy whistle makes a whistling sound, he should point to the telephone when he hears a "ring" and do nothing when he hears the whistle. We then know that he hears the difference between the sounds even though he cannot identify the sources of both.)

Comprehension: When the phone rings the child pulls a chair over, climbs up on it, picks up the phone, and says, "Hello." The child understands that the ringing means that someone is there to say "hello" to. This act of comprehension does not imply that the child will be able to understand what the caller is saying, or to successfully carry on a conversation by telephone. However, the child knows that the ringing of the phone means that answering it is required.

Example 2: Speech: "It's time for your bath."

Awareness: When the parent utters this phrase, the child may cease his activity, and look up or around toward the speaker.

Recognition: When the parent utters this phrase the child may go to, or point to, the bathtub. He has recognized the word "bath," associating it with the bathtub. (Evidence of his ability to *discriminate* between words would occur if the child heard,

"It's time for the movie," and he did nothing, since the word
"movie" is not in his recognition vocabulary.)
Comprehension: When the parent utters the phrase, "It's time
for your bath," the child goes to the bathroom, takes his
clothes off, and waits to be helped into the tub. He understands
the meaning of the phrase.

In learning to be aware of, discriminate, recognize, and comprehend
speech, hearing-impaired children gain immense benefit from the fact that
spoken communication occurs by combining a number of words. People do
not ordinarily communicate in single word utterances. Hearing-impaired
children, like normally hearing children, gain meaning from connected
language. The phrase, "Where's your shoe?," differs from the phrase, "Go
get your coat," in length, rhythm, and pattern of intonation. All of these
suprasegmental aspects of speech assist the child in deriving meaning from
what he hears. If, on the other hand, an adult simply says "shoe" or
"coat" to the child, the amount of information he has from which to derive
meaning is considerably less. It is important that the child receive as much
auditory information as possible to help him decode language. Talking to
him in short sentences, rather than in single words, is crucial.

SEQUENCE OF AUDITORY DEVELOPMENT OBJECTIVES

As stated earlier, the child will apply this hierarchy of auditory perceptual
skills — awareness, discrimination, recognition, and comprehension — to
the wide range of sounds to which he is exposed, including speech.
Specialists and parents will want to present auditory stimuli to the child in a
sequence that enables the child to achieve new skills by building on already
acquired skills. A developmental sequence of auditory perceptual skills is
presented in *Parent-Infant Communication* in the infant Auditory Objectives section. Activities for teaching each objective appear in the Activities
section. The auditory objectives incorporate both verbal and non-verbal
stimuli.

Specialists and parents generally work on two or three auditory objectives
at any given time through their interaction with the child in daily activities
and play. Since all children do not acquire the skills defined in the objectives
in exactly the same order, it is important not to be rigid in fixating on the acquisition of one objective before stimuli from the next is presented. Adults
must take care, however, not to attempt to teach a skill that requires prerequisite skills which the child has not yet attained. This is particularly true in
the auditory section where the eager teacher or parent may present an activity to the child in which he is asked to point to the animal that says, "meow"
(a *recognition* task) before they have exposed the child to many activities in
which the sound "meow" has been paired with the cat. The adult must also
have ascertained that the child is *aware* of the adult-produced sound

"meow" and that the child can *discriminate* that sound from other sounds in the environment before they test him for recognition of the sound.

Other descriptions of auditory development and suggestions for teaching auditory skills can be found in D. Pollack (1985), Northcott (1980), and Cole and Paterson (1984).

In teaching auditory objectives it is important to realize that listening does not occur as an isolated event for a child. Listening is part of all interaction, whether it be a daily activity such as changing diapers or a game such as "peek-a-boo." Any time you are producing sound in your interactions with the child, you are promoting auditory development *if* you have provided the props and the environment that enable the child to hear. Auditory skills can be taught constantly, during all of the child's waking hours, if you have assured that the child has the best possible opportunity to hear.

In addition to the informal auditory learning that takes place all day long, acquisition of auditory skills can be promoted by planning specific activities and games that focus on sound detection, discrimination, recognition, and comprehension. Having determined which auditory objectives the child has achieved, the specialist and parent can select the next objectives in sequence as the basis of auditory stimulation for the child.

Later objectives for infants in the sequence of auditory perceptual development found in *Parent-Infant Communication* focus on discrimination, recognition, and comprehension of speech. Many severely and profoundly hearing-impaired children who have attended IHR have graduated at the age of four years having achieved all of the auditory objectives in *Parent-Infant Communication*. These children are "auditory learners" in spite of their significantly reduced hearing thresholds. They are children who were identified early as hearing-impaired, on whom well-functioning hearing aids were regularly placed by their parents, and for whom listening was a pleasurable and meaningful activity that took place throughout the day.

TEACHING TWO SPECIFIC SKILLS WHICH PROMOTE LISTENING

The specialist and parents can teach the infant and young child two "games" which will help him focus on auditory stimuli and give a response to them when they occur. These techniques, called conditioned orienting response and conditioned response to sound, provide the specialist and parents with means of directing the child's attention to sound and with means to do an informal evaluation to determine what sounds the child is aware of at the time.

CONDITIONED ORIENTING RESPONSE

Infants four months and older can be taught to make an eye-shift or turn their head toward a brightly-lighted toy when a sound stimulus is presented. This behavioral conditioning process works because the infant associates or pairs the appearance of the brightly lighted toy with the presence of a sound. The infant hears the sound (the stimulus), and gives a response (the eye shift or head turn) because of the attraction of the brightly lighted toy (the reinforcer). Specialists at IHR begin teaching conditioned orienting response with the infant seated on the parent's lap or in an infant seat. We use a sound stimulus that we know the infant can hear, or hear and feel if the infant seems to respond only to sounds with a vibratory component. Beginning stimuli that we use are:

1. Low frequency (125, 250, or 500 Hz) pure tones delivered through sound field speakers at loud levels (40-90 dB depending on the frequency used).
2. Several rapid beats on a large drum.
3. A low frequency vocalization such as a sustained /o/.
4. Any other vocalization, noisemaker, or environmental sound to which we have observed the infant consistently responding.

One of the most effective visual reinforcers we have used is a large (10 inch) orange plastic Halloween jack-o-lantern. We cut a hole out of the bottom and placed it over a 40 watt light bulb which is mounted on a block with a cord leading to an external switch which we can push to turn the light on and off.

It works best for us to have the parent seated in front of the baby right next to the primary visual reinforcer, the intermittantly lighted toy. As the child learns to look to the toy in response to hearing the auditory stimulus, the parent becomes the secondary social reinforcer, applauding and smiling as the child looks at the lighted toy. This secondary reinforcement is very important since, as the child gets older, the reactions of his parents become extremely rewarding to him and have powerful impact in shaping his behaviors.

Step One in teaching a conditioned orienting response is to **pair the auditory stimulus with the visual reinforcer.** The visual reinforcer is placed in front of the infant while the auditory stimulus is presented outside of the infant's range of vision. (It is critical that the child is unable to see any movement that may be required to activate the auditory stimulus so that the adults can be certain that the child is responding to sound and not to movement.) *In the first step, the auditory stimulus and the visual reinforcer are presented simultaneously.* The toy is kept lighted for as long as the sound is presented and is turned off when the sound stops. After each presentation there is an interval of silence ranging from 5-15 seconds in duration. During this interval, the infant's visual attention may wander from the now unlighted toy. This is fine. After a period of silence the auditory stimulus

Conditioned orienting response. This 14-month-old turns to the pumpkin when he hears a pure tone delivered through sound field speakers. The pumpkin is lighted to reinforce the child's response.

and visual reinforcer are again presented simultaneously.

Step Two begins after the auditory stimulus and visual reinforcer have been presented simultaneously 5-10 times (the number of presentations will vary according to the infant's age and developmental level). **In the second step, there is a slight delay between the presentation of the auditory stimulus and the lighting of the toy which is still placed in front of the infant.** Specialist and parents will now make sure that the infant's attention is drawn away from the toy in the interval between presentations. With very young infants this can be accomplished by having the parent move a block or small toy into the infant's visual field and then move it slowly to the side as the infant follows it with his eyes. An older child (7-10 months) may require a bit more interesting toy to pull his attention away from the toy that is lighted intermittently. Once the infant's attention is drawn away, the specialist presents the auditory stimulus and both specialist and parent watch to see if the infant's eyes go back to the visual reinforcer. *As soon as the infant looks to the visual reinforcer, the light is turned on.* The auditory stimulus is maintained as the toy is lighted for 2-3 seconds, then the presentation of the sound is stopped and the light is turned off simultaneously. If the infant does not look to the visual reinforcer within 3-4 seconds of the onset of the auditory stimulus, three things should happen:

1. The specialist continues to present the auditory stimulus.
2. The parent drops the distracting toy out of sight.
3. The specialist begins to flash the light in the toy until the infant looks.

This process is repeated until the infant looks at the visual reinforcer immediately after the onset of the auditory stimulus. If, after 8-10 trials, the infant does not learn to turn his attention to the visual reinforcer following the onset of the auditory stimulus, the specialist may choose to cease the activity and plan to come back to it in the next session, using a louder or more vibratory stimulus.

Step Three is initiated when the infant is reliably looking to the visual reinforcer following the onset of the auditory stimulus. **Step three involves moving the visual reinforcer to one side so that the child is required to make an even more definite eye shift or head turn toward the visual reinforcer following the onset of the auditory stimulus.**

When the child has demonstrated repeatable and reliable responses to the initial auditory stimulus, the specialist can begin to vary the stimuli presented, e.g., decrease the loudness of the pure tone, present another frequency, or change to voiced stimuli. It may be necessary to repeat steps one and two for the new stimuli presented. If, after going through steps one and two, the infant does not give the same reliable turns to the visual reinforcer as were seen with the first auditory stimulus, the specialist and parent may conclude that the new stimulus is not audible to the child. Thus, *conditioned orienting response can be used as a tool to determine informally what pure tones, speech, and environmental sounds the child is able to detect.* This procedure is also excellent training for the child who will be participating in Visual Reinforcement Audiometry (VRA) when formal audiological evaluation is conducted. VRA also requires that the child pair a visual reinforcer with an auditory stimulus; however, the format for conducting a valid VRA assessment is formalized and requires that specific procedures be followed (Thompson and Wilson, 1984).

CONDITIONED RESPONSE TO SOUND

As the child approaches two years of age, the process of teaching him to give a conditioned response to sound can begin. Conditioned response to sound is the technique used when the child participates in play audiometry during audiometric assessment. When giving a conditioned response to sound, the child is performing a specified action, e.g., putting a ring on a stick, when he hears an auditory stimulus. Some bright children can learn this task at 17-18 months of age. Two years is the average age at which children learn this task, though some children have difficulty learning the task or being consistent and reliable until they are 2½.

Like the conditioned orienting response, this listening behavior is highly structured and teaches the child to listen actively for sounds. The well-trained two year old can respond to sounds which are at or very close to his auditory thresholds.

The length of time a child can attend to the conditioned response task and the number of responses he can give before he poops out varies with each individual. When working with 18 to 30 month-old children, the resourceful specialist will have a number of toys at hand that each require only 5-8 responses before they are completed. Frequently changing the toy means that the child gets to perform new tasks, a procedure that substantially increases his attention span for the activity. It is not wise to give the young child a 100-hole form board and expect him to stick with it for the duration of testing! As children grow older, they will be able to complete toys that require more responses, expecially when the toy is motivating. Putting marbles into the hole in the top of a small box is one of the activities we have found most motivating for the 2½ year old and older child.

The specialist's *goal* in teaching a child to give a conditioned response to sound is to gain information about the child's auditory thresholds at each frequency represented on the audiogram. The *challenge* in teaching a child to give a conditioned response to sound lies in finding activities for the child that motivate him to play the game. The child must want to play the games long enough for the specialist and audiologist to gain the audiometric information they need to set appropriate habilitation goals and make appropriate hearing aid decisions. Two year olds are not polite when they are bored with an activity. It is up to the specialist to entice the child into playing conditioned response games by providing him with motivating and reinforcing activities.

STEPS IN TEACHING THE CHILD TO GIVE A CONDITIONED RESPONSE TO SOUND

Specialists follow the steps below in teaching a young hearing-impaired child to give a conditioned response to sound.

1. Place the child, wearing his hearing aids, in a seated situation in which his movement can be controlled, if necessary. A high chair may be appropriate for wriggling two-year olds; relaxed or compliant toddlers do well at a small table and chair.

2. The specialist must have comfortable access to the child, to the equipment that will be used to present the auditory stimuli, and to the toys that will be used. (After the child has learned this skill, the specialist may also want paper accessible on which to record the child's responses.)

3. Have an appropriate selection of toys for the child to use in giving a response. At IHR we have a number of toys that are used *only* for conditioned response games. These toys are not given to the child for "free play" so that he is not confused by being able to play with them "his" way one time and having to use them "our" way the next time.

Conditioned response to sound. This two-year-old has learned to wait until she hears the pure tone, delivered through sound field speakers, before she puts the ring on the stick.

The child's response is met with enthusiasm from father and specialist.

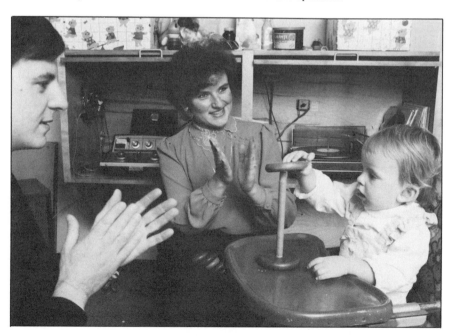

4. Prepare to present stimuli for which you are certain that at least *two* of the three following elements are available to the child: auditory, visual, tactile. (Very profoundly deaf children may first learn this task as a conditioned response to a visual or tactile event, and even when older, may be able to respond only to very loud sounds that have a vibratory component.)

5. Place in front of the child the part of the toy into or onto which he will put pieces, e.g., the stick on a stand. Place one of the pieces, e.g., a ring, into the child's hand and hold his hand around the ring. Move the child's hand (holding the ring) up to his cheek and hold it there until the stimulus is presented.

6. Present the stimulus, e.g., ring a cowbell or depress the lever on the audiometer, for 1-2 seconds. (Remember — the specialist must know that the child can perceive two of three elements of this stimuli: auditory, visual, tactile.)

7. Immediately following the onset of the stimulus, guide the child's hand in the desired response, e.g., help him put the ring on the stick.

8. Provide social reinforcement — clapping, smiling, patting his arm — immediately following completion of the response.

9. The specialist repeats this procedure until she can feel the child begin to move his hand toward the stick following the onset of the stimulus.

   If, after 6-8 trials, the specialist does not feel the child begin to initiate the movement toward the stick, stop the activity, smiling and clapping in appreciation for his willingness to participate. Repeat the activity, using the same toy, during the next two sessions. Use a louder, more vibratory or more visible stimulus, if possible. Keep the activity short. If, by the end of the third session, the child is not initiating movement on his own in response to the stimulus, he is not developmentally ready to learn this skill. Continue with other auditory stimulation activities and come back to teaching conditioned response to sound in a month or two.

10. When the child begins to move his hand toward the stick on his own, remove your hand from his, but keep it in the vicinity of his cheek so that you can halt any tendency he may have to put the ring on the stick without waiting for the stimulus. If child starts movement before the stimulus is presented, gently take his hand, move it back to his cheek, say, "Wait!" Hold the child's hand until the stimulus is presented, then release his hand and let him put the ring on the stick.

11. Once the child is responding reliably using at least two of three cues (audition, vision, taction), remove visual or tactile cues and present auditory stimuli alone, repeating the original method of

holding child's hand at his cheek.

12. When the child is consistently giving the appropriate response to the auditory stimuli, begin to decrease the volume of the signal to give the child practice in listening for softer sounds. If an audiometer and sound field speakers are used, the specialist can give the child practice in listening for pure tones across the frequency range. She can also remove the child's hearing aids and place pediatric earphones on the child to give him practice in listening for tones through earphones.

13. Every time a parameter in the conditioned response game is changed, the specialist should be prepared to assist the child in giving the first 1-2 responses. If a usually reliable child does not respond with help during the first two trials when a parameter is changed — e.g., the volume is decreased or a higher frequency tone is presented — quickly change back to a volume level or frequency at which the child has previously responded. The specialist must take care not to help the child continue to "respond" to something he cannot hear. Always end the conditioned response activity with a stimulus that you know the child can hear and respond to.

14. Stop the activity before the child does!

15. Record responses that the child gave to the stimuli presented.

WARNING: In teaching a child to give a conditioned response to sound, the specialist is not following the child's interest. This activity is one of few in which children at IHR are required to participate on *our* terms. Because the child's ability to give a conditioned response to sound enables the specialist and audiologist to continue to gain information about his auditory thresholds after he is no longer interested in participating in VRA activities, it is an essential skill for the child to acquire. Given the specialist's desire to teach the child this task and its rules and the two year old's desire to assert his newly found autonomy, the possibility for conflict is evident! It is sometimes the case that while teaching the child to give a conditioned response to sound IHR specialists find it necessary to utilize some behavior management strategies for the first time.

If, when the conditioned response game is introduced, the specialist detects resistance from the child — e.g., he resists her holding his hand at his cheek even after she has hurried through 2-3 responses to show him how much fun it is to put the ring on the stick — the specialist terminates the activity. She makes certain that she puts the toy used in the conditioned response game out of the child's reach so that he cannot play with it and gives the child another toy to play with while she talks to the parent(s). The specialist must make a judgment call at this point: Is the child's resistance a result of "can't do" because of immaturity, or "won't do?" If the former, the specialist will want to wait several weeks, then try the activity again. If the specialist feels that the child *is* ready to learn the task but is resisting for other reasons, she will want to reintroduce the task in a different way at the next lesson.

The next time the family comes in, the specialist selects a new toy, and begins "teaching" the parent to give a conditioned response to sound. She helps the parent give the appropriate response to the sound and lavishes attention and praise on him/her following the response. When the child edges toward the parent, the specialist lets him have a turn, then gives the parent a turn again, following all responses with praise. If the child wants to sit on the parent's lap, fine. The specialist is willing to do whatever is needed to entice the child into the task but she *does not* let him change the required response. Once the child has given three or four appropriate responses, the specialist terminates the game, leaving the child wanting more (that old theater adage!)

When the specialist and parents know that the child can do the task, the child's refusal to participate is handled in the same way as the adults have decided to handle any other of the child's non-compliant behaviors (see Chapter 14). In carrying out a behavior change program which is directed at the child's non-compliance in learning or participating in the conditioned response task, the parents and specialist will want to agree on a consequence to the child's non-compliance and reinforce heavily his cooperative behaviors.

Throughout any behavior management procedure, it is essential that the specialist acknowledge the parents' discomfort or embarrassment and reassure them that, if this situation is handled well, further episodes of non-compliance during this task will be rare. The child is testing the waters, asking, "Who's boss here?" If it turns out that he is, the effectiveness of habilitation is seriously diminished. Children do not always know best. They need guidance in learning to participate, even when they do not know why. Yet it is critical that the guidance is provided in a way that keeps the child's self-esteem intact. He will be angry when he is ignored or restrained. However, these behavior-specific consequences do not say to him, "You are no good," but instead, "These behaviors are not acceptable." There is an importance difference.

Once past any behavioral rough spots that may be caused by teaching the child to give a conditioned response to sound, the use of this stimulus-response procedure can be expanded to a variety of listening games: "Wake-up" when you hear the alarm clock; jump out of the box when you hear the drum; roll the car down the ramp when you hear "Go!"; jump off a platform when you hear "Jump!" All of these games help the child focus his attention on auditory stimuli, an important skill in the development of auditory perceptual skills.

THE ROLE OF THE AUDITORY FEEDBACK MECHANISM
IN THE INFANT'S DEVELOPMENT OF SPOKEN LANGUAGE

Audition plays a significant role in the infant's development of spoken language. One way in which audition is important in this process is the function provided by the auditory feedback mechanism. What is the auditory feedback mechanism? It is the process by which the infant receives auditory information about the vocal sounds he makes. His auditory feedback provides him with information about the characteristics of his vocalizations: their pitch, loudness, duration, and rhythm; about the differences between consonants; and about how co-articulation of consonants affects their production and their sounds. Using auditory feedback, the infant can experiment by varying these elements of his vocalizations while, at the same time, providing himself with endless hours of entertainment. Just as the sound of the voices of others is reinforcing to the child, the sound of his own voice is pleasurable and stimulates him to produce more vocalizations. The child's voice is produced only inches from the microphone of his hearing aids, an optimal distance for his own reception of sound.

Auditory feedback is as important — if not more so — to the child with hearing loss as it is to the child with normal hearing. It serves three major functions for him. First, while listening to his own voice, the infant strengthens his awareness of the relationship between the sound of his vocalizations and the way it feels to produce them (D. Pollack, 1984). Second, the auditory feedback mechanism allows the child to practice and to refine his own vocal productions. He can monitor his phoneme production as well as pitch, intensity, rhythm, and duration. Third, by listening to his own vocal productions and how they compare with those of others around him, the child experiences the joy of knowing that he can do what they do.

The auditory feedback mechanism begins to function very early. By the age of three months, behavioral changes are observed in infants with normal hearing which indicates their seeming delight in the sound of their own voices (D. Pollack, 1985). Vocalization is largely reflexive in the early months of a baby's life, so that babies do not *need* to hear the sound of their voice in order to vocalize. Between six and nine months their self-soliloquy (talking to themselves) increases. It is during this period that an infant who does not hear his own voice (has no auditory feedback) may decrease the self-soliloquy (Mavilya, 1969).

Our sense of urgency in fitting amplification on children with hearing losses before the age of six months stems from the desire to take advantage of children's potent, early period of reflexive babbling as well as their built-in mechanism for using auditory feedback to hear their own voices. The hearing-impaired four-month-old baby who is wearing amplification and who is still cooing reflexively is likely to hear and be reinforced by his own vocalizations (particularly the lower frequencies) and can approximate the sequence of vocal development followed by babies of his age who hear nor-

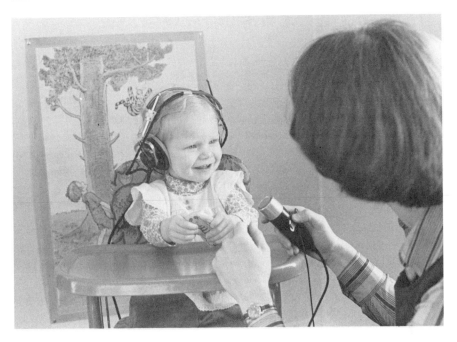

Babies love hearing their own voices!

mally. The hearing-impaired four-month-old baby who is not fitted with amplification does not benefit from the reinforcement to continue vocalizing that would occur if he were able to hear the sound of his own voice.

An additional value of early hearing aid fitting and the infant's resultant ability to hear some of the sounds he makes is the effect on the physical development of auditory mechanisms in the brain. During the first year of an infant's life, the cortex is growing rapidly. Full development of the auditory centers of the brain relies on sensory stimulation (sound) during these early months (see Chapter 4). The infant who, wearing amplification, vocalizes and "plays with sounds," hears his own voice and provides critical auditory stimulation to his brain. Parent-infant specialists at IHR believe that the high level of auditory skill development achieved by many children who are amplified very early in life may be attributed to more complete cortical development. This belief is supported both by our experience with hearing-impaired children and by studies (Ruben and Rapin, 1980) which suggest that lack of auditory input during a critical period of cortical development results in reduced auditory perceptual capabilities.

LEARNING TO LISTEN TAKES TIME

It is important to remain cognizant of the range of variability in auditory skills in children with similar audiograms and of the length of listening time some children require before they let us know they hear. Many profoundly deaf children show indications of their auditory aptitude right from the beginning of habilitation. IHR specialists have also worked with several profoundly deaf children who were fitted with hearing aids within the first year of life but who did not demonstrate consistent and reliable responses to voice and environmental sounds until age 2½-3½. Had specialists and parents given up and ceased stimulation activities because these children did not seem to hear, the children may not have developed the detection and beginning recognition skills they had acquired by graduation from IHR. The need for consistent and repeated stimulation in the face of apparent lack of response is particularly necessary for children with handicapping conditions in addition to hearing loss. The case histories of two IHR graduates are related here since these stories depict two different types of challenges that the parent-infant specialist may encounter while working toward developing an infant's auditory perceptual skills.

CHRIS: A PROFOUND HEARING LOSS AND SLOW DEVELOPMENT

Chris was born with a lung disease that necessitated his being in the hospital neonatal intensive care unit for the first three months of his life. During his first three years, Chris suffered from asthma attacks and was hospitalized several times for treatment of this condition. Chris's first auditory assessment, conducted when he was almost four months old, revealed responses to noisemakers, warbled pure tones, and narrow band noise at levels considered within normal limits for a child his age. Upon retest at age nine months, however, Chris did not respond to noisemakers or to pure tones except at 250 Hz and 2000 Hz at the limits of the audiometric equipment.

Chris and his family enrolled in the program of auditory and language habilitation at IHR when he was ten months old. At enrollment, Chris was fitted with two loaner hearing aids which provided approximately 53 dB HF average gain at use level. When tested wearing these aids, Chris demonstrated speech awareness at 60 dB HL and responses to the frequencies between 250-750 Hz at 55-100 dB HL. No responses were observed to frequencies above 750 Hz (Figure 9). After ten months of binaural hearing aid use, Chris was consistently demonstrating awareness of only a few loud, low-frequency sounds such as a drum and a door slam.

In his second year of enrollment at IHR, during which he had trial-use

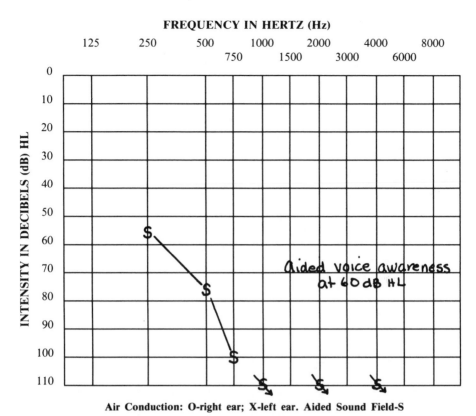

FREQUENCY IN HERTZ (Hz)

FIGURE 9. Chris' audiogram at age 17 months during his first year of enrollment at Infant Hearing Resource. Chris was wearing bilateral body aids (on trial-use basis) which provided 53 dB HF average gain at use level. He gave no responses to pure tones at the limits of the equipment while unaided.

periods with two additional sets of loaner aids, his responsiveness to sound increased very little. Developmental screening conducted using the "Early Intervention Developmental Profile" — EIDP — (Schafer, et al., 1985-86) revealed that Chris was operating several months below age level in most categories and twelve months below age level in cognitive skills.

At the beginning of his third and final year of enrollment, Chris was still being evaluated using loaner aids. About half-way through the year, when Chris was just over three years old and had been wearing high gain aids for more than two years, he finally began to demonstrate auditory skills beyond the level of awareness. He began to discriminate between fast and slow recorded music and between louder enviromental sounds. He also caught on to the concept of using his voice in response to the request, "Use your voice." His vocalizations changed from a great deal of lip-smacking to increased production of vowels, imitation of the vowels [u], [a], and [o], and imitations of the patterns [æ] versus [æ - æ - æ]. When tested at the end of the year with the aids which had been recommended for purchase, Chris showed aided awareness of voice at 35 dB and aided thresholds at 45 dB HL between 250-2000 Hz (Figure 10).

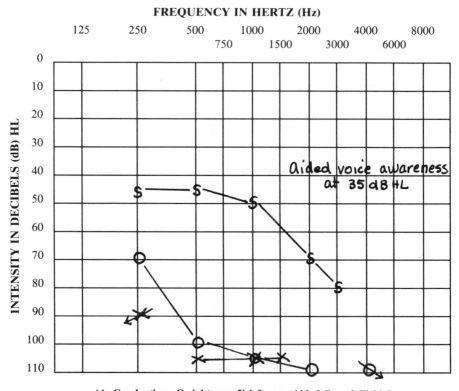

FREQUENCY IN HERTZ (Hz)

FIGURE 10. Chris' audiogram at age 3 years, 8 months, when he graduated from Infant Hearing Resource. He was wearing the binaural ear-level aids which had been recommended for purchase. These aids were adjusted to provide 59 dB HF average gain at use level.

Like the earlier screening with the EIDP, developmental screening conducted when Chris was 40 months old showed the same 12-month lag in cognitive development and lesser delays in other areas. As was true of all areas of his development, Chris's acquisition of auditory skills was slow. It took him a long time to learn to become aware of, discriminate, and recognize the auditory information he received. However, it was apparent from his ability to imitate some vowels that Chris does hear differences in speech sounds, and we believe that this ability to discriminate will continue to develop as he matures. Had we looked at his performance with aids after one year of use and said, "These are not helping. Let's not bother with aids," Chris would not have acquired the skills that he did.

Children whose overall development is delayed are likely to demonstrate slow acquisition of auditory skills. It is important not to give up on these children too soon!

DELILAH: HER PARENTS THOUGHT SHE COULD NOT HEAR

Delilah is the second child of hearing-impaired parents, both of whom use hearing aids. When each of their girls was born, Judy and Ross tested her hearing informally at the hospital and at home. Their assessments of their children's levels of responsiveness to sound were quite accurate. When the older girl was enrolled at IHR at age four months, Judy and Ross reported that she responded to Ross's voice at close range, to squeak toys close to her ear, and to the dog's bark. They believed strongly that this older girl had a great deal of usable hearing and they were strong advocates of her use of hearing aids and of her use of speech in combination with signed language.

By contrast, when Delilah's hearing was first tested formally at age four months, Judy and Ross told the audiologist and parent-infant specialist that Delilah, unlike her older sister, was not responding to any sounds at home. During her first audiologic test, Delilah gave reflexive responses to voice at 100 dB. Her sister, at the same age, had responded to voice at 65 dB. The parents' observation that Delilah's hearing loss was greater than that of her sister was confirmed by these test results.

Delilah was fitted with ear-level hearing aids on a trial-use basis at age five months. During Delilah's first year of habilitation at IHR, Judy and Ross were not as consistent in placing the aids on her as they had been with her older sister. Since Delilah responded less, the parents felt that her ability to hear was limited and that the hearing aids were not making any difference. They cited teething, fears that the aids would make Delilah's ears stick out, and the output of the aids being set too high/too low as their reasons for not putting the aids on Delilah.

The parent-infant specialist working with the family was in a delicate position. Audiological tests subsequent to the initial test showed that, while wearing hearing aids, Delilah was aware of voice at 45-50 dB HL and was responding to the frequencies 250-4000 Hz at levels between 35-70 dB. The specialist was certain that Delilah had residual hearing that would be of use to her in learning to understand and use spoken communication. She also observed that Delilah was demonstrating awareness of sounds during sessions. She felt it was important that Delilah have the opportunity to develop her auditory perceptual skills through consistent hearing aid use. However, the specialist also knew that she needed to listen to Judy and Ross. She described her interactions with the parents in the following words:

"Judy and Ross reported that they felt that Delilah was deaf while their older daughter was hard-of-hearing. Because of this perceived difference in their children's abilities to hear, their expectations for Delilah were very different from their expectations for their older daughter. Even when Delilah was very young, they related that they were using more signed language and less spoken language with her. They mentioned their plans to have Delilah attend the State School for the Deaf while their older daughter was in the local public school program for hearing-impaired children.

In habilitation sessions, I worked mostly on listening and vocal/speech activities because I knew that the parents were doing an excellent job with language stimulation. I set up many opportunities in which Delilah could practice listening to and responding to sounds and we talked about the responses to sound that we saw her making. Throughout our sessions, I listened to Judy and Ross and acknowledged their expertise about hearing loss and the validity of their opinions. Then I would state clearly my observations that Delilah was responding to sounds and my feelings that it was too early to make a decision that hearing aids would not be of benefit to Delilah.''

When a second set of trial-use aids were placed, Judy and Ross began to keep the aids on Delilah more consistently and began reporting to the specialist responses Delilah was making to sounds at home. During the next year, Delilah wore and was tested with three different sets of trial-use aids. As the audiologist and specialist obtained more aided and unaided information about Delilah's hearing thresholds, Ross and Judy's views about her ability to use hearing began to shift. They became more committed to Delilah's use of hearing aids and began to take pride in her frequent responsiveness to sounds.

In the final audiological test performed prior to Delilah's graduation from IHR, Delilah demonstrated aided awareness of voice at 35 dB HL and aided scores from 250-4000 Hz at levels of 25-45 dB HL (Figure 11). Comparisons of her unaided scores at age three years, five months with her sister's audiogram at age three years, two months revealed that Delilah's better ear average at 500, 1000, 2000 and 4000 Hz was 96 dB, while her sister's better ear average at these same frequencies was 88 dB, a difference of 8 dB. It is true that the older sister has more residual hearing available to her. At high levels of intensity a difference of 8 dB is a large difference in sound pressure level. It is also true that Delilah has residual hearing that will continue to be useful to her in her acquisition of listening and speech skills.

The parent-infant specialist who worked with Judy, Ross, and Delilah summed up this long-term conflict that was resolved in a satisfying way by saying, "I feel that my acceptance of their perspective and my honesty about my own views helped to keep our communication open. I did not force them to agree with me, nor did I necessarily agree with them. However, we listened to each other." Delilah left IHR to attend the same public school program in which her older sister was enrolled.

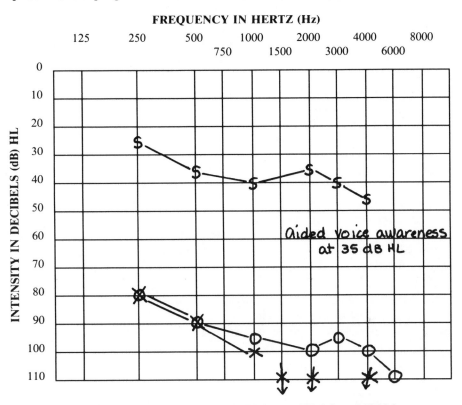

Air Conduction: O-right ear; X-left ear. Aided Sound Field-S

FIGURE 11.   Delilah's final audiogram at age 3 years, 5 months when she graduated from Infant Hearing Resource. She was wearing binaural ear-level hearing aids adjusted to provide 58 dB HF average gain at use level.

SUMMARY

It bears repeating that one of the most significant factors affecting the child's success in acquiring listening skills is the *attitude* held by the parents and specialist that the child can gain meaning from sound, regardless of the degree of his hearing loss. It may be true that for a child with no measurable unaided hearing, the information gained through the auditory channel may be so minimal that he may choose at some point not to wear hearing aids on a regular basis. *The point is, parents and specialists cannot make that decision for an infant.* If, after early placement of aids and consistent years of use, a hearing-impaired child makes the decision not to use hearing aids, that is his right. However, it is the experience of the specialists at IHR that for every IHR graduate who later eschews regular hearing aid use, 10-12 of his hearing-impaired peers rely on their hearing aids for everyday use.

Parents can acquire the information and skills they need to help their child learn to hear. They can do this by using a diagnostic teaching approach, by asking the right questions, by establishing an environment conducive to listening, and by teaching their child a sequential series of auditory objectives such as the sequence found in the curriculum, *Parent-Infant Communication.* Two teaching activities that promote the child's development of listening skills and facilitate the acquisition of information about his auditory thresholds are conditioned orienting response and giving a conditioned response to sound. Finally, a function of hearing that figures prominently in the child's acquisition of spoken language is his auditory feedback mechanism. Early identification and amplification permit the hearing-impaired infant to develop maximum use of this mechanism and of all of the other elements involved in good auditory perceptual skills.

CHAPTER 18

INFANT LANGUAGE ACQUISITION: IHR PHILOSOPHY AND GOALS

Goals and Philosophy

Choosing Communication Mode or Modes

In the next five chapters we discuss infant language acquisition. Chapter 19 deals with the role that cognitive development plays in the infant's acquisition of symbolic language. Chapter 20 addresses the significance of the infant's presymbolic communication system. Chapter 21 discusses parent behaviors that promote the infant's acquisition of symbolic language. Chapter 22 describes the IHR program for infant vocal and speech development. Chapter 23 describes the IHR program of teaching parents to use manually-coded English in combination with their spoken communication.

In this chapter we set the stage for these topics by outlining the goals and philosophy of the IHR program of infant language development. We also broach those scintillating topics that raise the blood pressure of educators of the hearing-impaired world-wide: choosing a communication mode and choosing a language system to use in communicating with, and thereby teaching language to, children with hearing loss.

GOALS AND PHILOSOPHY

The attainment of language competence is one of the major challenges faced by a deaf child. A normally-hearing infant is surrounded by language which is accessible to him through audition. His ability to hear and process language leads to his gradual acquisition of the symbolic language system used in his society. The child with hearing loss, on the other hand, does not generally have access to a complete language system. Hearing-impaired infants whose hearing-impaired parents use signed language have access to a visual symbolic language system and they *do* acquire symbolic language in ways similar to acquisition of spoken language by hearing children. In the United States, however, only 10% of deaf children have deaf parents (Roberts, 1979).

Most hearing-impaired children do not have access to a complete auditory or visual model of language from the time of birth or onset of hearing loss and will not acquire symbolic language without structured, systematic assistance. The timing, quality, and quantity of this assistance are critical. The age at which the child is identified and appropriate amplification is placed, the degree to which the child is able to use his aided residual hearing, and the accessibility and completeness of the symbolic language model to which he is exposed are all factors which affect the hearing-impaired child's acquisition of symbolic language. Most hearing-impaired children, even while wearing hearing aids, receive an incomplete representation of language through partial hearing and speechreading. It is not surprising that studies of hearing-impaired children's understanding and use of the English language reveal significant deficits. Quigley, Steinkamp, Power, and Jones (1978) stated that, "Few hearing-impaired children ever acquire even an adequate knowledge, let alone mastery, of standard English; and this affects all other aspects of their education."

Furth (1966) reported that only 12% of the hearing-impaired children ages 15.5 to 16.5 tested using the Metropolitan Achievement Test, Elementary Level, Form B, were reading at or above a grade level of 4.9, a level he described as a minimal functional level of literacy. The Gallaudet Research Institute's 1982-83 Annual Survey of Hearing Impaired Children and Youth revealed that the median achievement levels in reading comprehension barely exceeded 3.0 grade equivalent for the oldest children in the survey, who were 15-18 years of age (*The Endeavor*, 1985). Mid-fourth grade level is considered newspaper literacy level. Yoshinaga-Itano and Snyder (1985) found that in the 20 year span between 1958-1978, there was no appreciable difference in reading achievement of hearing-impaired children, "despite increased knowledge of language development, early childhood education, the introduction of sign language and oral/auditory training to the educational curriculum, increased professional staff, and individualized instruction" (p. 75). These investigators point out that the average reading achievement of children ages 10.5–11.5 was 2.5 grade equivalent and of children ages 15.5–16.5, 3.5 grade equivalent, only one year advancement in five years of school.

English reading mastery, which requires linguistic competence in English, is apparently achieved only by a minority of deaf children. Some individuals in the field of education of the hearing-impaired may interpret the results of these studies as proof that competence with the English language is neither a realistic nor appropriate goal for deaf children. Parent-infant specialists at IHR interpret these same results differently.

The philosophy of parent-infant specialists at Infant Hearing Resource is that comprehension and use of the English language are important and realistic goals for deaf children, and, further, that most deaf children have the potential to reach these goals. We do not believe there is anything about deafness itself which precludes deaf children from attaining competence in English language skills. Rather, we believe that the traditional ways in which language has been modeled for and transmitted to hearing-impaired children, whether through spoken or signed modes, have not provided these children with a complete model of the English language on which to base English mastery and subsequent achievement of age-level reading comprehension. We assert that the factors of late identification of hearing loss, the child's lack of access to a complete English language model during the critical first three years of life, and inadequately informed and unskilled teachers and parents are major contributors to the limited English language skills observed in many deaf children. The IHR habilitation program directly addresses these factors with a curricula for parents and for infants which focuses on the infant's development of auditory perceptual skills and on his acquisition of the English language.

The primary goal of the language habilitation program for hearing-impaired children at IHR is that they will acquire a functional communication system which is based on English language, the language used in the hearing society in which they live. Competence in English will give these children the opportunity to function effectively and competitively in schools and in society.

In support of this goal, the program of language stimulation at IHR is based on communicating with hearing-impaired infants in complete and accessible English language. This requires that the language used in communicating with the child — the model from which he learns his language system — be a correct model of English language which is available to the child. Three objectives were formulated to guide specialists and families in achieving this goal. They are:

1. To make maximum use of the infant's critical first three years of life for auditory and language input.
2. To provide the infant with the beginnings of a complete and effective communication system for use in the family and in society.
3. To provide the infant with the foundation for achieving competency in English language usage.

Having committed ourselves to the goal that hearing-impaired children enrolled at IHR will acquire a functional communication system based on the English language, specialists accept that they must assure that an English language model is available and accessible to all children enrolled. This commitment is our focus in working with parents to choose communication modes that meet these criteria.

CHOOSING COMMUNICATION MODE OR MODES

The auditory-oral mode of communication is used with *all* hearing-impaired children enrolled at IHR. Manually-coded English is added to auditory-oral communication with many of these children. Manually-coded English is a system which "supplements some ASL signs with invented signs that correspond to elements of English words (plurals, prefixes and suffixes for example). There is usually a set of rules for word (sign) formation within the particular system" (Gallaudet College, 1984).

The manually-coded English system used at IHR is based on Signed English. Our primary resource for sign vocabulary is the *Comprehensive Signed English Dictionary* (Bornstein, Saulnier and Hamilton, 1983).

The following factors are considered by parents and specialist as they determine whether or not a child will need a system of manually-coded English added to auditory-oral communication in order to have a complete model of the English language available to him.

1. **Degree of residual hearing:** It is evident from the time of the first audiologic evaluations that some hearing-impaired children have sufficient residual hearing to detect all the sounds of speech well above threshold when fitted with proper amplification. While it is true that this preliminary information does not provide the specialist and parents with knowledge of the child's ability to discriminate, recognize, and comprehend speech sounds, parents may elect to begin the habilitation process using spoken language as the only symbolic language system with the child. When this decision is made, parents and specialist agree to establish a series of checkpoints at which the child's progress in acquisition of listening and language skills will be evaluated. One of the yard-sticks that IHR specialists use to measure child progress is: a year's worth of progress in a year's time, i.e., we ask, "If the child started the year at the 13-15 month level of receptive language, is he functioning in the 19-21 month level 6 months later, and the 25-31 month level after a year's time?" Most hearing-impaired children are behind their age-peers in language acquisition at the onset of habilitation. When it is within our power to do so, we want to promote their catching up with their age-peers, not falling further behind.

   As is true with any decision parents must make during the habilitation process, decisions regarding communication modes are not etched in stone. Any decision made today can be re-evaluated in the light of new evidence and knowledge tomorrow or next year. Specialists make certain that parents are aware that changing their minds is an acceptable behavior! This permission reduces the parents' anxiety about making the "right" decision at the outset.

2. **Parents' goals:** Parents and specialist must be clear on whether or not the parents have set the goal of acquisition of a functional communication system based on the English language as a primary language goal for their child. Some parents do not set this goal, for very good reasons of their own. Some parents who are themselves hearing-impaired use systems of communication that are not English language based, such as American Sign Language (ASL), a visible language with its own vocabulary, idioms, grammar, and syntax which are different from English.

Parents who use ASL are likely to use this language system in communicating with their children, a decision which is entirely acceptable to IHR specialists. IHR specialists who are not skilled at ASL discuss this fact with parents and gain their consent to use manually-coded English in their interactions with the parents and the child.

Some parents have priorities for their children which preclude their making English competence in the preschool years a realistic goal for their child. We have worked with parents whose profoundly deaf children do not hear, even with powerful amplification, all or most of the individual sounds of speech. Some of these parents have elected not to add manually-coded English to their spoken communication with their child. IHR specialists state clearly to parents the effect this decision will have on their child's access to complete and available language, but *accept that it is the parents' right to make this decision*. IHR specialists operate from the premise that parents, once presented with the relevant data, must make the decisions on issues which affect themselves and their child. This premise allows the IHR specialist to be a supportive member of the parent-specialist partnership even when the parents' choice was not one the specialist would have made.

3. **Parental commitment to learning a new language:** When parents decide to add manually-coded English to their spoken communication with their child, they are choosing to learn a new communication system. It takes time, effort, and generally, money to learn to use signed English. These factors should not be minimized when discussing choice of communication mode with parents. Attainment of vocabulary and fluency in signed language is not a short and simple process. Parents who make this decision are making a lifetime commitment to building this skill. When parents — and siblings — work hard to become adept at using signed language, the payoff comes from the high quality of communication they are able to enjoy with the hearing-impaired child and from the child's growing mastery of the English language.

No families enrolled at IHR ever make the decision *not* to use the auditory-oral mode of communication with their child. All children enrolled use hearing aids. Spoken language is used in combination with manually-coded English, and vocalization/speech is expected as an expressive mode from the children. IHR specialists would not be comfortable working with a family who did not want their child to wear appropriate hearing aids and to be exposed to spoken English. Thankfully, this issue has not ever come up. It is true that some IHR graduates have themselves decided at a later age not to use hearing aids. That is their perogative. However, we do not feel that we have the right to make that decision for a young child, nor would we feel comfortable if parents were to make that decision before the child had an opportunity to try amplification.

Early in the habilitation process at IHR, specialists describe for parents the system of American Sign Language (ASL) that is used by many hearing-impaired individuals in the United States. We provide parents with the rationale for our decision to use a manually-coded English signed language system rather than ASL. This rationale encompasses the following beliefs:

1. Hearing parents of newly identified hearing-impaired children (90% of the parents with whom we work) can learn a manually-coded English system, which superimposes signed vocabulary on their already existing grammatical base, more rapidly than they can ASL, a language with a different grammar and syntax.
2. Hearing-impaired children who acquire language from complete and accessible English language model(s) will achieve higher competence with the English language, including the higher levels of reading comprehension essential to literacy.

We also share with parents our belief that ASL may, at some point, become another important communication system for their child. At whatever age the child has the opportunity to spend time with people, deaf or hearing, who use ASL, he will acquire elements from that language that will enrich his communication. ASL has a beauty, fluidity, and expressiveness that cannot be matched in a system of manually-coded English. We agree that most hearing-impaired children should learn ASL. We do not think that teaching it as their first language is feasible for or advantageous to the majority of hearing-impaired children who have hearing parents.

It is our experience that as soon as children begin spending time with each other in their early grammar school years, they begin to incorporate aspects of ASL into their communication. Parents of IHR graduates report that, as young as 5 and 6 years, their hearing-impaired child communicates differently with deaf and hearing people. We applaud this versatility. Our goal in teaching signed English to young hearing-impaired children is to provide them with an educational advantage, not to keep them from learning ASL. We convey this message to parents and hope that as their child learns ASL, so will they.

IHR specialists want to see parents and their infants and toddlers engaged in reciprocal communication of feelings, thoughts and ideas. In addition, we think that an older child who is not handicapped by difficulties with reading and academic work has educational and career options that allow him a greater range of choices in life. He can compete with his peers in academics and jobs, choosing to pursue a life's work that requires English competence, or he can opt not to rely on those skills but concentrate instead in a nonlanguage-loaded field. Were we not to provide every opportunity for learning English, our decision would preclude this broad range of choices for the hearing-impaired children we see.

The IHR program of language stimulation is geared to effective parent-child communication and to building the child's foundation in English language competence. The next five chapters describe the specific steps and techniques involved in this program.

CHAPTER 19

INFANT LANGUAGE ACQUISITION: THE ROLE OF COGNITION

Why Consider Cognition?

The Sensori-Motor Stage of Cognitive
   Development
- A Description of This Stage
- Sensori-Motor Assessment
- An Habilitation Approach Which Promotes Cognitive Development
  in the Sensori-Motor Stage
- How Infant Communication Objectives in *Parent-Infant
  Communication* Incorporate Cognitive Goals of the Sensori-Motor
  Stage

Beginnings of the Pre-Operational Stage of
   Cognitive Development
- Use of Signifiers and Symbolic Behaviors
- How Infant Communication Objectives in *Parent-Infant
  Communication* Incorporate Cognitive Goals of the Pre-Operational
  Stage

WHY CONSIDER COGNITION?

Any language development program for infants and toddlers must take into consideration important cognitive processes which occur during the first years of life. Language is one type of symbolic behavior that children acquire in the process of cognitive development. There are other types of cognitive behaviors, however, that infants and toddlers must acquire before they are able to use language. Young children learn through experience with their world. An effective habilitation program for the hearing-impaired child, therefore, is based on providing the child with experiences that enable him to explore the world safely, to develop positive feelings about his own competence, and to interact with others in ways that promote social and emotional growth.

Children's *experiences* are the precursors to their language. These interesting little people busy themselves observing and experimenting with their world and with their own role in it. They develop perceptions about how things work, about how competent they are, and about their relationships to other people and to objects. Each of these perceptions plays a role in the child's cognitive development, thereby influencing his acquisition of symbolic language.

Of the existing theories and descriptions of the development of cognition, Piaget's complex model is one of the most helpful to the parent-infant specialist. Piaget described his model in numerous books and articles, some more comprehensible than others (Piaget and Inhelder, 1969 is highly recommended). Other creative thinkers (Furth, 1970; Dunst, 1981) have interpreted and expounded on Piaget's theories. We will not duplicate those feats here, but will, instead, offer a simplistic description of the first two stages of Piaget's model of cognitive development. These stages, the sensori-motor stage and the pre-operational stage, describe the cognitive development taking place in children from birth to ages 7-8 years. We urge readers to procure more complete and learned explanations of Piaget's work from other sources.

Cognition, in its simplest definition, is the act or process of knowing (Webster, 1974). In discussing cognitive development, then, we are talking about what a person knows and how they attain that knowledge. The word "process" is an extremely useful word to keep in mind when thinking about cognition. "Knowing" something or having "knowledge" is not simply the random accumulation of information. While there are those esoteric bits of knowledge that we may retain simply for entertainment value, e.g., the weight of a bee's brain, most of what we know is a process of weaving newly acquired information together into relationships with other things we know. Our understanding of new information is facilitated considerably when we can relate that new information to other knowledge we already possess. Some of the most difficult learning occurs when we have no way to categorize, classify, or compare new information with already acquired information.

THE SENSORI-MOTOR STAGE OF COGNITIVE DEVELOPMENT

A DESCRIPTION OF THIS STAGE

The first information or knowledge that an infant needs to acquire is information that will help him interact successfully with his environment. Born a helpless, dependent being, he needs to acquire strategies to get along in this world. First, he needs strategies to get food, comfort, and attention. As he grows older, if his basic needs are met, he acquires more complex needs. All of an infant's and toddler's learning is directed toward finding more effective ways of getting his needs met. Babies do not sit around wondering, "How can I get Mom to change my diaper?" Babies act — emit a cry — and the world responds. Baby cries — Mom comes and changes the diaper. After several repetitions of this routine, baby gets the glimmer of an idea — a piece of knowledge or strategy: "If I cry, Mom will come." Baby accidently hits a toy and a noise results. He enjoys the sound, so he hits the toy again. Now he has acquired a strategy he can use to entertain himself. In short, babies learn by *doing*, by *acting*. If they act and nothing happens, that association is made, too.

Piaget calls this first stage of cognitive development, or learning to know, the sensori-motor stage. This stage, which spans the period from birth to 18-24 months, is one in which the baby acquires knowledge and strategies (which Piaget calls schemes) through interaction with his environment. In the sensori-motor stage, the infant interacts with the environment using his *senses* and *movement*. *What he knows is what he can see, hear, smell, taste and feel at the moment*. In the sensori-motor stage, if a baby does not have access to something through one of his senses (e.g., cannot see it, feel it), that thing does not exist for him.

Babies in this stage also act *on* their environment by moving their body. Sometimes an aimless movement results in an encounter with an object or person and something occurs. Baby moves his mouth into a smile, Daddy smiles back. Baby likes it! He does it again. Baby pushes a toy off his highchair tray. Sister runs over and replaces the toy on the tray. Baby likes this attention. He pushes the toy off the tray again. By acting on his environment and using his senses to detect the results, baby learns strategies for getting his needs met.

The more opportunity an infant has to act on and move in his environment and to use his senses to detect the responses that result from his actions and movements, the more knowledge he will acquire about his world. The more knowledge he gains from his experiences, the more strategies he will be able to formulate to help him get his needs met. Babies in the sensorimotor stage need to be able to see, touch, taste, hear, feel, and move in many different situations in order to learn as much as they can. **What they do not experience directly, they do not know.**

Infants with hearing loss are missing one of the senses through which babies normally acquire information about their world. Babies who hear learn to associate mother's voice with the person they can see. When mother, out of his range of vision, is talking or singing, baby's sense of hearing tells him that mother still exists. For babies who cannot hear, this is not the case. Rattles fascinate hearing infants; they move their hand which is clamped around a pink plastic thing and a sound is produced. Babies with hearing loss may find that pink plastic thing of little interest.

Learning that objects still exist even when partially or totally hidden is a thinking skill — "object permanence" — acquired during the sensori-motor stage of cognitive development.

Sound is a very important source of information to babies. In Chapter 4, we discussed four ways in which hearing impairment may affect an infant's development. Social, emotional, and cognitive development were discussed collectively as areas that are affected by hearing loss. Hearing loss prevents an infant from gaining complete information about how the world is. A baby who cannot hear has a different knowledge of the world than do babies who hear. While hearing-impaired babies may formulate different strategies for getting their needs met because they do not have access to sound, at least one study (Best and Roberts, 1975) has shown no difference in sensori-motor development of deaf and hearing infants except in the area of vocal imitation. This study also suggested, however, that when the same children were tested a year later, some differences in cognitive abilities that have ties to language began to emerge.

Knowledge of how babies in the sensori-motor stage of development learn is of great importance to the parent-infant specialist because most hearing-impaired infants are functioning in this stage at enrollment. Children with additional handicaps may remain at the sensori-motor stage long after they have passed their second birthday.

Piaget described several important mental processes that he observed taking place in children functioning at the sensori-motor stage. These have been interpreted by Uzgiris and Hunt (1975) as seven **principal cognitive achievements** of the sensori-motor stage:

1. Visual Pursuit and Object Permanence. This is the knowledge that objects exist as separate from oneself and that they continue to exist when out of sight. This is also the foundation of memory. For example, an eight-month-old baby will look to the floor when a cookie falls off the edge of his highchair tray. He can not see it, but he knows it still exists.

2. The Development of Means for Obtaining Desired Environmental Events. This includes eye-hand coordination, differentiation of means and ends, and beginning use of objects to achieve a goal. For example, an 11-month-old pulls a string attached to an out-of-reach toy to get the toy.

3. The Development of Vocal Imitation. For example, a 12-month-old imitates an adult's "musical" vowel and pitch patterns in the utterance, "uh-oh."

4. The Development of Motor Imitation. For example, a 10-month-old baby will open and close his mouth in imitation of an adult's modeling of the same movement.

5. Causal Relationships. This is the realization that a particular movement results in a desired effect. For example, a 17-month-old attempts to turn a key to activate a wind-up toy.

6. Spatial Relations. This includes the perception of distances (e.g., the need to reach to get something); how objects relate to one another in space; direction; and body awareness and position.

For example, the 12-month-old will turn an inverted bottle upright in order to direct the nipple toward his mouth.

7. The Development of Schemes for Relating to Objects. This includes the realization that objects can be thrown, hit, shaken, and have many other functions. Here representation (naming of objects) begins, as does symbolic play with objects. For example, the 24-month-old pretends to drink from an empty cup.

SENSORI-MOTOR ASSESSMENT

The Ordinal Scales of Psychological Development (Uzgiris and Hunt, 1975), can be used to assess an infant's level of achievement in each of the seven areas listed above. Other instruments useful for assessing sensorimotor function are, "Generic Skills Assessment Inventory" (McLean, Snyder-McLean, Rowland, Jacobs, and Stremel-Campbell, 1981), and "Sensorimotor Cognitive Assessment and Curriculum for the Multihandicapped Child" (Fieber, 1977). The Cognitive and Perceptual-Fine Motor Scales in "Early Intervention Developmental Profile" (in *Developmental Programming for Infants and Young Children,* Schafer, Moersch, and D'Eugenio, 1985-86) is a screening tool which specialists at IHR use to determine if an infant is functioning within the range expected for his age.

IHR specialists feel it is critical to involve parents in the assessment of their infant's cognitive skills, just as we do in assessing other areas of infant development. We explain to parents the importance of their child progressing through the stages of cognitive development in preparation for their readiness to acquire symbolic language. We recommend that parent-infant specialists discuss assessment goals and activities with the parents. Parents who understand the rationale behind cognitive assessment and the skills being assessed are invaluable members of the intervention team. Written handouts describing the sequence of cognitive development are helpful as the parents may require repeated exposure to new vocabulary and concepts before they are understood. Many parents enjoy performing some of the assessment tasks with the specialist. Their participation in the assessment can help parents understand and accept their child's present level of cognitive function.

AN HABILITATION APPROACH WHICH PROMOTES COGNITIVE DEVELOPMENT IN THE SENSORI-MOTOR STAGE

Assessment results determine habilitation goals. Once we know how the child is operating at present, we can select appropriate goals and activities which will stimulate acquisition of subsequent cognitive skills. Once the goals have been set, the specialist and parents provide *opportunity, materials*, and *language*. Because the child's cognitive development in the sensori-motor stage is based on his interaction with the environment, ample opportunities for interaction must be made available to him.

Most hearing-impaired children have normal potential for cognitive development, but because of their inability to hear prior to the placement of hearing aids and incomplete auditory input even after aids are placed, they may be delayed in acquisition of some cognitive skills. The challenge for parents and specialists is to structure the environment in ways that will allow the hearing-impaired child to *manipulate, explore,* and *experiment.* Setting up appropriate situations which provide opportunities at the child's readiness level facilitates the child's enjoyment, feelings of success and control, and motivation to continue.

It is critical to remember that **the process, not the product or the completed task, is the end goal.** The child makes gains as he experiments, puzzles over obstacles, and solves problems. For this reason, while it is appropriate to demonstrate and guide the child through a task occasionally, constantly doing so will limit the child's opportunity to engage in the exploration and manipulation that form the basis for his coming to know the world through his senses and his movement. When we can let go of our adult concern about the "right" way to perform an activity we are much more comfortable with letting the child acquire new knowledge and strategies at his own pace. Lehane (1976) suggests a variety of Piaget-based activities for the child functioning in the sensori-motor stage of cognitive development.

HOW INFANT COMMUNICATION OBJECTIVES IN *PARENT-INFANT COMMUNICATION* INCORPORATE COGNITIVE GOALS OF THE SENSORI-MOTOR STAGE

Two of the major cognitive achievements of the sensori-motor stage of cognitive development are the development of *motor imitation* and the development of *vocal imitation*. A sequence of imitative behaviors appears in the infant Presymbolic Communication section of *Parent-Infant Communication*. We have extracted a combined list of motor and vocal imitation behaviors from that section to include herein. The following list can be used by specialists and parents to evaluate the infant's imitation behaviors and to plan activities which focus on developing the skills he needs.

4 Months: "Child performs action in response to a familiar gesture, e.g., wiggles arms and legs when adult waves arm."

5 Months: "Child tries to imitate adult-produced changes in pitch and loudness."

7 Months:	"Child attempts to imitate speech sounds, e.g., child produces 'ga-ga-ga' when adult models 'a-a-a'."
	"Child correctly imitates one familiar movement, e.g., waving of arm, patting hand on tray."
8 Months:	"Child accurately imitates: 1) adult mouth, tongue, jaw movements; 2) adult babbling of consonant-vowel combinations already in child's repertoire; and 3) adult intonation patterns."
9 Months:	"Child imitates non-speech sounds already in his repertoire, e.g., cough, tongue click, lip-smacking, 'raspberry'."
	"Child attempts to imitate two familiar animal, toy, or vehicle sounds, e.g., 'boo' for 'moo'; 'oo-oo' for 'choo- choo'."
	"Child uses echolalia: consistently imitates, or echoes, words said by others. These imitated words do not have symbolic meaning for the infant."
10-12 Months:	"Child points to own body part in imitation of adult, e.g., child points to nose when adult points to nose and asks, 'Where's your nose?'"
	"Child imitates action when adult demonstrates function of object, e.g., rubs self with soap, feeds others with spoon."
	"Child imitates novel gesture if he can see himself perform it, e.g., can imitate patting hands on stomach, but cannot imitate patting on head."
13-15 Months:	"Child imitates one facial movement or expression accurately, e.g., rounds lips, raises eyebrows."
	"Child imitates most simple, new words."
19-21 Months:	"Child imitates phrases, short sentences, and questions (imitation needs to be exact)."
22-24 Months:	"Child whispers spontaneously or in imitation of adult whisper."

The first 120 activities in the Activities section in *Parent-Infant Communication* are appropriate for the child functioning in the sensori-motor stage of cognitive development. Two excellent books which will guide the parent-infant specialist and parents in selecting appropriate activities for the child who is operating in this stage are *Learning Through Play: A Resource Manual For Teachers and Parents* (Fewell and Vadasy, 1983) and *Infant Learning: A Cognitive-Linguistic Intervention Strategy* (Dunst, 1981).

BEGINNINGS OF THE PRE-OPERATIONAL STAGE
OF COGNITIVE DEVELOPMENT

USE OF SIGNIFIERS AND SYMBOLIC BEHAVIORS

Toward the end of the sensori-motor stage, as the child reaches 18-24 months of age, he develops a new cognitive function that is basic to the development of later behavior patterns (Piaget and Inhelder, 1969). This function is the ability to represent something using a **signifier**, such as language, a mental image, or a symbolic gesture. Use of a signifier enables the child to communicate about an event, object, or person that is not immediately present. Once the child can use signifiers — also called symbols — his knowledge of "what is" is no longer tied to what he can immediately see, feel, hear, taste, or smell. He is able to represent the absent with a specific symbol and thereby keep it in existence for himself. Piaget and Inhelder (1969) identify five symbolic behavior patterns which develop during the pre-operational stage, a period from 18-24 months to 7-8 years. These symbolic behaviors are deferred imitation, symbolic play, drawing or graphic image, mental image, and verbal evocation of events or language.

Deferred imitation occurs when the child performs a remembered action at a later time so that it communicates to others the previously observed act. A toddler who, upon approaching a steaming cup of coffee, shakes his head in the "no-no" action, is remembering the adults' use of this signifier at an earlier time.

Symbolic play is a way in which young children re-enact or recall earlier experiences but, through their play, change the experience so that the re-enactment represents how they want the experience to be. Thus, a two-year-old may play with a child's purse and pretend to apply make-up, go through a wallet, or comb her hair, all things she would like to do with mother's purse. Another child may shuffle along in father's shoes and end up in father's chair pretending to smoke a pipe as he reads a magazine. Through symbolic play, the child expresses how his life would be if he were in charge!

Drawing is another way in which a child begins to represent things that he has seen or experienced. His first lines and marks are meaningful only to the child, but later his drawings incorporate more commonly understood figures to represent thoughts and experiences.

Mental images during the preoperational stage appear to be copies of what the child has actually experienced or perceived. The toddler, for instance, has a mental image of how the scene is set for a certain activity or game and may insist that the scenario be exact prior to entering into the activity. Thus, if Mom always sits on the bed while putting the child's clothes on, the child may insist that Dad or Grandma dress him in the same place.

Verbal (or manual) evocation is the use of the symbols of language to represent an object or event not present or occuring at the time. One obvious advantage of the use of symbols or signifiers is the child's ability to communicate to others about objects not present and later about relative attributes and values that have no substantive form that can be perceived, e.g., relative attributes described by adjectives such as big and cold; values such as love and trust.

The transition from the sensori-motor stage to a different stage of knowing — the pre-operational stage — "is characterized by the child's capacity to recognize the independent existence of physical objects apart from his own personal actions on them" (Furth, 1970, p. 29). In place of thinking in personal action, children can now think in symbolic behavior. The use of the symbols of language makes possible not only *inter-individual* communication (communication between individuals), but also *intra-individual* communication (thinking). The intricacies of thought are much more manageable when children can use symbols to represent objects and actions and groups of objects and actions (Carroll, 1964).

During the pre-operational period, children begin to form ideas about how things work based on what they have seen and done. They acquire beginning notions of classification, conservation, seriation, and number that are based on their own perceptions and experiences. In this stage, what children see or perceive wins out over what reasoning or logic might tell them. Thus, their expectations and theories are frequently inaccurate because of their limited experience (Fewell and Vadasy, 1983).

The child with undetected hearing loss acquires some of the five symbolic behavior patterns described above. Deferred imitation of actions — imitation beginning after the model is gone — is a "natural" for the hearing-impaired child who is visually oriented. Imitation of gestures, which then acquire symbolic meaning for the child, is the basis for the "home-sign" communication system that develop when no formal language system is accessible to the child. The hearing-impaired child who has access to a symbolic language system — whether auditory or visual — will achieve all of the symbolic behavior systems characteristic of the pre-operational stage. Therein lies another challenge for parent-infant specialists and parents: making certain that a symbolic language system is available to the child so that he is able to move from thinking in actions to thinking in symbols.

Screening tools listed in Chapters 3 and 25 are utilized at IHR to assess children who are functioning in the beginning stages of pre-operational function.

HOW INFANT COMMUNICATION OBJECTIVES IN *PARENT-INFANT COMMUNICATION* INCORPORATE COGNITIVE GOALS OF THE PRE-OPERATIONAL STAGE

Cognitive activities for the child ages 18-24 months to 7-8 years should employ elements that will promote the child's acquisition of symbols and the mastery of elementary types of relationships. Sonquist and Kamii (1967) suggest a developmental series of activities that will promote symbolization and the development of cognitive relationships. These activities are described below and are related to appropriate teaching objectives in *Parent-Infant Communication* (Infant Hearing Resource, 1985).

SYMBOLIZATION

1. The child uses his body to represent objects or actions. For example, when he sees a drum, he begins to move his hands as if beating the drum. Gestures are typical of this stage. Activities that are useful are fingerplays, rhymes, songs, and "acting like," e.g., being a dog or a duck. *Parent-Infant Communication:* Presymbolic Communication Objectives #47, 50, 57; Receptive Language Objective #15; Expressive Language Objective #12; Activities #93, 97.

2. The child uses objects to represent other objects. The child pretends that a ball is an apple and attempts to eat it. Activities can include using blocks for cars, lining up chairs for a train, using a blanket over a table for a house.

3. The child uses utterances which characterize an object. The child uses sounds such as "meow" and "arf-arf" to represent the appropriate animal and sounds for objects such as "choo-choo" for the train. *Parent-Infant Communication:* Presymbolic Communication Objective #40; Expressive Language Objectives #2, 10; Activity #91.

4. The child recognizes objects and actions in pictures. Activities include experience stories, pictures of the child performing an action, books. *Parent-Infant Communication:* Expressive Language Objectives #7, 11; Activities #109, 110, 116.

5. The child makes representations of objects in two and three dimensions. Activities include drawing, playing with clay, pasting shapes, and building blocks. *Parent-Infant Communication:* General Play Activities.

6. The child uses symbols (spoken or signed words) to represent objects and actions. Because language has accompanied all of the interactions that adults have with the child in the types of activities described above, the child has learned to associate spoken and/or

signed words with objects and actions. He can now use these words to represent objects and actions when they are not present. *Parent-Infant Communication:* Objectives and related activities in all sections of infant curriculum.

COGNITIVE RELATIONSHIPS

1. The child learns to use logico-mathematical relationship groupings (pre-classifications). During the pre-operational stage, activities which promote the acquisition of the following concepts are appropriate: matching "same" and "different"; classification of similar attributes; "some" and "all"; class inclusion (e.g., words such as "animals" and "fruit"). *Parent-Infant Communication:* Receptive Language Objectives #24, 25, 30, 31, 43, 53; Expressive Language Objectives #39, 69.

2. The child learns to put materials in an order (pre-seriation) based on the least to greatest of some variable. The child must be able to discriminate size in order to perform ordering activities such as lining up cars from smallest to largest. *Parent-Infant Communication:* Receptive Language Objectives #41, 62; Activities #103, 109, 121, 122, 123, 124, 126, 127, 128, 132, 133, 156.

3. The child uses words that describe or define space and time relationships. The child is first able to manipulate objects into a specified spatial relationship, as in following the direction, "Put the cup *on* the table." He is also able to manipulate his body relative to objects as in following the direction, "Go under the table." At a more advanced level, the child is able to perceive and name spatial relationships, first in real life, then in pictures, as in saying, "The kitty is on the chair," or "The frog is in the water."

   Temporal relationship words include words such as "now" and "later" and also cause and effect descriptions such as "if-then" and "because." *Parent-Infant Communication:* Receptive Language Objectives #21, 29, 36, 45, 68; Expressive Language Objectives #27, 37, 53, 65, 72, 73; Activities #120, 137, 150, 154, 157.

Three additional resources for activities which will promote the child's development of pre-operational cognitive skills are *Thinking Is Child's Play* (Sharp, 1970), *A Teacher's Guide to Cognitive Tasks for Preschool* (Cahoon, 1975), and "Developing Thinking Skills in Young Hearing-Impaired Children" (Stone, 1980).

SUMMARY

Children who are presented with developmentally appropriate and meaningful experiences will acquire curiosity about their world, problem-solving strategies that help them cope successfully with their environment, and the motivation to explore and learn. The child's experiences are powerful determiments of his mental growth. Parent-infant specialists and parents who have an understanding of normal cognitive development are in an excellent position to provide the learning experiences that will promote the complementary growth of cognitive and linguistic skills in the hearing-impaired child.

Infants and toddlers first learn to know about the world through their direct action on and experience with their environment. In the sensori-motor stage, they "know" only what they are seeing, hearing, touching, smelling, or tasting at the moment. During the pre-operational stage of cognitive development, children learn to represent objects, actions, and events with a symbol or signifier. Use of symbols, including language, allows the child to "know" things that are not immediately present. Thus he can begin to compare, classify, and order, all early logical and mathematical skills.

Habilitation of the child with hearing loss must incorporate a wide range of activities that allow the child to gain extensive experience with his environment. Since sound is a characteristic of many of the events that occur in the child's environment, parents and specialists who help the child acquire listening skills are enabling him to better understand his world. Providing the child with an accessible and non-ambiguous symbolic communication system will allow him to learn to use symbols to represent objects and events, a skill essential to the acquisition of most cognitive skills beyond the sensori-motor stage.

CHAPTER 20

TEACHING INFANT PRESYMBOLIC COMMUNICATION OBJECTIVES

What is Presymbolic Communication?

Goals of the Presymbolic Communication Program

Presymbolic Communication: Stages and Functions
- Stages of Presymbolic Communication
- Functions of Presymbolic Communication

Effect of Hearing Loss on the Infant's Acquisition of Presymbolic Communication

Reinforcing Parent Behaviors that Promote the Infant's Use of Presymbolic Communication
- Assessing Existing Presymbolic Communication
- The Importance of Motherese and Fatherese

Preliminary Observations of Presymbolic Communication Resulting from Research with Infant Hearing Resource Families

WHAT IS PRESYMBOLIC COMMUNICATION?

Presymbolic communication is the way babies communicate their wants, feelings, and needs before they can use symbolic language such as spoken or signed words. Most normally hearing babies begin using symbolic language at around one year of age. Some people may think that babies have not been able to communicate before that time. Nothing could be further from the truth. Babies communicate through cries, grimaces, and body movement from the moment of birth. During their first year of life they learn to use an amazing assortment of facial expressions, vocalizations, and body movements to convey their needs and preferences to the people in their world. This complex communication system, called presymbolic communication, is the precursor to symbolic language.

Babies, both hearing and hearing-impaired, acquire communication skills through interaction with their significant caregivers. The more adults respond to a baby's presymbolic communication — conveyed through cries, smiles, gestures, facial expressions, and body language — the more motivated that baby will be to continue to communicate. Babies learn that by communicating, they can get their needs met and their point of view across to others. The development of a substantial, varied, and effective system of presymbolic communication is basic to the child's subsequent acquisition of symbolic language.

GOALS OF THE PRESYMBOLIC COMMUNICATION PROGRAM

As in the other areas of habilitation, parents of the hearing-impaired infant are in a position to have the most significant impact on their child's acquisition of communication skills. Achievement of the goals of both the presymbolic communication and the symbolic language programs at IHR are dependent on the intense participation of well-informed and skilled parents. IHR specialists and parents work toward achieving four goals related to presymbolic communication. These goals are:

1. That parents understand what presymbolic communication is, how and why their infant uses presymbolic communication, and the importance of presymbolic communication to the child's subsequent development of symbolic language.
2. That parents are aware of how their child's hearing loss can disrupt the development of a rich and varied system of presymbolic communication between themselves and their child and how this disruption may adversely affect the child's ability to develop subsequent symbolic language.
3. That parents acquire behaviors that will promote their child's acquisition of presymbolic communication.
4. That parents learn to observe, document, and appreciate the significance of their child's communication prior to the child's acquisition of symbolic language.

Parent-infant specialists can help parents achieve these goals by leading parents through the objectives in the Presymbolic Communication section of the parent curriculum in *Parent-Infant Communication* (Infant Hearing Resource, 1985), and by sharing with parents the information on presymbolic communication which follows.

PRESYMBOLIC COMMUNICATION: STAGES AND FUNCTIONS

STAGES OF PRESYMBOLIC COMMUNICATION

We are all aware that a child's expressive use of *symbolic* language begins with one-word utterances and progresses to two-word combinations, short phrases, simple sentences, and finally, to complex sentences. The child's presymbolic communication — the way he expresses his needs before he has the ability to use symbols such as signed or spoken words — also develops in a progressive fashion. Presymbolic communication can be observed in two stages: 1) Signal Stage and 2) Protosymbolic Behaviors (Robbins and Stenquist, 1967; Fieber, 1977). Both signals and protosymbolic behaviors encompass various types of communicative behaviors.

SIGNALS

Signals are the first way in which an infant communicates his immediate physical needs or his present state. Signals are concerned with objects and persons which are present and with situations presently occurring. **Behaviors such as cries, smiles, body posturing, eye contact, facial expression, hitting, swatting, touching, pulling, and vocalizing are all signals.** The infant learns to use signals from his previous experiences. His first signals are non-intentional communications which the adult interprets as signals of pleasure, comfort, discomfort, displeasure, or fear. After a period of time during which adults consistently respond to the infant's non-intentional signals, the infant begins to use the behaviors intentionally to convey his needs, wants, or feelings. A young infant learns that by making a certain movement, he is able to encourage the adult to behave in a certain manner. For example, baby Amber learned that by kicking at her mobile, she could get her mother to wind it up again. Joey's mom actually taught him a signal. While feeding Joey in the high chair, she would tap the tray with her hand as she said, "Here's some more!" Joey learned to hit the tray to signal to his mom that he wanted more food, thus communicating his desire.

There are three types of signals that the child may use: simple signals, complex signals, and combined signals. The first type of signal in the hierarchy is called a **simple signal,** in which only *one* communicative behavior — such as gazing, smiling, or touching — is used. In using a simple signal, the child acts either on an object or on a person; that is, he directs his signal to a person or to an object. Thus, the infant's simple signal can be further classified as either person-directed or object-directed. Remember Amber kicking her mobile? Since all she did was kick, she used a simple signal, one communicative behavior, to act on an object, the mobile. Therefore, Amber's simple signal can be further defined as object-directed. Another example of a simple signal is Joey making eye contact with his dad when he wants to be picked up. Joey used the one behavior of eye contact and directed it towards his father; that is, he used a simple signal that was person-directed.

A more advanced type of signal occurs when the child uses two or more behaviors in sequence to communicate. These communicative behaviors in sequence are called **complex signals.** A complex signal is made up of two or more child behaviors that are either object-directed or person-directed. Using our previous examples, we can see how, as Amber and Joey get older, their communications expand to include complex signals. To indicate her desire to have her mobile move, Amber kicked at it *and* she vocalized at it. She used two behaviors, a complex signal, both object-directed. Joey used three behaviors to get his dad to pick him up: he touched dad's hand, made eye contact with him, and vocalized at him. Joey's three behaviors are a complex signal that is person-directed.

In the third type of signal, called a **combined signal,** the child again uses two or more signals. However, this time he directs his signals to both an object *and* a person. Use of a combined signal occurs when the child uses two or more behaviors, at least one of which is person-directed and one of which is object-directed. Again, as they get older, Amber's and Joey's behaviors increase in complexity to meet this new criterion. Now to communicate her desire to have the mobile move, Amber kicks at it, vocalizes at it, and makes eye contact with her mother. She used three behaviors, which could qualify either as a complex signal or as a combined signal. One must look at the direction of her behaviors to determine if it is a complex signal or combined signal. She kicked the mobile (object); she vocalized to the mobile (object); she made eye contact with her mother (person). Her behaviors were directed at both an object and a person; therefore, Amber used a combined signal. Joey's latest sequence of communication behaviors consisted of touching his dad's hand, making eye contact with his dad, swatting at his "Johnny-Jump-Up," and leaning his body towards his dad. Since Joey used both person-directed and object-directed signals, his sequence of behaviors is a combined signal.

Objectives 1-37 in the Infant Presymbolic Communication section of *Parent Infant Communication* describe the increasingly complex signals that infants use to communicate.

PROTOSYMBOLIC BEHAVIORS

The second stage of presymbolic communication is comprised of protosymbolic behaviors. **Protosymbolic behaviors are representational behaviors which precede the use of symbols.** The use of protosymbolic behaviors is evidence of the child's developing cognitive skills because, being representational in nature, protosymbolic behaviors are the first signs of the child's potential symbolic ability. Protosymbolic behaviors indicate "some separation or distance of the child from concrete behavior" (Fieber, 1977). We cannot expect a child to use symbolic communication until he has used a variety of protosymbolic behaviors.

We will discuss four types of protosymbolic behaviors and relate them to Amber's and Joey's developing communication skills: pointing, pantomiming, gesturing, and vocalizing. One type of protosymbolic behavior is **pointing.** The infant uses the pointing gesture, which can be a bodily gesture, an eye signal, or a vocalization such as "da," to get something he wants or to direct attention to an experience he wants to share with another. Amber points to the toy out of her reach to indicate that she wants it. Joey points to the wind-up toy before he grabs it, again showing that he wants it even though he is able to get it for himself this time. At another time Joey gazes intently at a dog he sees through the window as a way of calling his sister's attention to the dog.

A second type of protosymbolic behavior is **pantomiming to self.** When using pantomime, the child employs body movement and facial expression to act out to himself elements of a familiar activity. This behavior is unconscious; the child is unaware that he is doing it and as such it is not an intentional interpersonal communication. However, the parent or specialist who observes a child pantomiming gets a quick look at the child's current thoughts! One example of pantomiming to self occurs when toddler Joey mimics, during solitary play with blocks, the exaggerated facial expression depicting surprise and alarm which his parents have used playfully on other occasions when his stack of blocks has toppled over.

Gestures are a third type of protosymbolic behavior. Gestures include behaviors such as "nodding 'yes' or 'no,' pointing from object to self to indicate wanting or ownership, pointing to tell where to put something or to indicate direction, pictorial gestures which describe the appearance of objects, and imitation of an action related to an object" (Fieber, 1977). The child's first gestures refer to his immediate physical situation. If the gesture refers to an object, then the object must be present. Amber uses the gesture of holding her cup out to a parent to show that she is thirsty. As the child's cognitive skills and her use of gestures develop, the child is able to refer to things that are not present and to more abstract ideas. Now Amber stands by the sink and pretends to drink without a cup in her hand to tell her mother that she wants a drink. This gesture represents the action of drinking and is made without an object — the cup — being present. In the next stage, gestures represent an attribute of the object. For example, Joey makes a gesture of turning a handle to encourage his mother to use a hand mixer to make a cake. He used the attribute of turning the handle to represent the mixer. Finally, the child may string several gestures together to produce "sentences" and even short "stories." Children frequently combine facial expression with their gestures in an effort to make their communication as clear as possible.

All children use gestures naturally as they pass through this protosymbolic stage on their way to producing their first spoken or signed word. Because certain concepts in signed language are identical to the natural gesture for that concept, children exposed to signed language may appear to be functioning at the symbolic stage when they use certain gestures expressively. In actuality, the child may be using a natural gesture or imitating a gesture, and is, therefore, still functioning in the protosymbolic behavior stage. Parents and specialists need to observe a variety of the child's communications to determine whether he is functioning in the gesture stage of protosymbolic communication or whether he has acquired some symbolic communication. Some natural gestures that are similar to their signed counterparts are "come," "want," and "drink."

The child does not discontinue use of these first three types of protosymbolic behaviors when he begins to use symbols. Even as adults, we continue to use gestures, pointing, and pantomime to communicate, e.g., a crooked finger for "come here"; pointing to show someone where to go; palm forward for "stop" or "wait"; or pulling a hand out of a pocket with a shrug of a shoulders to show "no money."

Vocalizing is a fourth type of protosymbolic behavior. Protosymbolic vocalizations are also referred to as "call-sounds." Some examples of vocalizations as protosymbolic forms are the child's consistent use of a vocalization in a specific situation such as, "anh anh anh" when he wants to be picked up. He may vocalize "mmmm" as he reaches towards an object,

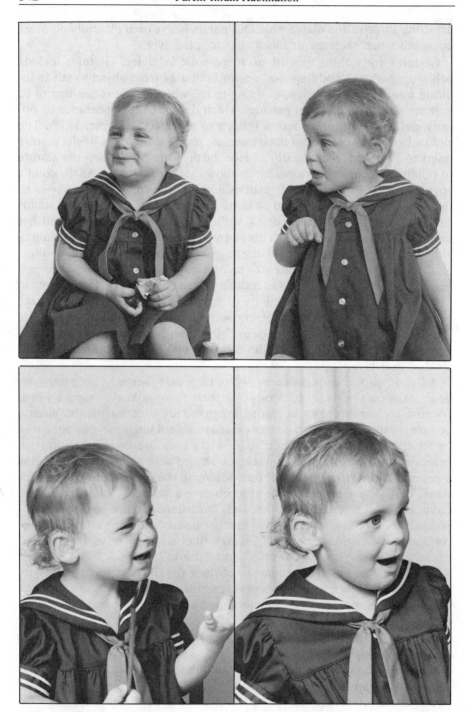

This toddler has so many things to "say" and so many ways of saying them without words.

meaning, "Please help me reach that." He learns that he can use his voice to attract others' attention; he yells from his crib in the morning and soon someone comes to rescue him. When he is angry, he is likely to vocalize his displeasure in an intense cry.

The infant is able to communicate requests, commands, and feelings through his vocalizations, which may or may not be combined with gestures. Even though the child's vocalizations have not yet reached the symbolic stage of actual words, the intent of his vocalizations is recognized both by the child and by the listener. These vocalizations are considered protosymbols since different children use different vocalizations to represent and express similar desires or needs. Protosymbolic vocalizations precede the child's acquisition of spoken symbolic language. Many of the objectives in the categories between 8-18 months in the Infant Presymbolic Communication section of *Parent-Infant Communication* describe protosymbolic behaviors.

We have been discussing "how" the young child communicates. We discovered that presymbolic communication can be divided into two stages: signals and protosymbolic behaviors. The first signals are called simple signals — single behaviors which are either person-directed or object-directed. When the baby combines the use of two or more simple signals he is using a complex signal. Complex signals, like simple signals, are directed either at objects or at persons. Finally, the child uses several behaviors in sequence, some of which are object-directed and some of which are person-directed. This sequence of signals is called a combined signal. As the child's cognitive skills develop, his communication behaviors become more representational and are called protosymbolic behaviors. Protosymbolic behaviors include pointing, pantomiming, gesturing, and vocalizing. Specialists and parents who are aware of and look for these early behaviors can respond to and reinforce the infant's use of a wide range of presymbolic communication behaviors that precede and promote the infant's acquisition of symbolic communication.

FUNCTIONS OF PRESYMBOLIC COMMUNICATION

It is important to look not only at "how" the infant is communicating but also at "why" he is communicating. We use the term "function" to label the child's communicative intent, or what he means to communicate. Examining the functions of the child's communications is important for two reasons. First, if we correctly identify the intent of the child's communication then we are more likely to respond appropriately to him. Second, if assessment reveals restricted use of functions, we can provide motivating situations or specific behavior shaping programs which will encourage the child's use of a variety of functions. Infants with delayed cognitive or motor development who have not yet learned that communication can give them power and help them get their needs met may need guidance in learning to use presymbolic communication for a variety of purposes.

Halliday (1973) enumerated a list of four functions of infant communication, each of which describes a different communicative intent: Instrumental, Regulatory, Interpersonal, and Personal. These functions, or purposes/intents of communication, apply to the signal and protosymbolic levels of presymbolic communication. (For a discussion of how the intents of a child's communication relate to the stages of cognitive development as described by Piaget, see Bates, 1976.)

INSTRUMENTAL FUNCTION

The function of the infant's first presymbolic communications is to communicate "I want" or "I don't want." This function is called the instrumental function. **In using the instrumental function the child may be responding to a presently occurring situation or he may be initiating communication because of his own present need.** We see a young infant using the instrumental function when he turns his head away from the bottle to communicate, "I don't want it." When baby Amber was kicking at the mobile with her foot, she was using the instrumental function of a simple signal to communicate, "I want more."

REGULATORY FUNCTION

The second function or intent of an infant's presymbolic communication is the regulatory function. This function is closely associated with the instrumental function and is described as the "Do this" function. **In using the regulatory function the child wants to achieve an end result by using a person to help him. It is the child's way of controlling others.** Since the child is acting on people, the "Do this" function is always *person-directed*. Sometimes it is difficult to decide if the child's intent is "I want" or "Do this" because the behaviors may tend to look similar. One way to distinguish between the two functions is that the regulatory, "Do this," function is stronger and more emphatic than the instrumental, "I want," function. If Amber were to kick wildly at the mobile, make prolonged eye contact with her mother, bat at her mother's hand, and vocalize loudly at her mother she would be using a stronger means of communicating than if she just waved her feet at the mobile and vocalized softly; when her "want" is expressed strongly and is mostly directed at a person, she is saying, "Mother, do this!", a regulatory function.

INTERPERSONAL FUNCTION

Amber has used signals and protosymbolic behaviors to communicate, "I want" and "Do this." In using the interpersonal function, she communicates "Me and you." **The interpersonal function is a social function and is used to establish bonds with others.** Examples of the interpersonal function are greetings and responsive smiles. When communicating the "Me and you" function, the child uses eye contact and body contact to demonstrate the sharing of a pleasurable experience between herself and another person. As Amber's mother wakes her up from her nap, Amber reaches out to touch mother's hand, smiles, vocalizes, and makes eye contact. Amber is using the interpersonal function to communicate, "Me and you, Mom!"

PERSONAL FUNCTION

Presymbolic communication can be used to convey a fourth function. This function is the personal or "I" function. **The infant uses the personal function to inform others of his feelings.** He may smile to show his pleasure in an activity, or he may fuss unhappily. One notable example of the personal function is the child's use of the "Aren't I smart?" expression when she learns how to control an event. Amber flashes the "Aren't I smart?" smile when she has learned that pushing down on the clown's hat makes him pop up again.

A young child's presymbolic communication can convey four meanings or functions: Instrumental ("I want"), Regulatory ("Do this"), Interpersonal ("Me and you"), and Personal ("I"). By determining the function or purpose of the communication, we can determine "why" the child is communicating. We can also answer several questions about the infant's communicative intents by examining the functions of his signals and protosymbolic behaviors. Is he using a variety of functions? Are the functions related to both objects and people? Does his use of the personal function indicate a growing sense of self-esteem? Is he developing an awareness of his own competence and his growing power to have some influence over what happens to him? Has he established a diversity of presymbolic communication behaviors and an assortment of functions which will serve as the foundation for the emergence of symbolic language?

EFFECT OF HEARING LOSS ON THE INFANT'S
ACQUISITION OF PRESYMBOLIC COMMUNICATION

In "normal" infant-adult interactions the infant's behaviors serve as the stimulus for the adult's responses. This behavior-response pairing is the beginning of the communication process for the infant. A handicapping condition, however, may interfere with an infant's ability to interact and communicate with adults in the way they expect him to. For example, an infant with a cleft palate may not be able to suck and swallow well, preventing the parent from feeling successful at providing him with the nourishment he needs. The adult's frustration may be communicated in the way she holds and responds to the infant. The infant with impaired vision may not make eye contact with his caregivers, depriving them of the warm feelings and bonds that emerge from mutual visual regard. The infant with impaired hearing may not be soothed by his parents' voices, and may not seek out their faces when they start talking to him. Parents of babies with impaired hearing may feel a subtle rejection from the child.

When a baby fails to behave in anticipated ways, skewed patterns of interaction between parents and infant are likely to develop. Parents may begin to worry that something is wrong, that the baby does not like them, that somehow they are not meeting the baby's needs. The baby's behavior or lack of behavior may be interpreted as a desire not to be handled, held, talked to. At this point an unfortunate cycle may begin between the infant and parent when neither one is providing the stimuli needed to motivate the other to communicate.

The varied and complex system of signals and protosymbolic behaviors that make up presymbolic communication were described earlier. The infant's use of signals and protosymbolic behaviors does not develop in a vacuum. As mentioned, the infant learns to use what were at first reflexive cries and movements as intentional signals because the reflexive behaviors were responded to and thus reinforced by the significant caregivers in the infant's life. A cry results in attention. A smile results in a warm smile in return. A chance wave of the arm results in the appearance of a toy. The responses of the adult create in the infant a desire to communicate more in order to get attention, smiles, food, toys. Eventually, as the infant's increasing cognitive and motor skills are combined with an environment rich in presymbolic communication, he learns to use the symbols of language to communicate. If, however, the infant's environment has not promoted his acquisition of presymbolic communication behaviors, his incentive to acquire symbolic language is lessened. An infant's hearing loss can be a factor which disrupts the development of presymbolic communication and his subsequent acquisition of symbolic language.

One of the specialist's early tasks in working with newly enrolled parents is to observe and point out to them the richness of the communication taking place between them and their baby and to explain its importance to all later learning. Reinforcing the already existing presymbolic communication between infant and parents is the subject of the next section.

REINFORCING PARENT BEHAVIORS THAT PROMOTE THE INFANT'S USE OF PRESYMBOLIC COMMUNICATION

We have discussed the fact that parents and their infants generally develop an extensive communication repertoire during the infant's early months of life. The baby's cries, squirms, smiles, and coos are powerful signals to the parents that the child has urgent needs or that he feels quite content. The parents communicate love and affection as well as nervousness or uncertainty to the infant through their manner of holding, cuddling, stroking, and positioning him. From the first days of life babies communicate with their parents through such behaviors as eye contact, posturing, and cooing. As the parent interacts with the infant a natural "conversational" *turn-taking* occurs with the infant gazing at the parent and cooing, then settling back while the parent takes a turn. These early communication activities cement the growing bond between parent and infant and establish a *reciprocal process* which is a necessary precursor to all subsequent language development.

Coached by the specialist, the mother conveys interest in her son's presymbolic communication by maintaining eye contact, leaning forward, and looking interested.

Early conversations, called "proto-conversations" (Bateson, 1975), are vocal exchanges which serve to affirm and maintain social contact between parent and infant. Proto-conversations, which become firmly established about the second month of life, have definite rules. *Eye contact* is nearly constant and the communicators *alternate* (take turns) with the mother or father settling back when the infant increases body movement and begins to vocalize. If the mother interrupts the infant his vocalizations will cease.

ASSESSING EXISTING PRESYMBOLIC COMMUNICATION

When a hearing-impaired infant and his family enroll in a program of habilitation they bring with them the system of presymbolic communication that they have developed. In some families this communication system is extensive, successful, and mutually reinforcing. In other families the communication system serves only to convey basic needs. Among the first tasks the parent-infant specialist will want to complete in working with a new family is an assessment of the presymbolic communication occurring between the infant and his parents. This assessment, which consists of four steps, is done as a part of the initial evaluation to determine where the infant and parents are functioning in terms of infant and parent presymbolic communication objectives as specified in *Parent-Infant Communication*. The steps of the assessment are:

1. Observe and describe the infant's presymbolic communication, noting stage and functions exhibited as well as the array of behaviors used. Following the developmental sequence of infant presymbolic communication objectives listed in *Parent-Infant Communication,* the specialist will check off on the Infant Curriculum Checksheet those objectives the infant has already attained.

2. Observe and describe the parents' communication behaviors used with their infant. The specialist will refer to the parent presymbolic communication objectives in *Parent-Infant Communication* and check off those objectives attained by each parent on the Parent Curriculum checksheet.

In each of these first two steps of assessing infant and parent participation in the presymbolic communication process, the specialist may elect to videotape the parent and child interacting. Parents can then view the videotape to observe the infant while not directly interacting with him and to observe their own communication with their baby. Some parents may need coaching in becoming good observers of their child. Techniques for helping parents learn to observe their child's behaviors are outlined in Chapter 13.

3. Observe and describe parents' and infant's responses to one another's communication. Reinforce the parents for the communication that is already taking place.
4. Referring to *Parent-Infant Communication,* the specialist points out to the parents presymbolic communication behaviors they can encourage in the infant and skills and information that the parents are ready to acquire.

Having observed and assessed the existing presymbolic communication taking place between parents and their infant, the specialist can point out to the parents the significance of this early communication. She can also commend the parents for interacting with their baby in ways that will promote his development of more complex and symbolic communication forms. The better understanding parents have of their role in their infant's language development the more likely they are to look for and respond to their baby's communication attempts. One critical aspect of the parents' participation in early communication with their infant is the use of Motherese and Fatherese.

THE IMPORTANCE OF MOTHERESE AND FATHERESE

Having helped parents gain an understanding of infant presymbolic communication, specialists at IHR then focus more specifically on the adult's role in the communication process. We highlight the use of a communication style commonly called "Motherese." Fathers also interact with their babies in very specific ways, using many communication behaviors characteristic of "motherese" but with their own unique style. Fathers may be less verbal and more physical than mothers in their interactions with their babies, employing playful tosses in the air and other acrobatic feats babies love. Fathers may play more teasing kinds of games involving tapping, touching, or poking the baby and making toys disappear and reappear.

We teach parents the importance of and characteristics of "motherese" and "fatherese" so that together we can assess their communication with their infant and determine ways it might be made more effective by the infusion of additional "motherese" or "fatherese" behaviors. "Motherese" and "fatherese" encourage the child to communicate. Parents need to use these communication styles to stimulate communication from their child.

Parents communicate with their child by the way they hold and touch him, talk to him, and with their body language. Young infants have the ability to perceive positive or negative communication intents from adults. "Motherese" communicates the parents' positive feelings towards the child. It is developed naturally by caregivers regardless of their social, cultural, or economic status and is used by both men and women.

"Motherese" has characteristics that have been compiled by Clark and Watkins (1978):

1. The pitch of the adult's voice is higher when communicating to infants than in adult conversations and may be so exaggerated as to be a falsetto voice.
2. The adult uses exaggerated intonation.
3. Short, simple, but grammatically correct sentences are used.
4. There are longer than normal pauses between sentences or phrases, with no pause-fillers such as "uh," "well," "you know."
5. Both the adult and infant engage in prolonged gazing at one another.
6. The adult uses repetition.
7. The adult uses special words ("baby talk").
8. The conversation tends to be about the here and now, whatever the child is seeing and doing.
9. Questions, many of them rhetorical, as in, "Does Mommy love her little girl? Yes, she does!" may be used in talking to the child and describing the child's activities.
10. There is an abundance of non-verbal signals, gestures, and facial expressions.
11. The adult imitates and expands the child's utterances, and prods to encourage the child to vocalize.
12. The type and quality of language input is changed by the adult depending upon the child's age and capabilities.

When an adult uses the characteristics of "motherese" or "fatherese" in conversations with a child he/she is providing an interesting, motivating style of speech to engage the child in a turn-taking type of communication. The "sing-songy" falsetto voice catches the child's attention — it is a cue to the child that, "Oh! This message is directed at me!" Repetitions allow the child the opportunity to hear new vocabulary over and over again. Facial expressions provide a visual message. Imitation of the child's vocalizations encourages him to continue his noisemaking. The use of "motherese" is a novel visual and auditory way of communicating to the child, stimulating him to participate in the communication cycle. This initial, shared experience of communication between the parent and child is necessary to ensure more advanced communications in the future.

OTHER SKILLS PARENTS CAN USE TO PROMOTE PRESYMBOLIC COMMUNICATION INTERACTIONS WITH THEIR HEARING-IMPAIRED INFANTS

1. Acknowledge and respond to the infant's non-verbal communication attempts.
2. Include non-verbal signals in conversations with the infant: peek-a-boo; smiles; a variety of facial expressions (eye-widening, eye-blinks, "surprised" look, "funny" mouth positions, tongue wiggling); hiding face; touching (poking, tapping, tickling, "creepy-crawling"); body movement.
3. Entice infant to look when directing conversation to him.
4. *Avoid forcing* infant's visual attention in intrusive ways.
5. Be dramatic and visually interesting in order to hold the infant's attention.
6. Take turns "conversing" with the infant; avoid interrupting his "conversation."
7. Avoid overtalking. Use pauses and give the infant time to rest and respond.
8. Imitate the infant's vocal and body movement communication.
9. Imitate the baby's rhythmic movements and vocalization and initiate rhythmic movement patterns for the baby to imitate.

The guide, *It Takes Two to Talk* (Manolson, 1985) provides some excellent ideas for parents and specialists who are working on the development of presymbolic communication interactions with a child.

The fourth goal for parents as they work to promote their child's use of presymbolic communication is that parents learn to observe, document, and *appreciate* the significance of their child's presymbolic communication. We have previously alluded to the tendency of some adults to discount the importance of a baby's communication prior to his acquisition of speech or signs. When parent-infant specialists and parents of hearing-impaired infants — especially those with additional handicapping conditions who may be slow to acquire symbolic language — fail to observe, promote, and appreciate the child's presymbolic communication, they can become very discouraged about the child's gains in communication skills.

It is apparent from the descriptions of the developmental stages of presymbolic communication which appear earlier in this chapter that a great deal of communication does, in fact, take place before a baby can talk. When the specialist helps parents focus on their child's presymbolic communication, she is providing parents with evidence of the progress that their child is making. When parents observe that one month their child is using simple signals and the next month is using complex signals, their communication interactions with their child are reinforced. Parents need tangible evidence of their child's progress to reinforce their efforts at stimulation. The hierarchy of development in presymbolic communication provides parents with a way to measure their child's progress and see that, "Yes, my child is moving forward!"

PRELIMINARY OBSERVATIONS OF PRESYMBOLIC COMMUNICATION RESULTING FROM RESEARCH WITH INFANT HEARING RESOURCE FAMILIES

When an infant has been diagnosed as hearing-impaired and the family has enrolled in the IHR program of habilitation, one program goal is to examine and reinforce the presymbolic communication which takes place between the infant and his parent. One question which has been raised is whether this early presymbolic communication between hearing-impaired infants and their parents is substantially different in content and effectiveness from similar communications between normally hearing infants and their parents.

Presymbolic communication interactions between hearing-impaired infants and their parents were examined over a period of one year in a study of four families enrolled at IHR (Bullard, 1981). Three of the infants were between four and ten months of age at the project's outset. The fourth infant was 18 months chronologically but functioning at the six-month developmental level. Three of the children had hearing parents and one child had hearing-impaired parents. One of the purposes of Bullard's study was to determine if hearing-impaired infants do communicate successfully with their parents in proto-conversations (using presymbolic communication) even though their hearing losses prevent their obtaining complete auditory information from the parent's interaction with them.

Bullard's report of preliminary results was presented at the 1981 International Sign Language Research Conference in Bristol, England, and is excerpted below:

"What is being examined at the present time in our project is the kind of behavior used by the parents or the child to initiate a proto-conversation, the kinds of simultaneous and sequential and turn-taking behavior used to sustain conversation, and the kinds of procedures used to end conversations. Recorded behavior includes facial expression, eye gaze, head movement, arm and trunk movement, general body orientation, hand and finger movement, leg movement, and vocalization. In the case of the parent, all of the above are included as well as the parent's use of spoken words and signs.

"Let me say at the outset that the proto-conversations between the parents and the children in our project are incredibly rich and productive. These conversations do not appear to differ much from the conversations between hearing children and their parents except when certain kinds of behavior are being looked for. In watching these rich communications it becomes apparent why parents do not discover their babies' hearing losses.

"The first thing that was very noticeable when viewing the videotapes was how rhythmical the behavior is when the parent and child are communicating. The following is an example of just such a movement. The mother took a block and banged it on a box six times, very rhythmically. Then the baby swatted at the box using the same rhythm as the mother had used. The mother, while the baby was swatting at the box, again started banging the block in rhythm with her child's movement. This type of rhythmical movement and rhythmical imitation is a very frequent occurrence. Another example was when one father began singing 'bababa' and the child began to simultaneously imitate the movement she observed and then continued the movement after her father had stopped the movement. The youngster, after mimicking the movement four times, also began to vocalize with movement.

"The rhythmic behavior appears to play an extremely important role in the conversations. It was used by our parents, as it is by other parents, to engage the child's attention (for example, by tapping the youngster), to cue the child into a familiar play sequence (for example, bouncing a toy across the table), to check whether the child is interested in a specific game, and to continue the conversation through imitating the child's behavior. Rhythmic behavior was sometimes started in one mode, such as vocalizing, and then imitated by the other partner in another mode, such as tapping.

"In addition to this type of rhythmic behavior is the kind of coordinated rhythmic behavior that takes place within the individual. For example, you'll see the parent tapping, vocalizing, and nodding her head all at the same time. For the hearing-impaired child who cannot hear such vocalizations, he will often get more than one cue that meaningful, rhythmical communication is taking place. The parent may be looking intently into the child's face, smiling, moving her mouth, and tapping the baby's arm all at the same time. The child, though deaf, becomes so familiar with this pattern that he will often wait until the mother is finished, watching his mother's behavior before he begins his own movement. When given this many cues the child seldom interrupts his mother's movement, waiting until she has finished if he's really watching his mother. One exception to this is when the child begins to imitate the mother's behavior. The child may begin the imitation pattern while his mother is still talking (as the mother may do with the child). In observing these patterns it seems quite clear why the parent may never discover that the infant has a hearing impairment, not realizing how many conversational cues are being used besides auditory ones.

"One example of how sensitive the child is to these visual cues is a pattern we observed with our one child who has hearing-impaired parents. The parents nearly always signed to the baby when talking to her. If they had the baby's attention she would watch them intently when they were signing to her. Both of the parents, when they had finished whatever they were signing to the baby, would drop their hands into their laps, accompanied by a slight lowering of the shoulders. The youngster at six months of age was so in tune to this cue that she would instantly drop her eyes to her toy or whatever she was playing with when she saw the parents drop their hands into their laps.

"It is probably worth noting that we saw one example of when turn-taking failed, which was a real irritant to the parent. One of the mothers would from time to time begin to talk to her child, calling his name fairly sharply, but out of the child's visual range. The child, because he was not attending to his mother auditorally or visually, would continue what he was doing and from time to time would even begin to vocalize midway through the mother's utterance. The mother would react to this interruption with annoyance. It is unclear to me if she realized what was annoying her.

"The fundamental role of this rhythmical behavior as the basis for successful communication just can't be over-estimated. The rhythmical aspect seems to be fundamental to human communication functioning, no matter what mode of communication is being used. While there are learned aspects to this behavior, some researchers such as Trevarthan (1979) feel that the rhythms are apparent so early that they must be built into the baby in one way or another.

"We made another observation concerning our younsters that rather surprised us. When infants are very young, up to three months of age, while they interact some with objects, objects do not play a very large role in conversations with their parents. As a colleague of mine stated, what the parent and infant at this stage do is play with each other's faces. However, as the child grows older, objects do begin to play a very large role in this play. The incorporation of objects in play had a very unexpected effect on the communication pattern. On our very first night of videotaping, very early on the parent began to play with the child while sitting behind him. I thought that the parent was trying to sit so both she and her son were facing the camera so I suggested to her that this was not necessary and that she could sit face-to-face with the youngster as I was concerned that the mother would be out of the child's line of sight. In no time, however, we discovered the mother back around behind the infant. That time I left well enough alone. The next day, in going back and looking at the literature on early communication behavior, we found just such a pattern described (Collis, 1979). Sure enough, as infants become heavily involved with objects, parents often sit behind the youngster. The parent communicates to the baby by talking to him, and then by leaning forward and peering into the baby's face to figure out where the child is in his communication. The pair then can become engaged in parallel movement with the mother helping the youngster as he plays with the toy rather than mirroring the child's play behavior as she might if she sat face-to-face with him. The unfortunate outcome for the hearing-impaired child is that a good deal of the mother's rhythmic communication behavior is then lost to the child as often when the mother is communicating in this position she is out of the child's line of sight. Two of the parents, interestingly enough, solved this problem by putting a mirror on the floor so that they could handle objects in a parallel fashion but the child could also see the mother's movements. Of course the mother did not always sit behind the baby when communicating, but it did occur occasionally.

"One area we have been interested in looking at is the parents' incorporation of signing as part of their communication strategies. We have been particularly interested in determining if such incorporation interferes with the rhythmical communication pattern. Two of the four families were new signers, one family decided not to use signing with their child, and the fourth family, because the parents were hearing-impaired, had used signing for some time. The two mothers who were new signers were quite different in the ease with which they incorporated signing. One mother seldom got flustered. Signs that she knew she generally included easily and freely in her play. When she did not know a sign she did not worry about it. She just used nothing and continued talking and playing with her youngster. On the whole, the signing on her part did not seem to interfere with her conversation.

"The other mother appeared to be much less easy with signing, using signs much less frequently at least while she was being videotaped. When she did use signs, they were not always well-coordinated with her ongoing dialogue. What would happen would be that a look would go across her face as if to say, 'Uh-oh. I'd better use a sign.' Then she would tend to rear back a little, get a very serious look on her face, and then use the sign. She would then lean forward, soften her face into her communication mode, and carry on with her communication. By the way, this was not the only time when we saw this particular movement. The parents in the program have been told that one way to encourage their children to vocalize is to imitate the child's vocalizations. Most of the time the parents did this very unconsciously and the imitation was very much integrated with their other play imitation patterns. However, every once in a while you would see the parent 'remember' that s/he was supposed to imitate. We'd see the same kind of slight rearing back and stiffening of expression for this contrived, non-conversational imitation.

"The children all seemed to be attentive to their parents' signing in one way or another. The child with the deaf parents paid the most attention, usually looking at the parent's face or hands until the signed message was completed. The other two children would not always wait until the signed communication was completed. We often saw, however, that if the child were looking at the parent's face and the parent started signing, the child would very briefly glance at the moving hands. We did not often see the children watching the hands through an entire message. They may, however, watch the face or at least keep the signs within their peripheral vision.

"To sum up our observations to this point, it appears that the communication strategies used by hearing-impaired infants and their parents differ little from that of hearing infants. The communication is very successful, very normal appearing. Conversations that are rewarding and fun take place between the parent and the child. While all of the children vocalized, vocalization was simply not the major carrying factor in these conversations. After observing the tapes, it became quite obvious that limited auditory information did not, at this stage of development, cause serious disruptions in the communication process. Most of the communication took place face-to-face with the child, with a few notable exceptions. Morever, the parent does not talk to the baby with a *bland* face. The parent gives many visual and tactile cues to the baby each time s/he says something. Significantly, when our mothers wished *not* to become engaged in a conversation with their babies, they did so by avoiding eye contact. While the introduction of signing does cause some interference in the communication process, this interference does not overwhelm conversation. The parents and the children in our study all had established very complex, rich, and rewarding conversational routines. It appears that if signing can be successfully introduced to the parent, it can simply be applied to a very successful, already established communication system.''

References

Collis, G. 1979. ''Describing the Structure of Social Interaction in Infancy.'' In *Before Speech: The Beginning of Interpersonal Communication*, ed. M. Bullowa. Cambridge, MA: Cambridge University Press.

Trevarthan, C. 1979. ''Communication and Cooperation in Early Infancy: A Description of Primary Intersubjectivity.'' In *Before Speech: The Beginning of Interpersonal Communication,* ed. M. Bullowa. Cambridge, MA: Cambridge University Press.

The families in the study described above were enrolled in an intervention program at the time they were observed. Thus, Bullard's observations that the communication strategies used by these families differed little from those used in families of normally hearing infants may not generalize to families who are not enrolled in a habilitation program like that at Infant Hearing Resource. However, it is useful for parent-infant specialists and parents to know that hearing loss does not have to disrupt the early ''conversations'' that take place between infants and their parents. Specialists and parents can make certain that they are employing several modalities in their communication with the hearing-impaired infant to assure that the rhythmical aspects of communication are available to the child. The study also indicates that some parents who are just learning to add signed language to their communication with their infant may need assistance in using signs in a relaxed way, a skill that may develop with increased familiarity with this new communication mode.

SUMMARY

Children grow and change so much during the first year of life! For parents, one of the most thrilling aspects of this growth is the child's increasing ability to communicate his wants, needs, and ideas. The importance and significance of a flourishing system of presymbolic communication for any child and his family cannot be over-emphasized. When the child is hearing-impaired, this early communication system, based as it is on many visual and tactile components of parent-child interactions, is tremendously important to the child. A hearing-impaired child who has enjoyed the benefits of communicating without symbols will be highly motivated to expand his communication to include symbolic language as his congitive and motor development permit and as his environment encourages him to do so.

CHAPTER 21

TEACHING INFANT LANGUAGE OBJECTIVES: PARENT BEHAVIORS THAT PROMOTE THE INFANT'S ACQUISITION OF SYMBOLIC LANGUAGE

The objectives in the Parent Receptive and Expressive Language section of *Parent-Infant Communication* (Infant Hearing Resource, 1985) specify major skills and information parents acquire during their two to three years at IHR. We will expand on these objectives herein by discussing in depth two major areas in which we work with parents to help them acquire the skills and knowledge we believe they need in order to help their child learn symbolic communication. These two areas are: 1) using non-directive language in communication interactions with the child, and 2) using specific communication techniques which facilitate the child's acquisition of symbolic language.

USING NON-DIRECTIVE LANGUAGE

One of the most effective techniques employed by IHR parent-infant specialists to promote language growth in young children is the adults' use of non-directive language in much of their communication with the child. Non-directive communication consists of descriptions, questions, comments, expansions, and praise and is free of commands, directions, and judgments. Our experience with families bears out what researchers have reported, that when adults use more non-directive language in their interactions with children, the children acquire language more rapidly. We are particularly interested in what the content of the adult's message conveys about his feelings for and relationship with the child. In this section we will discuss the importance of that relationship and how to enhance the parent-child interaction by helping parents look at and modify, if needed, their communication style.

WHY LOOK AT THE PARENT-CHILD RELATIONSHIP?

Communication grows out of the social interactions that occur between the child and the significant people in his life, particularly his parents. Through these relationships the child acquires a linguistic model, a value system, and a developing concept of who he is, his lovability, and his competence. The parent-child relationship begins to form at the time of birth and, from the infant's point of view, is based on the information that he can collect through his senses. He learns about his parents from the way they hold and touch him, look at him, talk to him. The infant contributes to the relationship with his cries, movements, and facial expressions. The way in which the infant and parents respond to one another in these early days is crucial to the growing parent-child relationship.

The hearing-impaired infant may be at a disadvantage as he attempts to gather information that tells him about his relationship with his parents. Almost all of the parents' interactions with the child include spoken messages. Deprived of much of the auditory component of the parents' messages, most deaf children miss the sounds of tenderness, reassurance, warmth, and calming that the parents convey through speech. When parents are not aware that their infant is hearing-impaired, they may not know the importance of emphasizing the affective content of their message in visual and tactile ways. Thus, the infant may not receive all this crucial affective information.

When children have a handicap which affects their ability to receive or initiate communication, the handicap may create a barrier to the developing parent-child relationship. The normal parent-child relationship is characterized by mutual responsiveness: each member in the pair initiates and reciprocates communication. This reciprococity, which is an essential element of early "conversations" between parent and child, must continue as the child grows. Many infants with impairments such as cerebral palsy, deafness, and mental retardation may not imitate or reciprocate communication during social interactions in the ways that their parents expect. They may present confusing cues to their parents and demonstrate reduced responsiveness to communication initiated by their parents. When the child does not respond as expected to the parents' communication, the parents are not reinforced and they may tend to decrease the number of communication attempts with their child. This disruption of the early interaction system between infants and parents has undesirable implications for the infant's later development of intentional communication (Appell, 1986).

McDonald (1985) reports that in his observations of handicapped children and their parents and teachers, the following behavioral profile of the parents and teachers emerged:

"They often talk in long sentences, far above the range of their child's communicative competence.

"They frequently attempt to communicate without gaining the child's attention.

"They communicate 'rhetorically,' without waiting for or cueing a child's response.

"They accommodate to the child's idiosyncratic communication instead of shaping more conventional performance.

"Primarily, they have short, 'dead-end' contacts with the child rather than balanced turn-taking interactions" (p. 92).

None of these adult communication behaviors is recommended as a way to promote a child's desire to communicate.

The results of four studies which examined communication between parents and their hearing-impaired children are summarized below. Goss (1970) looked at the language used in telling a story by mothers of young hearing-impaired children and mothers of young normally hearing children. He reported that "the results of this study show that mothers of deaf children are less likely to use verbal praise than mothers of the hearing and are more likely to show verbal antagonism" (p. 96). Schlesinger and Meadow (1972) compared the play interactions between mothers and their normally hearing preschool-age children and between mothers and their hearing-impaired preschool-age children on ten dimensions. They reported that:

"The behavior of mothers of deaf children differs radically from that of the mothers of hearing children . . . These differential behavior patterns are particularly pronounced when the deaf child lags behind his deaf peers in the development of a viable means of communication. In these instances, mothers are much more likely to appear inflexible, controlling, didactic, intrusive, and disapproving. Deaf children with fewer communicative skills appear to be less happy, to enjoy the interaction with their mothers less, to be less compliant, less creative and to show less pride in mastery than either their deaf peers with additional communicative skills or the hearing children" (p. 107).

Investigators at the Lexington School for the Deaf (Greenstein, Greenstein, McConville and Stellini, 1976) conducted a study of mother-child interaction that posed the question, "What is it that parents of very young deaf children do that facilitates or impedes speech and language development?" They reported that mothers of children with better language were rated lower in use of physical coercion (touching and moving toward the child) and that the mother's ability to motivate the child without coercion provided one of the best predictors of the child's language competence. Conversely, the investigators concluded, "The number of critical, inhibitory utterances by the mother and her use of (physical) coercive motivational techniques were highly correlated with low rate of language acquisition in the child'' (p. 32).

Nienhuys, Horsborough, and Cross (1985) compared the communication interactions between four groups of mothers and their deaf or hearing children, ages two and five, and concluded that the more restricted conversational interaction observed in mother-child pairs with deaf children seemed to be related to the lower linguistic ability of the deaf children. The study also suggested that the mothers of the deaf children initiated most of the verbal interactions, thus tending to dominate the conversations and that they talked to their children in sentences of lower cognitive complexity.

These studies suggest strongly that the presence of the child's hearing loss skews normal parent-child communication. This is not surprising since the child's hearing loss prevents him from receiving the complete message his parent is sending, unless a visual mode of communication is also used. When young normally hearing children do not respond to or comply with their parent's prohibitions or commands, the parent may escalate the strength of his/her request by using a stronger reprimand, removing an object, or by using physical punishment (Minton, Kagan, and Levine, 1971). Parents of hearing-impaired children, frustrated by their child's failure to respond to the communication they direct at him, have done what parents of normally hearing children do: escalate the strength of their communication in an attempt to get through. These less reinforcing and more directive and coercive parental behaviors have the unfortunate result of adversely affecting the child's interest in using these interactions as language learning opportunities.

Specialists at IHR are extremely interested in helping families avoid the problems created when there is not an effective communication system in place between parents and child. Over the years, we have noted a positive side-effect of early identification of infants with hearing loss which is related to parent-child interactions and communication. Families who enroll when their infant is very young have not established any non-helpful patterns of communication. Parents of young infants do not expect the infant to understand what they say or to respond to their verbal requests. Thus, their relationship with their child is free of the frustration that could later lead to use of directive, coercive communication patterns. By starting early in a habilitation program which emphasizes building an effective parent-child communication system, some of the problems described above may be by-passed.

There are three situations in which IHR specialists have observed parent communication behaviors which are at odds with their child's needs: in those families where, because of late diagnosis of the child's hearing loss, there is no viable communication system between the parents and toddler; in some families of early-diagnosed children when the child approaches the age of two years; and in families where parents are directive ''by nature.'' In the early enrolled families, we suspect that the two-year-old's emerging drive for autonomy, coupled with a possibly still limited communication system, presents some parents with a new challenge. They revert to a more directive communication style in order to maintain control over their newly rebellious child. Parent personality can also be a factor. Some parents are just not conversationalists. They are directive with all of their children. When families enroll already experiencing difficulties with communication interactions, and when families begin experiencing difficulty because of changes in their child, IHR specialists approach these difficulties by working to get an effective communication system established and by working with parents to modify behaviors they may be using that work against a good learning environment for their child.

MODIFYING PARENT-CHILD COMMUNICATION INTERACTIONS

The parent-infant specialist can play a positive role in enhancing the affective and communication aspects of the parent-child interaction first by assessing the need for changes in the interaction and then by modeling new behaviors.

The following language modification program for parents was developed to help parents who routinely used a more directive style of communication with their child become more aware of the effects of this style. This program was so well-received and so much fun to do that we began to utilize it with all families, if only to reinforce the more effective communicators and give them information about what they are doing well. The language modification program for parents is called Coding Language Interaction.

CODING LANGUAGE INTERACTION

The steps in utilizing this program are described in detail on pages 127 and 128 in *Parent-Infant Communication*. The steps are summarized below.

1. The specialist introduces the rationale for and benefits of using more descriptive language and fewer directions and commands with small children. The Parent Handout, PH-95, "Talking to Your Child: Does It Make A Difference What You Say?" in *Parent-Infant Communication* can be given to the parents to read.

2. The specialist introduces and gives examples of terms such as "descriptive language," "commands," and "directions." The definitions and examples on Parent Handout, PH-97, "Indirect Language Stimulation Techniques," in *Parent-Infant Communication* are very helpful. For the first exposure to this pro-

gram we introduce only the terms "descriptions" and "commands." Examples of descriptive statements that parents are encouraged to use when talking to their child are: "You put the block in the truck," and "You heard a dog bark, didn't you?" Examples of commands, the type of communication we encourage parents to avoid, are: "Put all the balls in *this* box," and "Tell me what this is."

3. The specialist introduces a form on which parents and specialist can tally the numbers of descriptions and the numbers of commands they hear used by the adult in a short videotaped adult-child interaction.

4. The specialist and parents view a two-minute videotaped segment of a parent-child interaction and both parent and specialist tally the adult's use of "descriptions" and "commands" on the form.

5. Parents and specialist discuss the results, compare notes, and watch the tape again, stopping the tape for discussion at points at which the parent and specialist disagreed on their characterization of the language used by the adult on the tape.

6. When the parents and specialist are in agreement on how to code the communication behaviors observed on the videotape, the parent codes the language the specialist uses as she interacts with the child.

7. If the parents feel comfortable, they are invited to practice using descriptive language in an interaction with their child.

8. After a few sessions of practice the parents may want to be videotaped so they can observe themselves and tally the descriptions and commands they used in talking to their child.

9. Many parents will be interested in watching for and tallying several additional types of communication. In subsequent sessions, parents can view videotaped interactions and note descriptions, commands, praise, admonitions, and questions.

It is critical to use this activity as a confidence builder. Because parents may be trying something new they may feel uneasy. The specialist can model relaxation, ease, and a spirit of fun. If there is a warm trusting relationship between members of the parent-specialist partnership this exercise will go very well. An example of how we worked with one family to modify the mother's communication with her son follows.

Elsa and her son, Sammy, who had a moderate hearing loss, enrolled at IHR when Sammy was two years old. At the time of enrollment, Elsa was using a high number of directive communications in her interactions with Sammy. Sammy was responding to his mother mostly by tuning her out. Julia, the parent-infant specialist working with Elsa and Sammy, videotaped them together in an activity in which Elsa was asked to play with Sammy like she ordinarily does at home.

After Julia had reviewed the videotape at a later time and tallied the behaviors she saw in this interaction, her suspicion was confirmed that it would be appropriate to introduce Elsa to the idea of a language modification program. In the next several sessions, she followed the steps in the Coding Language Interaction program, talking with Elsa about the benefits of using more descriptive language than commands and directions. She sent parent handouts home with Elsa, and talked with her about the terms "descriptive language," "commands" and "directions." Julia and Elsa practiced tallying these types of communication, first using a videotape Julia had made with another child, then using short videotapes of Julia and Sammy, and then of Elsa and Sammy playing together. Elsa and Julia compared their tallies and discussed the results of these practice sessions over a number of months. Julia began to notice an appreciable difference in the type of communication that Elsa used in her interactions with Sammy and in Sammy's responses to Elsa.

Seven months after Julia had first videotaped Elsa and Sammy, she videotaped another segment. The results from the first and second sessions are reported in Figure 12.

Segment I: In this 3.5 minute segment videotaped soon after the family enrolled, Elsa and Sammy were sitting on the floor playing with toys.

Parent to Child Communication

Questions	Commands	Non-Directive Communication
36	12	11

Child to Parent Communication

Vocalizations/Words	Looks toward Parent
10	6

Segment II: During this 4-minute interaction, videotaped seven months after the first segment, Sammy and Elsa were sitting side by side at a table, looking at a book.

Parent to Child Communication

Questions	Commands	Non-Directive Communication
5	0	57

Child to Parent Communication

Vocalizations/Words	Looks toward Parent
46	16

FIGURE 12.   The parent-infant specialist coded the communication interactions between the parent, Elsa, and her child, Sammy, prior to the introduction of a language modification program (Segment I) and after Elsa had practiced using non-directive language in her conversations with Sammy (Segment II).

The second interaction differed dramatically from the first. In the first segment, Sammy rarely looked at Elsa and, in fact, played with his body turned away from her. In the second segment, both Elsa and Sammy appeared to be relaxed and genuinely enjoying themselves. In the first segment, Elsa's communication to Sammy was predominately testing questions asked in a demanding tone of voice: "Where's the doggy?", "What's this?", "What's the doggy say?", "What's in there?" In the second segment, Elsa's communication was almost entirely descriptive sentences. She frequently imitated Sammy and nodded in agreement with what he said. The few questions she asked during the second segment were designed to provoke thinking, with no answer expected. During the second segment, Sammy's communications to his mother increased drastically. His looks to her and the length of eye contact between Sammy and Elsa both increased in the second segment.

In the seven month interval between these segments, Sammy was gaining auditory information from hearing aids that had been placed shortly before the first segment was recorded. His communicative abilities — both receptive and expressive — had improved during this period of time and his increased contribution to the communication interaction may be attributed in part to his improved language. However, the relaxed tone of the second segment signalled an enjoyment in the communication and interaction process that had been completely absent in the earlier segment.

It appears from this example and other instances in which we have used this procedure of modifying parents' language that:

1. It is possible to teach adults alternative ways of communicating with their hearing-impaired children.
2. When a parent decreases the amount of directive communication and increases non-directive utterances, the child's eye contact with the parent and number of communicative contributions are likely to increase.

At IHR we have found that making parents aware of the benefits of non-directive, descriptive language can affect their communication with their child, the apparent quality of the relationship, and very possibly the child's learning rate. If there is a high degree of tension and directiveness in the relationship, helping the parent change the content of his/her communication can change the nature of the interaction. It is very hard to be directive (adult is thinking to himself, "Put the block in the basket, not on the table") when the adult is saying, "You picked up the big block; you put it on the table."

We are not suggesting that parent to child communication be purged of all directions or commands. Parents *must* direct their children throughout the day: "Time to eat " "Get your coat " "Go wash your hands." What we are saying is that many parents do not naturally use non-directive language. When the adult increases his use of non-directive, descriptive language, the quality of the parent-child relationship and of the child's emerging symbolic language can be significantly enhanced.

USING COMMUNICATION TECHNIQUES WHICH FACILITATE SYMBOLIC LANGUAGE LEARNING

The content and timing of the communication of the adults around him will determine to a large degree what symbolic language the hearing-impaired child learns and when he learns it. An abundant background of presymbolic communication is a prerequisite. Once that has been attained, families and specialists can use specific techniques which foster the child's acquisition of symbolic language. Many of these techniques are also appropriate for children at the presymbolic communication level, but others are more structured and are intended for interactions with children of preschool age and older. The curriculum, *Parent-Infant Communication,* lists most of the techniques as parent objectives in the section entitled "Receptive and Expressive Language." That list is included here with a few additions.

Parents are encouraged to acquire and utilize the following skills, which are discussed in detail below, to promote their child's acquisition of symbolic language:

1. Use appropriate methods of gaining the child's auditory and visual attention.
2. Use effective methods of maintaining the child's attention.
3. Make communication relevant and interesting.
4. Use voice effectively.
5. Use repetition.
6. Encourage the child to use language to express his feelings, wants, and needs.
7. Use short sentences initially.
8. Emphasize the one or two important words in the sentence.
9. Include the child in family conversation.
10. Provide correct word when the child mispronounces or misnames.
11. Expand the child's incomplete words or sentences into complete words or sentences.
12. Once a language concept has been learned, help the child broaden it and generalize it to other situations.
13. Pose questions that elicit thinking and problem-solving.
14. Use active listening techniques in communicating with the child.

When a family first enrolls at IHR, the specialist carries out a baseline assessment. She observes the parents at play with their infant in order to determine which presymbolic/symbolic communication behaviors parents and child are using effectively and which of the skills listed above parents already practice. Specialist and parents then select communication behaviors to be encouraged and skills to be acquired in a priority order based on the infant's developmental level and needs at any given time, and upon the parents' interests. The Parent Involvement Method (Chapter 10) is utilized by the specialist to describe, model, and practice these techniques with the parents, all of which are described below.

USE APPROPRIATE METHODS OF
GAINING THE CHILD'S VISUAL AND AUDITORY ATTENTION

Effective methods for gaining the child's visual and auditory attention include: calling the child's name if he is "within earshot" (Ling, 1981); making novel audible sounds such as a handclap, whistle, or other vocal sound the child can hear; getting down on the child's level and talking within two feet of his hearing aids; moving hand or object toward speaker's face; moving into the child's line of vision; or ceasing movement until the child looks.

Most of these techniques are self-explanatory except perhaps the last one which can be illustrated with an example. When working with children eighteen months and older with whom gaining visual attention is a goal, the specialist can employ a short "attention conditioning" process. This process will teach the child that an adult's cessation of movement can be a cue to look at the adult. To the specialist this is a structured sequence. To the child it is just play. When the specialist uses this technique intermittently over 4 to 5 sessions the child learns to look to the adult for information without even knowing his behavior is being shaped!

In the following example the specialist, Julia, was playing with two-year-old Mandy who had not yet indicated auditory awareness of speech. Julia's goal was that Mandy would see her say "go" prior to watching a car go down the slide. In order to teach Mandy to look at her, Julia elected to control an activity in which a car was used. Julia held the car at the top of a slide, then moved her other hand up toward her chin. Mandy visually followed the hand movement and looked at Julia's face. Julia said, "Go," the car went down the slide, and Mandy squealed with delight. Next, Julia held her hand on the car which Mandy watched intently, waiting for it to go down. Finally, since nothing was happening, Mandy looked at Julia who said, "There it goes!" and immediately activated the car. Mandy giggled, scrambled over to get the car, and handed it back to Julia. Julia replaced the car on the slide and continued the process of waiting for Mandy to look at her. The length of time Mandy watched the car prior to quizzically looking at Julia began to decrease. On the seventh presentation Mandy looked at Julia as soon as the car was placed on the slide. Julia quickly rewarded Mandy's visual attention with, "Go car!" and released the car. This technique was repeated with different toys and situations over the next several sessions to generalize Mandy's concept of the need to look at Julia prior to the reward of seeing a toy activated.

After three weeks of effort by Julia and by Mandy's parents, Mandy had learned that when the adults stopped their movement mid-game, movement would resume after she looked at them. Of course the other valuable information Mandy gained was the important association between the auditory-verbal message and the activity or object. The adult's behavior of briefly ceasing movement to gain the child's visual attention becomes very natural and automatic. However, the behavior is always used with a purpose and

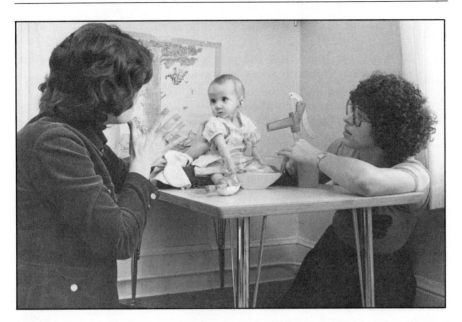

Making sure that the child is situated so that she can see the faces of the adults with whom she is interacting is essential to good communication.

with the awareness that it is an adult-directed behavior geared toward eliciting a specific child response. There are potential negative consequences in the excessive use of a technique like this, the primary one being the introduction of too much structure and adult control into communication interactions. Adults must keep in mind the need to keep their communication interactions with the young deaf child natural, low in frustration, and rewarding for the child. If done properly, attention-gaining techniques can meet the above criteria.

Mention must be made of one improper technique which is sometimes utilized by individuals unaware of its negative consequences. IHR specialists have intervened with family members who have mistakenly assumed that pulling the child's chin or face around is an acceptable means of getting his attention. A gentle reminder of the intrusive and demeaning nature of this technique, followed by careful modeling of other more appropriate techniques, is usually all that is needed to change this behavior.

When it is not feasible to place oneself within the visual field of a child who cannot hear the adult's voice, a light tap on the arm can be used. It is important to keep in mind, however, that the child who does not hear the adult approach may be surprised or even frightened by an unexpected touch on the arm.

There are specific situations in which IHR specialists utilize techniques which are aimed at directing the child's visual attention toward our face and hands. These are:

1. When presenting language to a child in early language-acquisition stages.
2. When the baby is at the presymbolic stage of communication development which relies so heavily on visual information.
3. When introducing new concepts to a child.
4. When we are certain the child's residual hearing requires that he use vision and hearing equally or that he rely primarily on visual information.

As children's auditory decoding skills grow, we give them increasing opportunity to listen without looking at us when we talk to them. Hence our instruction to some parents, "Talk both when your child is looking at you and when he is not looking." When a child can understand a message using both auditory and visual clues, it is time to remove the visual information and give him practice at decoding the message through audition alone. If the child has acquired receptive language through a combination of spoken and signed language, specialists and parents will first stop using signs when saying familiar messages, and will later make opportunities to talk so that speech-reading is also unavailable to the child. It is not our intent to prevent children from understanding our communication by removing visual information. It *is* our intent to give them the opportunity to comprehend speech through audition alone when that is possible for them.

USE EFFECTIVE METHODS OF MAINTAINING THE CHILD'S ATTENTION

Infants and young children are notorious for their fleeting attention. Adults who wish to capture their interest for the purposes of language input must exercise creativity and ingenuity. Since children learn best when they are motivated to attend voluntarily, it is important that adults attempt to provide interesting things for them to see and hear. Some helpful guidelines are:

1. Show enthusiasm. Keep your voice and facial expressions interesting.
2. Use clues to add meaning. Use natural gestures or show objects or actions along with spoken/signed words.
3. Use suspense, surprise, and appropriate teasing.
4. Give the child equal time to talk, to handle materials, and to participate in the activity.
5. *Show interest in what the child communicates.*

"That's a key. You want the key?" The specialist shows the parent how to use the baby's interest in his toy as an opportunity to model appropriate language.

MAKE COMMUNICATION RELEVANT AND INTERESTING

Learning theory tells us that children will learn what is developmentally appropriate, motivating, rewarding, and interesting. Parents, particularly those who are newly enrolled, experience frustration because they are unsure of how to talk to their child and of "what to talk about." It may seem to these parents that there is an unlimited number of words which could be used in any given situation. The following guidelines help narrow the choices somewhat:

1. Describe (talk about) what the child is seeing, doing, or feeling *right now*. Give him the words for objects he is seeing, places he is at, activities he is enjoying.
2. Use language appropriate to the child's developmental level. Begin with short, simple sentences and increase complexity as the child's understanding of language grows.
3. Respond to the child's communication. Show him you understand what he is communicating. Give him words for what he expresses non-verbally, e.g., "I don't want a bath, Daddy," as he refuses to let you remove his pants; "I like my puppy," as he strokes his pet.
4. Establish communication games around routine activities such as bathtime, bedtime, and meals. The child begins to anticipate the

parent's initiation of the game and learns to respond. For example, when preparing for a bath or bed, the parent may ask, "What comes off first, your shoes? Your shirt?" The child may point in response at first, but will later learn to use the spoken/signed words. As the child becomes more accomplished in his use of symbolic language, the adult can model more complex language in the routine.

5. Play the "child's game." Let him choose the activity, decide the rules of the game, and tell you what to do. This technique of using play as the learning milieu is discussed in detail in Chapter 12. Adults who provide the language that *describes* the child's play are optimizing the child's chances of learning.

6. Tell stories that incorporate pretend and make-believe as well as events that the child has experienced and people he knows. Make the child the main character in some of the stories. Encourage the child to tell stories, listen with enthusiasm, and respond with animated facial expression.

USE VOICE EFFECTIVELY

It is our experience at IHR that parents and specialists occasionally need feedback on the characteristics of the vocal stimuli they are providing to the child. Desirable vocal characteristics are appropriate loudness and projection of the voice, appropriate rate of speaking, clarity, and natural intonation patterns. Some adults with very soft voices need to learn to increase their vocal volume in order for their child to hear them. Practice and encouragement can help adults modify what might be an habitually soft voice. Specialists should also recognize that for some parents, insufficient loudness may only be a symptom of initial shyness which will diminish as the parent-specialist partnership grows.

A discussion of the adult voice as a critical auditory learning stimulus for the child can help parents see the value of their attention to how they talk. Ling's (1981) concept of talking within earshot — and what that means for their child — can be emphasized to raise parents' awareness of conditions under which their child is able to hear the sounds of voice and to discriminate speech sounds. Parents can learn that the hearing-impaired child gets important information from their use of pitch, loudness, and accent, and from the rate at which they speak.

USE REPETITION

Any child needs frequent exposure to words in a variety of settings and uses before he can attach meaning to them and begin to use them appropriately. Most children with hearing loss have dramatically reduced exposure to language because they cannot overhear all of the language that occurs in their environment as do normally hearing children. The adults around the hearing-impaired child must ensure that he is exposed to new words frequently enough to learn them. As his understanding and use of language grows, repetition in teaching will become less important.

Repetition can be utilized with young hearing-impaired children in important ways:

1. A new word is used in a variety of short sentences during an activity of limited duration. "That paper is *rough*. Does it feel *rough* to you? This sponge is *rough,* too."

2. The new word is used throughout the day in a wide variety of situations. "Do you remember that *rough* paper Julia used at school?" "Feel Bobo's feet. They feel *rough*." "The wood on this box feels very *rough*."

ENCOURAGE THE CHILD TO USE LANGUAGE TO EXPRESS HIS FEELINGS, WANTS, AND NEEDS

One of the perils of habilitation with the infant whose language development is delayed is the "talk trap." This results from the need felt by the over-zealous adult to make up for lost time by giving the child as much language input as air-time will allow. But what does this teach the child? Possibly it teaches him that he is an empty vessel waiting to be filled, that his role is a passive one, that his job is to attend silently, and that "conversations" with the folks are just no fun. Fifty percent of the communication process has been overlooked because the baby seldom gets a turn. Because the baby has no words yet the adult may think he has nothing to say. Not so. The baby has reactions, needs, ideas, desires, and questions, and if we listen and watch carefully we will understand them. He may show them in his eyes or by the shape of his mouth. He may coo, pull back, or point. The hearing-impaired baby, like all babies, has a lot to tell us. Tips for adults as they begin the exciting process of helping the baby acquire symbols for his "language" include:

1. During communication interactions with an infant, wait, look at him expectantly, and give him a chance to express himself.

2. Continue the conversational turn-taking established early in the presymbolic communication stage.

3. Attend to, interpret, and attach spoken and signed words to the baby's communication behaviors.

4. For the child who has some symbolic language, ask questions that you know he has the language to answer, thereby reinforcing his success with two-way communication.

5. Offer choices that elicit a language response such as: "Do you

want an apple or a banana?''

6. Convey through your interest, attention, and response that you value the child's contributions to conversations.

USE SHORT SENTENCES AT FIRST

Babies and young children will generally not attend to nor understand a grand assemblage of profuse vocabulary. The technique of communicating primarily in short sentences is logical because that is the amount of information babies can absorb and because the diminished receptive abilities of the baby with hearing loss require it. We need to limit and control stimuli at first and direct the infant's focus, knowing he must begin the arduous process of learning to decode verbal information that is ambiguous and confusing. Sentences of three to six words seem to be just right. ''Timmy, where's your kitty? You found him! Nice kitty. Shall we feed him? Yes? Okay, you help me. Where's kitty's food?''

The specialist will want to talk with parents about the importance of speaking in phrases and short sentences rather than in single words. Because one of our goals for the hearing-impaired child is that he understand conversational speech, we must model conversational speech from the beginning. Words spoken in isolation have different acoustic characteristics than they do when embedded in a sentence (Ling, 1976). Teaching words in isolation does not give the child information about how words must be ordered when placed in sentences and how they relate to each other. He can only learn how meaning is conveyed through word sequence and through the suprasegmental aspects of speech from hearing and seeing words used in sentences.

EMPHASIZE ONE OR TWO IMPORTANT WORDS IN THE SENTENCE

When working with families who are just starting out, IHR specialists model the technique of emphasizing one or two important words in the sentences directed to the baby. This highlighting of words can be done in two ways:

1. By placing the emphasized word at the end of the sentence, ''Here's your *milk*,'' ''Do you want to climb *up*?'', if you are working on teaching ''milk'' or ''up.''
2. By stressing the selected spoken word through accent, duration, or pitch emphasis and the signed word through use of larger sign and exaggerated facial expression. These techniques can be applied to the emphasized word when it lies at the end of a sentence or if it is placed elsewhere. In the example, ''Can you climb *up* the stairs?'' the parent pauses briefly before and after the word

"up," whether spoken or signed. The important word may also be spoken a little louder and with longer duration than usual. Care must taken not to cross that fine line between emphasis and distortion of the word through excess exaggeration.

It has been our experience that infants and toddlers sometimes naturally attend to the last word in a phrase and that they will attend to emphasized words because they contain more information. In the initial stages of sentence comprehension they may also learn to rely on their ability to pick out the one word they know and act on that information, failing to attend to unfamiliar words and thus failing to respond in the way the speaker anticipated. Adults can help the child at this point by understanding what a particular communication meant to the child and, therefore, why he responded the way he did; by patiently rephrasing; and by highlighting new words with emphasis.

This technique of highlighting words may seem to be at odds with data which says that young children, including those with hearing loss, do not learn discrete bits of language information, that they learn to decode phrases first, that they rely on suprasegmental information for meaning. This is all true. But at the same time as this is happening, they are learning single words. By using short sentences and supplying meaning through use of pitch, duration, rhythm, and intensity in spoken language, and through use of space and movement in signed language, we are giving children exactly what they need. But, in addition, by highlighting new words or important words, we are laying the groundwork for the subsequent stage of receptive language development, understanding single words.

INCLUDE THE CHILD IN THE FAMILY CONVERSATION

A disappointment commonly expressed by older deaf children and adults is that as children they were often shut out of family conversations because people talked too fast or unclearly, several members talked at once, speakers were not facing them, speakers were too far away to be heard, or the family did not sign at all or when the child was in the room (when sign was the child's primary communication mode) thereby preventing the child from "overhearing" the communication between others. Resultant feelings and attitudes are obvious: "They don't care " "I don't matter " "I'm too much trouble " "I don't like it here " "It hurts to be excluded " "It hurts to be deaf." Not only was the child relegated to the status of bystander or outsider, but wonderful language learning opportunities were lost.

It takes work for a family to change its communication style to accommodate the needs of a member who doesn't hear, but the payoffs in terms of family strength, cohesiveness, and joy — and in the child's view of himself and his value in the world — are vast. The parent-infant specialist can help parents think of ways to make family conversation meaningful and satisfying for the whole family. Some tips the specialist might give include:

1. Locate the hearing-impaired child so that he can see all family members.
2. Situate the hearing-impaired child next to someone who will repeat what was said by individuals out of the child's earshot.
3. When signed language is used, teach the entire family to sign.
4. Draw out the hearing-impaired child.
5. Gently encourage siblings to help each other be understood by and to understand the child with hearing loss.

It is unrealistic for a family to expect its members to make these accommodations 100% of the time. There is not the energy or the patience. But each family member does have the right to equal access to social interaction.

It is also important that the hearing-impaired child learns that his deafness is not the only cause of misunderstanding. He should learn that *other* children in the family do not understand all of what is going on, too. Not every conversation that takes place in a home is pertinent to, or intended for, a child's ears. In addition, communication is not always easy or clear even for people with perfectly normal hearing and excellent speech. The hearing-impaired child needs to learn to sort out what communication problems are caused by hearing loss and which are the result of the difficulties everyone experiences in communication interactions.

The family which strives toward full inclusion of their hearing-impaired child, without feeling guilt when that is not possible, will be rewarded by seeing the child mature into a self-confident, sociable, and interesting person.

PROVIDE THE CORRECT WORD WHEN THE CHILD MISPRONOUNCES OR MISNAMES

This is a modeling technique that, much to the surprise of many adults, is very effective in teaching the child to correct his own speech and signs. There are two cautions to keep in mind when the child mispronounces or misuses a word. **Caution 1:** Do not tell the child he was wrong. **Caution 2:** Do not repeat the child's mistake.

Illustration of an *improper correction*:

Child, looking at bear: "Doggy."
Adult: "No, that's not a doggy, it's a *bear.*"

The two mistakes in this example are: 1) The child's error was repeated so he may think he used the correct label, yet he also heard "no," leaving him confused, and 2) The child was told "no," so he thinks he did something wrong. **He did nothing wrong; he did not make a mistake.** He took a chance. He tried out the language for the concept he had. He gave us valuable information about what he knows. It is our responsibility to help him expand his concept about furry things with four legs. What a wonderful opportunity to begin that process on a positive note.

A much more effective way to help the child learn when he mispronounces or misuses a word is to **model the correct pronunciation or correct word yourself in a short sentence or two that acknowledge the child's communication intent and carry the conversation forward.**

Illustration of a *proper correction:*

> Child, looking at bear: "Doggy."
>
> Adult: "You see a *bear.* Wow, that's a big *bear*! Is that bear black or brown?"

The rules for modeling the correct word are:

1. Do not repeat the incorrect word or pronunciation.
2. Do not say "no," or "you are wrong."
3. Cheerfully provide the correct model.

Believe it or not, children learn to correct their own utterances from hearing the correct model. The rewards are:

1. They do not feel critized.
2. Their self-esteem remains intact.
3. They do not feel defeated.
4. They feel free to take risks.
5. They get the correct information they need.

USE EXPANSIONS

The use of expansions is often seen in the communication of parents whose children learn language early and well. These parents give the child information to augment his communication.

> Child: "Tree fall?"
>
> Adult: "Are you worried the tree might fall?"

> Child: "Ow, hot!" (pointing to driveway)
>
> Adult: "Yes, the pavement is hot because the sun has been shining on it. The sun is hot." (This is not a common observation in Oregon, however.)

ONCE A LANGUAGE CONCEPT HAS BEEN LEARNED, HELP THE CHILD BROADEN IT AND GENERALIZE IT TO OTHER SITUATIONS

Here are some examples:

1. When the child learns that the sun heats his driveway, show him that it also heats his toy cars, the sprinkler nozzle, the steel fence.
2. When you have shown a child that the animal in the picture is a

cow, point out the cow in the field, the brown and black cow, adult and infant cows, real and toy cows.

3. When the child has learned the word "shirt," help him learn the names of the individual parts of the shirt, e.g., collar, sleeves, cuffs.

4. When the child learns that he crosses a "bridge" on the way to church, point out that there are also bridges just for trains or just for people, that there are many different sizes and kinds of bridges.

If the child is not helped to generalize and broaden concepts, his restricted exposure to language will keep his understanding of concepts narrow and limited. This is the stage in the child's language development in which adults might become complacent and need a little nudge. We are often so thrilled that the child has finally learned the word "bridge" that we forget to help him with the next steps, the first being to fully understand "bridgeness" in its depth and breadth and the second being to acquire words, such as "overpass" and "foot bridge" that define different types of bridges. If we don't help him now, particularly for concepts which are more abstract than "bridge," it may not get done.

POSE QUESTIONS

The use of questions is frequently observed in parents whose children have extensive language. But these parents use a special brand of question. **It is not a test** as in the use of the question, "What's that?" to elicit the correct answer from the child. Instead, parents of language-competent children use questions which probe, which are not intrusive, and which the child may choose to answer or not. These questions stimulate thought, pondering, and more questioning by the child. The question, "What's that?" can be packaged with non-verbal and suprasegmental cues which convey, "What do you suppose that is?" or "Do you know what that is?". There is no right or wrong answer to this type of question. Other thought-inducing questions might be:

"What do you think happened to Fluffy's milk?"
"Where did that train go?"
"How can we make this thicker?"
"What do you think the Mama bird is doing?"

The toddler may not understand many of our questions at first, but he will learn to realize when a question is being asked. By using pauses, expectant postures, and facial expressions we have conveyed that the child may choose to respond or not. Adults will often pause for a moment following their question and then answer it for the child. Eventually, through experience, the child learns to decode questions, to respond, and equally important, to ask questions himself.

USE ACTIVE LISTENING TECHNIQUES

The field of interpersonal communication skills has much to teach us. Skills which clarify, enhance, and promote clear communication between adults (see Chapter 9) are also directly applicable to language stimulation with young children. Active listening responses serve to reinforce the communicator's behavior, to encourage him to talk more, and to elicit expansions of a past communication. They also create feelings of being accepted and understood and feelings of satisfaction with the communication process. Active listening behaviors that adults can use with young children include:

1. Paraphrasing
   Child: "Gramma house. Jimmy no."
   Dad: "You want to visit Gramma by yourself."
   As a result of his father's response, the child then knows that Dad understood him and he is likely to tell Dad more.
2. Minimal Encouragers
   These include nodding, leaning forward to show interest, eye contact, and facial expressions which convey empathy.
3. Reflecting Feelings, Attitudes, and Beliefs
   Child: "Buffy not outside. Where Buffy go? Not eat food."
   Parent: "You can't find Buffy and you are worried about him."
   Adults must take care not to take too broad a leap in guessing what the child might be feeling or thinking. It is unpleasant to have one's feelings or beliefs incorrectly labeled.

The use of non-directive language and of fourteen communication techniques which adults and siblings can use to promote a child's language acquisition have been discussed. These techniques are modeled by the specialist in her interactions with the child and can be demonstrated for parents during sessions using the Parent Involvement Method (Chapter 10). These techniques describe *how* family members can communicate most effectively with a hearing-impaired child. Equally important is the use of a developmental sequence of language objectives that guide the parent-infant specialist and parents in presenting the hearing-impaired child with language stimuli for which he is developmentally ready. The use of such a sequence is discussed below.

USING A DEVELOPMENTAL SEQUENCE OF INFANT LANGUAGE OBJECTIVES TO RECORD BASELINE, PLAN HABILITATION, AND ASSESS PROGRESS

IHR specialists use the receptive and expressive language sequences from *Parent-Infant Communication* in habilitation with hearing-impaired children. These objectives were drawn from norm-referenced tests and from other research-supported scales based on the language development of normally hearing children between the ages of nine months to four years. Using the objectives in *Parent-Infant Communication*, parents and specialist work as a team to:

1. **Determine baseline or current level of function:** What receptive and expressive language does the child already use?
2. **Set language goals:** What language concepts are next in the sequence? What language concepts are appropriate for the child to learn now? What language does he need to express his current interests and desires?
3. **Record progress:** What language objectives has the child achieved during the habilitation process?

Because new language is more readily and efficiently learned if it is based on former learning, we believe it is important to stay close to the sequence of language acquisition observed in normally hearing children. It makes no sense to attempt to teach names of colors to a 20-month-old child who is functioning at the 18-month level in receptive language when color names are not typically acquired by normally hearing children until age three. However, it is equally important to avoid becoming bound by the sequence of objectives in the curriculum. If a child has no interest in the activities, toys, or language associated with a specific concept, then select another objective to work on that is not dependent on acquisition of the first. Other cautions in using a scale based on normal development include:

1. Do not focus solely on language objectives which require more hearing or more listening experience than the child currently has, attempting to teach them just because they come next. The objective, "Child uses the sound made by an object to refer to the object, e.g., 'Choo-choo' for train, 'meow' for cat," is a 10 to 12-month skill. A 14-month-old hearing-impaired child who has been wearing hearing aids only one month may not be ready to acquire this skill. However, he may be ready for another objective in that or subsequent age-levels. Move on to teaching other objectives while continuing to model the former, without expecting it to be learned immediately.
2. Remember that any language scale or guide is merely that. It can only *sample* the breadth and depth of the language that is available. The adults' task is to use the guide as a reminder while

continuously drawing from within themselves a broad range of language to use with the child.

We encourage parents to have two sets of goals for themselves: 1) to expose the child to specific language concepts selected for emphasis, based on the child's developmental readiness; and 2) to have general language goals which encompass the things they naturally say to their child about whatever is going on at the time.

CHECKING FOR CHILD ACHIEVEMENT OF A LANGUAGE CONCEPT USING *PARENT-INFANT COMMUNICATION*

Children acquire language concepts in two ways. First, they *understand* a word, meaning that they can attach the word to the object, action, or person that it represents. Words that are understood are part of the child's *receptive language* vocabulary. Determining when the child has added a word to his receptive vocabulary requires that the adult observe some child behavior that demonstrates that the child has associated the word with an object, action, or person. Parents and specialists can set up situations in which the child is given the opportunity to demonstrate his understanding of a word. However, they must be certain that the child is, in fact, understanding the word as opposed to correctly interpreting situational clues.

It is difficult, for instance, to check for understanding of the word "open" since, when you hand the child a box or bag and say, "Open it!", that may have been his intent all along. Asking a child, out of the blue, to "Go open the door" requires understanding of more than just the word "open." It is generally easier to test for the child's understanding of nouns, including proper nouns, since the child can be given a choice of two objects or people as in the requests, "Get your *shoe*" and "Where's the *ball*?"; or "Give it to *Mommy*" and "*Daddy* has it." Even if the child does not understand the rest of the sentence, his eyes will go to the correct object or person if he has understood the emphasized word.

A warning is issued here to avoid the pitfall of constant testing of the child's receptive vocabulary. The child should not be asked to point to, show, find, or look at any object or person, or to perform any action unless you are confident that he has had enough exposure to the meaning of the word to have had a realistic opportunity to have learned it. The young child who is repeatedly requested to demonstrate language skills he has not yet acquired is put in the position of failing repeatedly and he will soon learn to tune out such requests and other verbal input from adults. Be aware that when you are asking a child, "What's that?", you are testing him. As was suggested in the section "Guidelines for Testing a Child's Abilities" in Chapter 16, if a child does not correctly identify an object after two requests, the adult should quickly switch from the testing mode to the teaching mode.

Once a child has acquired a spoken or signed word in his receptive vocabulary, he will add it to his expressive language vocabulary when he has a need to use it. The criteria for determining whether a word is a part of the child's expressive vocabulary are that the child uses the word *spontaneously* and *meaningfully*. Spontaneous usage means that the child is *not* imitating the word. In order to decide if usage is spontaneous it is necessary to wait for the child to use the word when it has not been modeled immediately prior to the child's use. Meaningful usage requires that the child use the word appropriately and with the correct referent. If the child says or signs "dog" perfectly but is pointing at a cow when he says it, that usage is not meaningful in the strict sense of the word. The child has generalized the four-legged characteristic of dogs to all four-legged animals, an important cognitive step. All the more reason not to admonish the child with, "No! That's not a dog." Providing the child with the correct referent for the object, "That's a *cow*!" will provide him with a way to expand his knowledge of four-legged animals.

As the child demonstrates acquisition of words in both his receptive and expressive vocabularies, the parents and specialist will record this acquisition in two ways. First, the individual word will be recorded on the appropriate vocabulary checksheet. Secondly, the receptive or expressive language objective that the child achieves with the acquisition of the word is checked off. In keeping these records — as well as records of connected expressive language when the child begins to combine words — the parents and specialist will be maintaining ongoing records of the child's linguistic achievements.

The receptive and expressive language objectives in *Parent-Infant Communication* are categorized into age-ranges according to the ages at which normally hearing children acquire each objective. This format enables the parents and teacher to know at what linguistic age the child is functioning at any given time and also to determine how much linguistic competence the child acquires over a given period of time. One goal of the specialists at IHR is that a hearing-impaired child acquires a year's worth of linguistic competence in a year's time. If we are not meeting or closely approximating this goal, the parents and specialist discuss the factors that are preventing the child from making more progress. It is not always the case that changes can be made to increase the child's rate of learning. However, it is important to determine if there are changes that, if made, are likely to increase the child's rate of progress so that parents can elect to make these changes if they like.

Each child's rate of achievement of language objectives is influenced by a unique combination of innate abilities, cognitive development, use of audition, and environmental factors — including stimulation from parents and other family members and the goals of the particular habilitation program in which the family is enrolled. An important part of any language program is the child's acquisition of language with which to express himself. The curriculum of all children enrolled at IHR includes a sequence of vocal and speech objectives that leads, optimally, to the child's use of spoken English as a communication mode. Many children also learn to use signed English as a communication mode. The IHR programs for the development of spoken English and signed English are described in the next two chapters.

CHAPTER 22

TEACHING INFANT LANGUAGE OBJECTIVES: PROGRAM FOR VOCAL AND SPEECH DEVELOPMENT

The IHR Speech Development Program

Principles Guiding the Vocal and Speech
Development Program for Infants at IHR

Prerequisites to Implementation of a
Successful Speech Program
- Placement and Use of Appropriate Amplification
- Establishing Optimal Listening Conditions

Strategies for Teaching Speech to Young
Hearing-Impaired Children
- A Five-Step Guide to Teaching Speech
- Involving Parents and Family Members in the Child's Speech
  Development Program

Stages of Speech Development: A Focus on
Stage 1
- Getting Started on Speech
- The Sequence of Vocal/Speech Objectives in *Parent-Infant*
  Communication

THE IHR SPEECH DEVELOPMENT PROGRAM

Vocal and speech development are areas of major emphasis for all children enrolled at Infant Hearing Resource regardless of the child's degree of hearing loss and of visual communication modes that may also be used with the child. **The goal of the IHR speech curriculum is that children will develop speech that will enable them to be understood by their family and friends and to have "interchange(s) in spoken language"** (Nittrauer and Hochberg, 1985, p. 491).

IHR parent-infant specialists regard intelligible speech as a communication tool of great importance to the hearing-impaired child, one which will enable him to engage in meaningful exchange of thoughts and ideas with the majority of individuals in his society. We also recognize that intelligible speech does not come easily for many young hearing-impaired children. These children may require several years of intensive training before speech is a viable communication mode for them. While working to acquire the skills that lead to intelligible speech, the young hearing-impaired child has a strong need to communicate. For this reason, the goal of intelligible speech does not override the IHR goal for infants of acquiring an effective communication system. During his first years the child's needs are best served when he and his parents share a mutually understood communication system. With some young children this system is based on spoken and heard language alone; with others it is based on spoken, heard, and signed language.

Communication skills in the areas of audition, language, and speech are taught to children at IHR in such a way that the development of skills in one area promotes and supports the attainment of skills in other areas. This approach is substantiated by research findings reported by Novelli-Olmstead and Ling (1984) which demonstrated that speech production training enhances the auditory skills of hearing-impaired children. The children in their study were divided into two groups: children who listened to and then vocally produced the speech stimuli they heard, and children who listened to and demonstrated discrimination of the speech stimuli presented without vocally producing the speech stimuli. The investigators found that those children who listened to and vocally produced the stimuli they heard made greater overall progress in both speech production and in auditory discrimination than did those children who listened but did not repeat the speech sounds heard. Parent-infant specialists must keep in mind that speech and auditory skills are interdependent, each one strengthening the other.

Successful use of speech requires that the user perform several intricate motor and cognitive tasks simultaneously. The two major categories into which these tasks fall are production of speech sounds and meaningful use of speech sounds. *Speech production* refers to the mechanics of using the breath flow and musculature of the throat, oral cavity, and lips to produce a specific speech sound and to produce speech sounds in rapid sequence to create words, sentences and paragraphs. *Meaningful use* of speech sounds refers to a person's ability to produce the sounds of speech in sequences that have meaning to others. This implies that the individual has learned the spoken code, or labels, for concepts and things that are used in his environment. Stated another way, meaningful use of speech occurs when the child can draw from a receptive vocabulary and orally produce meaningful words and combinations of words.

When we talk about the use of speech by hearing-impaired children, it is evident that for this population — as for any other child — successful use of speech is based on language. Speech is simply one way of expressing thoughts, ideas, and needs using the appropriate labels of a particular oral language. It is for this reason that language acquisition is a major emphasis of habilitation at IHR. Without an abundant language foundation a child with clearly developed speech may not have much to say. Conversely, a child who has a large receptive vocabulary but none of the skills necessary to express himself meaningfully is also at a severe disadvantage. A well-designed speech curriculum addresses this problem by guiding children through acquisition of a sequence of speech production skills which will result in meaningful spoken language.

Each session with families at IHR includes activities which focus on vocal and speech development, sometimes referred to as auditory-vocal and auditory-verbal learning. These latter terms are important since they emphasize the critical relationship between auditory and vocal and speech skills. For purposes of consistency with *Parent-Infant Communication* (Infant Hearing Resource, 1985), in this text we use the terms "vocal" and "speech development" to indicate auditory-vocal and auditory-verbal learning.

For speech to be learned optimally, it must be trained in concert with auditory skills. In Chapter 17 we discussed the importance of the child's auditory feedback mechanism, the way in which the child hears his own vocalizations. So closely tied together is the auditory-vocal feedback loop that it is impossible to say which stimulates which. The infant's development of listening skills promotes his vocal skill development and vice versa. When adults stimulate the infant with vocalizations that the infant can hear, they are promoting the infant's acquisition of both listening and vocalization skills. When the vocalization the adult produces is meaningful language, language acquisition is being promoted as well.

The IHR speech development program for young hearing-impaired children is based on the work of Daniel Ling (1976). The goals of Ling's program are to help the child acquire proficiency in producing both the patterns of speech and the individual sounds of speech through vocal play and babbling, and then to promote the child's use of these speech patterns and sounds in meaningful speech communication. Ling (1976, 1978) specifies a sequence in which speech sounds should be taught to the hearing-impaired child and discusses the principles on which successful use of his approach is based. Other resources that IHR specialists use to acquire crucial background understanding and to plan speech goals and activities are Calvert and Silverman (1975), D. Pollack (1985), and Stovall (1982).

PRINCIPLES GUIDING THE VOCAL AND SPEECH DEVELOPMENT PROGRAM FOR INFANTS AT IHR

The IHR speech program is based on three major principles:
1. The hearing-impaired child's acquisition of speech skills is determined by a number of factors which are individual for each child.
2. The skills parents learn to use to promote their child's speech development are very different from the skills used in speech correction. The parent-infant specialist must teach parents the difference.
3. The attitudes of adults toward the child's speech production attempts dramatically influence the child's ability to learn speech and affect his emerging self-esteem.

Each of these principles is discussed below.

Principle No. 1: The hearing-impaired infant/preschooler's acquisition of speech skills is determined by a number of factors which are individual for each child.

We can identify at least five factors which affect both the rate at which a hearing-impaired child acquires speech skills and the quality of his speech. These factors are:
   a. *The age at which the child's hearing loss is identified and amplification is placed* determines the age at which amplified speech sounds reach the child's brain. The first months and years of life are a critical time for the development of the neural pathways that carry information from the auditory nerve to the centers of the brain that process speech (Northern and Downs, 1984). In Chapter 17 we discussed the rationale, based on research, for early amplification. Extrapolating from animal

research on vision, we can infer that if an infant's brain does not receive auditory stimuli because of an impaired peripheral auditory system, these pathways in the brain probably do not develop in the same way as when stimulation of the auditory system is present from birth.

No one really knows when and for how long the critical period for sensory stimulation and development of auditory systems occurs in humans, but it is certainly prudent to assume that it encompasses the first year of life. Therefore, the child whose hearing loss is not identified early may have passed all or part of the period when amplified sound will promote neural development in auditory centers of his cortex. Our observations of profoundly deaf children who are amplified within the first 12 months of life point to auditory perceptual skills generally superior to those of children amplifed later. However, the connection between early amplification and superior auditory and speech skills is a difficult one to prove because of our inability to control all the variables that affect a child's learning.

b. *The degree of the child's hearing loss* is a second factor which affects his speech acquisition. A child with a moderate or severe loss may receive some speech input even before amplification is placed and, when wearing appropriate amplification, he most likely receives a fairly complete speech model on which to base speech production. The child with a profound loss who can hear amplified speech sounds throughout the high frequencies (where many consonant sounds occur) receives a more complete speech signal than the child with a profound loss who hears only low frequency sounds. It is obvious that the more complete the speech signal received through audition, the easier it will be for the child to reproduce speech sounds, words, and sentences.

Degree of hearing loss also affects the quantity of time during the day that the child hears speech. The profoundly deaf child who receives speech input only when the speech signal is delivered at a distance of three feet or less from his hearing aids will not experience the abundance of spoken information and repetition that is essential to early speech and language learning. This child will not learn speech incidentally through overhearing. Opportunity for speech input will have to be rigorously programmed to assure enough repetition for learning to take place.

c. *The child's built-in ability to use his or her aided residual hearing* is a third factor affecting his speech acquisition. All of us have worked with children whose aided audiograms indicate that they detect speech information at levels 20 to 30 dB above threshold. This is the level at which the child needs to hear speech in order to discriminate between speech sounds. However, over time we see that our expectations, based on audiological data, for these children's speech development are not being met. We are reminded here of the insufficient information regarding total functioning of the auditory system provided by the audiogram. Ling (1976) points out the following limitations of an audiogram: it provides information only about the frequency and intensity of sounds heard by the child and no information about how the child processes time relationships, about whether he can distinguish one frequency from another, can track formant transitions, or can judge whether one sound is louder or quieter than another; and finally, the audiogram depicts the child's responses to steady-state pure tones while speech is a complex and rapidly changing series of acoustic events.

d. *Etiology of the hearing loss and the presence of other handicapping conditions* make up the fourth factor affecting the child's acquisition of speech skills. Many hearing-impaired children demonstrate no additional problems that will impede their learning rate. However, a number of etiologies of hearing loss cause additional handicapping conditions which may affect the child's ability to process or produce speech (see Chapter 25). These handicaps may also affect general intelligence which is an important factor in the ability to use spoken language meaningfully.

e. *The child's learning environment* is a fifth factor affecting his acquisition of speech skills. If four criteria for the learning setting are present, learning is more rapid and efficient. These four criteria are motivation, readiness, interest, and reinforcement. Any interaction, activity, or game which includes all of these attributes will most likely promote learning.

Motivation: The child is motivated when he is excited about the activity or likes to play the game.

Readiness: The child is demonstrating readiness when he can successfully do at least part of the task. The task must be neither too difficult nor too easy.

Interest: The child is interested when he shows a natural curiosity and stays with the activity for a while.

Reinforcement: The child is reinforced when he will try the activity again and again. The most effective reinforcement for the child is the fun of the game. Adult attention, smiles, and applause are also reinforcing for many children.

Children learn through fun, non-stressful, interesting activities for which they are developmentally ready. Frequently, these are activities that they have selected and can control themselves.

We have discussed the first principle in teaching speech, that the child's speech skill acquisition is related to a number of factors that are individual for each child. These factors are: age of identification, degree of hearing loss, use of residual hearing, etiology and presence of other handicapping conditions, and the learning environment. In addition to these factors, a significant condition which affects the child's motivation to participate in speech activities is the parents' approach to their child's speech development. This brings us to discussion of the second principle which guides the IHR speech development program.

Principle No.2: Parents are taught skills which promote speech development rather than speech correction.

The parents' role in their child's speech development is vital. Parents can influence their child's speech development in two primary ways: through reinforcing their child's speech and through the quality of their own speech.

First, parents influence their child's speech development by reinforcing the child's communication attempts. The ways in which parents respond to their child's earliest communication attempts establish for the child the value, purpose, and effectiveness of his or her communication. When parents respond in positive ways to the infant's cries, grunts, wiggles, and smiles, and later to his coos and babbles, the child learns that his communication produces results, and his motivation to develop more sophisticated communication is increased. When the child first attempts to say words, his attempts will not be perfect; in fact, they may hardly resemble the words he intends. The parents' behavior at this point is critical. Parents who are working to promote their young child's *speech development* respond to their child's first word attempts with pleasure and understanding. "You said 'bottle'! You want your bottle!" In fact, the child had said "ba" as he pointed to his bottle. Parents who respond to this communication attempt with words such as "Not 'ba', 'bottle', 'bot-tle', say 'bot-tle'" are giving in to the temptation to *correct speech*.

IHR specialists believe strongly that speech correction is not an avenue that will promote early speech development. We feel that speech correction is NOT APPROPRIATE until the child is at least six years old and should ONLY be done by a trained speech teacher, not by family or friends. Each time an adult or another child corrects a young hearing-impaired child, the child is likely to think, "I made a mistake," "I can't do this right," "I am not competent," or "I am not okay." It will not take many of these corrections before the child gives up, becomes anxious about speech, fears trying, and begins to resist. Why this reaction? Because he has been asked to do something that is too hard and inappropriate for his age. He is too *young* to be able to *control* his speech production, or to *remember* to use that "good" [t] that we know he "can produce" in a word.

Undesirable results of speech correction with a hearing-impaired preschooler may be:
1. Resistance. The child may select speech as a battle ground. It is one thing adults cannot make him do.
2. Low self-confidence. The child feels he is unable to do something right, and that something is obviously very important to his parents.

Speech development activities are fun for children when their vocalizations make the train go around the track!

Since speech training will continue throughout the child's educational career, it is critical that the hearing-impaired child feel courageous, be able to make mistakes and still feel good about himself, and be willing to receive help in this very sensitive area — speech.

IHR parent-infant specialists teach parents to use **speech development** activities which differ from speech correction activities in three major ways. First, the speech development activities that parents are encouraged to use are **incorporated into two-way communication** with their child. Parents learn that part of motivating their child to want to communicate is motivating him to communicate using his voice. Parents learn to promote vocal communication by using their own voices and by showing interest in and reinforcing *what* the child has to say rather than focusing on how perfectly he says it.

Secondly, parents learn to stimulate their child with speech development activities which **provide speech models** for the child at appropriate phonetic and phonologic levels. During the two-way speech development activities, the child has ample opportunity to hear the suprasegmentals of speech, speech sounds, and words as they are modeled for him in playful ways. The child is encouraged to take his turn in the communication interaction but he is *not required* to produce a specific sound or word in order to keep the activity going. When the child *does* approximate or imitate the speech sounds, suprasegmental patterns, or words that the parent has modeled, the parent responds with enthusiasm and with an appropriate rejoiner that keeps the activity and communication interaction going. When the child does not produce a vocalization during his turn, the adult remains pleasant and playful as he talks for the child and provides a model of the sound again.

The third way in which speech development activities taught to parents differ from speech correction activities is that the **speech development activities are based on a sequential progression of skills.** Each speech skill modeled for the child builds on previously attained skills. Parents know what speech skills the child has already acquired and learn to model for the child speech objectives that follow in developmental sequence. The child is not expected or urged to produce sounds for which he is not developmentally ready.

A final way in which parents influence their infant's speech development is through the quality of their own speech and language. Parents can promote their child's speech development by talking to their child at distances and under conditions in which he is most likely able to hear them, by using descriptions and conversational questions in their interactions with the child, and by frequently modeling speech skills appropriate to their child's developmental level. Parents whose "conversation" with their child is limited to demands, commands, and reprimands do not create an environment conducive to furthering the child's speech or language growth. Alternatively, parents who play with speech and language as they play with their child are modeling the stimulating, humorous, and interesting thoughts and ideas that can be conveyed though words. Speech itself can be a playground for the child.

Parents learn to use speech development activities with their child to promote his speech skill acquisition. Equally important are parents' attitudes about their child's speech production attempts. These attitudes are discussed in Principle No. 3.

Principle No. 3: Adult attitudes toward the child's speech production attempts dramatically influence the child's ability to acquire speech skills and affect his emerging self-esteem.

Speech is often an emotionally loaded topic for parents. Their concern, "Will my child talk?" may be ever-present and may affect how they interact with their child. The fact is, learning to speak intelligibly is a difficult task for most hearing-impaired children. Many deaf children do develop speech that is intelligible, but some do not. We believe that professionals must be very open with parents about the realities of deafness. Yes, early training, hard work, and skilled instruction pay off, but these optimal conditions still may not be enough to allow prelingually deafened children with little or no residual hearing to learn to speak well. Unless we forecast to parents the entire range of possibilities for a profoundly deaf child, we are withholding important information that those parents need in order to come to grips with the realities of deafness.

Interestingly enough, the child whose parents understand his possible limitations as well as his potential levels of achievement is most likely to develop optimum speech skills. Why is that? Perhaps because his family and teachers convey to him their acceptance of him and of his speech attempts. He does not feel anxiety, pressure, or ridicule during vocal and speech activities. These activities are fun and rewarding. Adults like him and they like what he does, consequently he likes himself; he develops confidence in his abilities. He becomes a risk-taker: He is motivated to try, even if it means making mistakes, in order to learn.

The three principles discussed above strongly influence the way in which parent-infant specialists and parents promote the child's acquisition of vocal/speech skills. In the next section we review two elements in the child's habilitation program which also influence his ability to acquire speech skills.

PREREQUISITES TO IMPLEMENTATION
OF A SUCCESSFUL SPEECH PROGRAM

There are two important prerequisites to the implementation of a successful speech program: placement and use of appropriate amplification for the child and the establishment of optimal listening conditions. These prerequisites, which were discussed in detail in Chapters 6 and 17, are reviewed below.

PLACEMENT AND USE OF APPROPRIATE AMPLIFICATION

When a sound occurs at or slightly above threshold the child can barely detect the sound; he is hardly aware that a sound is present. Like normally hearing children, the hearing-impaired child needs to hear speech at least 20 to 30 dB above his threshold in order to be able to discriminate (tell the difference between) speech sounds. The goal in selecting and placing hearing aids is to amplify all frequencies of the speech signal so that this signal is at least 20 to 30 dB above the child's thresholds, without exceeding the child's threshold of discomfort. (It is not possible to achieve this goal when working with children with some types of profound hearing losses.)

At Infant Hearing Resource we use a system of trial-use amplification in order to select the most appropriate hearing aids for a child. The child is fitted with a set of trial-use hearing aids immediately following enrollment. He is observed over time and his responses to sound are noted in the home, agency, and during audiological evaluation. After a series of different models of aids are worn by the child, the audiologist recommends for purchase those aids with which the child functions best. This approach to selecting amplification is described in detail in Chapter 6. *In addition to being appropriate, amplification must be used.* The child should wear his or her personal hearing aids during all waking hours so that hearing becomes a constant function, as it is for the normally hearing child.

ESTABLISHING OPTIMAL LISTENING CONDITIONS

Establishing and maintaining optimal listening conditions for the child is another prerequisite of a successful speech program. Three factors which must be monitored in order to establish conditions under which the child can best hear speech are distance of the sound source, loudness of the signal, and the presence of competing noise. Keeping in mind that the signal must occur above the child's auditory threshold before the child can discriminate it, the parent and specialist will want to manipulate these three factors, which are discussed in Chapter 17, to assure that the child has the best possible chance to hear speech. Ling's article "Keep Your Hearing Impaired Child Within Earshot" (1981) is an excellent reference for parents and specialists.

Once the child has been fitted with appropriate amplification and the specialist and parents have carefully considered how to structure the child's listening environment, a systematic program for teaching speech can be initiated.

STRATEGIES FOR TEACHING SPEECH TO YOUNG HEARING-IMPAIRED CHILDREN

A FIVE-STEP GUIDE TO TEACHING SPEECH

Parent-infant specialists at IHR follow a five-step guide in promoting the hearing-impaired infant's development of vocal and speech skills:
1. Evaluate the child's aided capability to hear speech.
2. Evaluate the child's present level of vocal/speech skills.
3. Determine speech teaching goals.
4. Select activities to teach immediate speech goals.
5. Teach immediate speech goals.

The purpose of this five-step guide is to give the specialist a framework for knowing how to approach the task of teaching speech. Each of the five steps is discussed below.

STEP 1. EVALUATE THE CHILD'S AIDED CAPABILITY TO HEAR SPEECH.

When working with infants, it is not possible to say, "We must know everything about this child before we can begin habilitation activities." Most of the habilitation activities which are presented to the newly identified and enrolled hearing-impaired child are designed to provide the parent-infant specialist and parents with information about the child's abilities. The specialist and parents alike are both extremely interested in discovering what the child will be able to hear when he is wearing appropriate hearing aids. They will need to gather a great deal of data about the child's hearing and listening responses in order to know under what conditions the child will be aware of and can attend to and discriminate the sounds of speech.

Specialists and parents can acquire information about the child's ability to hear and listen to the sounds of speech from three sources: his audiogram, through observation, and from the Five-Sound Speech Test (Ling and Ling, 1978).

RELATING THE CHILD'S AUDIOGRAM TO THE ACOUSTICS OF SPEECH

Some vital information that specialists and parents need to acquire is the distances within which the different sounds of speech are audible to the child. The child's audiogram will provide information about the child's aided thresholds for pure tones across the frequency range. These thresholds can be related to the loudness of the sounds of speech by using the "speech banana" (see p. 105) and the following guidelines spelled out by Ling and Ling (1978). These guidelines enable the parent-infant specialist to use the child's audiogram to make a best guess about the child's ability to hear the individual sounds of speech.

1. If a child has measurable hearing up to 1000 Hz and is wearing appropriate amplification, he should be able to hear the three vowels [u], [a], and [i] uttered in a quiet voice at a distance of at least 5 yards.
2. Children with hearing up to 2000 Hz should hear the consonant [ʃ] as well as the three vowels.
3. Children should be able to detect the consonant [s] from at least two yards if their aided thresholds at 4000 Hz are better than 40 dB.
4. The suprasegmental aspects of speech — intonation, stress, and rhythm — are carried primarily by the vowels and voiced speech sounds. If the child hears the three vowels [u], [a], and [i], the specialist can be certain that suprasegmental patterns are also audible to the child.

5. When vowel sounds have a similar first formant (such as the [i]
and [u] sounds), the second formants must be audible in order for
the child to be able to *discriminate* one vowel from another. The
primary energy of the second formant of [i] is at 2000 Hz; thus
the child with no hearing at 2000 Hz is not likely to be able to
discriminate [i] from [u] through audition alone.

OBSERVING THE CHILD'S RESPONSES TO SPEECH

The second source from which specialists and parents can gain information about the child's ability to hear speech is observation of the child.
Utilizing a diagnostic teaching approach (see Chapter 16) in which the
adults present stimuli to the child and watch for and record his responses is
an excellent way to gain some of the information necessary to planning
speech development activities that are appropriate for the child. Since very
young children are not able to participate in formal *speech reception* tests
(although a *speech awareness* threshold is usually obtained), it is very
helpful to use a variety of diagnostic teaching activities through which the
child's responses to speech sounds can be observed.

As the parents and specialist play with the child they can model a variety
of speech sounds, e.g., "rʌ -rʌ " and "ki-ki," and watch for the child to
look up, stop playing, or even attempt to imitate the sounds as an indication
of his ability to hear them. As the adults talk to the child from varying
distances they will get an idea of the range within which the child is most
responsive. Nonsense sounds employing unusual patterns of vocal intonation and pitch and adult-produced animal sounds may be intriguing to some
children. As was mentioned in Chapter 17, adults must be inventive and
observant as they sleuth out the child's ability to detect and discriminate the
sounds of speech.

USING THE FIVE-SOUND SPEECH TEST

The third source of information about the child's ability to hear speech is
the Five-Sound Speech Test (Ling and Ling, 1978). To administer this test,
the adult presents, one by one, the sounds [u] as in "wh*o*," [a] as in "s*a*w,"
[i] as in "b*ee*," [ʃ] as in "*sh*oe," and [s] as in "*so*" and watches for an indication from the child that he hears each sound. These sounds sample
points across the frequencies in which all speech sounds occur. Ling and
Ling (1978) recommend presenting these sounds within a distance at which
speech is most likely to be audible to the child. The sounds should be
presented in varying order from test to test. The specialist can experiment
with distance, background noise levels, and voice intensity to determine how
the test should be given each time. When the test procedure is standardized

for each child, inter-test differences in the child's responses can be easily spotted and the reason for these differences (e.g., low battery voltage, middle ear effusion) tracked down.

The Five-Sound Speech Test can be administered quickly to infants and toddlers who cannot yet perform play audiometry tasks by noting whether the child turns, looks up, or shows some change in behavior in response to the sounds. The response of a young child can be reinforced with a lighted or moving toy as is done in VRA procedures (see Chapter 6). The test can be conducted rapidly with older children by having the child clap his hands or give a conditioned response (such as putting a ring on a peg) when he hears the sound. Children who hear all of the speech sounds in the Five-Sound Speech Test will hear all of the phonemes of English under the conditions in which the test was given. This is extremely valuable information for the specialist.

The specialist can use the information about the child's ability to hear speech gained from his audiogram, through observation, and from using the Five-Sound Speech Test to select the most effective mode(s) by which to present speech sounds to the child: through audition alone, or with the addition of visual and/or tactile cues. It is essential to keep in mind that children's responses to sound may vary from one hearing test to another or from one day to the next for various reasons. As a result, it is important to evaluate the functioning of the child's complete auditory system before each habilitation session. A procedure that works well for us at IHR is:

1. Evaluate the child's hearing aids electroacoustically on a hearing aid analyzer at least weekly, checking to determine that the output and distortion of the aids have remained at the levels set for the child. If a hearing aid analyzer is not available, the specialist should listen to the hearing aids through her own earmold and measure the voltage of the hearing aid batteries.
2. Administer the Five-Sound Speech Test (Ling and Ling 1978).
3. Perform tympanometry when indicated.

STEP 2. EVALUATE THE CHILD'S PRESENT LEVEL OF VOCAL/SPEECH SKILLS.

IHR specialists use the *Cumulative Record of Speech Skill Acquisition* (Ling, 1978) to assess the vocal and speech skills of children enrolled. We have found it most helpful to videotape or audiotape the child during play sessions so that analysis of the child's vocalizations can be done after the session. Parents who are good observers and reporters of their child's behaviors can also make note of vocalizations which their child produces at home. This evaluation does not need to be completed in one session; it may take several sessions to gather enough data on a very young child to assess vocal and speech production accurately.

When sufficient data on the child's vocalizations have been gathered, the child's predominant stage or stages of operation in Ling's model can be determined. The child's vocal/speech production achievements are recorded on the evaluation form by checking off skills the child exhibits.

STEP 3. DETERMINE SPEECH TEACHING GOALS.

The Ling model establishes seven stages of speech acquisition. The stages are sequential and each builds on skills acquired in the previous stages. Specialists work with children on the sequence of stages at both the phonetic and phonologic levels. Working on speech at the phonetic level involves the production and differentiation of non-meaningful sounds. At the phonologic level, the child works to produce and differentiate these same sounds in meaningful communication. In Ling's model, both the phonetic and phonologic levels have several target behaviors or target sounds on which to focus. The child achieves the target behaviors by mastering a series of subskills. By using the evaluation tool (Ling, 1978) and the sequence of stages (Ling, 1976) in combination, the teacher is able to determine which skills proceed from the skills the child already has. These subsequent skills — both targets and subskills — become the immediate speech teaching goals. New goals are set as the child achieves the immediate goals. We refer readers to Ling's texts (1976, 1978) for detailed description of his speech instruction program.

STEP 4. SELECT ACTIVITIES TO TEACH
IMMEDIATE SPEECH GOALS.

Working on speech goals with a child under the age of four is not a "sit down and repeat after me" proposition. Characteristics of successful speech activities are:

1. They meet the criteria of being interesting, motivating, readiness-appropriate, and reinforcing to the child.
2. The production of a vocalization need not appear to the child to be the major focus of the activity.
3. The vocalization aspect of the activity is a natural part of the two-way communication that takes place during the activity.
4. The specialist and parents are clear about which of the child's vocal behaviors or speech productions meet their criteria for reinforcement and about how they will be reinforced.

Specialists and parents should be alert for opportunities to add speech stimulation to any activity the child is engaged in if this can be done without assuming control of the activity.

STEP 5. TEACH IMMEDIATE SPEECH GOALS.

Not all planned speech activities or spontaneous opportunities for speech stimulation will result in the child's producing the desired speech subskill or target behavior. Every child requires opportunities to hear speech sounds again and again in order to learn to discriminate and produce the sounds. The specialist who takes a diagnostic approach to the child's behaviors is likely to determine what needs to be done to help the child learn target skills. Diagnostic teaching is a process of presenting stimuli to the child and observing how the child responds. If the child's response is not what the specialist and parents have predicted, they must be able to evaluate why the outcome was different, and determine what changes they must make in presenting the stimuli in order to evoke the desired outcome.

Parent-infant specialists are familiar with a variety of techniques which can be used to encourage a child to work on speech objectives. Not all of these techniques work with all children. The specialist can experiment with several techniques to discover which ones are most helpful to the child. For instance, the specialist, Julia, is working with 11-month-old Mona on production of repeated and sustained vowels. Julia presented the three following activities to see which one best engaged Mona's interest and provided her with the most motivation to attempt imitation of the model Julia was providing:

1. Julia hopped a small toy on the floor as she vocalized, "o-o-o"; she alternated this with moving the toy smoothly on the floor while she vocalized, "ooooo". Mona showed no interest in this activity, so Julia quickly switched to another technique.

2. Next, Julia held Mona on her lap, with Mona leaning against her chest as they both faced a mirror. Julia again modeled the vocalizations, "o-o-o" and "ooooo", talking so that Mona could hear, see, and feel these vocalizations. Mona watched with interest as Julia repeated these sounds but made no attempt to try the vocalizations herself. Julia switched to yet another technique.

3. The next activity Julia tried was to turn Mona around so that, while still seated on Julia's lap, they were now face to face. This time as Julia vocalized "o-o-o", she gently bounced her knees. After a pause, she vocalized "ooooo", and swayed her knees from side to side. Mona was very excited about this game! After several repetitions, Julia waited a little longer than usual and Mona began to bounce herself, vocalizing " ʌ - ʌ - ʌ ". Julia nodded and smiled in response. When Mona finished vocalizing, Julia took her turn bouncing and vocalizing "o-o-o". The child and specialist repeated their playful interaction several times before Julia ended the game.

After she set Mona down, Julia turned to Mona's delighted father and suggested that he might want to incorporate this activity into his play with

Mona at home during the next week. Julia also referred back to Mona's interest in the activity using the mirror and indicated that the parents might want to repeat that type of activity at home, too, as they modeled vowels and the suprasegmentals of speech for Mona.

Once the child has achieved a speech goal, the specialist records this achievement on the child's Ling evaluation form and establishes new immediate goals, thus cycling through the Five-Step Guide to teaching speech again.

We have discussed the importance of parents' attitudes and approaches to their child's speech development and the parents' participation in the five-step cycle of teaching speech skills. Specific ways in which parents and family members are involved in the speech development program for infants at IHR are discussed below.

INVOLVING PARENTS AND FAMILY MEMBERS IN THE CHILD'S SPEECH DEVELOPMENT PROGRAM

INVOLVING PARENTS IN SPEECH DEVELOPMENT ACTIVITIES DURING SESSIONS

Skills aimed at helping the child acquire speech objectives are modeled for parents in two ways: First, through planned activities designed specifically to encourage speech development like those Julia presented to Mona in the example above, and second, through awareness of and attention to vocal and speech goals during interaction with the child at other times. Speech activities are typically kept short to maximize the child's attention span and interest level. Often the child's interest will dictate how long the activity lasts. He practices speech sounds while engaged in activities that are age-appropriate and motivating for him.

IHR specialists use several techniques to help parents feel comfortable and competent as they participate in their child's vocal/speech development activities during habilitation sessions. These techniques are:

1. Demonstrating to parents how stimulation of their child's vocal and speech production can be easily incorporated into the child's routine, during both play and daily activities such as feeding, diapering, or bedtime. Establishing a pattern of short and frequent periods of stimulation of speech skills is advocated by Ling (1976), who stated that, "teaching specific speech skills should be allocated to brief blocks of two or three minutes' duration for each child, four or five times a day, rather than to longer lessons" (p. 4).

2. Showing parents that the traditional "sit down at the table and

drill'' type of speech activities are not the most motivating and exciting ones for their young child.

3. Encouraging parents during habilitation sessions to take an active part in their child's speech development at whatever level they feel comfortable. Ways in which parents can participate include:
   - joining in activities
   - reinforcing child's vocalizations
   - recording child's speech attempts
   - modeling specific speech sounds and suprasegmentals of speech during vocal play and in words.
4. Using parents' suggestions for speech activities.
5. Giving parents specific feedback on the quality of speech they use in interactions with their child, e.g., loudness, pitch, rate.
6. Giving parents instructions about which speech sounds to model currently, and about specific techniques for modeling them.
7. Discussing with parents the importance of accepting their child's successive approximations as he works to produce speech sounds. Specialists demonstrate for parents the technique of providing the child with a combination of social reinforcement and the correct model of the sound he is attempting to produce: "Yes! You tried 'la-la!' La-la-la-la-la, Dennis. Your turn.''

It is the specialist's responsibility to keep parents current on what speech skills to model for their child and to point out which of their child's speech productions they should reinforce. For instance, when an infant is just beginning to vocalize, the specialist and parents will want to reinforce all of the child's vocal productions. As the child's speech skills develop, the specialist and parents will want to reinforce only the highest level skills of which the child is capable. If, for instance, the child has produced an alternating "ba-da" sound in order to elicit a movement of a toy, the parent and specialist would not reinforce a lower level vocalization, for example, a sustained /a/, by moving the toy. It is also critical to avoid speech correction: "No, Johnny, not 'a'! Say 'ba-da'.'' Instead, model "ba-da,'' move the toy, then indicate it is Johnny's turn to try again.

Parents are encouraged to incorporate the babbling and speech sounds that the specialist has modeled in sessions into their interactions with their child at home. Specialists *want* parents to repeat speech development activities at home. However, the specialist must tell parents clearly that as they are modeling a new speech sound or babbling pattern for their child they must not in any way *require* the child to imitate the vocalization nor should they attempt to *correct* vocalizations the child produces. Continuing to model new sounds and babbling patterns even when the child responds with a different vocalization is the best way for parents to give the child maximum exposure to new speech goals.

It may seem to parents that the goal of establishing an attitude of acceptance of their child's attempts at speech production is incompatible with the goal of encouraging a child to try different ways of producing a sound. It is not. We believe that the *role of parents is to model, to reinforce, and to enjoy communication interactions with their child*. It is only the *parent-infant specialist* (and later, the child's teacher) who *applies some structure* to the communication setting when she is stimulating speech. The specialist must be very clear with parents about how her role differs from their role, otherwise parents may think that the more structured speech development techniques being used by the specialist are ones they should carry out at home.

GUIDELINES FOR SPEECH DEVELOPMENT ACTIVITIES AT HOME

Family members can do an excellent job of providing speech development activities for the hearing-impaired child. The guidelines which follow point out the importance of the roles of family members in the child's achievement of speech competence.

EXPECT SPEECH FROM THE CHILD

Expect that the child will use vocalizations and, eventually, speech to communicate. This expectation means that you give the child time to "talk," that you look at him expectantly when you have finished your side of the conversation, that you tune in to his vocalizations. You are expecting him to produce sounds so you listen for them and then reinforce the child by truly hearing what he says, even if, at the beginning, what he produces is not intelligible speech. Keep in mind that your first utterances didn't sound perfect either!

ACCEPT AND REINFORCE THE CHILD'S SPEECH EFFORTS

When beginning a speech development program, accept and reinforce all of the child's attempts at speech sound production. The child is more likely to attempt vocal productions and imitations if he has experienced reinforcement rather than correction from family members.

Accept and respond appropriately to word attempts or mispronounced words if you can understand them. You want the child to learn that his speech works for him as a communication tool. Give the child lots of praise for his attempts at new words. When the child knows that his speech attempts are accepted he continues to be willing to take risks in talking.

MODEL SPEECH

Model for the child in babbling games the particular suprasegmentals of speech, vowel, or vowel-consonant combinations the specialist is presenting in sessions. If the child responds with a different vocalization, the adult can choose to imitate his vocalization then switch back to the original model. When the child begins to attempt words, his attempts may be incorrect. *Model the correct word* as you respond. Modeling allows the child to match his production against yours as he is able, e.g., Child: "Goggie?" Parent: "Yes, I see the doggy." This does *not* encourage the child to continue inaccurate production. It *does* increase the child's chances of developing intelligible speech as his successive approximations come closer and closer to the accurate model.

One final thing that parents must do to promote their child's speech development is to make certain that the child's teachers use a sequential program of *speech development* throughout the child's educational career. The beginning of such a speech development program is the topic of the next section.

STAGES OF SPEECH DEVELOPMENT: A FOCUS ON STAGE 1

IHR parent-infant specialists use Ling's (1976) speech development program with the hearing-impaired infants enrolled. This model for speech acquisition delineates seven sequential stages through which hearing-impaired children learn speech skills. Each of the seven stages has subskills and target behaviors for both the phonetic and phonologic levels.

In this text we will discuss only the first stage in Ling's model. In Stage 1 the child learns to vocalize freely and on demand (phonetic level) and to use vocalization as a means of communication (phonologic level).

GETTING STARTED ON SPEECH

Many of the beginning parent-infant specialists with whom we have talked have expressed particular interest in techniques and activities that can be used with very young hearing-impaired children to get them started in their acquisition of speech skills. We refer the reader to Ling (1976, 1978) for discussion of and evaluation and teaching strategies useful in subsequent stages.

STAGE 1: CHILD VOCALIZES FREELY AND ON DEMAND
AND USES VOCALIZATION
AS A MEANS OF COMMUNICATION (Ling, 1976).

Achievement of the target behaviors in Stage 1 means that the infant or young child is vocalizing spontaneously and will vocalize when asked to imitate or in response to a question, and is consistently using voice to attract attention. The child's vocalizations should be natural-sounding and pleasant. At this beginning level it is not necessary for the child to produce any particular vowel or vowel-consonant combination, as long as he produces an *abundance* of vocalization.

At the phonologic level of Stage 1, the child is utilizing vocalization as a means of communication. For example, the child might vocalize [ʌ - ʌ - ʌ] while pointing to his cup to indicate he wants more milk, or emit a loud "ba ba ba" upon awakening from a nap to tell Mom that he wants to be removed from his crib. The specialist and parents encourage and reinforce the child's communication attempts at the highest level at which he or she is capable. It is important to reinforce the child in a number of different situations so he will more likely want to communicate under a variety of circumstances and with a variety of individuals.

Almost every child is producing vocalizations of some kind when they enroll for habilitation at IHR. These vocalizations may include laughing, crying, coughing, sneezing, "yelling" during rough housing and so on. If a child is producing very few vocalizations spontaneously, the specialist and parent must brainstorm a number of situations and activities that are most likely to elicit vocalization — preferably of pleasure as opposed to a cry of annoyance — from the child.

The following guidelines can be used in selecting activities designed to elicit vocalization from the child. **First,** determine which modality (auditory, visual, tactile, or a combination) should be used to stimulate the child to vocalize; **second,** engage in an activity, e.g., tickling, making faces, that is likely to promote involuntary vocalization; and **third,** reinforce whatever vocalization the child produces. When the child is producing a number of vocalizations involuntarily, the specialist can work on developing vocalization on demand. It is helpful at this stage to pair occurrence of the child's involuntary vocalizations with a gesture or cue, such as pointing to your ear, that accompanies your words and smiles and tells the child you heard something he "said." This cue can later be used as an indicator to the child that you are waiting to hear him vocalize.

Let us consider for a moment a newly enrolled hearing-impaired child who rarely vocalizes. Vocalization is a natural part of social interactions for the baby who hears. The first step in working with a hearing-impaired baby who rarely vocalizes is to determine what he *does* do when stimulated with warm, smiling, vocal input from a significant adult. Does he maintain eye contact? Smile in return? Imitate facial expressions? If none of these

A visual reinforcer such as the oscilloscope is an excellent reinforcer for a child who is practicing the production of different consonant-vowel combinations.

behaviors are present, then working to elicit them is the first step (see Chapter 20). If the infant is smiling, can the smile be escalated into a laugh which can be reinforced with expressions of pleasure and a "I hear you" cue? If the infant is imitating some facial expressions, can those be extended to include the mouth movements used in producing "ma-ma" or "ba-ba?" As the parents and specialist work with a baby who rarely vocalizes, they will want to hold him so that he can feel the vibrations in their chest cavity produced as they vocalize and talk. Holding the infant also assures that the adult is talking close to the microphones of the child's aid.

When a young child vocalizes only rarely, it may be because he has not in the past, or does not now, hear the voices of others or hear his own voice. When a baby is fitted with hearing aids, he will need time to learn that some of the sounds he hears are produced by people, including himself. The more opportunities he has to experience social interactions, the more rapidly he will make these associations. Young children who, even while wearing aids, hear voice only under very optimal conditions, if at all, will need tactile information that they can attempt to imitate by producing vocalizations. Holding the child's hand against your throat as you play vocal games and sing, then placing his hand against his own throat and looking expectantly at him will help the child understand that there is something he can do to produce the same tactile sensation.

Young children must experience that vocalizing produces results for them. They need reason to vocalize. If their vocalizations have been ignored in the past or if they have been met with disappproving frowns because they are loud or "unpleasant" sounding, the child has not been reinforced for using this form of social interaction. The child must have frequent opportunities to experience vocalization as part of pleasurable social interactions.

Adults who respond to a young child's vocalizations teach the child to use his voice as a stimulus to get the response he wants. When a family enrolls with a hearing-impaired infant who is vocalizing very little, the specialist will want to observe how the parents respond to the vocalizations the infant *does* produce. If the parents are generally inattentive to all but the baby's loudest cries, the specialist will want to start a program in which the parents learn to respond to, and thereby reinforce, *all* vocalizations the baby produces. Before an infant will learn to use his voice to attract attention he needs to learn that this is a procedure that, in fact, works for him! It is extremely reinforcing for a baby to learn that, simply by saying "ah," he can gain attention from adults, causing them to point to their ears, widen their eyes, smile broadly, and talk back.

As a baby starts producing more spontaneous vocalizations, the specialist and parents can model vocalizations selected for their audibility and visibility (e.g., "ma-ma" or "buh-buh") and encourage the infant to attempt to imitate these vocalizations by giving him a turn in the communication interaction. Encouraging and reinforcing imitation behaviors is one of the early steps in the speech program. One of the first ways to start imitation reciprocity with a baby is to imitate him, play his game, wait for him to act, then respond. Imitate his laughter, lipsmacking, facial expressions, tongue-clicks; show pleasure and enjoyment in response to the sounds he produces. Diapering is a perfect time for these games, when parent and baby are face to face. These imitations of the baby provide important early practice for the adults in giving the child with hearing loss *power* in communication interactions. So many of us have been trained to "talk," "stimulate," "bombard" the child with language. We do this so well that we overpower and discourage him. Babies love it when we copy them and their vocalizations. This is highly reinforcing. They will repeat their behavior again and again.

THE SEQUENCE OF VOCAL/SPEECH OBJECTIVES IN *PARENT-INFANT COMMUNICATION*

Because an infant's pre-speech vocal behaviors are an important part of his presymbolic communication, these skills are located in the section "Infant Presymbolic Communication" in *Parent-Infant Communication*. Early presymbolic communication vocal behaviors are designated with "Sp" preceding the number of the objective. These behaviors can be modelled for and reinforced in the child as part of the Stage 1 process of encouraging the child to vocalize freely and with communicative intent, and as part of later stages in which diphthongs, vowels, and consonants are elicited.

It is helpful to refer to the sequences of motor and vocal imitation behaviors as they develop in normally hearing babies. These sequences are found in *Parent-Infant Communication* and in Chapter 18 of this volume. Equipped with a guide to the sequence of vocal imitation and with ideas for eliciting vocalization from the child, the specialist is ready to carry out activities which will stimulate those babies for whom imitation is age and developmentally appropriate. Some of the techniques we have found useful in reinforcing an infant's vocalization include:

1. Reinforce the child's *spontaneous*, voluntary vocalizations by activating a lighted or moving toy.
2. Model vocalizations that activate a lighted toy; encourage the child to vocalize in order to activate the toy himself.
3. Associate specific vocalizations with small toys (airplane, boat, cow) by moving the toy simultaneously with "its" vocalization (D. Pollack, 1985).
4. Use an unpowered microphone as a prompt to encourage imitation of vocalization, "singing" into it yourself, then handing it to the child for his performance.

D. Pollack's (1985) chapter, "The Development of Speech," and Stovall's (1982) book, *Teaching Speech to Hearing-Impaired Infants and Children* contain valuable information and suggestions for encouraging early vocal/speech production in the hearing-impaired child.

As the child advances through acquisition of presymbolic communication objectives and merges into the use of symbolic language, the parent-infant specialist will continue to help the child expand his vocalizations from the phonetic to the phonologic level. At this point the expressive language objectives in the "Infant Receptive and Expressive Language" section of *Parent-Infant Communication* will guide the specialist in selecting appropriate language to use in the child's speech training program.

ACTIVITY IDEAS FOR SPEECH-RELATED GAMES

In addition to the speech stimulation activities described in *Parent-Infant Communication*, IHR specialists have compiled the following list of motivating games for stimulating speech sound production and for reinforcing vocal/speech behaviors:

Play with puppets who "talk"

Move cars, boats, airplanes to vocalizations

Use wind-up toys that jump or move as you vocalize

Use fingerplays, songs, and nursery rhymes

Turn lights on to reinforce vocalizations and speech

Move toy animals up and down child's arms/legs while changing the pitch and intensity of your vocalizations

Play games to wake up people or dolls, changing intensity of
voice to put them to sleep and wake them up

Play hide and seek or calling games, varying the intensity of
your voice

Match painting and drawing movements to different durations
and pitches of vocalizations

Paint the outside of the house with water while vocalizing

Move cars on a play road while vocalizing

"Sing" while swinging and sliding

Play motor imitation games such as Thumbs Go Up, Hokie-
Pokie, and Pat-A-Cake

Tell stories, changing pitch, intensity, and rate of voice as different characters "talk"

Blow feathers/ping pong balls/candle/paper/cotton balls

Pour water/corn meal while vocalizing

Press play-doh through Fun Factory toy while vocalizing

Clap to vocalizations

Walk or march dolls and stuffed animals as you "sing"

Tie a toy to a string which goes through a loop screwed into the
ceiling and raise or lower the toy while changing pitch of
your voice

Move pieces to game (e.g., blocks, stack toys) after child
vocalizes

Hold hands and move bodies rhythmically while vocalizing

Ride on rocking horse while "singing"

Move vehicles fast/slow as you change the rate of your
vocalization

String beads and let them slide down, changing the pitch of
your voice

Use microphone and tape recorder to encourage vocal
"performance"

Vocalize into mirror

"Make" person walk or jump to vocalization

Pop bubbles as you say "pop!"

Finger paint with pudding while you hum

Push and pull toys, strollers, wagons, as you chant or sing

Roll balls or tear paper to match vocalizations

Bernstein and Svarc (1983) describe a number of games and activities
which can be used to promote speech skill acquisition in young children.

SUMMARY

Our final words on the subject of speech acquisition in the hearing-
impaired child are intended to serve as a reminder — and a warning — that

the child with a considerable hearing loss will not acquire intelligible speech without frequent, consistent, and sequential speech training *throughout his educational career*. The people who are in a position to assure that the child gets the training he needs are his parents. It is our observation that many — if not most — children with severe or profound hearing losses do not get the type and amount of speech training that they need to acquire intelligible speech. The parent-infant specialist can help parents become potent facilitators of their child's speech development by working with parents to:

1. Help parents define their personal goals for their child's acquisition of speech skills.
2. Familiarize parents with sequential speech development programs that have been designed for hearing-impaired children.
3. Keep parents involved in and informed about the speech skills their child is acquiring during his years in the parent-infant program.
4. Provide parents with a description of the child's immediate speech goals at the time they leave the parent-infant program, e.g., write these goals into the child's final report.
5. Help parents appreciate their role in developing their child's individual education plan (IEP) in the child's public school program. Help them understand that this process is one of the opportunities they have to firmly outline their expectations for their child's individualized speech development program.
6. Encourage parents to learn to work *with* educators and administrators in their child's educational setting in order to promote optimum educational programming, including effective speech development instruction.
7. Prepare parents for the possibility that it may be necessary for them to obtain and pay for private speech tutoring if their child is not receiving speech training in school that will permit him to meet their personal goals for his speech intelligibility.

Children with impaired hearing have a great deal to learn during their educational careers. The values and goals of the child's school will not always coincide exactly with the parents' values and goals for their child. When parents find that this is the case and when they have been unable to work with the system to effect the changes they want for their child, it may be necessary to procure what they want outside school hours. Parents with an ingrained pattern of involvement in their child's education will be well-equipped to determine what elements may be missing from their child's school program and to work to supply them during non-school hours. If frequent, consistent, and sequential speech development training is not made available to the child at school, parents who have been well-educated in a parent-infant program will be aware of this fact and will have the knowledge they need to seek high-quality speech training from other sources.

CHAPTER 23

TEACHING INFANT LANGUAGE OBJECTIVES: PROGRAM OF SIGNED LANGUAGE DEVELOPMENT

Rationale for the Use of Signed English in Conjunction with Speech with Young Hearing-Impaired Children
- Tenets Supporting the Use of Spoken and Signed English at Infant Hearing Resource

Discussing with Parents the Option of Using Signed English

Teaching Language through a Combination of Speech and Signed English
- Techniques to Use When Communicating with the Child
- Signed Language Classes
- Challenges in Teaching Signed Language to Parents of Young Hearing-Impaired Children

RATIONALE FOR THE USE OF SIGNED ENGLISH
IN CONJUNCTION WITH SPEECH WITH YOUNG
HEARING-IMPAIRED CHILDREN

The many issues surrounding the use of signed language with children are complicated, difficult, and fascinating. Even when the emotional issues long associated with the advisability of using signed language with children are set aside, there are today no clear and universally accepted "facts" that describe the effects of the use of signed language on all aspects of a hearing-impaired child's development. A great deal of research is currently being conducted and reported with regard to the use of signed language in educational settings. It is not our intent in this chapter to report on the literature — we can hardly keep up with what is current ourselves! What we do intend is to describe the IHR rationale for the use of a system of manually coded English and our experiences in teaching this system to parents.

Some of the questions that have been raised in the literature are concerned with what we should be calling what it is we are presenting to children when we use a manual communication method. Wilbur (1979) uses the term "systems" to designate "those manual methods that have been developed for educational purposes which permit concurrent signing and speaking using English context but which are not *language* in the sense ASL and English are" (p. 203). We are in agreement with this semantic differentiation, yet we persist in using the term "signed language" and in referring to what we use with children as "spoken and signed language," or "an auditory-oral approach with signed English." Other educators refer to the system they use as "total communication" or as a "simultaneous method." We probably all believe that, however we label the system we use, it is clear to others exactly what we are doing, and, unfortunately, it is not!

All IHR specialists use a system of manually representing English that is based on *The Comprehensive Signed English Dictionary* (Bornstein, Saulnier, and Hamilton, 1983). Signed English is defined by Bornstein, et al., as "a reasonable manual parallel to English . . . meant to be used while you speak . . ." (p. 2). Of the signed language systems available, IHR specialists feel signed English is most compatible with our communication goals for young hearing-impaired children and their parents. Signed English incorporates the use of 14 sign markers to designate changes in words, such as verb tense, plurals, and possession. The number of markers that IHR specialists use at any given time with a family varies depending on factors such as the parents' facility with signs, the child's age, and other handicapping conditions the child may have. It is our goal to represent our messages in English, but not at the expense of the child understanding our communication. Therefore, it is generally true that the longer the child has been in habilitation, the more accurately the signed component of the message is rendered in English. As in other aspects of habilitation, the input to each child is gauged by his developmental levels and needs.

TENETS SUPPORTING THE USE OF SPOKEN
AND SIGNED ENGLISH AT IHR

As we trust is the case in every parent-infant habilitation program, our ideas about how we can best teach communication skills to young hearing-impaired infants change as we accumulate experience and acquire new information. However, IHR specialists have maintained three tenets which have been supported over time by our experience and by new information. These tenets form the basis of our rationale for the use of signed language in conjunction with speech in teaching language to young hearing-impaired children. These tenets are:

1. The use of signed English in conjunction with spoken English enables many young hearing-impaired children with severe and profound losses to acquire a system of symbolic communication more rapidly than if spoken English is used alone.
2. The use of signed English is compatible with the IHR goal of helping young hearing-impaired children acquire functional speech when certain conditions are met.
3. The use of signed English in conjunction with spoken English promotes the young hearing-impaired child's acquisition of English language competence.

Each of these tenets is discussed below.

THE USE OF SIGNED ENGLISH IN CONJUNCTION
WITH SPEECH PROMOTES THE CHILD'S
MORE RAPID ACQUISITION OF SYMBOLIC COMMUNICATION

The significance of the communication interactions that develop between an infant and his parents was discussed in Chapter 20. Hearing-impaired babies born into families with hearing parents who use auditory-verbal symbolic language are at a severe disadvantage in acquiring symbolic language at the age and rate that normally hearing infants do. When a child's hearing loss is diagnosed and hearing aids are placed, most children begin to hear some of the sounds of speech. However, the auditory information received by many children with severe and profound hearing losses is very soft and incomplete. Years of listening and speech practice may be required to enable them to discriminate, recognize, and comprehend the speech of others and to speak intelligibly themselves.

Signed language, however, is presented to an intact sensory system, the child's eyes. While it is true that the child's visual attention must be directed at the individual who is using signed language, when the child is looking he is able to receive a complete signal. It has been our experience that hearing-impaired children who do not hear speech easily can understand and use the signed symbol for an object, person, or concept before they are able to understand and use the spoken symbol. When signed English is used in conjunction with speech, the child has the opportunity to understand and use signs to communicate while he is still sorting out the speech signals he can hear. This access to a symbolic communication system greatly facilitates the child's cognitive development and his inclusion in communication within his family with all of the positive consequences that this communication produces.

THE USE OF SIGNED ENGLISH IS COMPATIBLE WITH THE GOAL OF TEACHING CHILDREN TO TALK WHEN CERTAIN CONDITIONS ARE MET

Our experience in using a combination of spoken and signed English with young hearing-impaired children has demonstrated that when both spoken and signed language are modeled for a child, he will use both signs and vocalizations/speech in his beginning expressive communication. However, as mentioned above, speech does not come easily to many hearing-impaired children, especially those with profound hearing losses. **Simply using or modeling speech consistently in our communication with hearing-impaired children does not guarantee that the child will acquire intelligible speech.**

Most hearing-impaired children need to be involved in a rigorous and consistent program of auditory and speech development in order to acquire intelligible speech. This is true both of children using an aural-oral approach and of children using an aural-oral with signed English approach. It is our observation that when hearing-impaired children are communicating well through signed language, many teachers and parents fail to provide the intense, sequential speech development training that is necessary to allow the child to acquire intelligible speech. This failure on the part of the adults has a negative effect on the child's use of speech.

Young hearing-impaired children sign and vocalize simultaneously when that is the model provided by their parents and teachers. Signing is easier for the child with a profound hearing loss to learn than is speech, so communicating in signs is more effective for the child whose speech efforts are not understood by others. Unless teachers and parents apply continuous effort to helping the young child develop and use his speech skills so that speech also becomes an effective communication mode for the child, he will stop using his voice. Thus, the child, who is initially motivated to communicate orally because that is what his significant role models do, loses his motivation when he discovers that his spoken communication does not work for him.

Parent-infant specialists, parents, and the children's subsequent teachers must work together to assure that hearing-impaired children do not reach the point at which they determine that their speech is not helpful to them in their communication with others. We can do this by meeting the following conditions:

1. Making certain that the hearing-impaired child is fitted with and consistently wears the amplification system that best permits him to hear and discriminate as much of the speech signal as possible.
2. Consistently using speech when communicating with the child under conditions that permit the child to hear it.
3. Regularly instructing the child in a rigorous, sequential program of speech development.
4. Encouraging and reinforcing the child for using speech to communicate his needs and ideas.

IHR parent-infant specialists acknowledge that there are some hearing-impaired children who do not learn to talk even when all of the conditions that promote acquisition of listening and speech skills are in place. It may be that these children have an auditory processing quirk that prevents them from using the information they receive or a problem with oral expression unrelated to the hearing loss. There are also some profoundly deaf children who, despite the use of appropriate hearing aids, gain no auditory information related to speech. Some of these children do not acquire intelligible speech even when provided with years of excellent speech training.

IHR specialists believe that intelligible speech is an extremely useful tool for the hearing-impaired child. Therefore, we feel that everything possible should be done to give the child the optimum opportunity to acquire functional speech. **We do not believe, however, that the worth of the child is related to his ability to speak clearly.** While the child should be given the optimum opportunity to acquire speech, he should never be given the impression that functional speech is what defines him as a worthwhile individual. The child for whom intelligible speech is not possible needs to know that he does other things well and that his inability to speak clearly does not detract from his inherent value.

Parent-infant specialists at IHR communicate with most of the hearing-impaired infants enrolled using both spoken and signed language. We also meet the conditions listed above — and teach parents to provide these conditions — that promote the child's opportunity to learn to use spoken language. When, because of limited residual hearing, acquisition of vocal and speech skills is slow for a child, we try to ascertain that the child does not perceive himself as failing to measure up. We applaud his speech attempts and acknowledge the effort he puts into learning speech skills. We also make sure that he is able to communicate his thoughts, feelings, and ideas successfully through a manual mode until such time that he can communicate successfully in speech, if that is a possibility for him.

IHR specialists work to make certain that parents are aware of and support the four conditions that will promote their child's acquisition of speech when he is also using signed language. Some parents of IHR graduates, seeing that these conditions are not being met to their satisfaction in the child's school program, pay for individual speech tutoring for their child. It is unfortunate but true that many educational settings do not provide enough of the rigorous and sequential speech development training that gives hearing-impaired children optimal opportunity to acquire functional and intelligible speech. Parents may need to find sources for this training outside of the school program.

THE USE OF SIGNED ENGLISH IN CONJUNCTION WITH SPOKEN ENGLISH HELPS HEARING-IMPAIRED CHILDREN LEARN ENGLISH

The key to acquisition of any language is repeated exposure to complete and non-ambiguous use of that language in situations where the language is meaningful. Spoken English is the language used in the majority of American homes. Normally hearing children learn to use the English language to communicate because they hear it day in and day out. Hearing-impaired children learn language in the same way. They learn what is modeled for them. If a hearing-impaired child can not hear English, he will not learn to use it unless it is modeled for him in a complete and accessible visual mode. If a hearing-impaired child receives an incomplete spoken or signed version of English, that is what he will learn. A child who receives communication in English only part of the time learns to use English very slowly.

Acquisition of English as a first language is one of our goals for children at IHR. The challenge for the family of a hearing-impaired infant is to find ways to expose the child to meaningful use of the English language on a regular basis and in a complete and non-ambiguous way. Some children, wearing appropriate hearing aids, hear well enough to receive all the sounds of English frequently enough to learn English though hearing alone. Other children, whose losses are severe-profound to profound, may not hear all the sounds of language well enough, even when wearing proper amplifica-

POPCORN!

tion. Specialists at IHR believe that this latter group of deaf children can receive English on a regular basis when their families use signed English in combination with speech.

There are some educators who argue that using signed English is a problem because babies may not see, much less understand, the movements or hand positions that signify inflectional endings such as plurals or verb tenses. These educators might also argue that it is pointless to sign "little" words such as "and" or "to" which do not have a visible referent to which the baby can attach the sign. It is true that using signed English is a problem — it is a problem for most adults who are trying to learn to use it! Like learning any new skill, learning signed English requires that an adult make a commitment of time, money, and energy. Adults learning signs must make conscious the usually unconscious process of communication until the newly learned skill of signing while talking becomes automatic.

It is also true that normally hearing babies do not understand all the "little" words or endings used in spoken English. Normally hearing babies do not understand a word of English when they are born. They learn to understand it through repeated exposure to English in meaningful situations. Hearing-impaired babies learn to understand signed and spoken English in the same step-by-step way when they are exposed to it on a regular basis. IHR specialists believe that unless a young hearing-impaired child can consistently receive frequently repeated and non-ambiguous language information through his aided auditory system, his acquisition of English — and of speech — will be facilitated by the addition to spoken English of a signed language system that visually represents the English language.

DISCUSSING WITH PARENTS THE OPTION
OF USING SIGNED ENGLISH

When families enroll at IHR they are aware that they have the option of using an auditory-oral approach or an auditory-oral with signed English approach in communicating with their child and helping him acquire symbolic language. Some families have already decided by the time they enroll which approach they want to use. Other families want more information before they make this decision. As is true in every area of habilitation, most parents have strong feelings associated with the issue of the communication approach they use with their child. Some parents have talked to people who have told them there is only one "right" way to communicate with their child. Then they talk to someone else who tells them only another approach will *really* work. These parents may not be ready to make an immediate decision about communication mode.

Specialists at IHR tell all parents that the first decision they make about communication approach does not necessarily have to be their final decision: What they decide today can be changed if circumstances change or if they acquire new information. Specialists discuss with parents the variables that should be taken into consideration in deciding what communication approach to use with their child. **The child's need to have a functional communication system within his family is maintained as the focus of the discussion as the variables are applied to each child.** It is a given, in this process at IHR, that the *decision* as to communication approach used by the family *belongs to the parents*. It is *their* child.

Professionals cannot honestly tell parents that any one approach works best with all children with hearing loss. Professionals *can* tell parents what they know about the advantages and disadvantages of each communication approach and relate these advantages and disadvantages to the following variables as they apply to the child:

1. **The child's age.** The older the child is when he is identified as hearing-impaired, the further behind he will be in the process of language acquisition and the stronger his immediate need is to have a system to communicate his ideas and feelings.

2. **The etiology of the loss.** If the child's hearing loss was acquired after he had gained some functional receptive and expressive spoken language, this factor must be considered. The immediate goal will be to help the child retain the spoken communication he already has.

3. **The characteristics of the child's hearing loss.** The greater the degree of the hearing loss, the more time it will take for the child to acquire language through audition. If the child's aided residual hearing does not allow him to hear speech, expecting that the child will acquire language through an auditory approach is unrealistic.

4. **The rate at which the child acquires language over time.** One goal for children enrolled at IHR is that they can make one year's worth of gain in acquisition of language concepts in one year's time. The communication approach used with a child must make language accessible enough to him that he can meet or approximate this goal.

5. **The family's ability to learn signed language.** Parents who express interest in using signed English in combination with spoken English are making a commitment to learning a second language. Gaining fluency and competence in signed English requires time, considerable effort and dedication, and usually money. Some families are not able to make this commitment.

Parents are told that a goal for all children enrolled at IHR is beginning competence in spoken English and that, regardless of the communication approach chosen, the same emphasis is placed on helping children reach the goals of maximum use of their residual hearing and of intelligible speech. When signed English is added to the auditory-oral approach, signed language is regarded as a means to accomplishing these goals, not as a barrier to these goals.

Newly enrolled parents who are just beginning to deal with the fact of their child's hearing loss and who are trying to learn how to interact most effectively with their deaf baby may find that the addition of a new language system (signing) is overwhelming. We advise parents who want to begin adding signed language to their spoken communication with their baby that using just a few signs at first is fine. It is critical that the natural, non-verbal parent-child communication system be maintained and enriched. The teacher who advocates a strict adherence to "correct" or "complete" use of signs when these skills are beyond the ability of a beginning signer imposes a structure and self-consciousness on the parent that greatly diminishes the effectiveness of parent-infant communication interactions. The specialist must know when to encourage more signing and when to encourage the parents to relax and just enjoy interactions with their baby.

TEACHING LANGUAGE THROUGH A COMBINATION OF SPEECH AND SIGNED ENGLISH

TECHNIQUES TO USE WHEN COMMUNICATING WITH THE CHILD

The specialists at IHR follow the same steps in communicating with infants and young children while using a combination of speech and signed English as we do when using speech alone. The way we talk to young babies is telegraphic and repetitive, features that make the production and practice of signed English a little easier for the beginning parent. The following suggestions can serve as a guide to parents who are just starting to add signs to their communication with their child:

1. Talk/sign about what the child is seeing and doing.
2. Keep sentences short.
3. Use repetition.
4. Sign the words in the same English word order as you say them.
5. Speak complete English from the very beginning, starting with very short sentences, even if you cannot sign all the words in the sentence at the start. Young children learn English grammar and the use of abstract and relationship words through constant exposure to their correct usage.

    We have found that most parents can learn to use the following elements in their signed language early on:

    a. "-s" for signed plurals; the contracted "'s," as in "it's," the possessive "'s," as in "Timmy's ball."

    b. "-ing" with present progressive verbs.

    c. the articles "a," "an" and "the," and the conjunction "and," (later add "or" and "but").

    d. the prepositions "in," "on," "under," "over," "by," "to," etc.

    e. the "to be" verbs "am," "is," "are," "was," etc.

6. Sign when talking to the child even if the child is not looking. If the child glances up he may catch a word or two and begin to realize that communication is taking place. (See Chapter 21 for suggestions on how to gain the child's visual and auditory attention).

7. Talk/sign for the child using words that give him the power to control his environment. "More," "up," "on," "off," "want," "stop," "go," "no," and "help me" are all words that give the child power in his communication.

8. The optimal situation is to sign everything that is said in the child's presence, whether the communication is directed to the child or not. In beginning sessions with a family who is just learning signs we start by signing only the communication that is directed to the baby. As the parents become more comfortable with signed language, we sign more and more of what is said in the session.

9. Have the parents practice the words and sentences that will be used during an activity prior to starting the activity, reviewing the sign vocabulary that the parents will be using and practicing short sentences to increase fluency and achieve a closer correspondence between production of spoken and signed words. "Here's your toy!" "It's a mouse." "That mouse is small." "He feels soft." "You like your mouse." "Bye-bye mouse." "Where's your mouse?" "Here he is!"

10. Acknowledge and reinforce the child's early sign approximations. As you would with early spoken language, try to understand and respond to what the child is communicating; model the correct sign, without correcting the child. Do not adopt the child's "baby signs" for your own use.

11. Help the child make signs if he is amenable to your manipulation of his hands. Never force him to sign or talk.

12. Select for beginning use two or three words that symbolize the child's favorite activities or toys and create frequent opportunities in which you can say/sign these words meaningfully to the child.

13. As soon as the child demonstrates understanding of a word/sign, add one or two additional words to your emphasized vocabulary. Do not wait for the child to use the sign himself as a test of his understanding — he may understand it long before he uses it himself.

14. Always use language that is a step beyond what the child is using expressively to provide a model for the child to learn. Remember that children, like all of us, understand more language than they use.

There is no set sequence of words that a child will or should learn, whether in speech or in speech and signed language. Parents and specialist will do best when guided by the child's interests. If he is looking at lights, say/sign, "Light! The light is on! It's a bright light." If he's watching the dog, talk/sign about the dog. There is no "right" sequence for learning vocabulary and language. It is an individual process that varies with every child and every family. Every child, however, will need to learn to use a variety of types of words: verbs, nouns, power words (e.g., "want," "more," "up), and adjectives. There is a general sequence of acquisition of words in normally hearing children which reflects cognitive growth, need, frequency of occurrence, and ease of learning. This sequence appears in the language sections of *Parent-Infant Communication.* The record-keeping system included in this curriculum allows specialists and parents to record the child's receptive and expressive vocabulary by category of usage. This system clearly demonstrates what types of words the child is learning to understand and use expressively and to what types he needs more exposure.

SIGNED LANGUAGE CLASSES

Three nine-week courses of signed language instruction are offered each year at IHR to those families and friends of young hearing-impaired children whose parents have chosen to use the auditory-oral with signed English approach. These classes, which are taught by IHR staff, deaf adults, and local educators of the hearing-impaired hired by IHR, are held one evening a week for an hour and a half. Attendees are divided into three groups: beginning adults, intermediate adults, and children. One teacher leads the children's group and one or two teach the adult groups, depending on the number of people enrolled. Parents who are ready for advanced signed language classes, or who want to learn ASL, are referred to classes offered by the local community colleges.

Signed language classes at IHR are offered to meet two needs:
1. To help family members and friends learn to communicate using signed English in conjunction with speech.
2. To provide a forum in which parents, extended family, and friends can develop a support group for discussion of their concerns and feelings regarding handicapped children.

The classes are purposely structured in a relaxed, non-academic way to promote this second function. Many of the parents who attend do not have regular contact with other parents of hearing-impaired children and the signed language class is their only opportunity to share observations, questions, and concerns about their child. Instructors for the classes are selected for their ability to facilitate discussion among parents as well as for their skill in teaching signed English.

One of the first goals of a beginning signed language class at IHR is to help parents become aware of all the non-verbal forms of communication that they are already using and to help them become comfortable with the idea of using their bodies and facial expression even more effectively to communicate. Focusing on these two factors can help parents lose the self-consciousness and anxiety common to individuals who are first learning to sign. A crucial spin-off of beginning the class with an emphasis on universally understood communication behaviors is that it clearly states to parents the importance of communicating meaning by whatever method one can devise. It is our intent that, given this understanding, parents will communicate with their child whether or not they know the formal sign for a concept. When this first step is overlooked and the signed language instructor jumps immediately into teaching a formal sign system, parents get the unfortunate message that, "One does not communicate unless one can use the correct signs in the correct order." Both parents and children suffer unnecessary frustration if this message is conveyed.

Games such as "charades" can encourage parents to relax and enjoy themselves as they practice communicating without words. Starting classes with games that promote pantomime and interpretation of pantomime help create the relaxed, fun-filled environment in which people learn best. One such game is to pin a list of three descriptive adjectives, e.g., "tall," "mean," "slow," on the back of each class participant as they arrive. As people mingle, they act out for each other the words on someone else's back until everyone knows all three of their adjectives.

One innovative instructor has used a "magic wand" which is passed from person to person, with each person using the wand as something else — a toothbrush, a cane, a violin. Another excellent activity — and one that will demonstrate how many signs evolve from natural and familiar gestures — is to give a class participant a situation and ask how they would convey what they want: "You are in Egypt. You want to ride a camel around the pyramids. You need to ask where you can rent a camel." After someone has successfully conveyed their need or interest, the instructor can point out any formal signs that the person has inadvertently used in his/her effort to communicate. This is a wonderful way to initiate exposure to signed language. The parent pantomimes; the instructor notes which of the parent's movements are signs or approximations of signs. Presto! Those signs are remembered!

The book currently used as the source of signs taught at IHR is *The Comprehensive Signed English Dictionary* (Bornstein, et al, 1983). This book is used by the total communication classes at the Columbia Regional Program for the Hearing Impaired, the public school program into which most IHR graduates enroll. Once more formal instruction begins in the IHR signed language classes, the vocabulary taught is specifically geared to the interests and communication needs of children, 0-4 years of age.

Sign class sessions include body awareness activities, discussion of signed language systems, and teaching components of American Sign Language (ASL) that contribute to and convey meaning, such as signing space, sign movement, and handshape. The teacher also incorporates activities which promote practice in reading signs (receptive practice), practice in using signs in sentences and paragraphs (expressive practice), and introduction of and practice with new vocabulary.

Some instructors videotape class participants intermittently so that each person can evaluate his/her own performance. Videotape may also be used at the beginning and end of the course so that participants can appreciate the progress they have made when they see the "before" and "after" tapes. Some instructors use a self-graded "quiz" format in the receptive practice during each class so that participants can evaluate their own recall of signs previously learned. At the end of each course, participants complete a written evaluation of the course and instructor. The information gained from these evaluations is used when hiring instructors for subsequent courses and by the instructors as they plan the content of the next nine-week course.

The children's classes are extremely popular with siblings and neighborhood friends of the hearing-impaired child. These classes can present a challenge to the instructor because of the wide range of ages and signing abilities of the children enrolled. Instructors have found that snacks are a strong motivator for the children when interspersed with the games they use to teach signs. Children learn signs very rapidly and often serve to motivate (and remind) their parents to use signs at home.

IHR signed language instructors utilize three tips that appear to promote efficient learning on the part of class participants:

1. Parents are urged to review new vocabulary before going to bed the night of the class and to use the new signs with their child during the week.
2. At the beginning of the course, the teacher establishes one rule which (s)he asks enrollees to follow: The teacher is the only person who can "correct" signs used by class participants. This rule is designed to minimize the conflict that inevitably arises between spouses, one of whom is generally a better signer.
3. Class participants are told that when there is more than one sign for a concept, they can select the one they feel most comfortable using. They are encouraged not to think of any signs as being "right" or "wrong."

CHALLENGES IN TEACHING SIGNED LANGUAGE
TO PARENTS OF YOUNG HEARING-IMPAIRED CHILDREN

Learning to use a new communication mode simultaneously with speech is a difficult task, as several researchers (Baker, 1978; Marmor and Petitto, 1979) have shown. Swisher and Thompson (1985) studied the simultaneous use of spoken and manually coded English of six mothers of young hearing-impaired children. Each of the mothers had been using simultaneous communication for an average of three years and had taken an average of three signed language courses after "graduation" from an early intervention program in which signed language usage was introduced. The investigators found, among other things, that "on the average, just 40.5 utterances per 100 utterance sample were signed in full" (p. 213), and that the mean length of utterance directed at their children (ages 4.5 to 6 years at the time of the study) during the interactions studied was only 3.89 morphemes. The investigators concluded that the difficulty of simultaneous communication for parents may have been underestimated and that methods used in teaching parents to sign may need to be reevaluated.

In their discussion, Swisher and Thompson eloquently describe some of the difficulties associated with parents learning to use signed language.

> ". . . we need to remember that mothers of deaf children, unlike teachers of the deaf, are not a population selected for having academic skills or college degrees. The necessity of analyzing language form to decide what ending to choose for an /s/ sound or an ' -er ' ending may be a baffling addition to a new world that includes the jargon of audiologists and teachers, the intricacies of hearing aids, and the difficulties of trying to communicate with a hearing-impaired child. Again, unlike most teachers, most parents have been forced by circumstances to learn to sign. Parenting a deaf child is not a profession that they have chosen, and the need to sign is thrust upon them whether or not they have the language aptitude, the intelligence, or the physical coordination to acquire the skill easily. In addition to this lack of choice, they may have deep, unresolved conflicts about having a child with disabling conditions, and these conflicts may affect their disposition to learn. Deciding to acquire sign language implies some degree of acceptance that the child is disabled and that the condition is not going to go away. Furthermore, the decision requires overt demonstration of this acceptance to the world at large. The mother who signs to her child in public will surely be watched and may well be approached by interested bystanders whether she is gregarious by nature or not. A part of her life that may feel very private is necessarily made public for the sake of her child" (pp. 214-215).

In addition to the obstacles described by these investigators, IHR parent-infant specialists have identified five challenging areas which frequently arise when teaching signed language to families of hearing-impaired infants. These areas are:

1. Motivating families to use signs at home.
2. The existence of different signs for the same concept.
3. Striking a balance between teaching vocabulary and teaching fluency.
4. Dealing with families who elect to use signed English in conjunction with spoken English with their child, but who cannot/do not attend signed language classes.
5. Teaching signed language to multi-handicapped infants.

Each of these areas is discussed below.

MOTIVATING FAMILIES TO USE SIGNS AT HOME

Learning signed language is like learning any other language — the more a person is exposed to it and uses it, the more rapidly he/she will become competent. Because parents are themselves just learning to sign they often experience frustration and feelings of incompetence when they try to add signs to what they are saying to their child. Since no one enjoys feeling incompetent, it is easier to "forget" to sign at home than to struggle with using this new skill.

The signed language instructor and parent-infant specialists can encourage families to use signs at home with the following suggestions:

1. As new vocabulary is taught, ask parents to tell you how they would be likely to use the vocabulary with their child. If the sign for "bath" is taught, ask parents what they say to their child when it is bathtime. *Help them practice signing the phrase that they normally say.* Parents may say, "Time for your bath," or "It's bathtime," or "Mommy's gonna put you in the tub," or "You ready for your bath?" If the only phrase you teach them is, "Let's have a bath" and that's not what they normally say, the chances of their using the new language is minimal. Encourage parents to think about new vocabulary as it is taught so that in their mind they see themselves using that vocabulary at home with their child. Assure parents that it is worth using signs with their child even if, at first, they can only remember one sign in the sentence they are saying.
2. Encourage families to set aside one 10-15 minute period each day during which they communicate without using spoken language, but instead use signs, pantomime, and gestures. If associated with a positive family time, such as dessert after dinner, and the time limit is strictly adhered to, this could become a family high-point.

Suggest that each person relate one event of the day so that other family members have practice "reading" non-verbal communication. Be sure the hearing-impaired child is included in these daily gatherings.

3. Suggest that families plan activities into which they can incorporate their signing practice. Trips to the store, the zoo, the car-wash, church, can all become opportunities to practice vocabulary and phrases relevant to that particular event. Families can also make a point of learning specific signs that relate to anticipated family activities such as a trip to Disneyland, going to Grandma's, or planting a garden.

4. Ask each class participant to report back (in gestures, pantomime, and signs) to the signed language class one short event which took place during the week in which they used signs with their child, e.g., "I said to Brenda, 'Please get your coat.'"

THE CONFUSION CAUSED BY DIFFERENT SIGNS FOR THE SAME CONCEPT

Some people who are learning signed language find it very difficult to tolerate the fact that different signs exist for one concept. The frustrations people experience when learning signed language are frequently expressed as irritation when the instructor, either intentionally or inadvertently, uses a sign that is not the same as the one parents learned earlier. Almost all new signers feel hopeless about becoming fluent in signed language after the first few lessons they attend. Anger and hostility are common reactions associated with feelings of hopelessness. Because it does not feel safe to express these feelings directly, beginning signers, especially parents who are experiencing self-engendered pressures to learn, may use occasions of confusion over signs to vent some of their feelings of anger.

Our staff has also noticed that adults who are just beginning to gain minimal competence in signed language may be very resistant to learning alternative ways of expressing an already learned concept. Having acquired a small measure of competency, they are unwilling to experience the "ordeal" of learning alternative ways to communicate the same message. The instructor needs to perceive that this seeming rigidity on the part of adult learners is an attempt to hang onto their feelings of competence and accomplishment. It may help if instructors tell class participants at the outset that they will be seeing signs used that are different from the one they learned for a particular concept. The instructor can encourage participants to tolerate these differences and accept the fact that there is more than one way to sign many concepts.

One of the best ways to help beginning and intermediate signers overcome their resistance and anger about the fact that signs are not universally (or even locally!) standardized is to provide as many opportunities as possible to communicate in signed language with a variety of accomplished signers under enjoyable and non-threatening circumstances. The ideal situation is to utilize hearing-impaired adults as instructors. If that is not possible, encouraging social interaction with hearing-impaired teenagers or adults is an excellent way for parents, friends, and siblings (not to mention teachers) of hearing-impaired children to expand their signed language horizons. Some instructors choose to invite hearing-impaired adults to signed language classes every third or fourth week, at which time both informal social interactions and group activities can be planned to promote the use of signs in conversation. Part of the proceeds from sign class tuition can be used to pay these guests for their help if plans are made in advance to include these costs in the charges.

STRIKING A BALANCE BETWEEN TEACHING VOCABULARY AND TEACHING FLUENCY

Once parents have acquired a core signed vocabulary that they are accustomed to using with their child, and especially after they see their child beginning to understand and use signs, they become more motivated to sign everything they say. This period of motivation often produces a strong desire in parents to learn vast numbers of new signs. As adults begin using more and more connected signs, they notice that their rate of signing lags seriously behind their rate of speaking. An obvious solution may be to omit some signs for the "little words" so that the signs can coincide with the corresponding spoken words. The problem with this solution is that the "little words" frequently convey the significant relationships between the other words in the sentence. In order to speed up their signing, adults may leave out prepositions, articles, and word endings. Since these parts of speech are not always audible to the hearing-impaired child, he may miss them altogether. Not having been exposed to a complete model of English, the child will acquire an inadequate English language base, creating subsequent difficulties in learning to read and use English expressively.

It is necessary for signed language instructors to attach equal importance to fluency (the rhythm, rate, size, and flow of signs, and economy of motion between signs) as well as to vocabulary development in order to promote the parents' use of a complete language system in their communication with their child. Practice with familiar material is essential. Viewing videotapes of themselves signing can provide adults with valuable feedback about their sign production and can help them compare various aspects of their signing with more advanced signers.

FAMILIES WHO ELECT TO USE SIGNED ENGLISH IN CONJUNCTION WITH SPOKEN ENGLISH BUT WHO CANNOT/DO NOT ATTEND SIGNED LANGUAGE CLASSES

Some families have a sincere interest in using signed English in conjunction with spoken English in their communication with their child but are unable to attend signed language classes in order to learn signs. In these cases, the parent-infant specialist becomes responsible for teaching signed language to the family in addition to all the other necessary information and skills she must teach. One way to accomplish this task is to extend the length of each regularly scheduled habilitation session, with the added time (e.g., 30 minutes) dedicated to learning signed language. The specialist may find it most efficient to use 15 minutes before the session to introduce new signs that will be used with the child during activities planned for the session, and to follow the session with another 15 minutes for further practice and review of signs. If the specialist is signing/talking throughout the session, the parents will have additional opportunity to see signs repeated and to imitate and use new signs themselves.

Parents who cannot attend signed language classes should be strongly encouraged to purchase the signed language book used by the agency or school and to study it on their own. If a parent-infant habilitation program has signed language lessons available on videotape, parents should have access to the tapes to use at home, if possible. (The SKI*HI Institute in Logan, Utah, has produced a set of 20 signed language instruction videotapes which are designed for use by families of young hearing-impaired children.)

As mentioned in another discussion in this volume, some parents who believe they are using a total communication approach with their child never, in fact, acquire the signed vocabulary or fluency so essential to providing the visual component of total communication. The low language levels and poor academic achievement of some children trained in alleged "total communication" environments can be attributed to lack of exposure to a complete language system in the home, school, or both during the child's first several years of life.

TEACHING SIGNED LANGUAGE TO MULTI-HANDICAPPED INFANTS

This challenge is present when the parent-infant specialist is helping a family with a multi-handicapped infant establish communication through a combination of signed and spoken systems. Chapter 26 of this volume contains general suggestions regarding teaching signs to multi-handicapped infants.

When considering the five challenges discussed above, it becomes apparent that teaching signed language to parents/friends of hearing-impaired infants is not a simple task. For many parents, the trip made to signed language classes at IHR is their third or fourth weekly trip to the agency. The classes are conducted during the evening so that parents must make babysitting arrangments for their hearing-impaired child and for any siblings not attending the children's class. If signed language classes are not fun and reinforcing, attendance drops. The instructors must structure classes so that parents can learn signs relevant to their child's needs in a relaxed, enjoyable, and non-punitive environment, and must motivate parents to use the signs they learn when communicating with their child.

SUMMARY

The decision to ''use signed language'' when communicating with a young hearing-impaired child is not as simple as it seems. Our experience with some of the issues surrounding this decision — which signed language system to use, how the use of signs affects the child's acquisition of speech and of the English language, how best to teach signed language to parents — have been discussed in this Chapter. Parent-infant specialists need to attempt to keep abreast of the research that is being published so that we can help parents make informed decisions about using signed language with their hearing-impaired children.

CHAPTER 24

IDEAS FOR BEGINNING SESSIONS WITH A NEWLY ENROLLED FAMILY

Determining the Sequence of Activities

Activities Which Take Place During the First
Sessions with a Newly Enrolled Family

DETERMINING THE SEQUENCE OF ACTIVITIES

The chapters which have preceded this one in Part Five have focused on the broad spectrum of knowledge, techniques, and skills that the specialist will teach to parents so that the parents can help their child with hearing loss acquire listening and language skills. Most families are enrolled at IHR for two years and attend around 70 sessions each year. Thus, the IHR specialist has approximately 140 hours in which to transmit to parents a vast amount of information related to listening, language, speech, behavior, etc.; to model a large number of techniques and skills related to specific objectives; to attend to the parents' emotional needs; to build the parent-specialist partnership; to evaluate parent and infant baseline behaviors; and to assess ongoing achievement of objectives.

When a newly enrolled infant crawls through the door of an agency for the first time, he is followed by anxious parents who may want to know and do everything at once in order to fix this newly diagnosed problem or by parents who may want to know and do nothing because they are hurting too much to act. The specialist can, at this point, be an anchor of stability for parents who have been thrust into the unknown and bewildering arena of habilitation for young hearing-impaired children. One of the most positive things that can happen to these parents is to encounter a calm, competent specialist who can assure the parents that she knows what needs to be done and that she will guide them in doing it.

Easy to say! However, in order to feel calm and competent and to convey these qualities to parents, the specialist must, in fact, know how to prioritize the activities that will take place during first sessions with new families. Initial sessions are important 1) because the manner in which they are conducted sets the tone for the parent-specialist partnership, and 2) because the activities which the specialist chooses to focus on will indicate to parents whether or not their own priorities will be considered in the habilitation process.

The importance of the content of initial sessions and how parents react to this content can be seen by describing what happened during the first several sessions of one newly enrolled family. Ted and Pat had recently enrolled with their seven-month-old daughter, Ariel. Ariel had been tested twice by the audiologist and had been seen by an otologist, who saw no abnormalities in Ariel's ears during his exam. Based on the auditory thresholds obtained using VRA during Ariel's first two visits, the audiologist had determined that Ariel had a profound, bilateral sensorineural hearing loss.

During their first visit with the IHR parent-infant specialist, Julia, both Ted and Pat mentioned their desire to learn the cause of Ariel's hearing loss. Julia had reviewed Ariel's history and saw that there were no conditions noted which would place Ariel at risk for hearing loss. She mentioned this fact to Ted and Pat and observed that in some cases it may be very difficult to pinpoint the cause of the hearing loss. Julia told Ted and Pat that it would be important for them to meet with a genetic counselor who would do a more thorough study of Ariel's history. She promised them that she would give them the name of an agency through which they could arrange an appointment with a genetic counselor.

However, Julia's priorities for Ariel centered on further audiologic testing and on beginning hearing aid placement. During the first several sessions with this family she failed to attend to the parents' need to explore the cause of Ariel's hearing loss. When Ted and Pat failed to keep an appointment to have earmold impressions made for Ariel, Julia was concerned. She telephoned Ted, who had said earlier that he would be bringing Ariel in to have the impressions made.

> Julia: "Ted, I'm concerned because you missed the appointment to have Ariel's earmolds made. Did we get our signals crossed?"
>
> Ted: "Oh, was that today? Yeah, here it is on my calendar. I'm sorry, we've got so much on our minds. I guess that having the earmolds made just slipped by."
>
> Julia: "What is it that you and Pat have been thinking about most, Ted?"
>
> Ted: "We sure want to know why Ariel is deaf. Nothing else seems real important to us right now. I guess we feel immobilized until we know what made her deaf."
>
> Julia: "I'm sorry, Ted! You and Pat told me the first time we met that that was important to you. I really dropped the ball, didn't I. Let me give you the name and phone number of a genetic counselor right now. It sounds like talking to him is your first priority. I apologize for failing to follow up on that for you."

Once Ted and Pat had made an appointment with the genetic counselor, they became increasingly more involved in the activities that Julia presented during the habilitation sessions. Julia learned from this experience that failing to attend to the parents' priorities may result in diminished parental attention to the habilitation activities that she planned. She made certain, from that point on, to ask the parents what activities were most important to them and to include time for dealing with their concerns in her lesson plan.

There is no one sequence of activities that can be followed for each new family since situations and circumstances will vary with each family. However, there are a series of activities which must be carried out with each family at the onset of habilitation. Determining the order of priority in which these activities are conducted is one of the first things a parent-infant specialist will do in meeting with a new family. She will use information gathered from the audiologist, physician, and parents to help her make prioritization decisions.

What follows is a list of activities that are conducted during first sessions with families at IHR. Specialists at other agencies will need to alter this list to suit their own habilitation settings. As mentioned earlier, the sequence in which these activities are carried out is determined by the specialist for each family with which she starts working.

ACTIVITIES WHICH TAKE PLACE DURING THE FIRST SESSIONS WITH A NEWLY ENROLLED FAMILY

The content of each session during a family's first weeks of enrollment can be planned prior to each session, but the specialist must remain flexible so that the activities that actually take place are a reflection of the parents' immediate needs for support and information. The parents may leave one session saying they want to learn more about hearing aids during the next session. They may come into the next session with a stronger need to talk about some feelings evoked by a remark made by a friend or relative. There *will* be time for everything, though it may not seem so at first.

The following areas should be covered, if only at an introductory level, during the first several sessions with a family.

1. Outline the habilitation program for the family:
   a. Confirm lesson times and sites (clinic, home, audiodiological suite).
   b. Discuss who may attend sessions (siblings, grandparents, babysitters, friends).
   c. Describe the role parents and other adults will play in the sessions, i.e., participants rather than observers.
   d. Preview the infant curriculum and the parent curriculum that will be the sources of learning objectives for the family.
   e. Request that parents purchase a binder and dividers in which to organize and keep parent handouts and reports on their child.
   f. Briefly describe activities at the agency in which the family will be involved, e.g., parent groups, child groups, special sessions for fathers and extended family, signed language classes.

2. Introduce the first set of loaner hearing aids that their child will be using for a trial period:
   a. Go over the parts of the aid and how they are assembled.
   b. Demonstrate a listening test for the aid to check function prior to inserting the aid in the child's ear and give parents related hand-outs from *Parent-Infant Communication.*
   c. Discuss the type of battery used in the aid, where batteries can be purchased, and how frequently they will need to be replaced.
   d. Demonstrate use of a battery tester.
   e. Demonstrate placing hearing aids on the child and observe parents as they place aids on child.
   f. Discuss the length of time the child will wear the aids as he begins usage and set goal for full-time usage (at IHR we aim for full-time use during waking hours within two weeks of first placing aids).
   g. Provide parents with a form on which to record the child's first use of aids, including length of time worn for each time placed, problems that occur while the child is wearing aids, and responses to sound that the child makes while wearing aids.
3. Keep in touch with the parents' feelings and concerns:
   a. Ask if they have questions about information discussed at earlier sessions.
   b. Ask how they are *feeling* about information you have discussed.
   c. Ask how they are doing.
   d. Ask how their extended family members, siblings, friends are reacting to the diagnosis of their child's hearing loss.
   e. Attend to their non-verbal behaviors and remark on them, e.g., "You seem quiet today — what kinds of things are you thinking about?"; "You are energetic today!"
   f. Follow up on off-hand remarks parents make, such as a parent saying, "This is hard," as she attempts to put the earmold in her child's ear. The specialist might acknowledge, "Yeah, it's tricky getting the earmold in. Are you also finding it a little hard to think of Timmy needing to wear hearing aids at all?"
4. Introduce parents to the parents of other children with hearing loss.
5. Learn about the child's interests and abilities from the parents:
   a. Ask parents to describe the child's favorite activities.
   b. Ask how the child communicates his wants and dislikes.
   c. Encourage parents to tell you about the child's moods, reactions to favorite people, reactions to new situations, to

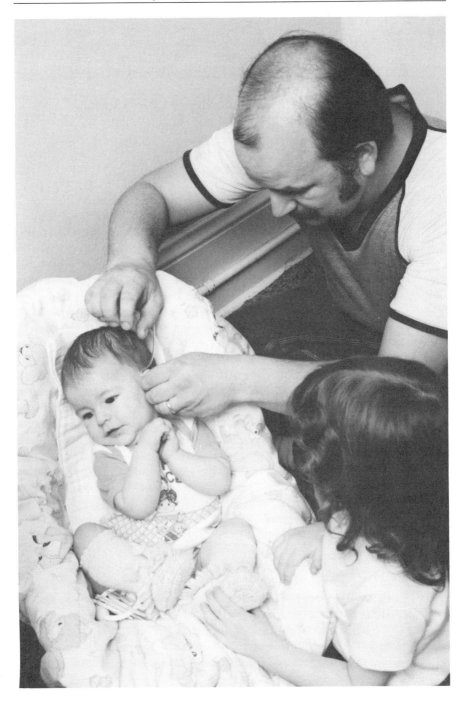

Learning to put their baby's first hearing aids on is a memorable moment for parents who are just beginning the habilitation process.

describe what the child's personality is like.

  d. Ask parents to predict how the child will respond to new activities, unfamiliar people.
6. Observe and record communication already occurring between parents and infant:
  a. Observe how parents bring the child into sessions.
  b. Observe how they hold the child, place child down, prepare child for session.
  c. Observe frequency and length of eye contact and physical contact between parents and child.
  d. Note the types of non-verbal and spoken or signed language the parents use with the child and the presence/absence of characteristics of "motherese" in their spoken language.
  e. Note how the child responds to adult-initiated communication.
  f. Note how the child uses body positioning to get close to or avoid parents. If child is mobile, note how dependent/independent he is of parents.
  g. Note types of vocalizations and gestures the child uses to get his parents' attention, to communicate wants and needs, to communicate dislike or refusal.
  h. Observe how parents respond to child-initiated communication.
7. Model beginning observation and recording skills by talking as you observe the child's behavior. Describe the child's actions and vocalizations as you observe them and point out to parents the significance of the child's behaviors as you record them on your lesson plan.
8. Establish infant baseline behaviors in auditory, presymbolic communication, and receptive and expressive language using the objectives in *Parent-Infant Communication*:
  a. Interview parents.
  b. Observe the child during sessions.
  c. Use diagnostic teaching approach during play activities with the child.
  d. Select beginning objectives in each curriculum section.
9. Establish parent baseline behaviors using the objectives in *Parent-Infant Communication:*
  a. Observe parents interacting with the child.
  b. Ask parents to describe their need for information or their understanding of informational areas such as the audiogram, audition, language, etc.
  c. Select several parent objectives to begin working on based on parent need for information and skills (e.g., related to hearing aid use, getting and maintaining the child's attention, interpreting the audiogram).

10. Coordinate habilitation goals for multi-handicapped infants with other professionals seeing the child; acquire as much information as possible about the child's level of function from other professionals who work with the child.
11. Discuss the options of using auditory-oral or auditory-oral with signed English as communication modes; describe advantages and disadvantages of each *as they relate to the child's individual characteristics and needs and the family's characteristics and needs.*
12. Provide beginning parent handout materials to all parents and additional books and/or periodicals to parents who are interested in acquiring information through reading.

Sometimes it may feel that the first month or two of sessions with a family are disorganized or lack cohesion. These sessions must cover a wide variety of topics at a fairly cursory level in order to select and start working on appropriate infant and parent learning objectives. This introductory approach actually works well with parents who are having to learn a great deal of new vocabulary and many new concepts related to hearing loss and the habilitation process. Dealing as they are with the emotional issues related to their child's hearing loss, many parents are not ready for information in great depth. Approaching important topics at an introductory level with the knowledge that the details of information and skills will be addressed later is a comfortable compromise for specialists and parents alike.

If we looked at a specialist's lesson plans for the first three or four sessions with a new family, we would most likely see many of the following activities:

- Answer parents' questions, respond to parents' needs to talk about their feelings.
- Discuss the parts of the hearing aid, and describe its general function; practice putting parts of aid together; discuss type of battery to use and where it can be purchased.
- Hand out calendar of agency activities and directory of families enrolled.
- Discuss the child's favorite toys, foods, games.
- Look at and explain the child's first audiogram(s).
- Show parents the curriculum used in habilitation, explaining how objectives are selected and how record sheets are used.
- Ask parents to buy 3-ring binder for handouts they will receive.
- Explain loaner hearing aid policy.
- Place hearing aids on child and let parents practice putting aids on.
- Demonstrate cleaning the child's earmolds.
- Do informal auditory assessment, aided and unaided, using noisemaking toys.
- Do initial videotape of parents and their infant playing together.

- Begin modeling techniques for observing the child's awareness of sounds.
- Ask parents to keep records of their child's auditory responses noted at home.
- Begin teaching conditioned response to sound if the child is ready (18-30 months).
- Begin modeling appropriate techniques for getting the child's auditory and visual attention.
- Note and reinforce non-verbal communication observed between parents and infant and explain its importance.
- Begin modeling techniques for imitating the child's vocalizations.
- Begin modeling techniques for using repetition when talking to the child.

As each of the topics outlined above is covered during the beginning sessions, the specialist can check off the objectives accomplished on the appropriate infant or parent Curriculum Checksheet. The specialist can then confer with the parents to select subsequent objectives to work on in sessions and at home. As the parents' initial anxiety diminishes, they are able to participate more fully in sessions and to be more certain about which areas they need more help with and learning areas they would like to emphasize in future activities with their child.

First sessions with a newly enrolled family are а challenging and stimulating time! The specialist is juggling a number of tasks that need to be accomplished; the parents bring in their own needs to be added to that list. The specialist must keep in mind — and convey to parents the attitude — that there *is* time for everything. The most important and effective way for the specialist to proceed in these sessions is to follow the lead of the parents, just as in later sessions the parent-specialist team works to follow the lead of the child. If the parents find that their needs and concerns are given priority, they will feel motivated to enter into the parent-specialist partnership with the goal of helping their child acquire the listening and language skills and positive self-esteem that he needs in order to function happily in his family, school, and society.

PART VI

WORKING WITH FAMILIES OF HEARING-IMPAIRED INFANTS WITH ADDITIONAL HANDICAPS

CHAPTER 25

IDENTIFYING THE HEARING-IMPAIRED INFANT WITH ADDITIONAL HANDICAPPING CONDITIONS

Some of the Effects of Other Handicapping Conditions on the Hearing-Impaired Child and His Family

- Describing Handicapping Conditions: The Importance of a Positive Stance
- The Effects of a Combination of Handicapping Conditions
- Parents' Reactions to the Identification of Additional Handicapping Conditions in Their Child

Detecting the Presence of a Handicapping Condition in Addition to Hearing Loss

- Etiology and Incidence of Other Handicapping Conditions
- Use of Developmental Scales to Detect Signs of Other Handicapping Conditions
- Alert Lists: Child Behaviors That May Signal the Presence of Handicapping Conditions Other Than Hearing Loss
- Use of the Diagnostic Teaching Approach

Continued on following page

Procedures the Parent-Infant Specialist Can Follow if She Suspects that a Child has a Handicap in Addition to Hearing Loss

A Framework for Guiding the Parent-Infant Specialist in Acquiring Information

- Acquiring Information About Other Handicaps
- Acquiring Information About the Child
- Acquiring Information About the Family
- Acquiring Information for Yourself

It is not the intent of Part VI to provide all the information a parent-infant specialist requires in order to meet all the needs of the young multi-handicapped hearing-impaired child and his parents. While IHR specialists have worked with a number of infants who have handicapping conditions in addition to hearing loss, we do not consider ourselves experts on intervention with these children. We suspect that we have done what many readers do: As we enroll a child with handicapping conditions in addition to hearing loss, we set about learning what we need to know to help that specific child. It is fortunate that, in the past few years, experienced educators who have worked with large numbers of children with different combinations of handicapping conditions have written books and articles in which they share their knowledge and approaches with us. Chapter 26 concludes with a list of suggested readings that the parent-infant specialist is encouraged to use to expand her knowledge of a variety of handicapping conditions.

The goal of the chapters in Part VI is to give the parent-infant specialist 1) an introduction to the effects of multi-handicapping conditions on the child and his family; 2) an awareness of some child behaviors that may signal the presence of a handicapping condition in addition to hearing loss; 3) an outline of the procedures to follow if the parent-infant specialist suspects that an undiagnosed handicap is present; 4) a framework for helping the parent-infant specialist acquire information about other handicapping conditions; and 5) a description of specific techniques used successfully by the IHR staff in working with young multi-handicapped children and their parents during audiological testing, in hearing aid use, and in habilitation sessions.

We want to emphasize again that this is not an exhaustive discussion of the characteristics and intervention needs of multi-handicapped children. We refer the reader to the Sugggested Reading list at the end of Chapter 26 for descriptions of some of the work others have been doing with multi-handicapped children.

SOME OF THE EFFECTS OF OTHER HANDICAPPING CONDITIONS ON THE HEARING-IMPAIRED CHILD AND HIS FAMILY

DESCRIBING HANDICAPPING CONDITIONS: THE IMPORTANCE OF A POSITIVE STANCE

The issue of selecting terms to use in describing handicapping conditions is not a simple one. As is true with hearing loss, other disabilities can be described as mildly to severely or profoundly handicapping. The severity of a handicapping condition can be measured and described in two ways: 1) according to the degree to which the function of the impaired sensory system is inhibited; and 2) according to the degree to which the handicapping condition increases the individual's dependency on others. The way in which a child's handicapping conditions, once diagnosed, are described or labeled may have a tremendous impact on the parents' reaction to the diagnosis and on the reaction of the educators encountering the child and his family. The statement, "This child is deaf-blind," produces a very different reaction from the statement, "This child is hearing-impaired and partially sighted." Specialists at IHR feel that it is helpful to provide parents with terms that acknowledge their child's residual capabilities rather than describe their child's deficits. Nowhere is this more necessary than in the case of a child who has more than one handicapping condition, since it is true that the attitudes and beliefs of the significant adults in the child's life will either add to or help overcome the effects of the handicaps.

The general public's understanding of terms such as "deaf," "blind," and "mentally retarded" is that all function is gone. This perception is demonstrated by one person's question, "Well, if he's deaf (blind), why bother with a hearing aid (glasses)?" Another person may ask, "Why does he go to school if he's retarded?" The use of words that imply absence of function can have a strongly negative effect on parents' and teachers' attitudes and beliefs about what they can expect the child to achieve. On the other hand, use of terms such as "limited residual hearing," "partially sighted," "developmentally delayed," "limited control of movement," describe a sensory system that is present, even if impaired.

It is important not to ignore the presence of residual capabilities that the child can learn to utilize; it is equally important not to deny the existence and effects of handicapping conditions. The individual who diagnoses a handicapping condition in a child and the specialist who works with the family in a habilitation program may feel that they teeter on a thin line when it comes to providing the parents with an accurate picture of the consequences of their child's handicapping condition(s). Professionals do not want to give the parents a rosy picture that defies the gravity of the situation and encourages the parents to adopt unrealistic or false expectations regarding their child's potential. On the other hand, professionals do not want to paint a picture so bleak that the parents abandon all hope and with it their enthusiasm for working to assure that their child will achieve his maximum potential. One of the most helpful paths to take in talking to parents is to focus on the child's present strengths and limitations and on the habilitation objectives that will minimize the limitations imposed by the handicapping conditions. Specialists who convey positive attitudes and professional competence are a real source of comfort to anxious parents.

It is impossible for a professional to predict accurately how an infant with a disability will be functioning in five or ten years' time, even though parents are eager to have that information. The child's future achievements are highly dependent on steps that are carried out in the present. Providing parents with frequent updates on skills their child has achieved in all areas of his development as the habilitation process proceeds is infinitely more helpful than providing them with labels that attempt to define the child's areas of limitation.

THE EFFECTS OF A COMBINATION OF HANDICAPPING CONDITIONS

Any condition that limits the infant's or child's ability to acquire information from his environment or that increases his dependency on others is a handicapping condition. A child, for example, who has limited control over his movements and mobility will not experience the types and degrees of interactions with objects and with space that give the normally developing child information about his environment. When this informational deficit is combined with the diminished amount of information the child receives as a result of impaired hearing, the effects are more than simply additive. This is true of any combination of handicaps. When two of the child's sensory modalities are impaired, not only is his sensory input reduced, but methods that are generally used to minimize the effect of one handicap may not be effective because of the second handicap. Three potential effects of combined handicapping conditions are described below: multi-sensory deprivation, learned helplessness, and insufficient parent-child attachment.

MULTI-SENSORY DEPRIVATION

McInnes and Treffry in their excellent text entitled *Deaf-Blind Infants and Children: A Developmental Guide* (1982) describe deaf-blind children as "multi-sensory deprived," a description that would fit any child who is receiving limited input from more than one sensory channel. Many of the problems McInnes and Treffry describe as resulting from the dual handicap of impaired hearing and impaired vision would apply to other combinations of handicaps. These children may:

- "lack the ability to communicate with their environment in a meaningful way,
- have a distorted perception of their world,
- lack the ability to anticipate future events or the results of their actions,
- be deprived of many of the most basic extrinsic motivations,
- have medical problems which lead to serious developmental lags,
- be mislabeled as retarded or emotionally disturbed,
- be forced to develop unique learning styles to compensate for their multiple handicaps,
- have extreme difficulty in establishing and maintaining interpersonal relationships'' (McInnes and Treffry, 1982, p. 2).

LEARNED HELPLESSNESS

The problems listed above can be magnified when parents habitually respond to their multi-handicapped child with actions colored by grief, anger, or guilt. Parents who have not dealt openly with these feelings may respond to their child by withdrawing emotionally from the child or by trying to compensate for the handicaps by doing everything for the child. Either of these reactions may create a syndrome in the child that Seligman (1975) calls "learned helplessness."

Learned helplessness results when a person feels or expects that he has no control over the important events or outcomes in his/her life. This syndrome itself can become an additional handicap for a child. Think of a multi-handicapped child who, because of cerebral palsy, cannot lift his head to turn it in the opposite direction. What he sees and how comfortable he feels is entirely out of his control. His head is turned when someone else thinks it is time to do so. Children with impaired vision in addition to impaired hearing may be restricted by their caregivers to a confined play area for their own safety. They may have limited control over choice of activities or range of mobility. All they know is what is brought to them by others. Learned helplessness results from the child's experience that things happen to and for him, independent of his own actions or responses.

Seligman (1975) suggests three broad effects of learned helplessness:

1. It reduces people's motivation to control outcomes. They stop trying (or never learn) to control events in their lives. They become passive recipients of whatever happens to them.
2. Learned helplessness, once acquired, interferes with a person's ability to learn that he can control outcomes related to himself. Responses easily learned by non-helpless individuals are very

slowly learned or not learned at all by the helpless.
3. Long experience with being helpless (or perceiving oneself as helpless) produces depression. The person's affect is flattened and the symptoms of neurotic depression occur.

Teachers and members of the medical profession may unwittingly model behaviors and attitudes that promote the child's acquisition of feelings of helplessness. The professional who regards the multi-handicapped child with pity, revealed through expressions such as, "You poor little thing," may encourage parents to take care of everything for the child, to be overly protective of the child, and to maintain low expectations for the child's achievement. Pity is not fertile soil in which growth can take place and is of no use in the habilitation process. A more helpful attitude is one of confidence that, with appropriate help, the child has potential for determining and controlling many aspects of his life. Schlesinger (1985) discusses the related concept of powerlessness, a state which evolves out of an individual's inability to influence and shape his own environment. The individual's capacity and motivation to learn are negatively influenced by feeling powerless.

Parent-infant specialists are in an excellent position to assist parents in determining areas of their infant's life over which the infant can assert control and power. The more handicaps the child has, the more resourceful the specialist and parents will need to be in determining how they can allow the child's actions to produce a desirable outcome. The concept of the child's contingency awareness is extremely useful to specialists and parents in their approach to the child with multiple handicaps. Watson (1966) hypothesized that, from birth, infants are able to detect and understand the contingent (or cause-effect) relationships between their behaviors and resulting outcomes. Studies (e.g., Watson and Ramey, 1972) have demonstrated that infants increase behaviors that produce desirable outcomes and that the motivator for the infants was their *control* over the production of the outcome. Much of what happens in healthy parent-infant interactions reinforces the infant's feeling that his actions can affect the environment. He cries, an adult appears; he smiles, an adult smiles and talks in return. These contingency experiences create a feeling of power and effectiveness in the child that motivates him to try other behaviors in other situations. Habilitation activities that promote the infant's contingency awareness are essential to the multi-handicapped child's future learning.

INSUFFICIENT PARENT-CHILD ATTACHMENT

In addition to the difficulties created by multi-sensory deprivation and by learned helplessness, the infant with one or more handicapping conditions faces a third potential area of difficulty, that of the bonding or attachment which takes place between an infant and his primary caregiver, usually his mother. The attachment between mother and infant is regarded as a mutually reciprocal relationship in which the actions of one affects the reactions of the other. "The mother-infant relationship has come increasingly to be viewed as a system in which both partners are engaged in a continuing process of mutual modification" (Thoman and Trotter, 1978, p. xviii). The mother-infant attachment is one that begins to form immediately after birth (Klaus and Kennell, 1976) and continues to grow during the first months of life as each mother-infant pair develops its own particular style of interaction filled with rhythms and routines unique to the pair (Thoman and Trotter, 1978).

Both infant and mother come with individual traits which will affect the attachment process. The infant brings to the bonding process his temperament, his capabilities and methods of signaling his wants and needs, and his ability to make eye contact with and posture his body toward his parents. Since all babies differ in these aspects, even parents of "normal" infants must learn to read and interpret their baby's signals, to adjust to their baby's temperament — whether it is basically "demanding," "happy," "irritable" or "placid" — and to communicate through mutual gazing and smiling with their infant. It is obvious that any one or combination of handicapping conditions will affect the infant's temperament, signals, visual regard, body posturing, and responsiveness to his caregivers.

Some handicapped babies are constantly irritable and cannot be soothed. Others, because of limited control of body movement, cannot mold their body to their parents' bodies in ways that feel comfortable, with the result that parents may feel that the child does not like being held or like being held by them. Other infants may have difficulty maintaining eye contact because of poor head control or may not seek out eye contact at all because of limited vision. Some handicapped infants do not smile because of limited muscular control or because they are not reinforced by being able to see others smiling at them.

The mother brings to the attachment process her expectations, perceptions, and interpretations of the infant's behaviors. Mothers feel close to their babies when they can soothe their cries by feeding, holding, or rocking the infant. They become attached to the infant because he cuddles against them, looks intently at them, smiles at them. When, as a result of their handicapping conditions, infants fail to produce the expected signals that promote attachment or bonding, parents may withdraw without being aware of doing so, thus intensifying the infant's deprivation and resultant problems. It is easy to see how this cycle might develop, especially when the infant has handicaps that are undiagnosed. Unable to understand their infant's failure to respond to them, parents may assume that the baby doesn't like them, is resisting them, has no interest in them or that they, as parents are doing something wrong. If the baby's behaviors do not reinforce the parents' expressions of warmth and caring, parents are likely to diminish these positive actions with the unfortunate result that bonding and attachment are not fully realized.

One of the most visible aspects of parent-infant attachment is early presymbolic communication that occurs between the pair. The parent-infant specialist is in an excellent position to observe this communication and to evaluate how the child's handicapping conditions are affecting the attachment process. The infant's early presymbolic communication behaviors such as gazing, body posture, and smiling, promote attachment. When these behaviors are absent or skewed the parents experience disappointment and anxiety. These feelings, in turn, affect how they communicate with the child: the number of their communications directed to the child may diminish, their tone of voice may reflect their sadness and discouragement.

The specialist can encourage parents of children with handicapping conditions in addition to hearing loss to begin rebuilding communication with their infant. Utilizing the information on Presymbolic Communication in Chapter 20 of this book and in the infant and parent "Presymbolic Communication" sections of *Parent-Infant Communication*, the specialist can help parents acquire behaviors that will draw their infant into reciprocal communication, thus strengthening the parent-infant bond. When the specialist provides parents with information about their child's handicapping conditions, parents can see that certain of their child's behaviors which they have been interpreting as signs of rejection are instead a result of the child's handicapping conditions. Parents can then learn effective ways to work around the behaviors so that parent-infant attachment is fostered.

PARENTS' REACTIONS TO THE IDENTIFICATION OF ADDITIONAL HANDICAPPING CONDITIONS IN THEIR CHILD

The discovery of a first handicapping condition in their child is devastating for most parents. When, at a later time, a second, or third, handicapping condition is identified, most parents once again experience strong feelings of hopelessness, helplessness, and fear — fear that there are yet more disabilities that will appear one by one. Some parents are filled with a tremendous sadness and with feelings of alienation from their child whose handicaps will cause him to experience the world differently than they do. Parents who are feeling powerless and fearful are likely to be angry. Sometimes the anger is suppressed, resulting in depression which includes feelings of increased hopelessness and powerlessness. Sometimes the parent's anger may be directed at the child even though the parent knows this is "wrong" or not fair. So, in addition to feeling angry, they also feel guilty about their anger.

At the very time that parents may be feeling very low, they are being asked to carry out a series of tasks on behalf of their child: make appointments, go to various diagnostic facilities, participate in therapy assignments, carry on with life. They are inundated with new terminology and technical descriptions which leave them confused and frustrated. They are very likely to feel besieged by the seemingly endless training needs of their child.

Specialists working with parents of young multi-handicapped children will be most effective when they openly acknowledge the severe stress under which the parents may be operating. The specialist can acknowledge the parents' stress both by recognizing it in words and by minimizing the requirements and requests placed on the family at the beginning of habilitation. Many parents feel guilty about their anger, depression, and rejection of their child and find it difficult to initiate conversations in which these feelings are mentioned. The specialist can facilitate discussion by saying, in a matter-of-fact way, that these are feelings that many parents experience and that they are normal and acceptable feelings. Learning that they are not perceived as "unnatural" parents by the specialist because of their feelings brings relief to many parents.

Parents of newly identified multi-handicapped children may feel vulnerable, fearful, guilty, hopeless, and angry all at the same time. The specialist who attends to these feelings as part of the habilitation process is providing an extremely important service to parents.

DETECTING THE PRESENCE OF A HANDICAPPING CONDITION IN ADDITION TO HEARING LOSS

ETIOLOGY AND INCIDENCE OF OTHER HANDICAPPING CONDITIONS

Schildroth (1986) stated that, "Approximately 20% of the students under age 6 in the Annual Survey (of Hearing-Impaired Children and Youth, Gallaudet College) for 1984 were reported as multiply handicapped" (p. 89-90). This statistic tells the parent-infant specialist that one of every five children in her caseload is likely to have a handicapping condition in addition to hearing loss. At Infant Hearing Resource close to 30% of the hearing-impaired children we enroll have additional disabilities.

Vernon (1982) discussed the five known leading causes of deafness in children in the 1960's — rubella, prematurity, meningitis, genetics, and Rh factor — and the incidence of other handicapping conditions in addition to hearing loss associated with each of these etiologies. Awareness of this information enables the parent-infant specialist to be alert for other handicapping conditions when working with a young child whose hearing loss is a result of one of these etiologies.

Vernon (1982) points out that children whose hearing loss is hereditary seem to be relatively free of other disabilities, except for the one-third of genetic deafnesses associated with syndromes which include other handicaps, such as Treacher-Collins Syndrome and Usher's Syndrome. The prevalence of other anomalies associated with each of the four remaining etiologies is summarized below (Vernon, 1982):

1. Rubella: visual defects — 29.8% of sample study
                       aphasoid disorders* — 21.9%
                       mental retardation (IQ below 70) — 8.1%
                       orthopedic defects — 4.8%
                       cerebral palsy and/or hemiplegia — 3.8%
                       seizures — 0%

    * Aphasoid disorders are defined by Vernon (1982) as "a marked difficulty with language greater than that expected due to deafness or level of intelligence" (p. 20).

2. Prematurity: aphasoid disorders — 36.2%
                       visual defects — 28.3%
                       cerebral palsy and/or hemiplegia — 17.6%
                       mental retardation (IQ below 70) — 16.5%
                       orthopedic defects — 8.9%
                       seizures — 1.7%

3. Meningitis: aphasoid disorders — 16.3%
                       mental retardation (IQ below 70) — 14.1%
                       cerebral palsy and/or hemiplegia — 9.7%
                       visual defects — 5.7%
                       orthopedic defects — 5.4%
                       seizures — 3.2%

4. Rh Factor: cerebral palsy and/or hemiplegia — 51.1%
                       visual defects — 24.4%
                       aphasoid disorders — 22.8%
                       seizures — 6.6%
                       mental retardation (IQ below 70) — 5.1%
                       orthopedic defects — 2.2%

Schildroth (1986) reports data on etiology gleaned from two Annual Surveys of Hearing Impaired Children and Youth (Gallaudet College). He compares the etiologies of deafness in the children ages 0-5 who were reported in 1977 and in 1984. He found that maternal rubella, as a cause of hearing loss in children, is declining. While heredity and meningitis continue to be the most frequently reported causes of hearing loss in young children, the etiologies of prematurity and unspecified "other" have both increased. Schildroth (1986) notes that cytomegalovirus was written in as an etiology on a number of the 1984 survey forms.

At Infant Hearing Resource we enrolled six children in the five years between 1980-85 whose hearing loss was caused by congenital cytomegalovirus infection (CMV). Eichorn (1982) reports that 27,000 infants are born each year in the United States with clinically inapparent CMV, 4,000 of whom will have impaired hearing. The same neurological damage caused by CMV that results in deafness can also result in mental retardation, delayed motor development, and learning disabilities in children.

The multi-handicapped children examined by Vernon (1982) were school-aged. It is interesting to note the relatively low percentage of other disorders, especially aphasoid disorders, associated with the etiology of meningitis in school-aged children. Having worked with many children who were deafened by meningitis sometime during their first two years of life, IHR specialists have seen a very high incidence of learning difficulties in these children during the year or two following the illness. While a few of these children, upon recovery and with the placement of aids, proceded right along with their language acquisition and cognitive and motor development, the majority of meningitis deafened children lost ground in almost all developmental areas and had difficulty regaining the skills. It seemed that the disease had caused some kind of cortical disorganization so that skills acquired right before the onset of the illness were lost and previously used avenues for learning new skills were no longer available to the child. Many of these children appeared initially confused and angry and, with time, depressed. Other educators (Pappas and Houston, 1984) have noted similar sequelae to meningitis in children who contracted the disease during their first years of life.

In the case of some IHR graduates with meningitis etiology, specific learning disabilities for academic material have appeared when the children reached school age or difficulties with behavioral control have remained an issue through the child's first years in school.

USE OF DEVELOPMENTAL SCALES TO DETECT SIGNS
OF OTHER HANDICAPPING CONDITIONS

Specialists trained to work with hearing-impaired infants can anticipate some of the child's hearing-related behaviors about which the parents may express concern: "He ignores me"; "He isn't vocalizing/talking"; "He doesn't turn when I call his name"; "He doesn't mind me." It is also helpful for specialists to be aware of characteristics associated with other handicapping conditions, for two reasons: 1) so that they can convey to parents that behaviors they might be observing in their child are related to an already diagnosed handicap, and 2) so that they might recognize signs of an undiagnosed problem.

Fortunately, the specialist does not need to memorize a long list of characteristics that may signal visual problems, motor development problems, overall developmental delay (including delays in development of cognitive, social-emotional, and self-help skills), learning disabilities, or emotional disturbance. There are many excellent scales which, when administered to the child even informally, will alert specialists and parents to the need for further evaluation. It is also true that the more experience an observant specialist has had with young children, the more likely she is to detect that child whose developmental patterns are deviating from the norm in ways that are hindering his development.

The range of "normal" development varies among young children, but developmental scales can be invaluable in helping specialists and parents assess the child's levels of development in all areas in order to design an educational program that meets all his needs. One of the scales that our staff has found extremely useful is *Developmental Programming for Infants and Young Children* (Schaefer, Moersch and D'Eugenio, 1985-86). This program consists of five volumes: Volume 1 — "Assessment and Application"; Volume 2 — "The Early Intervention Developmental Profile" (EIDP), a compilation of major developmental milestones in six areas from ages 0-36 months; Volume 3 — "Stimulation Activities"; Volume 4 — "Preschool Assessment and Application"; and Volume 5 — "Preschool Developmental Profile." The EIDP, the developmental profile contained in Volume 2, is easily administered and indicates specific areas of development in which the child under the age of three may be lagging behind and need extra stimulation or further evaluation. A second tool that is very useful in assessing and programming for multi-handicapped children is *Assessment in Infancy: Ordinal Scales of Psychological Development* (Uzgiris and Hunt, 1975).

Other tools our staff uses all or parts of for assessment with multi-handicapped children are:

1. *The Oregon Project for Visually Impaired and Blind Preschool Children* (Brown, Simmons, and Methvin, 1979).
2. *Generic Skills Assessment Inventory* (McLean, Snyder-McLean, Rowland, Jacobs, and Stremel-Campbell, 1981).
3. "Sensorimotor Cognitive Assessment and Curriculum for the Multihandicapped Child" and "The Profoundly Handicapped Child: Assessing Sensorimotor and Communication Abilities" (Fieber, 1977, 1978)
4. *Callier-Azuza Scale*, Scale G (Stillman, 1978).
5. *Brigance Inventory of Early Development* (Brigance, 1978).

Some of the scales listed in Chapter Three are also used with multi-handicapped children if the scale can be adapted to provide specific information related to one or more areas of the child's function.

ALERT LISTS: CHILD BEHAVIORS THAT MAY SIGNAL THE PRESENCE OF HANDICAPPING CONDITIONS OTHER THAN HEARING LOSS

Using the scales mentioned above, the following "Alert Lists" have been compiled to give the parent-infant specialist an idea of the types of behaviors, or absence of behaviors, that may, during the child's first year of life, signal a handicapping condition in addition to hearing loss.

ALERT: POSSIBLE VISION PROBLEMS

0-8 weeks
- Does not focus on faces or objects within 10-13 inches by 8 weeks of age.

2 months
- Eyes do not fixate, converge, focus.

3 months
- Does not track moving objects.

4 months
- Does not reach for objects.
- Does not smile at moving faces or recognize familiar faces.

6 months
- Does not recognize familiar faces up to 6 yards away.
- Is not aware of things happening across the room.
- Does not shift visual attention from one object in a field of two or more objects.

7-8 months
- Does not close eyes on approach of object to face.
- Does not visually explore objects held in hands.

General
- Holds head to one side or back, or holds objects in a particular position relative to eyes in order to examine them.
- Eyes have jerky movement (nystagmus).

ALERT: POSSIBLE MOTOR PROBLEMS

0-2 months
- Does not lift head momentarily or turn head from side to side.

3-4 months
- Does not have any control of head.
- Does not open mouth in anticipation of feeding.

5-6 months
- Does not support self on arms when lying on stomach.
- Does not sit with support.
- Does not roll from stomach (prone) to back (supine) over both sides.
- Does not have efficient suck/swallow pattern.

7-8 months
- Does not roll from back (supine) to stomach (prone).
- Does not sit without support.
- Does not go from stomach to sitting to hands and knees.

Other warning signs during the child's first year (Denhoff, 1967)
- Tremulous or jittery movements.
- Jerky movements, sudden twitches.
- Asymmetrical movements — one arm/leg used much more than the other.
- Is very stiff, difficult to pick up, resistant to being held, slides or pushes out of infant seat.
- Is unable to use arms for play when lying on back.
- Curls toes and stiffens hips and knees when placed in a weight bearing position or held in standing.

ALERT: POSSIBLE DEVELOPMENTAL DELAY

General
- Follows normal developmental sequences but at a noticeably slower rate.

3 months
- Does not attempt to keep a toy (e.g., mobile) in motion by repeated hand or leg movements.

4 months
- Does not grasp for toy held in view.

5 months
- Does not search for partially hidden object.
- Does not transfer toy from hand to hand.
- Does not reach to familiar people (fails to discriminate strangers).

8 months
- Does not look for dropped object.
- Does not hold bottle to drink.
- Does not imitate sounds or hand movements already in his repertoire.
- Does not laugh at peek-a-boo games.

12 months	• Does not pull string to obtain object attached to it.
	• Does not show discomfort when separated from mother in strange environment.
	• Does not hold, bite, and chew cookie.
	• Does not cease drooling.

ALERT: POSSIBLE NEUROLOGICAL PROBLEMS CAUSING LEARNING DISABILITIES (Kass, 1982)

0-18 months	• Looks at anything and everything without really discriminating; frequently drops eyes; does not study objects or people visually.
	• Does not maintain equilibrium — does not arch up head and legs when held under stomach.
	• Is commonly irritable, distractible, and restless.

18 months	• Is hyperexcitable, cannot pay attention.
	• Echoes words/imitates signs indiscriminately long past time expected.
	• Is easily frustrated, gives up task if cannot do immediately, does not demonstrate any problem-solving skills.

ALERT: POSSIBLE EMOTIONAL DISTURBANCE

General	• Does not make eye contact.
	• Has extremely flat affect — no response to voices or smiles of significant adults, dreary cry, cannot be comforted.
	• Pulls away from contact with others.

While not intended as all-encompassing lists, the above "Alerts" demonstrate clearly that babies who are developing normally exhibit all kinds of signs of normal sensory function. Absence of these signs is cause for further evaluation.

USE OF THE DIAGNOSTIC TEACHING APPROACH

Use of the diagnostic teaching approach as described in Chapter 16 is a very effective way for the specialist and parents to focus on defining the child's abilities. By following the first four steps of the diagnostic teaching process — input, processing, output, and analysis of output — the parents and specialist can observe and record the child's actual behaviors and responses in a variety of situations. They can then compare these behaviors with their own expectations of what the child might do and with standardized norms of child behavior. Specialists who routinely use the diagnostic teaching approach with children will become practiced at noting both subtle and more extreme deviations from "normal" behavior. Because she documents and records her observations of the child's behaviors over time, the specialist is well-prepared to describe specific behaviors when she refers the child for further evaluation.

PROCEDURES THE PARENT-INFANT SPECIALIST CAN FOLLOW IF SHE SUSPECTS THAT A CHILD HAS A HANDICAP IN ADDITION TO HEARING LOSS

If a parent-infant specialist needs to refer a child for evaluation, the procedures that she follows will differ depending on the situation in which she works. If she works in an agency which has an assessment center, a referral to that center is indicated. If her agency utilizes one of the full service cooperative approaches such as the "transdisciplinary approach" (Connor, Williamson, Siepp, 1978), then multi-faceted assessment may be a routine part of every child's program. Many agencies serving hearing-impaired children do not have personnel on staff who can provide formal assessment of motor, vision, neurological, or social-emotional development. These agencies frequently refer children to outside assessment centers, selecting one that can assess the developmental area of concern. In many rural or remote regions, assessment may need to be scheduled well in advance and families may need to travel some distance to participate in evaluation.

Wherever assessment is done there are four steps the specialist can carry out to make certain that the evaluation will actually address the concerns she and the parents have, to assure that the parents' and child's experience with the evaluation is as positive as possible, and to assure that the specialist receives the results of the evaluation. The steps the specialist can follow are: 1) write a letter of referral; 2) acquire information about the schedule and procedures that will be followed during the evaluation process; 3) attend the evaluation, if appropriate; and 4) ask the parents to authorize release of evaluation results to her or her agency.

1. **Write a Letter of Referral:** The letter of referral will include information from two areas in addition to the basic child-identification information that the specialist provides. These areas are described below.

  a. *State Reason(s) for Referral and What You Want from the Evaluation.*

    Be clear about the reason for the referral and about what information, services, or both, the specialist and parents want to result from the referral. If, for example, the child is being referred for evaluation of motor function and development, the specialist might write, "I am referring John Jones for evaluation of his motor function and development," and then specify which of the following is needed:

• A diagnosis only; any necessary therapy services will be provided at the referring agency; or

• A diagnosis *and* an outline of a recommended course of therapeutic treatment for a therapist at the referring agency to follow; or

• A diagnosis *and* a recommendation for an agency that can provide therapy; or

• A diagnosis and, because the family lives in an area where no physical therapy services are available, specific information about what the specialist and parents can do to address the child's problems as diagnosed. In this case, the specialist will want to establish whether regular consultation could be obtained from the evaluation agency, either by telephone or by visits to the agency at whatever time intervals are possible for the family to arrange.

If the parents have asked the specialist to serve as case manager to coordinate the child's therapeutic needs, she will want to state that she expects to be involved in planning therapy needs that become apparent as a result of the evaluation. If the evaluation agency to which the specialist is referring the family is unfamiliar with the habilitation services the child is receiving related to his hearing loss, a brief description of the specialist's involvement with the family will be helpful.

If the child who is being referred for evaluation communicates in a symbolic language mode other than speech (e.g., signed language), the specialist will need to inform the evaluation staff of this fact. If the evaluation staff cannot communicate effectively in the child's mode, arrangements should be made to have a qualified interpreter present.

b.   *Be Specific in Describing the Child's Behaviors About Which The Specialist and Parents are Concerned.*

In the letter of referral, provide the evaluator with a list of the child's behaviors, or lack of behaviors, which have provoked the concerns. This list should consist of observations that the specialist and parents have made regarding the child. Be as specific as possible. For instance, rather than writing, "We are wondering if his vision is normal," the specialist will describe why she is concerned: "Jimmy, at age six months, does not yet appear to differentiate his mother from other people; he does not reach for objects placed in front of him unless they are large and bright; he likes to look at lights." The specialist will also want to provide the evaluator with a brief description of the child's already diagnosed handicapping condition(s) and his general level of function.

2. Determine the Schedule and Procedures That Will Be Followed During the Evaluation Process: If it is possible for the specialist to talk to a professional who will be participating in the evaluation of the child, she can learn what kinds of tests or procedures will be used during the evaluation and what information the evaluator(s) will be able to give the parents at the end of the evaluation. The specialist can also determine whether the professional(s) who will be conducting the evaluation have had any experience in evaluating hearing-impaired children. An evaluator who is unfamiliar with deafness may not realize that this handicap may make it difficult or impossible to administer some tests, expecially those that are language-loaded, to some hearing-impaired children.

Parents should know how many professionals will be evaluating the child and how they will coordinate their recommendations. Parents should also know when and how they will be informed of the findings of the evaluation: Will they learn the results through discussion with an evaluator immediately following the evaluation? Will a staffing take place after the family has left the assessment center so that results/recommendations are not available until later? Will the evaluation findings be provided to parents (and to the professionals they designate) in a written report? Some evaluation agencies will not release any results directly to parents and instead send results to the child's physician who then becomes responsible for interpreting them to parents (a practice IHR does not condone).

Parents' feelings about the value of the evaluation are strongly affected by how their expectations for the evaluation are met. The more information parents have about evaluation procedures prior to the assessment, the more likely it is that they will formulate realistic expectations that will lead to feelings of satisfaction rather than of disappointment.

3. Attend the Evaluation and Subsequent Discussion of Evaluation Results If Appropriate: The specialist may want to accompany the family to the evaluation as she can both provide and gain information that is related to habilitation with the family. Some parents may feel that the specialist is better able to articulate mutual concerns and to ask pertinent questions. Other parents may want the specialist along as moral support.

From the specialist's discussion with the evaluator prior to the actual assessment, the specialist and parents will have learned when and how the evaluation results will be transmitted to the parents. If the results will be reported to the parents at the conclusion of the assessment, the parents and specialist may want to brainstorm a list of questions they might have if an additional handicapping condition is diagnosed in the child. Several factors — the parents' feelings about the diagnosis, the style of the evaluation team, unfamiliar terms used in reporting results — may make it difficult for the parents to learn everything they want to know at the time results are reported to them. The specialist can make sure that the parents get the name and phone number of one of the evaluators so that they can call with questions at a later time.

4. Ask the Parents to Authorize Release of Evaluation Results to the Habilitation Agency: The specialist should ask the parents to be certain to sign a release of information form at the evaluation site that will authorize the site to send a copy of the results and recommendations to the specialist as well as to other pertinent people, such as the child's physician.

The referral for evaluation may be the first step in establishing a working relationship with another agency or therapist in order to meet the needs of the multi-handicapped child. By taking time to provide information and expectations to the evaluator prior to the evaluation, the parent-infant specialist can ascertain that the evaluation is most likely to produce the information and recommendations that she, the parents, and other professionals need in order to implement an effective program for the child.

A FRAMEWORK FOR GUIDING THE PARENT-INFANT SPECIALIST IN ACQUIRING INFORMATION

Part of the frustration involved when attempting to learn new information in any area is not knowing enough to know what questions to ask to obtain the information one needs! When the parent-infant specialist is faced with the need to learn about a handicapping condition that has been diagnosed in a child with whom she is working, she will find it easier to approach the problem of gaining knowledge if she knows what to ask. This section will provide the specialist with a series of questions she can direct to other professionals, to the parents, and to herself and her colleagues. The answers to these questions will give her a foundation for beginning to deal with the unfamiliar handicapping condition. Sometimes gaining the information the specialist needs is as easy as asking a question, if the specialist knows what question to ask and of whom to ask it. The following section contains questions listed under four major areas:

1. Acquiring information about other handicaps.
2. Acquiring information about the child.
3. Acquiring information about the family.
4. Acquiring information for yourself.

These questions are designed to help the specialist get the information she needs to design a habilitation program that will make maximum use of her skills in helping the multi-handicapped child and his family.

ACQUIRING INFORMATION ABOUT OTHER HANDICAPS

There are six questions the parent-infant specialist can ask in order to gain information about other handicapping conditions. These questions are discussed below.

1. What is the degree of the handicap and how does it affect the child's function? This question should be asked of the individual who diagnosed the handicap. The specialist needs to acquire at least the following information for the child who is:

Visually Impaired
Can he see light?
Can he see large, bright objects?
How close do objects need to be for him to see them?

Motor Impaired
Does he have voluntary control of his head? neck? eyes? lips and
    tongue? limbs?
Is he more disabled in certain states, e.g., when excited?
Is he more disabled in certain positions?

Developmentally Delayed
Are all areas of development equally delayed?
Is the child "delayed," implying that he will eventually catch up or
    "retarded," meaning that development will proceed at a slower
    pace with limited achievement in all areas to be expected?

Neurologically Impaired
Is the child unable to differentiate pleasant from unpleasant stimuli
    so that all stimuli are experienced as irritation, resulting in a con-
    stantly crying or fussy baby?
Is the child unable to inhibit certain behaviors?
Is the child unable to recognize or remember, to attach meaning to
    events?
Is the child unable to maintain attention without being distracted?

In talking to the individual who diagnosed the child's handicapping condition, the specialist should attempt to get as much information as she can about conditions under which the child's function will be better or worse. The specialist should be prepared to ask medical professionals (by telephone, usually) for an explanation of unfamiliar medical terminology used in their reports.

2. What type of sensory input or information does this handicap affect? The specialist knows the effect that hearing impairment has on the child's ability to gain information from his environment. When another sensory avenue is impaired, the specialist needs to consider what kind of other information will now be limited or inaccessible to the child.

Visually Impaired: The child's second distance sense is affected. He may have difficulty determining his position in space, his relationship to other people and objects, his "separateness" from other people and objects.

Motor Impaired: The child may be limited in the amount of tactile information he can receive. He may have difficulty moving himself into positions so that he can see or reach. He may not be able to smile in response to familiar faces. He may not be able to "cuddle" against his parents' bodies.

Developmentally Delayed or Neurologically Impaired: The child may not be able to organize or make use of the sensory information he receives through intact systems. He may experience normally pleasurable stimuli as an irritant. He may not perceive his environment as ordered, sensible, or safe.

3. How will the effects of this handicap combine with the effects of the child's hearing loss? In working toward an answer to this question, the specialist and parents can make use of the information they have gained from medical professionals about the degree of the child's second handicapping condition and about his residual capabilities. They will also want to talk with professionals who are experts in the field of the child's other handicapping condition, and read all of the literature to which they have access. The combination of handicapping conditions is likely to have an effect on the child's ability to communicate and on other areas of the child's development. These issues are addressed in the next two questions.

4. How will this combination of handicaps affect the child's ability to convey information about his wants and needs to the significant others in his life? Specialists and parents will need to look closely at each multi-handicapped child to determine what systems the child can make use of to receive and generate communication.

Visually Impaired: Since both the child's distance senses are impaired, he may not have access to information that is not directly impinging upon him. He may not be able to see or hear that people communicate to him and to others. Parents and specialists will need to determine whether either the child's auditory system or his visual system is available as a mode through which he can acquire communication skills. If neither of these systems is intact enough to serve him, they will need to learn tactile modes of communicating with him while he is in infancy. As the child grows, other communication systems used with persons who are both hearing and vision impaired will become appropriate (see "Choosing an Appropriate Communication System for the Child with More Than One Handicapping Condition" p. 494).

Motor Impaired: A child who does not have control over the movements of his body parts or over his mobility may have difficulty getting what he wants or needs. He may not be able to extend an arm in the direction of a toy he desires or roll to re-gain a bottle that got away from him. Parents and specialists will need to look for other clues that the child gives — an eye shift, a head turn, an extended leg — with a part of his body over which he does have control to understand what he wants. The adults may need to seek out or develop simple gestural systems that incorporate hand, limb, and body shapes or movements that the child can use intentionally to convey his needs.

Developmentally Delayed or Neurologically Impaired: Some infants with these handicapping conditions may appear to have no interest in communicating. The challenge for specialists and parents is to engage the child, to entice him into social interactions that will promote his interest in the give and take of non-verbal communication. It may be necessary to start with capturing the child's visual attention for more than a fleeting second. The concept of "resonance phenomenon" (Van Dijk, described in Curtis, Dunning, Meese, Westover, Yost, and Perotti, 1978) may be a useful technique for getting interaction started with these children.

5. How will this combination of handicaps affect the child's development in areas that are not directly impaired? Specialists are aware of the effects that impaired hearing has on the child's early interactions with his parents, on his development of language skills and the resultant effects on cognitive development, and social and play skills. A second handicapping condition is likely to compound these effects. Parents and specialists will need to study, among other things, the concepts of learned helplessness (Seligman, 1975), mother-child attachment (Klaus and Kennell, 1976), and contingency intervention (Schweigert, 1986) in order to understand the effects these double handicaps can have on the child and to learn ways to minimize these effects. When any handicapping condition is added to that of deafness, the specialist and parents will need to become aware of potential effects on the child's cognitive development, awareness of self, relationships to people, and communication. Parents and specialists who are aware of the roles that the child's sensory systems play in his development in each of these areas will be highly motivated to help the child acquire the information he needs through whatever sensory avenues are available to him. Resources such as those listed in Suggested Reading, Chapter 26, are essential tools to the adults in the life of a multi-handicapped child.

6. Will changes occur in the handicapping condition(s) and, if so, how does the specialist figure those in? Specialists and parents will need to get guidance in dealing with questions related to potential changes in the child's status. For instance, a child with atresias and occluded ear canals but normal middle ear systems may be able to have surgery to correct this condition when he is older. The specialist and parents need to know that use of a bone-conduction hearing aid in combination with speech and language habilitation will enable the child to acquire communication skills prior to the surgery. When the child has a condition which may be degenerative, e.g., vision in the case of the child with Usher's Syndrome, the parents and specialist will want to teach the profoundly deaf child using signed language since this system will still be available to the child through the tactile-kinesthetic mode as his vision diminishes. The specialist must also be prepared to help parents deal with their feelings when the child loses skills he once had as a result of his handicap becoming more severe or when additional handicapping conditions become apparent.

ACQUIRING INFORMATION ABOUT THE CHILD

Once the specialist has a beginning understanding of the additional disability and its effects on the child, there are four questions she can ask others — and herself — to gain information about the child.

1. **What are this child's special needs and how can they be met?** All children have needs for food, shelter, companionship/communication, and love. Children with handicapping conditions almost always have additional needs. Seriously handicapped children may have medical needs that require intensive and long-range care. Parents may need help in seeing how they can integrate and adapt habilitation strategies into the life-sustaining medical activities they must perform for their child. The specialist and parents may want to list all the child's needs and plan activities that meet several needs at one time. A child with a tracheotomy may require frequent suctioning to keep his breathing tube clear; a child with cerebral palsy may require that his body and limbs be regularly moved in certain ways to facilitate muscle development. Parents can learn to incorporate presymbolic/symbolic language usage into these necessary interactions with their child so that parent-child attachment and communication development are also promoted.

2. **What is the child's perception of the world?** Parents and specialists can gain new understanding of what the world is like for the multi-handicapped child by setting up situations in which they can attempt to simulate the effects of the child's handicaps. What does it feel like to be unable to hear or to see or to control the movement of your limbs? Adults who experience, even in a short-term simulation, what the child experiences all the time may have a greater understanding of the child's behaviors and more appreciation for the need to adapt the child's environment so that it feels more predictable, controllable, and safe to him.

3. **What is the child like to be around?** Every child has a distinct personality, regardless of handicapping conditions. Babies come with all types of traits: friendly, cranky, humorous, bland, irritable, active, passive, affectionate. Some are people-oriented, others are loners. Handicapping conditions may exaggerate or flatten out the child's personality traits, but these traits still exist. Parents and specialists need to watch the child so they can learn what motivates him to interact with people and objects, to smile, vocalize, and reach out. They need to know what annoys or irritates the child, makes him withdraw, makes him cry. If the child seems to be passive, withdrawn, or depressed much of the time, the parents and specialist can brainstorm ways to make changes so that the child is enticed into becoming more active and can learn that he has more control over and effect on his environment.

4. **Where is this child functioning in each area of development?** Specialists and parents can administer screening tools that sample the child's development in several areas. This information can be factored into all the other data they have on the child so that developmentally appropriate activities can be planned for the child.

ACQUIRING INFORMATION ABOUT THE FAMILY

The specialist can ask four questions that will help her acquire information about family members.

1. **How are the parents doing?** Every parent needs a support system, and for parents of children with handicaps, spouses, friends, and relatives who provide support are essential. Specialists can encourage parents to call on their relatives and friends for help, even when it is just a listener they need. The parent-infant specialist needs to be particularly tuned in to parents whose non-verbal behaviors — missing appointments, lackluster participation in sessions, not following through on mutually agreed upon activities — indicate that parents are feeling overwhelmed. The specialist can also gain clues about the parents' feelings by watching the way they handle the child. Are they gentle and affectionate with the child or is frustration or impatience revealed by the way they hold, touch, or lead the child? Parents who are feeling good about their child talk with pride about his accomplishments; an absence of positive talk about the child may indicate that parents are experiencing some unresolved feelings related to the child.

2. **Have the parents been able to make the changes necessitated by having a multi-handicapped child?** Parents almost always have to make changes in their lives in order to meet the needs of their handicapped child. Professionals should do everything they can to consolidate services so that every

waking minute of the parents' day is not spent in traveling to and from appointments for their child. However, parents react differently to the demands placed on them by their child and the way in which they react will provide the specialist with valuable information about the parents' states of mind. Some parents seem pleased to get help for their child; others appear resentful of the extra time the child requires. Some parents have no difficulty in asking their supervisor or boss to adjust their work schedule so that they can attend habilitation sessions and appointments. Other parents resist making such a request, asking instead that the specialist come in early or stay late for sessions. At IHR we are willing to accommodate parents who make efforts to meet their child's needs. However, we also realize that the majority of the effort on behalf of the child must come from the parents if the child is to reach his potential. Our job is to help parents learn what they can do for their child and to motivate them to do it.

3. **How are the parents processing the information that they are getting from professionals in different disciplines?** Parents of children with more than one handicap are in an even more difficult position than parents of children with a single handicap when it comes to the amount of information and number of skills they must acquire in order to help their child. Specialists should be on the look-out for signals that parents are becoming overwhelmed: Are they forgetting what they are told? Are they having difficulty accurately relating information from other professionals? Are they resisting suggestions to incorporate therapy activities from one discipline into activities related to another handicapping condition, e.g., listening goals into physical therapy activities?

Specialists should take care that they do not unknowingly place parents in the position of having to choose between the suggestions or advice of two professionals. Asking parents, ''How does this fit in with what the vision specialist suggested you do?'' gives them the opportunity to describe potentially conflicting requests.

4. **What is happening with other children in the family?** The specialist who is working with the family can keep an eye out for the interests of the other children in the family as well as for those of the multi-handicapped child (See Chapter 15). Siblings can be a resource and support system for the multi-handicapped child and for the parents *if* their own needs are being met. If siblings feel shunted aside by the demands of their handicapped brother or sister, their resultant behaviors can create additional problems for the parents. Specialists, while acknowledging how difficult it is to find time for everything, can encourage parents to take time, even if only 15 minutes each day, for individual attention for each sibling. The payoff in terms of the child's attitudes and self-esteem can be remarkable. Specialists can also take care not to promote parental tendencies to require that older siblings become little ''mothers'' or ''fathers'' for the multi-handicapped

child or to always have to give up what they want on his behalf. Siblings should be included in instruction related to special communication techniques or handling procedures necessitated by the child's handicapping conditions.

ACQUIRING INFORMATION FOR YOURSELF

It is apparent that the parent-infant specialist who is working with the family of a child with handicapping conditions in addition to hearing loss has her work cut out for her! In fact, it is not uncommon for the specialist to feel overwhelmed right along with the parents. Usually, the specialist is working with a number of families and she does not have much spare time in which to acquire new information and skills herself. Specialists who work in rural or remote areas may have limited access to resources, be they people or written materials. These specialists may find it very difficult to get the information they need to feel competent in working with a multi-handicapped child. It *is* a problem, but given some time, a telephone, and some money for the written materials that are available today, one that is surmountable.

The specialist may want to ask herself the following questions as she prepares to work with the multi-handicapped child and his family.

1. **Is this agency the most appropriate delivery setting for the child?**   This is obviously not an appropriate or useful question if yours is the only agency in town. In that case, the answer is a resounding, "Yes!" However, if the family lives in an urban area with a number of facilities available to them, it is important that the professionals who meet with families of multi-handicapped children be honest about where each particular child and family can best be served.

One way to consider the question is to ask if your staff is trained to deal with the child's most severely handicapping condition. If the child has severely impaired vision and a moderate hearing loss, the child obviously needs good auditory management, including appropriate hearing-aid selection. The parents will need training in the use and care of the child's hearing aids and guidance in teaching the child to attend to sounds. While it is critical that the child learn to make excellent use of his aided residual hearing, it is equally important that he learn to use his residual vision. This child may be better served in a program, if one is available, where teachers are trained to work with both handicapping conditions. Parents need to be aware of all the services available to them so that they can choose the one that best meets their needs. Specialists can not make that decision for families.

2. How can specialists get the information they need about the multi-handicapped child and his family? In addition to using their own observation skills, the specialist can use the following resources for information: the parents, other specialists, professionals who are knowledgable about other handicapping conditions, medical professionals, books (see Suggested Reading, Chapter 26), journals, workshops, classes, universities, and social service agencies.

3. How do specialists set goals for the multi-handicapped child? It may not be possible for the specialist who is just starting to work with a child with more than one handicapping condition to set goals such as, "By the end of the year, Tina will be operating at such and such a level." More important than trying to predict future achievement is assessing the child's present levels of function and establishing objectives to work on in each area of development. The tools the specialist requires are good assessment instruments (whether she administers them herself or they are administered by someone else) and curricula that specify sequential learning objectives for the child.

The specialist will also need to know what information and skills to teach parents and to have an organized method of keeping track of both child and parent achievements. For many of us, these needs require that we reach out for help. We can talk to other professionals, hit the books again, call agencies in other cities for information. The place to start is with the professionals who diagnosed the child's handicapping condition(s). Gaining the answers to the questions posed earlier will give the specialist some confidence that she is beginning to understand the child's needs. Bolstered with this information about the child, the material in books and curricula becomes more meaningful and useful. Which brings us to the final question:

4. How do you learn everything you need to know on top of everything else you have to do? It takes time. The longer a specialist works with a multi-handicapped child, the more she learns about his capabilities and how to help him build new skills on top of those he already has. One of the specialist's most effective skills may be her ability to put herself in the child's position and ask, "What would I want to be able to communicate if I were this child? What can this child already do and how could he use those skills to tell other people what he wants?" Be inventive and creative — this child needs our best efforts. Finally, we need to be as patient with ourselves as we are with the children; we allow them time to learn — it is the least we can do for ourselves!

CHAPTER 26

A DESCRIPTION OF SPECIFIC TECHNIQUES THAT IHR SPECIALISTS HAVE USED SUCCESSFULLY IN WORKING WITH YOUNG MULTI-HANDICAPPED CHILDREN AND THEIR FAMILIES

Audiological Testing and the Multi-Handicapped Child: Adapting the Test Environment and Procedures

- Two Test Variables That Apply To All Multi-Handicapped Children
- Test Variables as They Apply to the Hearing-Impaired Child with Visual Impairment
- Test Variables as They Apply to the Child with Motor Impairment
- Test Variables as They Apply to the Child with Developmental Delay or Neurological Impairment

Continued on following page

Hearing Aid Use and the Multi-Handicapped Child

- Hearing Aids: A Family Priority?
- Placement of Hearing Aids: Comfort and Feedback

Habilitation and the Multi-Handicapped Child

- General Considerations for Habilitation with Families of Young Multi-Handicapped Children
- Getting Communication Started with the Young Multi-Handicapped Child
- Suggestions for Working with the Hearing-Impaired Child with Impaired Vision
- Beginning Techniques for Working with the Hearing-Impaired Child with Motor Impairment
- Beginning Techniques for Working with the Hearing-Impaired Child with Developmental Delay or Neurological Impairment

Suggested Reading — Multi-Handicapped Children

Information and teaching techniques related to audiological testing, hearing aid use, and habilitation which have been used by specialists at IHR will be discussed in that order, though many of the techniques described in one area apply to the other areas. We freely acknowledge that there are many extremely useful techniques used with multi-handicapped infants which are not described herein. We have not attempted to report on techniques other than those with which we are familiar. Again, we refer the reader to books and journals for the information that is constantly forthcoming from other professionals who work with multi-handicapped children.

AUDIOLOGICAL TESTING AND THE MULTI-HANDICAPPED CHILD: ADAPTING THE TEST ENVIRONMENT AND PROCEDURES

When testing the hearing of a young hearing-impaired child with other handicapping conditions, it is necessary to analyze all aspects of the test environment and test procedures used in order to adapt test variables to fit the child's needs. The audiologist and parent-infant specialist need to consider the following six variables when preparing to test the multi-handicapped child: how the child will be situated in the test setting, ways in which the test environment and procedures may need to be modified, how the parent and specialist will participate, what types of responses the child is likely to give or can be trained to give, how the child will be reinforced for his responses, and how long testing will last.

TWO TEST VARIABLES THAT APPLY TO ALL
MULTI-HANDICAPPED CHILDREN

Parent and specialist roles in the test procedures and determining the duration of audiological tests are handled in the same way, regardless of the child's handicap(s).

1. **Parent and Specialist Participation:** As is true in all situations where parents are involved, it is imperative that they be told what their role during the test will be. Parents are anxious to see their child respond to the sounds presented during the testing process and may unwittingly give the child clues that something has occurred. The child may then respond to the parent's body movement or even to the parent's voice presented close to the child's ear, rather than to the test stimulus. Thus parents need clear directions about what they should and should not do during the test. Parents can help distract the child's attention between presentations of test stimuli, can help keep the child positioned correctly, and can provide reinforcement for the child's responses. Agreeing on the extent of the parent's participation prior to the beginning of the test prevents embarrassing "corrections" having to be made during the test.

The specialist should be equally clear about what her role will be during the testing. If the testing is being conducted by an audiologist with whom the specialist has already established mutual roles, discussion of roles at the time of testing will be brief. The parents should be informed as to the role the specialist will play so that they can see how their functions complement that of the specialist.

2. **Duration of Testing:** The duration of testing is most frequently determined by the child's failing attention, increasing fussiness, or outright refusal to sit any longer! Nothing is gained by forcing the young child to continue once he has tired. It is far better to anticipate that a series of short evaluation sessions will be necessary and schedule them accordingly. Since reliable test results are essential to the placement of appropriate amplification, the specialist and audiologist should not hesitate to schedule frequent test sessions (in place of habilitation sessions, if necessary) when the child has first been identified as hearing impaired in order to determine the child's auditory thresholds.

The remaining variables in the audiological test situation will be considered for hearing-impaired children with three different additional handicaps: impaired vision, motor impairment, and developmental delay or neurological impairment.

TEST VARIABLES AS THEY APPLY TO THE HEARING-IMPAIRED CHILD WITH VISUAL IMPAIRMENT

ORIENTING THE CHILD TO THE TEST ENVIRONMENT

One of the most important things to remember when interacting with a child with both auditory and visual deficits is that the child receives diminished information from these senses about where he is. Every time he is taken into a new or different environment, he must be given time, and possibly assistance, to explore that environment tactilely in order to learn to recognize it.

If the infant is still being carried, place his hands on objects in the environment that can become identifying landmarks for him. In the audiological suite, the landmarks may be the audiometer with its dials and buttons, the headsets hanging on the wall, or the sound field speakers. If, upon bringing the child into the audiological suite, his hands are placed on and allowed to explore these objects, he will learn to associate them with the place and the procedures which will follow. If the child is crawling or walking, it is essential to permit him time to explore the room as his way of gaining information about where he is, thus permitting him to anticipate what will be happening next. As the child is moved into the sound-treated booth and placed in position for the test, he should also be allowed to explore the high-chair or chair and table at which he will be seated. Before earphones are placed on his head they should be placed in front of him so he can handle them and explore their shape.

It is a good idea to have used earphones with the child prior to the test situation. One mother enrolled at IHR bought a set of small earphones which her son, who is hearing-impaired and visually-impaired, used at home to listen to music. When earphones were presented in the audiological suite, he readily accepted them because of his prior pleasant experience. Any toys that will be used in testing also should be made available to the child for exploration prior to the test, or he may ignore test stimuli to investigate the toy.

DETECTING THE CHILD'S RESPONSES TO SOUND

The young visually-impaired child's responses to sound may be difficult to observe, especially if even very loud stimuli are barely audible to the child. The child may still momentarily, may smile briefly, may shift his eyes, tilt his head slightly, or may vocalize in response to the sound. If the child is engaging in self-stimulation behaviors such as rocking or eye poking, the astute observer may detect a slight pause in the behavior when the child hears the auditory stimulus. The parent and specialist will want to reinforce any child behavior that occurs immediately following the sound stimulus with a previously identified successful reinforcer in order to encourage the child to repeat that behavior whenever the sound occurs.

REINFORCING THE CHILD'S RESPONSES TO SOUND

If visual reinforcement audiometry (VRA) is being used, the light source may need to be intensified, either by using a brighter light or by moving the reinforcer closer to the child, or both. If the child sees better from one eye or in one quadrant, the light should be placed where it is most easily seen by the child. If the child has learned to participate in play audiometry, the toys used in the test situation should be familiar to him.

If the child's visual impairment is so severe that a light source will not serve as a reinforcer, it is necessary to provide another type of reinforcer when he responds to the sound. The parent and specialist should establish prior to the testing session what kind of reinforcement is most rewarding to the child. A toy that can be activated can be put in front of the child with his hands placed on it. The specialist or parent can activate the toy when the child gives a response to the auditory stimulus, thus reinforcing the response. However, reinforcing a response from the child, e.g., a head turn, with a toy or interesting object can backfire too, since the toy must then be removed prior to the auditory stimulus being presented again. When the toy is removed, the child may cry, making further testing difficult. A taste of a favorite food (e.g., pudding) may be reinforcing, though some visually impaired children do not enjoy eating, making food an inappropriate reinforcer. A stroke on the body or momentary presentation of an interesting object (e.g., a feather) can be tried as reinforcers.

One reinforcer that has worked well at IHR for a two-year-old visually impaired child with hearing loss was a small, battery-operated fan purchased at a novelty store. The child quickly learned to lift his face and turn his head slightly to the side when he heard a sound in order to receive the reinforcing "breeze." Specialists need to experiment with all types of reinforcers for use with visually impaired children, using the parents' expert input on their child's likes and dislikes.

TEACHING THE CHILD TO GIVE A CONDITIONED
RESPONSE TO SOUND

Teaching a two-year-old or older child who has a severe loss of vision to participate in traditional play audiometry techniques is difficult. There is no intrinsic value in putting a ring on a stick or a ball in a tube when the child cannot see what is happening. When the partially-sighted child is old enough to learn to give a conditioned response to sound (between 20-30 months), it may be necessary to teach him the task in steps. Since the child may not be able to see the specialist when she performs a task in response to the sound, she may need to teach him first how to release a toy, such as a block, into a bucket. It increases the motivation of some visually impaired children to use a translucent bucket with a light under it so that they can see the outline of the blocks once they are dropped in.

It is sometimes effective to teach the conditioned response task using a vibratory, low frequency stimulus produced through the bone oscillator of the audiometer. The parent can hold the bone oscillator against one of the child's arms or hands while the specialist helps the child hold the block in the other hand. When the tone is produced, causing the oscillator to vibrate, the specialist can help the child drop the block into the bucket. Once the child can perform the task without assistance, a pure tone delivered through sound field speakers or earphones can be substituted for the bone oscillator and, following a short period of practice with the new stimuli, testing can be initiated.

The specialist and parent should be certain that the activity they teach the child to use in response to the stimulus is enjoyable for the child so that he is motivated to "play" the conditioned response game.

TEST VARIABLES AS THEY APPLY TO THE CHILD WITH MOTOR IMPAIRMENT

Cerebral palsy is the motor impairment seen most frequently in conjunction with impaired hearing in children. Thus, the information and teaching techniques discussed in this section will refer to the child with cerebral palsy (CP). Cerebral palsy is a condition caused by damage to the brain, usually occuring before, during, or shortly following birth. This damage results in abnormal coordination of muscle action, not in paralysis of muscles.

"Cerebral Palsy is characterized by an inability to fully control motor function. Depending on which part of the brain has been damaged and the degree of involvement of the central nervous system, one or more of the following may occur: spasms; involuntary movement; disturbance in gait and mobility; seizures; abnormal sensation and perception; impairment of sight, hearing or speech; and mental retardation. There are three main types of cerebral palsy: spastic — stiff and difficult movement; athetoid — involuntary and uncontrolled movement; ataxic — disturbed sense of balance and depth perception. There may be a mixture of these types for any one individual." (UCPA, 1982)

The major difficulties involved in testing the hearing of children with cerebral palsy are 1) positioning and supporting the child in a way that *in-*

hibits involuntary movements and *permits voluntary movement*; 2) establishing an action that the child can produce voluntarily in response to the auditory stimuli; and 3) reinforcing the child's responses.

POSITIONING AND SUPPORTING THE CHILD

If the child has a wheelchair or other seating device that has been designed for his use, this is probably the most appropriate seating arrangement for the child during audiological testing. Specialists and audiologists should also keep in mind that there is nothing sacred about the seated position; if the child is most relaxed while lying on his back or side or propped on a wedge, these positions are fine as long as the child's face can be seen clearly by at least one trained observer. Make certain that the child is not having to work to keep himself in position, since this effort may preclude his responding to the sounds presented.

ESTABLISHING AN ACTION THAT THE CHILD CAN VOLUNTARILY PRODUCE IN RESPONSE TO THE AUDITORY STIMULUS

The responses that a child with cerebral palsy gives to sound are likely to be subtle and delayed. The exaggerated latency of the child's response creates a problem since the observers may fail to associate it with the stimulus. The response may be a subtle movement such as a smile, eye widening or eyeblink, a cessation of movement (e.g. sucking), a guttural vocalization, or a movement of some body part. The specialist, parents, and audiologist must take the time to observe the child's behaviors prior to the onset of stimuli and then watch the child for much longer than usual following the presentations of stimuli in order to detect consistent — though perhaps delayed — responses.

Whenever a particular response is required from the older toddler or preschooler with cerebral palsy, the audiologist and specialist should make certain that it does not require so much effort that the child tires rapidly or "drops-out" of the test because of the difficulty. When utilizing VRA, the testers must place the visual reinforcer at an angle and height that make it easy for the child to respond with an eye movement only, or with a minimal head movement. Conditioned response audiometry should not be used if the task of grasping and releasing a toy requires so much effort that the child has no attention left for the stimulus. As is true with any young hearing-impaired child, it is most efficient to teach the child with cerebral palsy the task of giving a conditioned response to sound during habilitation sessions which precede audiological testing.

REINFORCING THE CHILD'S RESPONSES

Caution must be observed in giving social reinforcement for his response to the child with cerebral palsy. Our staff has noticed that the normal amount of enthusiasm shown and praise given a young child following an appropriate response to a stimulus may have an adverse affect on the child with cerebral palsy. Excitement is contagious and some children with CP tighten up when excited, preventing them from repeating a previously successful response. Reinforcing the child's behavior with a calming stroke on the arm or cheek may be more appropriate for a child with CP.

TEST VARIABLES AS THEY APPLY TO THE CHILD WITH DEVELOPMENTAL DELAY OR NEUROLOGICAL IMPAIRMENT

AWARENESS OF DEVELOPMENTAL LEVELS AT WHICH THE CHILD IS FUNCTIONING

The most critical aspect of testing the hearing of a child with delayed development or neurological impairment is awareness of the developmental level at which the child is functioning, regardless of his chronological age. If most of the child's behaviors are at the 12-month level, then the audiologist and specialist will look for and reinforce the type of responses to sound expected from a year-old child, even if the child's chronological age is two years. Likewise, familiarity with the child's typical behaviors (even if this familiarity is gained rapidly by observing the child during the initial interview with the parents) will cue the audiologist and specialist to make modifications in the test environment that will enable them to get the information they need about the child's hearing levels.

ESTABLISHING/DETECTING THE RESPONSE THE CHILD WILL GIVE TO THE AUDITORY STIMULI

It may be necessary to plan a longer period for training the child who is developmentally delayed or neurologically impaired to respond to VRA, and frequent retraining during the testing session may be necessary. Like a child with cerebral palsy, the responses to sound given by the delayed or neurologically-impaired child may have an increased latency, requiring that the audiologist and specialist watch for responses that occur several seconds after the presentation of the stimulus. Responses from these children may not only occur late, but may be minimal in magnitude so that the testers must look for small changes in behavior which indicate that the sound was heard.

Delayed or neurologically impaired children may perseverate in their responses, a trait which results in the child giving a large number of false positive responses (responses that occur when no stimulus is presented). Some children are so entranced by the lighted and moving reinforcer used in VRA that they turn to it frequently without waiting for the auditory stimulus. Other children "pattern" easily, requiring that the audiologist take particular care not to fall into the child's response rhythm in presenting stimuli. Short and frequent sessions that permit the child to become familiar with the test environment and procedures are most effective in producing auditory threshold information.

MODIFYING THE TEST ENVIRONMENT

It is necessary to keep the test booth free from distractions that call the child's attention away from the task. Toys used between presentations of stimuli to get the child's visual attention away from the reinforcer must be carefully selected: if their appeal is too strong, the child may ignore the auditory signal because of his interest in the toy. Some children can be permitted to handle a toy; others become too involved with the toy and fail to attend to subsequent sounds.

Like other young children, some children with developmental delay may be frightened by the moving, lighted toy that is commonly used as a reinforcer in VRA. Some children may become overly excited by the appearance of such a toy and find it difficult to tear their eyes away from the spot where it will appear. If either of these situations exist, a small (15-25 watt) colored light bulb which can be flashed can be substituted with excellent results.

A few of the young hearing-impaired children with developmental delay who have attended IHR have reacted with intense fear upon being taken into the sound-treated audiological test room. When this has occurred, the specialist and family have conducted all or part of several subsequent habilitation sessions in the test room. The child was allowed to explore the room thoroughly and to play interesting games in the room before audiological testing was scheduled again. Taking the time to allow the child to feel comfortable in the test environment makes good sense since the child's comfort contributes considerably to reliable test results.

HEARING AID USE
AND THE MULTI-HANDICAPPED CHILD

HEARING AIDS: A FAMILY PRIORITY?

It is essential for the parent-infant specialist to acknowledge that some young multi-handicapped children have so many problems, some of which may be life-threatening, that the parents simply cannot make hearing habilitation the top priority at the time the hearing loss is identified. In such cases, we have found it necessary to adapt the frequency and focus of habilitation sessions to the needs of the family.

In the beginning, parents may not need information specific to hearing loss and hearing aids as much as they need to talk to someone about their feelings related to their child. Sessions may also give the parents a chance to "take a breather" while someone else interacts with the child. Even though the stated purpose of sessions is to increase the parents' effectiveness in interacting with the child, sometimes the best way to do that is to let them relax and watch the parent-infant specialist engage the child in play that promotes acquisition of listening and language skills. As the child's health status stabilizes and the life-threatening handicaps are under control, his parents will become increasingly able to participate in sessions and learn about hearing loss and hearing aids.

Prior to the time that parents are ready to take the hearing aids home, the child can be wearing the aids during habilitation sessions. The parent-infant specialist can familiarize the parents with the aids during sessions in preparation for the time that they feel able to add use of hearing aids to the child's daily routine. The last thing parents need when dealing with a multi-handicapped child is guilt-inducing pressure from a professional to do something for the child that feels impossible to do.

PLACEMENT OF HEARING AIDS:
COMFORT AND FEEDBACK

One problem that often arises in dealing with multi-handicapped children is placing the aids so that they are comfortable for the child, who may spend much of his time lying down or propped in an infant seat. In either of these positions, the child's head may be turned to one side so that the earmold is uncomfortable or the proximity of the earmold and receiver to a surface creates feedback. We have no stock solution for this problem. If the child is wearing body aids it may be possible to put longer cords on them and place the body of the aid or aids on a surface near the child. Increasing the distance between the earmold/receiver and the microphone of the aid will decrease the likelihood of feedback. A similar arrangement can be worked out for ear-level aids by using lengths of thick-walled tubing between the aids and the earmolds that permit the aids to be worn pinned on the child's upper chest in lightweight bags (an infant sock works well). Since longer tubing will decrease the intensity of the signals that reach the child's ears, the aids must be tested with the selected tubing lengths on them in order to adjust the volume settings to provide the amount of gain the child needs.

When a combination of factors promotes the production of feedback — small body size, poor neck and head control, an ear or ears frequently held against a surface — the audiologist may want to utilize a CROS arrangement. In the CROS, the microphone, which is placed on one ear, is connected by a cord to the amplifier-receiver placed on the other ear. Sound is picked up on one side of the head and delivered to the opposite ear. This separation of microphone and receiver is likely to eliminate the feedback problem.

The key to hearing aid placement on the multi-handicapped child is a willingness to be flexible and inventive. The first amplification systems placed may not be optimal from a purist's point of view, but getting consistent sound to the child is the most important task. As the child grows, hearing aids and hearing aid placement can be changed until the child can utilize the most adequate and appropriate systems.

HABILITATION AND THE MULTI-HANDICAPPED CHILD

There are several considerations that apply to working with all families of young multi-handicapped hearing-impaired children. Following a discussion of these general considerations, teaching techniques for each of the three types of multi-handicapped child discussed above will be presented.

GENERAL CONSIDERATIONS FOR HABILITATION WITH FAMILIES OF YOUNG MULTI-HANDICAPPED CHILDREN

PRIORITIZE THE NEEDS OF THE FAMILY AND CHILD

In the previous section dealing with hearing aid use, it was pointed out that it may not be possible to implement hearing aid usage with multi-handicapped hearing-impaired children in the same way as with hearing-impaired children who have no additional handicaps. Some parents may not consider their child's hearing impairment to be the condition requiring the most time and attention at the present time. There is nothing wrong with this decision. However, problems may arise if this decision is not discussed and the specialist establishes her goals and expectations as if hearing impairment *were* the parents' first priority. It is very important to discuss openly with parents all the requirements that are being placed on them as a result of their child's handicaps, and to agree on an habilitation approach that requires only the amount of time and effort that the parents are able to exert at that particular time. As time passes, the family's circumstances and needs will change and their ability to commit more time, energy, and interest to the child's hearing loss will most likely increase.

One possible outcome of acknowledging and supporting the needs of the multi-handicapped child and his family is delaying the initiation of auditory and language habilitation until other needs can be met. The parents and specialist may agree, for instance, to wait for two months before starting habilitation sessions so that the family can attend to their most pressing initial concerns regarding the child. When habilitation does begin, the parents' readiness will make them more efficient learners and more motivated participants.

It is sometimes difficult for professionals, who know the importance of auditory input during the child's first years of life, to let go of their sense of urgency about auditory stimulation when working with multi-handicapped children. However, if the specialist's interests and concerns regarding the child do not coincide with those expressed by the parents, the development of the parent-specialist partnership, so essential to a productive habilitation program, is jeopardized. If, on the other hand, the specialist acknowledges and supports the parents' concerns and interests — even if these fall outside the range of auditory and language habilitation per se — the developing partnership is off to a good start.

REFER/DEFER TO OTHER PROFESSIONALS
WHEN APPROPRIATE

The parent-infant specialist is not expected to know how to diagnose and treat handicapping conditions in addition to hearing loss. Appropriate procedures for referring a child to other professionals for evaluation and therapy were outlined in Chapter 25. Nothing is gained by failing to refer a child for evaluation if the specialist or parents have questions about the child's growth or development. When the specialist suspects, for instance, that the child's motor development is delayed, it is not helpful to dodge the issue for fear of alarming or upsetting parents. The parents may have suspected motor problems themselves but have hesitated to say anything. One parent of a hearing-impaired child (Shepherd, 1973) has suggested that professionals may "underestimate the toughness of parents. It is hard to convince those who are in authority that it is far better that a parent be told of a suspicion of a handicap which may later prove to be ill-founded than to reassure him and later have a handicap proven'' (p. 242).

It is also a possibility that the specialist will raise her concerns with parents only to be met with resistance to the idea of yet another handicapping condition. The specialist can acknowledge the parents' fears while not backing down from her concerns about the child and her impression that a referral for evaluation is indicated.

SET GOALS THAT ARE MEANINGFUL
FOR THE CHILD AND FAMILY

The needs of each multi-handicapped child are specific to him at any given time. As his needs and capabilities change, specialists and parents must be certain to adjust both his environment and their expectations and goals for him. Setting meaningful goals for the multi-handicapped child requires climbing inside his skin, seeing the world from his perspective, determining what it is he can do now, and how he might build new skills on top of existing skills to get his needs met and his ideas, interests, and feelings expressed. Sometimes by making simple changes in the child's environment, parents and specialists can provide the child with the means to meet some of his own needs. He can learn to push a button or bar that rings a doorbell to summon a parent, that turns on a T.V., radio, or light, or that activates a toy. He can learn to pull a string to regain a toy he has pushed off his high chair tray.

It is important for the specialist and parent to make every effort to determine the multi-handicapped child's level of cognitive function. They can then use cognitive development scales and curricula to ascertain what activities are appropriate for children functioning at that level. These activities may need to be adapted for the multi-handicapped child, but activities for which the child is cognitively ready will be both motivating and reinforcing for the child. The books and curricula found in the "Suggested Reading" list at the end of this chapter will be invaluable to the specialist who wants to establish realistic objectives and goals for the child.

Equally critical is determining how the child is interacting with his significant others. McInnes and Treffry (1982) delineate eight stages through which the child may pass in responding to interaction: resists, tolerates, cooperates passively, enjoys, responds, imitates, and initiates independently. Objectives for the child must acknowledge at which of these stages of interaction the child is currently functioning. It may be appropriate to initiate a program that will help the child move through these stages.

It is as important to set expectations and behavioral limits for the multi-handicapped child as it is for a child with no known handicaps. If specialists and parents expect nothing from the child, he learns to expect nothing from himself, and a debilitating pattern is established. Do not set limitations

("He will never be able to walk, so why bother helping him stand up?''), but *do* set limits ("I cannot allow you to tear the book") so that the child is not further handicapped by unacceptable behaviors that are within his control.

KEEP PARENTS MOTIVATED TO STIMULATE THEIR CHILD

A multi-handicapped child may learn and develop slowly. Parents need help in finding ways to stimulate and interact with their child so they do not grow bored and discouraged when they do not see rapid results. Many times parents fail to perceive small changes that occur in their child's behaviors, changes which signal that progress is being made. The specialist may notice and point out that the child is gazing at the parent for longer periods of time, is imitating an arm movement made by the parent, or is vocalizing as if wanting the parent's attention. Nothing better motivates parents to keep working than having progress pointed out to them. They need to hear, "What you are doing makes a difference! You're doing a great job!" Breaking the child's goals down into smaller, more easily achieved steps allows parents and specialists to experience the positive feelings that come from seeing the child succeed.

HELP PARENTS INTEGRATE THE INFORMATION THEY RECEIVE FROM A NUMBER OF PROFESSIONALS

Parents of young children whose sole handicap is hearing loss sometimes find it difficult to find time to tend to their child's special needs. The family of a child with handicaps in addition to hearing loss has this difficulty compounded. Usually the parents must see professionals in addition to the parent-infant specialist who works with the child's hearing impairment. These other professionals also provide parents with assignments ("Read this"; "Get his glasses fixed"; "Time to check on the level of his medication.") as well as with information. Sometimes the information the parents receive from professionals in different fields is, or appears to be, contradictory. When this happens, the parents may be justifiably confused or angry.

The parent-infant specialist can help parents integrate the information and instructions they receive from all the professionals with whom they work by:

1. Showing parents how auditory and language objectives can be combined with movement exercises, visual stimulation, or developmental activities.
2. Encouraging parents to check back with professionals if they are unclear about any of the instructions or information they have received.

3. Asking parents to tell her when information or instructions she gives them appear to be in conflict with that given them by other professionals.
4. Calling a meeting of all the professionals working with the family if the parents feel a need to have services and information better coordinated and integrated.

The parent-infant specialist can often provide a valuable service to families by acting as the "case manager" and assisting the parents of multi-handicapped children as they juggle appointments, assignments, and information.

INCLUDE NURSES, BABYSITTERS, AND GRANDPARENTS IN HABILITATION SESSIONS WHEN POSSIBLE

Raising a multi-handicapped child requires a tremendous amount of energy, patience, and perseverence. Even the best-intentioned parents will run out of these valuable commodities if they have no time for themselves away from their child. The more people who feel comfortable and productive while interacting with the child, the more resources the parent will have to call on for respite care. Specialists should not encourage parents to feel that they are the only people who can provide the care and training that their child needs. Instead, the specialist should encourage parents to take time for themselves on a regular basis. Parents who make their multi-handicapped child the sole focus of their lives soon exhaust their supply of perspective, along with their enthusiasm and creativity.

BE VERY CLEAR WITH ADULTS WHO ATTEND HABILITATION SESSIONS ABOUT THEIR ROLE IN THE SESSIONS

When parents or caregivers attend therapy sessions at more than one agency, they may assume that all professionals want them to participate in the same way. However, a physical therapist may want parents to sit away from the action and watch; a vision specialist may have parents watch intervention through a one-way mirror. Parents coming to auditory and language habilitation for the first time may assume that the parent-infant specialist wants them to remain uninvolved in sessions. The specialist must be clear about the parents' roles, showing them, as well as telling them, how she would like them to participate, and reinforcing them when they participate actively. Many parents and other involved adults feel vulnerable and inadequate as they begin habilitation with the child. They need reassurance from the specialist that they are performing appropriately and well.

GIVE THE MULTI-HANDICAPPED CHILD TIME TO RESPOND TO THE STIMULI PRESENTED TO HIM

It may take the child with multi-handicapping conditions longer to process information, to get messages to his muscles, to work out the meaning of a situation. Adults will want to fill their interactions with the child with long pauses to give him a chance to react and respond to what has been done or said. Don't always act *on* the child. Involve the child in what is going on by telling him ahead of time that he will be picked up, turned over, have his shirt removed, fed. Tell him, then wait for his response, then go ahead with the action. Act *with* the child by letting him know what is happening rather than by manipulating and moving him without explanation. As time goes by, adults will begin to see responses on the part of the child that tell them how he is feeling about what is about to happen: He arches his body toward the adult to be picked up, turns his head in preparation for being turned over, raises his arms to have his shirt removed, looks toward the kitchen where the food is. Or maybe he tells the adult that he isn't interested in the activity being proposed and the negotiation process can begin.

When toys are presented to the multi-handicapped child he may need a period of time to explore the toy before he is ready to do anything *with* it. One hearing-impaired child with developmental delay watched the IHR specialist model putting a necklace into a milk bottle as part of a cognitive assessment. When the necklace and empty bottle were given to the child he played with the bottle alone for four to five minutes. He pretended to drink from it, turned it over, dropped it. Only after he had finished exploring the bottle did he pick up the necklace and attempt to put it in the bottle. This child needed *time* — his previous concept of a bottle was that it was something you drink from; it took him five minutes to act out that concept and then to expand his play to include a new use for the bottle.

GETTING COMMUNICATION STARTED WITH THE YOUNG MULTI-HANDICAPPED CHILD

Working with young children with diminished sensory capabilities requires that specialists be acutely aware of the reasons that communication between individuals exists in the first place, and of the basic functions that communication serves. Getting down to this elementary level may help us determine what to teach the infant and how to teach it.

First of all, communication exists because we live in a world peopled by others. Communication is one of the major ways in which we interrelate with others. It is, therefore, a social phenomenon that allows us to convey and receive messages to and from those around us. Secondly, we communicate for a purpose. We want to ask, tell, describe, protest, or maintain contact through communication. If we view communication as a bridge between people that allows them to get their needs met, we have a simple starting point for our work with the multi-handicapped child: We can help the child build the bridges that will help him get his needs met.

Two initial criteria, then, that can be applied to any communication curriculum used with the multi-handicapped child are 1) that parents and specialist help the child develop communication through their social and caregiving interactions with him, and 2) that we help the child acquire communication strategies that are functional for him, meaning that they help him get his needs met. There are, as always, a number of other considerations and principles related to communication instruction and how it works best. Many of these considerations and principles, as well as curricula for teaching communication to severely handicapped children, are discussed by the contributors to *Teaching Functional Language* (Warren and Rogers-Warren, 1985), and by contributors to *Communication Development in Young Children with Deaf-Blindness: Literature Review II* (Bullis, 1986), as well as by Reichle and Keogh (1985), Musselwhite and St. Louis (1982), and McLean, Snyder-McLean, Rowlands, Jacobs, and Stremel-Campbell (1981).

CHOOSING AN APPROPRIATE COMMUNICATION SYSTEM FOR THE CHILD WITH MORE THAN ONE HANDICAPPING CONDITION

Mathy-Laikko, Ratcliff, Villarruel, and Yoder (1986) provide a concise summary of the nonspeech, or augmentative, communicative systems that have been developed for use by persons who cannot use speech as their primary means of communication. Augmentative communication systems are divided into two types:

1. Unaided systems, meaning that no special equipment or devices are used. Signed language and gestural codes are unaided augmentative communication systems.
2. Aided systems, meaning that some type of non-electronic or electronic device or equipment is used by the handicapped individual to communicate. Non-electronic augmentative communication systems include cards, books, or simple communication boards that display pictures, letters, or words that the individual can select to convey his message. Electronic augmentative communication systems include devices that are activated by switching mechanisms, and have a user display, control electronics, and some form of output, e.g., printed language or synthesized speech.

There are businesses which sell augmentative communication systems for use with individuals who are non-speaking. State departments of vocational rehabilitation or local associations serving people with handicaps (e.g., United Cerebral Palsy Association) may be resources for specialists and parents who want information about the kinds of devices that are available.

A complete discussion of the considerations and issues involved in the choice of the appropriate augmentative communication system for a child is beyond the scope of this section. Readers are referred to "Suggested Readings" at the end of this chapter for a listing of some sources of information about augumentative communication systems.

AN INSTRUCTIONAL SEQUENCE FOR TEACHING SIGNED LANGUAGE TO YOUNG MULTI-HANDICAPPED CHILDREN

The use of signed language is an appropriate communication system for some multi-handicapped children. Schaeffer (1982, Parts I and II) proposed an instructional sequence for teaching signed language to multi-handicapped children that is based on a sequence of linguistic functions which develop in both normal infants and non-verbal children. The instructional sequence begins with language that expresses desires, and moves to reference or people's names, person concepts, inquiry skills, and abstraction.

1. **Expression of desires:** The Parent Handout entitled "Presymbolic Communication — How a Child Communicates Before He Uses Words" found in *Parent-Infant Communication* (Infant Hearing Resource, 1985), describes four functions of a young child's earliest presymbolic communication. The first two presymbolic functions, the instrumental function ("I want" or "I don't want") and the regulatory function ("Do this") fall into this language category, expression of desires. Schaeffer (1982, Part II) lists three non-verbal prerequisites to the use of signs which express desire, prerequisite behaviors which he states many profoundly retarded children may need to be taught before they will learn to use a symbol such as a sign to express their desires. These prerequisite behaviors are 1) reaching for desired objects, 2) turn taking, and 3) awareness of differences between self and object.

Schaeffer (1982, Part II) proposes that instructors follow three steps in teaching a child to *reach for desired objects*. These steps are:

1. To encourage all hand movements or movement of any body part which the child might learn to use to signal desire.
2. To encourage all grasping.
3. To help the child grasp specific objects, such as foods.

He suggests that a child may not be ready to learn a sign for an object until he has been consistently reaching for it for a month or longer.

Turn taking is the second skill prerequisite to the use of signs that express desire, since implicit in asking someone for something is the expectation of a response. Simple games in which the adult and child imitate and alternate movements and vocalization are an excellent way to promote turn taking.

The third prerequisite skill to using signs to express desires is the *child's awareness of himself as different from the objects and people around him.* Schaeffer (1982, Part II) suggests that "the profoundly retarded child is likely not to have had enough experience with discrepancies and resistances to so define himself, because of his physical and psychological incapacities" (p. 405). Many multi-handicapped children are limited in their experience of themselves in their environment and have difficulty perceiving themselves as separate from significant people and objects around them. We have worked with children at IHR who perceived their mothers' hands as an extension of their own body. Instead of reaching for a toy, they picked up their mother's hand and directed it to the toy they wanted.

It makes sense that a child will not use a symbol to request an object or person if the object or person is not perceived as a separate entity. Once the child does perceive himself as separate, he can be taught to use signs such as "want" and "more" in combination with reference words (e.g., names of objects) to express his desires.

2. **Reference:** The second category of linguistic functions to teach a multi-handicapped child includes signs that describe or name objects or people. Examples of these words are, "milk," "Ma-Ma," and "play." When being taught this function of language, children learn that they can use language that answers the questions, "What is that?" or "Who is that?" The ability to name objects, activities, and people is based on four prerequisite skills: initiation of social interactions, language (or sound) play, exploratory behavior, and imitation, all of which may be deficit in severely handicapped children. Activities which promote development of these skills will also promote the child's readiness to use symbols to name objects.

3. **Person Concepts:** Schaeffer (1982, Part I) defines person concepts as including "people's names, people's names as possessive terms, labels for human actions, labels for emotions, direct address by name, calling to someone by name (the vocative) and so forth; in short, those concepts normal infants use when initiating or talking about social interactions" (p. 300). He suggests three techniques for teaching person concepts:

1. Link instruction in person concepts to the expression of desires, e.g., "Ronnie's bear" or "Mommy cookie" meaning, "Mom, I want a cookie."
2. Place the child in situations where possessiveness, pride in performance, boastfulness, and frustration at not being understood motivate him to use person concepts. For example, designating objects such as toys, bottles, or blankets as the child's own will foster feelings of possessiveness that the child may express using symbols.
3. Promote the child's use of names and action labels by showing him how use of these symbols gives him control over the actions of others. Playing games in which the child can produce a desired

result in another person by using that person's name is an effective way to introduce this function.

4. **Inquiry Skills:** Schaeffer defines inquiry skills as using language to gain information about the location and identity of objects that are not visibly present. He suggests teaching three inquiry skills in the following order: search for hidden objects at another person's request, answering questions about the location of hidden objects, and asking questions about the location of hidden objects and the names of unknown objects. The child can be stimulated to ask questions by making an unexpected change in his environment, e.g., by moving a favorite toy usually located in the same place in the room, so that the child is motivated to ask, "Where's the monkey?"

5. **Abstraction:** Schaeffer suggests that teachers can teach abstractions useful to the child such as colors, personal pronouns, presence and absence, and truth and falsity. Abstract language is a basic component of conversation and of symbolic play which incorporates the imaginative function. The child who has little interest in social interaction is not motivated to use the abstractions that underlie conversation and symbolic play. This child will need stimulation to evoke his interest in developing these linguistic functions.

The specialist and parent can select signs that apply specifically to the child's interests and needs as they work through each of these five sequenced steps. Adults who are willing to be flexible, consistent, and patient will promote acquisition of a communication system that will enable the child to participate in meaningful social interactions, control aspects of his world, and convey his feelings, needs, and interests.

SUGGESTIONS FOR WORKING WITH THE HEARING-IMPAIRED CHILD WITH IMPAIRED VISION

Many children who are both hearing and vision impaired have one sensory modality that has more residual capability than the other. It is important to identify the child's better modality and to consider the usefulness of information the child receives through both modalities in selecting the communication system that will be used with the child. Specialists and parents who have the orientation of identifying and promoting maximum use of the child's residual capabilities are likely to see the child as someone who "can," rather than someone who "cannot." An attitude of empowering the child to speak for and act for himself is of immense benefit to the child. Specialists and parents may find the following suggestions useful in their interactions with the child with a combination of visual and auditory impairments.

TALK TO THE CHILD'S VISION SPECIALIST

If a vision specialist is working with the child, ask him/her if he/she is using a particular program to help the child learn about himself in his world. Van Dijk developed an approach to communication development that spells out a progression of learning stages for the child. Van Dijk's approach is described by Siegal-Causey, Sims, Ernest, and Guess (1986), Hammer (1982), and Curtis, Dunning, Meese, Westover, Yost, and Perotti (1978). Another type of curricular approach to the deaf-blind child utilizes contingency awareness strategies (Brinker and Lewis, 1982; Dunst, 1981; McCormick and Noonan, 1984; Robinson and Robinson, 1983; Schweigert, 1986). The specialist and parents should request that the vision specialist provide them with the information and skills they need to successfully implement and reinforce whatever communication development strategy is being used with the child during vision therapy.

Ask for and follow other suggestions provided by the vision specialist. He/she may have determined that the child has a small window of light/dark discrimination for objects held at a certain angle relative to one of the child's eyes. He/she will have ideas about programs for mobility, motor development, cognitive and perceptual development, and social-emotional development. The parent-infant specialist and parents can keep the vision specialist up-to-date on the child's progress in auditory development and hearing aid use and in acquisition of skills in other areas.

USE TOUCH CUES TO TELL THE CHILD WHAT IS HAPPENING

There are two major ways in which the hearing-impaired child with limited vision can get information through taction: *touch on* his body and *touching with* his body. It should be mentioned that many infants and children with auditory and visual deficits do not like to be touched and a program which follows a set sequence leading to acceptance of touch may need to be initiated (McInnes and Treffry, 1982). Once the child is comfortable with being touched and with having his hand guided to touch objects in his environment, the parents and specialist can begin using cues, adapted signs, and symbols (i.e., an object or part of an object associated with an activity or event that represents the entire activity or event) that give the child information about whom he is interacting with, where he is, and what is happening to him and around him.

Laura and Jack selected the following sequence of cues, signs, and symbols to use with their hearing and vision impaired daughter, Mimi, when they were ready to go to sessions at IHR. Before leaving the house they clapped one of their hands on her hand twice to tell her she was going to "school". When they arrived at IHR, they repeated this cue for "school." The IHR parent-infant specialist, when approaching Mimi, signed a "J" on

Mimi's cheek and said, "Hello! This is Julia." When Julia and the family went upstairs to the teaching room, they helped Mimi feel the doorjamb and a round ball that was always placed by the door prior to her arrival. Having oriented Mimi to her environment, they were ready to begin the habilitation activities.

Touch can be used to inform, reassure, and reinforce. It is an essential part of every interaction with the visually impaired child.

USE LIGHT IF THE CHILD CAN DISCRIMINATE LIGHT VERSUS NO LIGHT

If the child can perceive light, think of as many ways as possible to utilize light to give the child visual information and to reinforce desirable behaviors. Light can be flashed to reinforce staccato vocalizations, held steadily on to reinforce sustained vocalizations. Parents can turn on a light as they call the child's name to train him to locate the source of a sound (if he has adequate aided hearing to hear voice). Objects can be silhouetted by light to give the child information about their size and shape in addition to that gained from handling the object.

HELP PARENTS STRUCTURE THE CHILD'S HOME ENVIRONMENT TO BE CONSISTENT FROM DAY TO DAY

When both distance senses are impaired, it is difficult for the child to establish his orientation in space. He may be unable to use vision or hearing to identify either his location or his position relative to obstacles as he moves around in a room. The home setting is one environment that can be kept consistent for him — the furniture in a set place, his bed and toys always in the same location. The child can learn to plan his movement in a room based on his memory of the location of furniture, doorways, carpets, heating ducts, etc. Providing a consistent physical environment at home is an important way to help the child feel secure and to have a feeling of mastery over some aspects of his life.

The habilitation setting at the agency can also be made consistent for the child. Sessions should be held in the same room each time and objects in the room, such as tables and chairs, can be placed in the same place. As the child is ready, he can be prepared for changes. At the end of one session, he can help the specialist move the table to a new location. He can practice, with help, coming into the room and locating the table in its new position. Prior to his entering the room for the next session, the specialist or parent can remind him that the table has been moved and help him locate it if necessary. When the child is ready, the sessions can be moved to a different room. Providing the child with adequate preparation for change and with support and time to explore in a new environment will promote his sense of security and of ability to adapt to change.

IDENTIFY CHILD'S SELF-STIMULATION BEHAVIORS AND AGREE WITH THE PARENTS ON PROCEDURES TO DISTRACT THE CHILD

Hearing and vision impaired children may engage in activities such as rocking or pressing their knuckles into their eye sockets because these activities provide sensory stimulation. The stimulation provided, however, is not helpful to the child, and engaging in these behaviors may prevent the child from participating in activities that would promote learning. An effective, non-punitive strategy to discourage self-stimulation behaviors is to gently remove the child's hand(s) and give him a toy, or gently still the child and engage him in social interaction. Some children use behaviors such as rubbing objects on their upper lip to explore or identify an object. The child should be allowed to use this method for identification but discouraged from persevering in the behavior past a reasonable amount of time. It will take almost constant monitoring on the part of parents and others who interact with the child to eliminate perseverative behaviors but the benefits to the child are well worth the effort.

BEGINNING TECHNIQUES FOR WORKING WITH THE HEARING-IMPAIRED CHILD WITH MOTOR IMPAIRMENT

TALK TO OTHER THERAPISTS WHO ARE WORKING WITH THE CHILD

The physical therapist can give the specialist and parents information related to the child's posture and movement. He/she can demonstrate the positions in which the child is most relaxed, positions to avoid because they cause the child to tense, positions that are best for speech activities, and ways in which to move the child from one position to another. Specialists and parents will learn whether objects should be presented to the child at midline or to one side, and at what level relative to the child's eyes objects should be held so that he can focus on them or reach for them with the least amount of effort. The physical therapist can also relate how to situate the child so that his attention is free for learning rather than focused on maintaining his position. The therapist may say that the child needs to be stabilized with straps in a high chair or may indicate that the child does best when propped on his side on a wedge.

The occupational therapist and speech pathologist can describe the degree of the child's oral-motor involvement and how it will affect his ability to control his breath stream, lips, tongue, and teeth for the production of speech. The occupational therapist can also recommend techniques that are being used to help the child accomplish daily activities independently or with as little assistance as possible. The clinical psychologist can provide information about the child's intellectual function and suggest ways in which to stimulate his cognitive development.

Infants and toddlers express their developing cognitive skills through their response to and manipulation of objects in their environment. When a child's ability to give a motor response or initiate a movement is impaired, it is difficult for specialists and parents to assess his cognitive function. It is important to continue to provide the child with stimulating input even if, because of his motor handicap, it is difficult to determine how he is processing the input.

USE CALMING REINFORCEMENT

Use reinforcement techniques that are calming if excitement causes the child to tense so that it is difficult for him to continue with the activity. Strokes and smiles let the child know you appreciate him and what he does.

BE CREATIVE IN FINDING WAYS
TO HELP THE CHILD COMMUNICATE

If the child has limited control over oral movements as well as arm and hand movements, he will have difficulty developing a spoken or signed expressive language system. Talking with a speech/language therapist who is knowledgeable about working with individuals with cerebral palsy (or stroke) may give specialists and parents some ideas of what communication options are available (see, "Choosing An Appropriate Communication System for the Child," p. 494). Some ways that parents and specialists can help the child develop beginning communication skills are:

1. Develop a system of signals or gestures that the child can use to say "yes" and "no." Watch what he does naturally to indicate "yes" and "no" and build on these signals to establish a formal signal. It may be very simple — a smile or head lift for "yes", a head turn or eye closing to indicate "no." Verbalize/sign that you understand his desire, e.g. "You said 'no', I understand," to establish that you are reading his signal.

2. Pair pictures with familiar activities, toys, and foods. The child can learn to use a glance at a picture to indicate what he wants.

3. If signed language is being used with the child, adults will want to

watch for the child's use of the sign in a modification or approximation that he can produce. For instance, while the parents and specialist use the standard open-handed configuration for the signs "mother" and "father," the child who cannot move an open hand to the chin and forehead may make these signs with a fisted hand in the appropriate position. IHR specialists feel it is wiser for adults to use standard signs with the child and allow the child to make his own modifications, rather than having adults modify their signs to match the child's output. When the child learns to comprehend standard signs, he will be able to receive information from a larger number of people.

When a child with whom signed language is being used is extremely limited in his voluntary movement, the parents and specialist will want to identify those movements or positions that the child can produce with some part of his body and begin to help the child associate the movement or position with an object, action, or event. If the child can voluntarily cross one ankle over the other, adults can help the child learn to use this signal to express "food," "play," or some other need the child has. It is essential that all adults who interact with the child learn to interpret the child's signals so that the child gains the feeling that he does have some control over his environment and some way to communicate his needs.

Adults will want to select a name sign for the child that he can make, even if something as simple as an arm laid across the chest. Adults should use the child's name sign when they talk with — and for — the child so that he can learn to use it to refer to himself.

BEGINNING TECHNIQUES FOR WORKING WITH THE HEARING-IMPAIRED CHILD WITH DEVELOPMENTAL DELAY OR NEUROLOGICAL IMPAIRMENT

OBSERVE THE CHILD

Specialists and parents need to observe the child to determine how his developmental delay or neurological impairment affects his behavior. The adults can then select teaching strategies that circumvent the child's non-productive behaviors. Specialists and parents may find that the child with one of these disabilities simply needs more time and more exposure in order to learn a task or a concept. He may learn a task in one situation or with one set of materials, e.g., putting blocks in a can, that he is unable to generalize to other situations, such as putting bean bags in a box. He will need to be taught each task. This same child may learn the word "dog" for his own pet but may fail to generalize it to other dogs until he is exposed to a variety of activities incorporating other dogs. Another child may do well attaching symbols to actual objects but have trouble with more abstract concepts such as "good," "hungry," or "tired," or with attaching meaning to pictures of objects.

One of the major challenges of working with children who learn slowly is keeping parents encouraged and motivated to continue with stimulation activities even though they do not see immediate response from their child. The parent-infant specialist can show the parent how a variety of daily activities, toys, and games can be used to teach a concept so that the parent does not get into a rut and lose enthusiasm for a task.

Observation of a child may reveal behaviors that make it difficult for him to participate in a normal learning environment. A child who has limited ability to control impulsive behaviors needs external controls to help him stay still long enough to learn. Short and frequent activities in a high chair, broken up with periods of activity on the floor, may help slow the child down enough to enable him to direct his attention to a task. Children who are easily distracted may need to be taught in a room devoid of stimuli other than those associated with the planned activity. Children who cannot apply "brakes" to their level of activity, who accelerate a ball-rolling activity into a wild game of throwing and running and laughing, need help from observant adults who can carefully control the activity and stop it before the child gets stimulated to the point of losing control.

At the other end of the spectrum is the child who shows no curiosity and is not motivated to interact with people or to explore objects. Developmentally delayed children often appear disinterested in the world around them. They may show very little spontaneous interest in exploring their environment. These children may have to be physically led to explore and manipulate toys and helped through games that encourage interaction with people. Parents can be encouraged to play interaction games such as "peek-a-boo" and "I'm gonna get you!" They can hide toys under blankets and under the child's shirt to provide an element of suspense and surprise. These children need help in learning that the world is an exciting place!

Observing the child, identifying his behaviors that inhibit or disrupt learning, and using teaching strategies that circumvent the child's disruptive behaviors are three essential steps in working with the developmentally delayed or neurologically impaired child.

ANALYZE TEACHING OBJECTIVES AND BREAK THEM DOWN INTO SMALL, SEQUENTIAL STEPS THAT CAN BE TAUGHT ONE AT A TIME

The suggestion to break objectives into smaller teaching steps can be applied, for example, to Presymbolic Communication objective #21a (from *Parent-Infant Communication,* Infant Hearing Resource, 1985) which states, "Child uses body movement and posturing to communicate; shows anticipation, e.g., waves and raises arms to be picked up." The parent and specialist can break this objective down into the following steps:

1. Child (lying on back) looks at face of adult who is standing by crib.
2. Child looks at adult's hands as adult extends them down toward child.
3. Child wiggles body or smiles in anticipation of being picked up.
4. Child extends own arms toward adult.

The parent and specialist can work together to help the child accomplish these steps. One adult may physically move the child (e.g., in Step 1, one adult turns the child's head toward the other adult, who then moves her face into the area where the child's gaze is directed). The adults will move the child through an action several times, then lift the child out of the crib. Once the child accomplishes Step 1 by being consistent in voluntarily looking at the face of an adult standing by his crib, the adults can work on the next step. In the second step, one adult can help direct the child's attention to the hands of the other adult which are extended toward him, perhaps bringing the child's hands up to touch them. As the child accomplishes each step, his progress is applauded and both parent and child are reinforced for their persistence.

ADJUST EXPECTATIONS TO REFLECT THE CHILD'S RATE OF DEVELOPMENT

The distress experienced by the adults in the life of the child with developmental delay or neurological impairment is usually created when the child's performance does not match their expectations. The adult's distress causes problems when it spills over onto the child in the form of anger, frustration, or impatience. If the child experiences rejection from the significant adults in his life because of his slower pace, the attendant deprivation of love will increase the child's disability, potentially to the point that he loses all motivation to interact, grow, and learn. Adjusting expectations for the child does not mean you are giving up on him, but rather that you are accepting that he will do the best he can at his own speed with your help. Professionals will want to ascertain, however, that the child's slow progress is not a consequence of the child being stimulated with inappropriate learning activities. Ongoing assessment, use of well-developed curricula, and selection of appropriate activities for stimulation will ensure that the child is being given the best possible opportunity to develop as rapidly as he can.

SUMMARY

The hearing-impaired child with additional handicapping conditions presents a challenge to specialists and parents alike. The challenge lies in the adults' ability to set aside their perception of the world and attempt to imagine how the child experiences the world. The most helpful habilitation plans are those that are formulated when you sit inside the child's skin and imagine what you would want if you were without sound and sight, or without sound and freely controlled movement, or without sound and an intact central nervous system. Parents and specialists who can empathize with the child, and who can build on the child's abilities rather than focus on his disabilities, are in the best position to formulate a habilitation plan that will help the child reach his potential as a happy, independently functioning human being.

Each of the handicapping conditions discussed in this chapter will, when combined with loss of hearing, present unique challenges to parents and specialists as they work with multi-handicapped children. IHR specialists are certain that there is a great deal of expertise regarding the habilitation of multi-handicapped infants which resides in the minds and plan books of teachers who work with this population. In the past, we have been frustrated by the inaccessibility of information to help us help children who present complex learning needs. There are now available a number of books and journals that are very helpful to us. However, we urge those readers who have techniques to share to burn the midnight oil one more time and write an article for publication!

SUGGESTED READING
MULTI-HANDICAPPED CHILDREN

Extremely useful books that provide information and/or training curricula for handicapping conditions other than hearing loss are listed below.

ALL HANDICAPPING CONDITIONS

Batshaw, M. L. and Perret, Y. M. 1981. *Children with Handicaps — A Medical Primer.* Baltimore, MD: Paul H. Brookes Publishing Co.

Bricker, D. 1986. *Early Education of At-Risk and Handicapped Infants, Toddlers and Preschool Children.* Glenview, IL: Scott, Foresman and Co.

Campbell, B. 1982. *Severely Handicapped Hearing-Impaired Students.* Baltimore, MD: Paul H. Brookes Publishing Co.

Darby, B. L. and May, M. J. 1979. *Infant Assessment: Issues and Applications.* Seattle, WA: Western States Technical Assistance Resource.

Dunst, C. J. 1986. *Infant Learning: A Cognitive-Linguistic Intervention Strategy.* Allen, TX: Teaching Resources Corporation.

Fewell, R. and Vadasy, P. 1983. *Learning Through Play, A Resource Manual for Teachers and Parents.* Allen, TX: Teaching Resources Corporation.

Fewell, R. 1986. *Families of Handicapped Children.* Austin, TX: Pro-Ed, Inc.

Garwood, S. and Fewell, R. 1983. *Educating Handicapped Infants.* Rockville, MD: Aspen Systems.

Hare, B. A. and Hare, J. M. 1977. *Teaching Young Handicapped Children, A Guide for Preschool and the Primary Grades.* New York, NY: Grune and Stratton.

Morrison, D., Pothier, P., and Horr, K. 1978. *Sensory-Motor Dysfunction and Therapy in Infancy and Early Childhood.* Springfield, IL: Charles C. Thomas.

McLean, J. 1978. *A Transactional Approach to Early Language.* Columbus, OH: Charles E. Merrill.

Neel, R. 1983. *Impact.* Seattle, WA: CDMRC, University of Washington. (Curriculum for teaching autistic children.)

Pearlman, L. and Scott, K. A. 1981. *Raising the Handicapped Child.* Englewood Cliffs, NJ: Prentice-Hall.

Tweedie, D. and Shroyer, E. H., eds. 1982. *The Multi-Handicapped Hearing Impaired, Identification and Instruction.* Washington, DC: Gallaudet College Press.

Uzgiris, I. and Hunt, J. 1976. *Assessment in Infancy: Ordinal Scales of Psychological Development.* Urbana, IL: University of Illinois Press.

Vincent, L., Davis, J., Brown, P., Broome, K., Funkhouser, K., Miller, J., and Gruenewald, L. 1983. *Parent Inventory of Child Development in Non-School Environments.* Madison, WI: Madison Metropolitan School District.

Warren, S. and Rogers-Warren, A., 1985. *Teaching Functional Language.* Austin, TX: Pro-Ed, Inc.

VISUALLY IMPAIRED

Brinker, R. and Lewis, M. 1982. "Contingency Intervention." In *Curricula for High-Risk and Handicapped Infants.* J. Anderson, ed. Chapel Hill, NC: University of North Carolina — Chapel Hill, Technical Assistance Development Systems.

Brown, D., Simmons, V., and Methvin, J. 1979. *The Oregon Project for Visually Impaired and Blind Preschool Children.* Medford, OR: Jackson County Education Service District.

Bullis, M., ed. 1986. *Communication Development in Young Children with Deaf-Blindness: Literature Review II.* Monmouth, OR: Teaching Research Division.

Curtis, C., Dunning, L., Meese, B., Westover, L., Yost, K., and Perotti, N. 1978. *A Prelanguage Curriculum Guide for the Multihandicapped.* Washington, DC: Gallaudet College Press.

Hammer, E. 1982. "The Development of Language in the Deaf-Blind Multihandicapped Child: Progression of Instructional Methods." In *The Multihandicapped Hearing-Impaired: Identification and Instruction.* Washington, DC: Gallaudet College Press.

McCormick, L., and Noonan, M.J. 1984. "A Responsive Curriculum for Severely Handicapped Preschoolers," *Topics in Early Childhood Special Education*, 4: 79-96.

McInnes, J. M. and Treffry, J. A. 1982. *Deaf-Blind Infants and Children: A Developmental Guide.* Toronto, Ontario: University of Toronto Press.

Mills, A., ed. 1985. *Language Acquisition in the Blind Child.* San Diego, CA: College Hill Press.

Otos, Maurine, ed. 1983. *Nonverbal Prelinguistic Communication, A Guide to Communication Levels in Prelinguistic Handicapped Children.* Salem, OR: Oregon State Dept. of Education.

Robinson, C. and Robinson, J. 1983. "Sensorimotor Functions and Cognitive Development." In *Systematic Instruction of the Moderately and Severely Handicapped*, 2nd Edition, M. E. Snell, ed. Columbus, OH: Charles E. Merrill Publishing Co.

Scott, E. P., Jan, J. E., and Freeman, R. D. 1977. *Can't Your Child See?*. Baltimore MD: University Park Press.

CEREBRAL PALSY

Bigge, J. L. and O'Donnell, P. A., eds. 1976. *Teaching Individuals with Physical and Multiple Disabilities*. Columbus, OH: Charles E. Merrill Publishing Co.

Connor, F. P., Williamson, G. G., and Siepp, J. M. 1978. *Program Guide for Infants and Toddlers with Neuromotor and Other Developmental Disabilities*. New York, NY: Teachers College Press.

Finnie, N. 1975. *Handling the Young Cerebral Palsied Child at Home*. New York, NY: Dutton.

Hansen, M. 1986. *Teaching the Young Child with Motor Delays*. Austin, TX: Pro-Ed., Inc.

Kriswold, P. A., *Play Together: A Program Outline for Parents and Their Children, Ages 3 months to 3 years, Having Cerebral Palsy*. Indianapolis, IN: United Cerebral Palsy of Central Indiana.

Scherer, A. and Tscharnuter, I. 1982. *Early Diagnosis and Therapy in Cerebral Palsy*. New York, NY: Marcel Dekker, Inc.

DEVELOPMENTAL DELAY/NEUROLOGICAL IMPAIRMENT

Funderburg, R.S. 1982. "The Role of the Classroom Teacher in the Assessment of the Learning-Disabled Hearing-Impaired Child." In *The Multi-Handicapped Hearing Impaired: Identification and Instruction*. D. Tweedie and E. Shroyer, eds. Washington, DC: Gallaudet College Press.

Johnson, V. and Werner, R. 1975. *A Step-By-Step Learning Guide for Retarded Infants and Children*. Syracuse NY: Syracuse University Press.

Linde, T. F. and Kopp, T. 1973. *Training Retarded Babies and Preschoolers*. Springfield, IL: Charles C. Thomas.

Smith, D. W. and Wilson, A. A. 1973. *The Child with Down's Syndrome (Mongolism)*. Philadelphia, PA: W. B. Saunders Co.

AUGMENTATIVE COMMUNICATION

Carlson, F. 1982. *Prattle and Play — Equipment Recipes for Non-Speech Communication.* Omaha, NE: Meyer Resource Center, Meyer Children's Rehabilitation Institute.

Mathy-Laikko, P., Ratcliff, A., Villarruel, F., and Yoder, D. 1986. "Augmentative Communication Systems." In M. Bullis, ed. *Communication Development in Young Children with Deaf-Blindness: Literature Review II.* Monmouth, OR: Teaching Research Division.

Musselwhite, C. and St. Louis, K. 1982. *Communication Programming for the Severely Handicapped: Vocal and Non-Vocal Strategies.* San Diego, CA: College Hill Press.

Reichle, J. and Keogh, W. 1985. "Communication Instruction for Learners with Severe Handicaps." In R. Horner and L. Meyer, eds. *Education of Learners with Severe Handicaps.* Baltimore, MD: Paul H. Brookes Publishing Co.

Schiefelbusch, R., ed., 1980. *Nonspeech Language and Communication: Analysis and Intervention*, Baltimore, MD: University Park Press.

Silverman, F. 1980. *Communication for the Speechless.* Englewood Cliffs, NJ: Prentice Hall.

Vanderheiden, G. and Grilley, K., eds. 1976. *Non-Vocal Communication Techniques and Aids for the Severely Handicapped.* Baltimore, MD: University Park Press.

PART VII

GRADUATES OF INFANT HEARING RESOURCE

CHAPTER 27

OBSERVATIONS AND IMPRESSIONS OF IHR GRADUATES

A Preliminary Report from an IHR Survey
Liza and Her Family

A PRELIMINARY REPORT FROM AN IHR SURVEY

A question that IHR parent-infant specialists are frequently asked is whether or not the early intervention we provide to young hearing-impaired children and their families has any lasting positive effects. Most people want to know if our graduates are doing any better in school than do children whose families did not have early help. These are valid inquiries; anything that requires considerable investments of time and money should bear some fruit. In this final chapter we will address briefly the question of child achievement.

Over the past 15 years our staff has kept track of the activities and achievements of many of our graduates through personal contact with their families, through talking with the children's teachers, and through school

The graduation ceremony at IHR celebrates the achievements of parents and their young children. "I'm ready for anything!" this graduate says.

newsletters. In spring, 1986, we mailed out a survey to 40 graduate families. The survey consisted of questions related to the child's academic achievement and communicative function, and parents' attitudes. The three-part survey was completed by the parents, the child's current teacher, and the child. The families selected as recipients of the survey met the following criteria: The child was now seven years of age or older; the child had a severe or profound hearing loss and no known seriously handicapping condition in addition to hearing loss; and the family had been enrolled at IHR for at least one year. Twenty-two sets of families and teachers completed and returned all three parts of the survey.

We have not yet analyzed all the information we gathered through this survey. We were interested, however, in looking at the standardized reading achievement scores and at the written language of the children in the survey. We feel that these areas reflect one of our goals for children at IHR, competence with the English language. We were pleased to find that the reading scores of the majority of children in the survey were at or above grade level and that almost all the children were writing in English language word order and correctly incorporating many of the grammatical markers of English.

We are aware that we must do a more rigorous study that involves a larger number of IHR graduates in order to arrive at valid findings relating later academic achievement to early habilitation. We are also aware that it is not possible to postulate a direct relationship between the early intervention in which these children participated and the fact that more than half of this small group is reading at or above grade level, particularly since these children have been in a variety of school settings over which we had no control for five to twelve years. However, as we combined our data on these children from three sources — their current reading achievement, their performance while at IHR, and our observations of the children in the intervening years — one factor emerged which appears to be significant in determining child achievement. This factor will be discussed later in this chapter.

We present below some information about four of the oldest children who responded to the survey. At the time of the survey, all of these children were reading well above the national average for hearing-impaired children. We recognize that the descriptive summaries of the children include only a fragment of the factors which have influenced their development. However, we think it is important to include here an outcome of this survey that was very instructive to us, as well as some of our thoughts about this finding and the challenge it presents to parent-infant specialists.

SHELLY

Shelly's profound, genetic hearing loss was identified when she was two years of age, shortly before she and her family enrolled at IHR (Figure 13). The family attended three sessions per week at IHR for two years. Shelly's family has always used spoken English alone in communicating with her. Her first several years of school were in classrooms in which only oral communication was used. At age nine, while in the third grade, signs were added to the use of speech in her educational setting.

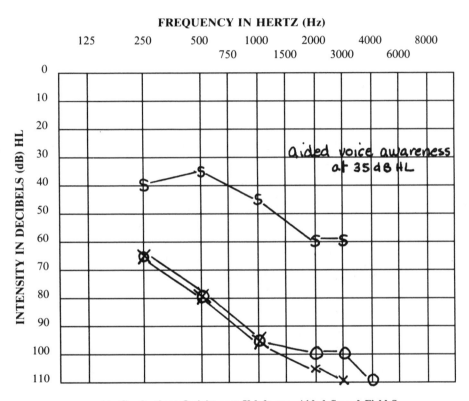

Air Conduction: O-right ear; X-left ear. Aided Sound Field-S

FIGURE 13. Shelly's audiogram

At the time of the IHR survey, Shelly was 16 years old and in 10th grade. At school she was in a self-contained classroom for the hearing-impaired part-time and mainstreamed with a sign language interpreter for three academic subjects. Shelly wears binaural hearing aids full time. She was described by both her parents and her teacher as talking in complete sentences using English word order and grammatical markers 80-100% of the time. Her speech was described as 80-100% intelligible to strangers.

While in the 10th grade Shelly's reading comprehension score on the S.A.T. (Advanced Test) was 8.6. Her written response to the survey question, "If you could go anywhere in the world, where would you go and what would you do there?" follows:

> "I would go to Europe. I love to go there because it is so different than United State. Europe is a place that I wanted to go. I wanted to go there to find alot of new things like the things that I never see. I am so sick of living in United States because everything in United States look the same. I wanted to learn how to speak French. But the language of France would be so hard for me to speak because I am hard of hearing. I would like to live there to meet new people and try to learn to social with them."

RONALD

Ronald is the child of two deaf parents who communicate in American Sign Language (ASL) and Pidgin Sign English. His hearing loss was identified before he was one year of age. He was enrolled in another parent-infant habilitation program for one year before coming to IHR at age two. Ronald and his parents attended two to three sessions each week at IHR for two years. Ronald has a profound bilateral sensorineural hearing loss (Figure 14).

Ronald, now in the 8th grade, has attended a state school for the deaf since the second grade. He wears one hearing aid about 25% of the time. His parents and teacher both describe Ronald's spoken and signed language as mainly in English word order but missing more than half the grammatical markers of English. The parents and teacher also both describe his speech as somewhat difficult for strangers to understand. His mother reports that Ronald uses ASL at home, while at school he is described as using more signed than spoken words.

At the time of the survey Ronald was 13 years old and in the 8th grade. His reading comprehension score on the S.A.T. (Hearing Impaired) was 11.0. His response to the survey question, "If you could go anywhere in the world, where would you go and what would you do there?" follows:

> "When I graduate, I would like to go to Gallaudet University. If I don't like, I'll go to N.T.I.D. After the college is over, I would like to have family. Maybe I'll live in Oregon. Not for sure. Maybe other state."

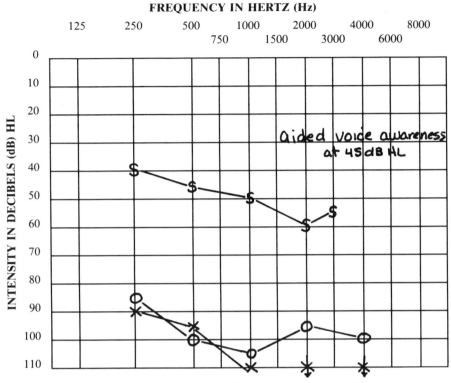

FREQUENCY IN HERTZ (Hz)

Air Conduction: O-right ear; X-left ear. Aided Sound Field-S

FIGURE 14. Ronald's audiogram

KIRSTEN

Kirsten's profound, bilateral hearing loss was detected when she was a year old. Etiology of the hearing loss is unknown (Figure 15). Kirsten attended a parent-infant program in another city between the ages of 15-22 months, at which time the family moved to Portland and enrolled at IHR for three sessions a week. Kirsten's final report from IHR, written when she graduated at age four, describes her early language learning.

"At age 2 years 4 months Kirsten understood 20 words through speech reading and said 16 words. At that point the use of signed language was added to communication with Kirsten. Within a month she learned four times as many words, there was a marked increase in her amount of vocalization, and her parents reported a dramatic change in her motivation to learn and to express herself orally."

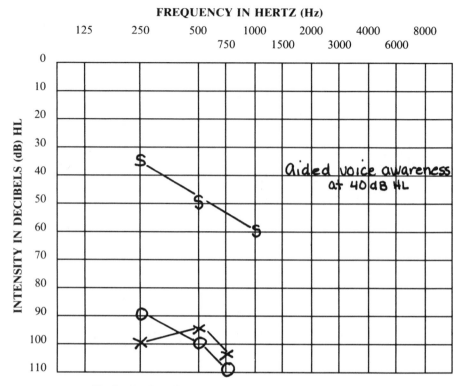

Air Conduction: O-right ear; X-left ear. Aided Sound Field-S

FIGURE 15. Kirsten's audiogram

At the time of the IHR survey, Kirsten was 14 years old and in the 9th grade. She is no longer wearing hearing aids, a decision she made at age ten. Her parents describe her as talking and signing in complete sentences using English word order and grammatical markers 80-100% of the time. Her parents describe Kirsten's speech as somewhat difficult for strangers to understand; her teacher says that strangers cannot understand Kirsten's speech.

While in 9th grade, Kirsten's reading comprehension score on the Woodcock Johnson Psycho-Ed Battery was 8.8 and her mainstreamed reading level was 9th grade. She was mainstreamed with a sign language interpreter for all classes except English. Kirsten responded to the survey question, "If you could go anywhere in the world, where would you go and what would you do there?" by writing:

> "There are alot of places I would love to to visit! One of them
> is Scotland Highlands. Others are such as Ireland, Sweden,
> Germany, Norway, Denmark, and others more. There are lots

of things I could see at Scotland. I would like to rent a cottage somewhere on the Scotland Highlands. I really like green pastures and nice serenity. I plan to go to Scotland when I get out of school, with some friends. It probably would be easier if I went with friends, that way each person would be alert and having fun! Also, I want to tour Glasglow and Edinburgh throughout. I expect to live temporarily there for a while before I take on a serious career.''

MITCH

Mitch's severe-profound hearing loss resulted from maternal rubella (Figure 16). He and his family enrolled for habilitation when Mitch was 14 months old. The family attended two to three habilitation sessions a week at IHR for two and one half years. During his last year of enrollment, Mitch

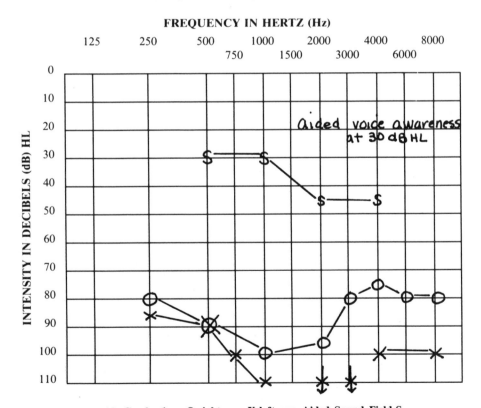

FIGURE 16. Mitch's audiogram

was also attending a nursery school program for normally hearing children three mornings a week. In Mitch's final report from IHR, written when he was 3 years 7 months of age, the following comment is notable: "Mitch's nursery school teacher reported that he was a willing group participant and that her only problem with him was his desire to talk when it was another child's turn."

Mitch was educated in a classroom for hearing-impaired children through preschool and kindergarten. He has been integrated in a regular classroom full time since 1st grade. He had special education tutoring during his first several years of grade school.

At the time of the IHR survey, Mitch was 14 years old and in regular 8th grade classes. His speech was 100% intelligible and his English usage like that of a normally hearing person. He had a large and colorful vocabulary and was reading at grade level. His response to the survey question, "If you could go anywhere in the world, where would you go and what would you do there?" was:

> "I would go to Disneyland, and Knotts Berry farm. I've wanted to go back there since my family trip there in 81. Unforuneately, we don't have that kind of money. If we did, I'd go back. Once there, I'd have some fun in the 30 years old-fashioned way. This time I would bring my friend Kevin. I would go to arcades, restaurants, etc. Then I'd catch a train, airplane or cruise back here. I've also been wanting to go on a cruise, to. Disneyland is where I would want to go back to."

DISCUSSION

These four children were selected for discussion because the factors to which we might be inclined to credit achievement vary so widely among them. One child, Mitch, has a severe-profound hearing loss with residual hearing throughout the frequency range. The other three children have profound hearing losses, but the use of this term blurs the differences in the amount of residual hearing available to each child. Both Shelly and Ronald have measurable hearing throughout the frequency range, but Shelly's better thresholds in the frequencies 250-1000 Hz appear to have been of advantage to her in understanding and using oral language. It should also be noted that Ronald has never used hearing aids 100% of his waking hours. He has had constant access to signed communication from his parents but has not had a model of intelligible speech at home. Kirsten has a "corner" audiogram. While hearing aids brought her thresholds for the low and mid frequencies up considerably, she found it extremely uncomfortable to wear these high gain aids, possibly because of recruitment.

Of the three children in this group who have learned through signed language, one child, Ronald, had deaf parents who provided him with visual communication since his birth. Kirsten had signs introduced after her second birthday and Shelly when she was nine years old, and then only at school. Thus, we cannot point to the early use of signed language as the primary factor leading to these children's reading achievement and English language competence.

When we looked at these four children and at the other survey respondents who were reading within a year of grade level or better, we realized that while there were many differences among them, we could identify one factor that they all had in common. **These children all had sufficient access to language to acquire a solid foundation of a symbolic language system in their preschool years.** Ronald had access to visual symbolic language from the time of birth. Mitch's aided residual hearing enabled him to hear spoken language frequently and clearly enough to learn the spoken language code. Since Shelly's high frequency hearing was not as good as Mitch's, spoken language was not as accessible to her. However, Shelly's parents made her early language learning a priority in their lives and provided her with repeated exposure to carefully structured language input under conditions in which she could hear it. Finally, Kirsten's parents recognized early in Kirsten's life that she was not receiving enough language information through audition to acquire language competence. They chose to add the use of signed language to their communication with her so that she was able to receive language through an intact sensory modality. They, too, provided Kirsten with intensive and structured language input as they communicated with her in spoken and signed English.

This factor — access to a frequent and non-ambiguous symbolic language code — is common to all the children in the survey who are reading at, near, or above grade level. For those children whose aided residual hearing did not provide this access, it appears that intense and structured parental language input through speech, signs, or both is essential. The children in the survey who are reading at, near, or above grade level all had at least one parent, usually the mother, who was able to take full advantage of the information and skills taught her at IHR and was able to transfer what she learned to daily home activities. **We recall these mothers as having an urgency to communicate with their child and time during the day to communicate and teach language.**

Looking at the families of the children in the survey who were reading more than a year below age level, we recognize that we knew at the time the family was enrolled at IHR that the parents were not able to make communication with the hearing-impaired child and his language acquisition a priority. In some of these families, both parents held jobs in addition to parenting. In other families, several small children at home diluted the quantity and quality of the time that the caregiving parent could spend with the deaf child. In some families the energy required from the parent or parents to provide for the family's physical needs meant that there was not time or emotional energy to provide for the extra needs of the child with hearing loss. Finally, in some families we recognized that communication, beyond that required by essential daily tasks, was not highly valued.

This information from our survey confirms the belief of IHR specialists that it is critically important that children have frequent, accessible, and non-ambiguous early language input in order to acquire a solid foundation of a symbolic language system in their preschool years. When this type of early language input is not available to children with severe and profound hearing losses, diminished reading achievement may result.

This finding, tentative as it is, presents a challenge to parent-infant specialists at IHR. We work with many families in which a single parent or both parents hold jobs in addition to parenting. This fact in itself limits the amount of time which parents have to spend in communicating with the child and in carrying out activities designed to promote the child's acquisition of listening, language, and speech skills. It limits the amount of time parents have available to learn and practice signed language so that they can become skilled signers. It also reduces the parents' ability to provide for their own emotional needs and for those of their children. When parents are not available to care for the child, this function is filled by a caregiver in the child's home or in a group daycare setting. Few of these caregivers have the expertise or the time to make communication with the hearing-impaired child a priority.

IHR specialists have made an effort to meet the needs of families in which both parents work by holding sessions late in the day, by offering signed language classes in the evening, and by doing home visits at the site where the child is receiving daycare. These efforts have not been sufficient to compensate for the lack of a full-time individual who is communicating with and teaching the child.

Having confirmation that access to frequent and non-ambiguous language models appears to have an impact on the one area of child achievement that we have looked at — reading achievement — our next responsibility is to convey this information to parents who are presently enrolled at Infant Hearing Resource. While some parents may be unable to make changes that may benefit their child, other families may decide to change their circumstances so that the child's acquisition of language becomes a family priority during the first years of his life.

Our second responsibility is to consider what IHR and the individual parent-infant specialists might do when families are unable to make their child's learning a priority. One potential solution is to go into the daycare business ourselves at IHR. Another approach might be to find a daycare provider who is willing to make listening and language, both spoken and signed, a focus of the daycare setting and to encourage working parents of hearing-impaired children to use this facility. Any potential solution would need to be carefully coordinated with the services provided to parents at IHR since we would not regard language-loaded daycare as a substitute for intensive parent involvement.

Feedback from families and teachers of our graduates and our observations of the children as they grow have supported our conviction that we are doing many things well in our parent-infant habilitation program. We try hard to keep our minds open to new avenues that will benefit the families with whom we work. We are frequently frustrated by the reality that what we are doing already fills the entire day and there is so much more to be learned and to do. For instance, the informal survey we conducted of a few of our graduates has provided us with some interesting data that raise more questions than they answer. One of our next projects may be to focus in a more scholarly and organized way on what has happened to our graduates. It is clear to us that we can only continue to grow and improve by looking critically at what we have done in the past and are doing in the present.

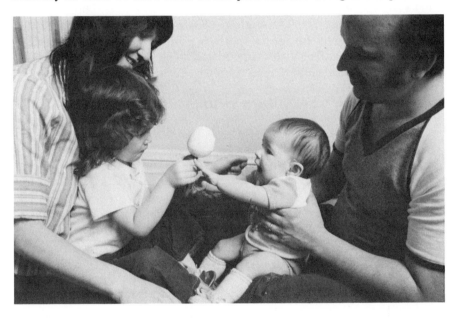

An effective program of habilitation is designed to help parents of young hearing-impaired children meet their children's needs for love, security, communication, positive self-esteem, and family values.

We also hope to hear from the readers of this book. What do you agree with and disagree with? What are you doing that works well for your families? How are your graduates doing? What are some of the factors you see affecting the achievement of your graduates? What are some of the issues you are struggling with? We look forward to hearing from you!

The final section of this chapter describes a family formerly enrolled at Infant Hearing Resource. Like many other families with whom we have worked, this family has been able to make their child's learning a priority. The results are an inspiration to us.

LIZA AND HER FAMILY

Several of the families who have participated in the IHR program of habilitation have provided what IHR specialists consider to be exemplary family and learning environments for their children, including their hearing-impaired child. We will focus on one of these families, in order to describe their hearing-impaired child's progress over time and to discuss the elements that we feel have contributed to the flowering of this little girl, Liza.

Liza was the fourth child born to Ann and Pete. They began to suspect that Liza had a hearing loss when she was three months of age. However, since Liza had frequent ear infections during her first months of life, it was not until she was nine months old that her profound, bilateral hearing loss was diagnosed (Figure 17). The etiology of Liza's loss is unknown. Three months after the family enrolled for auditory and language habilitation at IHR, the parent-infant specialist administered the Denver Developmental Screening Test to Liza. Now 12 months of age, Liza was functioning slightly

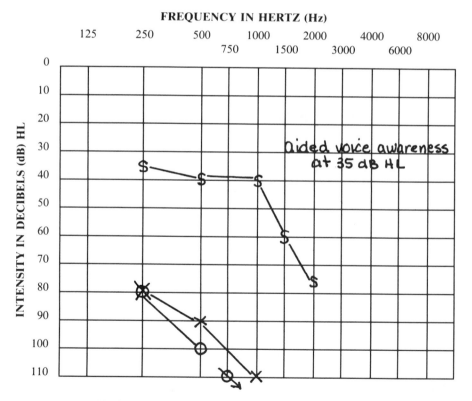

Air Conduction: O-right ear; X-left ear. Aided Sound Field-S

FIGURE 17. Liza's audiogram

below age level in the areas of personal-social, fine motor-adaptive, and gross motor and, predictably, more than six months behind in language.

Three years later, Liza and her family graduated from IHR. Liza, now age four, had been tested with the Leiter International Performance Scale and was functioning in the bright average range of intelligence. Her achievements in auditory and communication skills were recorded in her Final Report as follows:

Auditory Perceptual Development: "Liza is aware of many environmental sounds and recognizes some of them, e.g., a dog bark, the stereo, the dishwasher, the washing machine, the vacuum cleaner, and car and airplane engines. She is aware of voice at distances up to 10 feet. She can discriminate some single words, short phrases, and sentences through audition alone."

Receptive Language Development: "Now four years of age, Liza is functioning at the 43 to 48-month level according to the scale in *Parent-Infant Communication*, which is based on norms for hearing children. She understands comparative adjectives such as 'bigger' and 'biggest', can answer questions about herself and her family appropriately, and is able to answer questions such as, 'What do you do when you're hungry? tired? thirsty?' She understands everything said to her during routine activities."

Expressive Language Development: "Liza has passed nearly all the expressive language objectives at the 31 to 36-month level according to the scale in *Parent-Infant Communication*. She is able to communicate her thoughts about events occurring in the past as well as in the future. Her signed communication is always accompanied by vocalization, with some words being intelligible. Liza does not use signs if she knows the words are familiar to the listener(s) or if she is excited or angry. She uses the conjunction 'and'; the negatives 'not', 'won't', and 'don't'; and the third person pronouns 'it', 'her', and 'he'. She uses the 'to be' verb as an auxilliary, e.g., 'are sleeping', 'is coming'. She uses the word 'tomorrow' to denote future and is using both regular and irregular past tense markers."

"Liza vocalizes constantly and utilizes some information from the suprasegmental aspects of speech (intensity, pitch, duration, rhythm) meaningfully in her spontaneous utterances. She can produce several consonant-vowel combinations in single, repeated, and alternated syllables with variations in intensity. She can produce the consonant [b] in combination with ten vowels."

At age seven, Liza was in the second grade, reading at the second grade level, signing complete sentences using English word order and grammatical markers 80-100% of the time, and talking in sentences that were mainly in English word order but omitting one-fourth to one-half of the grammatical markers. Her second grade teacher noted that Liza "is an extremely empathetic listener, truly understanding what is being said. When entering into a conversation, Liza uses polite opening strategies, waits her turn, and is able to maintain and contribute to the conversation." She concluded by remarking that few of the deaf children she has known have demonstrated these kinds of conversational abilities.

At age seven, Liza responded to the IHR survey question, "If you could go anywhere in the world, where would you go and what would you do there?" by writing:

> "I went to Geernsboro to go swimming, have my brith day, go shopping, look at toys, play with GrandDad, Learn to knit from my GrandMom, Watch Videos, play with the little swings, bike, fire truck."

The following signed and spoken exchanges were transcribed from a videotaped conversation with her father when Liza was eight years old.

Liza: "You know, Expo, they have a lot of things. You know, one ride that Bill and Jana wanted to go on — Wow — they wanted to go on the Scream Machine."

Pete: "The Scream Machine?"

Liza: "Yes, you know, when Jana went on the Scream Machine she got her, she got her fingernail hurt. It was bleeding!"

Pete: "That's why it came off, right?"

Liza: "Yes."

Pete: "Okay, I understand now."

Liza: "And then she went to the first aid . . . and (unintelligible) hurry up!"

Pete: "What did they do at first aid?"

Liza: "At the first aid . . ."

Pete: "Wrap it up or something?"

Liza: "Wrap it up — with Kleenex. And then we went on other rides."

Liza, presently eight years old, is a charming, vibrant, and interesting child. IHR specialists have worked with and observed Liza and her family over the past seven years. We have noted several characteristics of this family that we feel account for the excellent progress that Liza is making. Many of these characteristics are shared by other families whose hearing-impaired children are also doing very well.

1. The family simply accepted Liza, hearing loss and all, from the time her hearing loss was diagnosed. Theirs was always an attitude of moving ahead and of getting on with what needed to be done.

2. Both parents and one of Liza's sisters who was not yet in school herself regularly participated in habilitation sessions. Her two school-aged siblings attended sessions occasionally even when it meant missing part of their school day. The entire family attended signed language classes during their three years enrollment at IHR. The family demonstrated a high level of commitment to communicating with Liza in signed and spoken English. Family members continued to expand their signed vocabulary and to increase their fluency by looking up words in the signed language dictionary and by learning new signs from Liza. Family members do not use signs 100% of the time and, as a result, Liza has learned to understand commonly used language through audition and speechreading.

3. Pete and Ann do a superb job of promoting their children's acquisition of positive self-esteem. Liza, like her siblings, hears frequently that she does things well. She also hears — and experiences — that she is loved and appreciated. At the same time, Pete and Ann set firm rules for how their children will behave. The children do not get away with behaviors that are not acceptable to their parents. Liza gets no slack in this area because of her deafness. Her parents correctly assumed that she was able to learn the same behavioral limits that her siblings are held to.

4. Liza's sister, Jana, is two years older than Liza and the two of them are very close. Jana is constantly interpreting and explaining the world to Liza from her own child point-of-view. As a result, Liza has not missed out on that perspective of the world that children generate and share among themselves. Child-to-child communication creates a special magic that adult-child communication rarely provides. Liza has benefitted immensely from the fact that Jana and her other sister and brother have learned to communicate with her.

5. Imaginative play and fantasy have always been a part of family activities. Liza learned early to take a role in fairy tales, to play "dress up," and to play imaginative thinking games. Her ability to fantasize and pretend, coupled with her ability to use abstract language concepts, enables her to understand and communicate about many things other than the concrete "here and now."

6. Pete and Ann have always kept appropriate and well-maintained hearing aids on Liza. She wears her aids 100% of her waking hours. In addition, the parents have provided Liza with a private speech tutor who has followed the sequential speech program developed by Daniel Ling (1976). Her parents value intelligible speech and Liza has acquired the habit of speech. Ann reports that Liza is dropping her use of signed language more and more and that family members have to ask her to use signs when they cannot understand her speech. Liza's speech is improving year by year, and while still not rated by parents and grade school teachers as "80-100% intelligible to strangers," she is approaching that level of intelligibility. People familiar with Liza can understand her speech in face-to-face conversations with the clues added by speech-reading and body language.

In Chapter 17 we mentioned three factors which affect the child's acquisition of symbolic language: 1) early identification of hearing loss; 2) the degree to which the child is able to use his aided residual hearing; and 3) the accessibility and completeness of the symbolic language system to which the child is exposed. In Chapter 21 we delineate three additional conditions that are essential to the child's acquisition of intelligible speech: 1) consistently modeling speech for the child under conditions that permit the child to hear it; 2) instructing the child in a rigorous, sequential program of vocal and speech development; and 3) encouraging and reinforcing the child for using speech to communicate his needs and ideas.

All of these factors have been present for Liza. Even more important, Liza has a family which treats her no differently than they do other family members — they communicate with her, love her, and expect the best for her and from her. It is our goal that all hearing-impaired children with whom we work will experience these same advantages to the highest degree that their family situation will allow.

REFERENCES

Alpiner, J. 1975. "Hearing Aid Selection for Adults." In *Amplification for the Hearing-Impaired*, ed. M. Pollack. New York: Grune and Stratton, 145-205.

Anderson, J. 1968. "Giving and Receiving Feedback." *Personnel Administration* 31:21-27.

Appell, M. 1986. "Mother-Child Interactions and the Development of Preverbal Communication." In *Communication Development in Young Children with Deaf-Blindness: Literature Review II*, ed. M. Bullis. Monmouth, OR: Teaching Research Division, 85-106.

ASHA, 1978. "American Speech and Hearing Association Guidelines for Manual Pure-Tone Threshold Audiometry." *American Speech and Hearing Association*, Vol. 29.

ASHA, 1986. "Report of the Ad Hoc Committee on 'Cochlear Implants'." *American Speech and Hearing Association* 28:29-52.

Atkins, D. Fall 1984. "Siblings of Hearing-Impaired Children." In *Our Kids Magazine*, International Parents Organization. Washington, D.C.: Alexander Graham Bell Association for the Deaf, 8.

Baker, C. 1978. "How Does 'Sim Com' Fit into a Bilingual Approach to Education?" In *Proceedings of the Second National Symposium on Sign Language Research and Teaching*, ed. F. Caccamuse. Coronado, CA.

Bates, E. 1976. *Language and Content: The Acquisition of Pragmatics*. New York: Academic Press.

Bateson, M. 1975. "Mother-Infant Exchanges: The Epigenesis of Conversational Interaction." In *Developmental Psycholinguistics and Communication Disorders*, eds. D. Aaronson and R. Rieber. New York: The New York Academy of Sciences, 101-113.

Bernstein, A. and Svarc, J. 1983. "Toys and Games as Rewards in Listening and Speech Lessons." *Volta Review* 85:36-40.

Bess, F. and McConnell, F. 1981. *Audiology, Education, and the Hearing Impaired Child*. St. Louis, MO: C. V. Mosby Company.

Best, B. and Roberts, G. 1975. Research Report No. 92: "Cognitive Development in Young Deaf Children." Minneapolis, MN: Research, Development and Demonstration Center in Education of Handicapped Children.

Bloom, L. and Lahey, M. 1978. *Language Development and Language Disorders*. New York: John Wiley and Sons.

Bodner-Johnson, B. 1985. "Families That Work For the Hearing-Impaired Child." *Volta Review* 87:131-137.

Boothroyd, A. 1971. "Acoustics of Speech." In *Speech for the Deaf Child: Knowledge and Use*, ed. L. Conner. Washington, D.C.: Alexander Graham Bell Association for the Deaf, 3-44.

Bornstein, H., Saulnier, K., and Hamilton, L., eds. 1983. *The Comprehensive Signed English Dictionary*. Washington, D.C.: Gallaudet College Press.

Brigance, A. 1978. *Inventory of Early Development*. North Billerica, MA: Curriculum Associates, Inc.

Brinker, R. and Lewis, M. 1982. "Contingency Intervention." In *Curricula for High Risk and Handicapped Infants*, ed. J. Anderson. Chapel Hill, NC: Technical Assistance Development Systems, University of North Carolina.

Briskey, R. 1978. "Binaural Hearing Aids and New Innovations." In *Handbook of Clinical Audiology*, 2nd edition, ed. J. Katz. Baltimore, MD: The Williams and Wilkins Company, 501-507.

Brockway, B. 1974. *Training in Child Management: A Family Approach*. Dubuque, IA: Kendall/Hunt Publishing Company.

Brown, D., Simmons, V., Methvin, J. 1979. *The Oregon Project for Visually Impaired and Blind Preschool Children*. Medford, OR: Jackson County Education District.

Bullard, C.L. 1981. "An Examination of the Communication Inter-actions Between Hearing-Impaired Infants and Their Parents." A paper presented to the International Sign Language Research Conference, Bristol, England.

Bullis, M., ed. 1986. *Communication Development in Young Children with Deaf-Blindness: Literature Review II*. Communication Skills Center for Young Children with Deaf-Blindness, Monmouth, OR: Teaching Research Division.

Cahoon, O.W. 1975. *A Teacher's Guide to Cognitive Tasks for Preschool*. Provo, UT: Brigham Young University Press.

Calvert, D., and Silverman, S.R. 1975. *Speech and Deafness*. Washington, D.C.: Alexander Graham Bell Association for the Deaf.

Carroll, J. 1964. *Language and Thought*. Englewood Cliffs, NJ: Prentice-Hall, Inc.

Cevette, M. 1984. "Auditory Brainstem Response Testing in the Intensive Care Unit." In *Seminars in Hearing: Early Identification of Hearing Loss in Infants*, Vol. 5, No. 1, eds. J. Northern and W. Perkins. New York: Thieme-Stratton, Inc., 57-69.

Clark School for the Deaf, 1971. *Auditory Training*. Northampton, MA: Clark School for the Deaf.

Clark, T. and Watkins, S. 1978 and 1985. *SKI*HI Curriculum Manual: Programming for Hearing Impaired Infants Through Home Intervention*. North Logan, UT: Hope, Inc.

Clarke, J. 1978. *Self-Esteem: A Family Affair*. Minneapolis, MN: Winston Press.

Cole, E. and Mischook, M. 1985. "Survey and Annotated Bibliography of Curricula Used by Oral Preschool Programs." *Volta Review* 87:139-154.

Cole, E. and Paterson, M. 1984. "The McGill University Project." In *Early Intervention for Hearing-Impaired Children: Oral Options*, ed. D. Ling. San Diego, CA: College Hill Press, 119-179.

Condon, W.S. and Sander, L.W. 1974. "Neonate Movement is Synchronized with Adult Speech: Interactional Participation and Language Acquisition." *Science* 183:99-101.

Connor, F.P., Williamson, G.G. and Siepp, J., eds. 1978. *A Program Guide for Infants and Toddlers with Neuromotor and Other Developmental Disabilities*. Columbia University, New York: Teacher's College Press.

Coplan, J., Gleason, J., Ryan, R., Burke, M., and Williams, M. 1982. "Validation of an Early Language Milestone Scale in a High-Risk Population." *Pediatrics* 70:677-683.

Crary, E. 1979. *Without Spanking or Spoiling*. Seattle, WA: Parenting Press.

Crowley, M., Keane, K., and Needham, C. 1982. "Fathers: The Forgotten Parents." *American Annals of the Deaf* 127:38-40.

Curtis, C., Dunning, L., Meese, B., Westover, L., Yost, K., and Perotti, N. 1978. *A Prelanguage Curriculum Guide for the Multihandicapped*. Colorado Springs, CO: Colorado School for the Deaf and Blind.

Darbyshire, J.O. 1977. "Play Patterns in Young Children with Impaired Hearing." *Volta Review* 79:19-26.

DeCasper, A. May 22, 1984. "Infants Have Memory — Even Before Birth." *Oregonian* newspaper. Portland, OR: Oregonian Publishing Company.

DeCasper, A. and Fifer, W. 1980. "Of Human Bonding: Newborns Prefer Their Mother's Voices." *Science* 208:1174-1176.

Demany, L., McKenzie, B., and Vurpillot, E. 1977. "Rhythm Perception in Early Infancy." *Nature* 266:718-719.

Denhoff, E. 1967. *Cerebral Palsy: The Preschool Years*. Springfield, IL: Charles C. Thomas.

Dowell, R., Brown, A., Seligman, P., and Clark, G. 1985. "Patient Results for a Multiple Channel Cochlear Implant System." In *Cochlear Implants*, eds. R. Schindler and M. Merzenich. New York: Raven Press, 421-431.

Dreikurs, R. 1964. *Children: The Challenge*. New York: Hawthorne Books, Inc.

Dunst, C.J. 1981. *Infant Learning, A Cognitive-Linguistic Intervention Strategy*. Hingham, MA: Teaching Resources Corporation.

Eddington, D. and Orth, J. 1985. "Speech Recognition in a Deaf Subject with a Portable, Multi-Channel Cochlear Implant System." In *Cochlear Implants*, eds. R. Schindler and M. Merzenich. New York: Raven Press, 277-282.

Eichhorn, S. 1982. "Congenital Cytomegalovirus Infection: A Significant Cause of Deafness and Mental Deficiency." *American Annals of the Deaf* 127:838-843.

Eisenberg, R. 1976. *Auditory Competence in Early Life*. Baltimore, MD: University Park Press.

Englehart, L. 1985. "He Changed." *Sibling Information Network Newsletter*, Vol. 4, No.3. Storrs, CT: University of Connecticut.

Feinmesser, M., Tell, L., and Levi, H. 1984. "A Combination of High-Risk and Mass Screening: A Follow-Up of 40,000 Infants." In *Seminars In Hearing: Early Identification of Hearing Loss in Infants*, Vol. 5, No. 1, eds. J. Northern and W. Perkins. New York: Thieme-Stratton, Inc., 79-84.

Fewell, R.R. and Vadasy, P.F. 1983. *Learning Through Play*. Hingham, MA: Teaching Resources Corporation.

Fieber, N. 1975. "Movement in Communication and Language Development of Deaf-Blind Children." *MCRI Working Papers, No. 5*. Meyer Children's Rehabilitation Institute, Omaha, NB: University of Nebraska Medical Center.

Fieber, N. 1977. "Sensorimotor Cognitive Assessment and Curriculum for the Multihandicapped Child." *MCRI Working Papers, No. 7*. Meyer Children's Rehabilitation Institute, Omaha, NB: University of Nebraska Medical Center.

Fieber, N. 1978. "The Profoundly Handicapped Child: Assessing Sensorimotor and Communication Abilities." *MCRI Working Papers, No. 8*. Meyer Children's Rehabilitation Institute, Omaha, NB: University of Nebraska Medical Center.

Flexer, C. and Wood, L. 1984. "The Hearing Aid: Facilitor or Inhibitor of Auditory Interaction?" *Volta Review* 86:354-361.

Frank, R. April 1985. "Self Esteem Building." *Interact*. An Oregon Special Education Newsletter. Portland, OR: Portland State University.

Furth, H.G. 1966. "A Comparison of Reading Test Norms of Deaf and Hearing Children." *American Annals of the Deaf* 111:461-462.

Furth, H.G. 1970. *Piaget for Teachers*. Englewood Cliffs, NJ: Prentice-Hall, Inc.

Gabbard, S. 1982. "Reference for Communication Disorders Related to Otitis Media." In *Seminars in Speech, Language and Hearing*, Vol. 3, No. 4, eds. J. Northern and W. Perkins. New York: Thieme-Stratton, Inc., 351-353.

Gallaudet College/National Information Center on Deafness. 1984. "Deafness: A Fact Sheet." NICD/NAD Washington, D.C.: Gallaudet College.

Glover, M., Preminger, J., and Sanford, A. 1978. "Early-LAP: The Early Learning Accomplishment Profile for Developmentally Young Children, Birth to 36 Months." Winston-Salem, NC: Kaplan Press.

Goss, R.N. 1970. "Language Used by Mothers of Deaf Children and Mothers of Hearing Children." *American Annals of the Deaf* 115:93-96.

Greenstein, J., Greenstein B., McConville, K., and Stellini, L. 1976. *Mother-Infant Communication and Language Acquisition in Deaf Infants.* New York: Lexington School for the Deaf.

Griffiths, C. 1967. *Conquering Childhood Deafness.* New York: Exposition Press.

Halliday, M. 1973. *Explorations in the Functions of Language.* London: Edward Arnold.

Hammer, E. 1982. "The Development of Language in the Deaf-Blind Multihandicapped Child: Progression of Instructional Methods." *The Multi-Handicapped Hearing-Impaired: Identification and Instruction,* eds. D. Tweedie and E. Shroyer. Washington, D.C.: Gallaudet College Press, 193-200.

Hedrick, D., Prather, E., and Tobin, A. 1984. *Sequenced Inventory of Communication Development,* revised edition. Seattle, WA: University of Washington Press.

Higginbotham, D.J. and Baker, B.M. 1981. "Social Participation and Cognitive Play Differences in Hearing Impaired and Normally Hearing Preschoolers." *Volta Review* 83:135-149.

Hlibok, B. 1981. *Silent Dancer.* New York: Messner, Division of Simon Schuster.

Howell, R. 1984. "Maternal Reports of Vocabulary Development in Four-Year-Old Deaf Children." *American Annals of the Deaf* 129:459-465.

Infant Hearing Resource, 1985. *Parent-Infant Communication: A Program of Clinical and Home Training for Parents and Hearing-Impaired Infants,* 3rd edition. Portland, OR: Infant Hearing Resource.

Jerger, J., ed. 1975. *Handbook of Clinical Impedance Audiometry.* Dobbs Ferry, NY: American Electromedics Corporation.

Joint Committee on Infant Hearing. 1982. "Position Paper." *Pediatrics* 70:496-497.

Kaplan, E. L. 1969. "The Role of Intonation in the Acquisition of Language." Unpublished doctoral dissertation, Cornell University, Ithaca, NY.

Kass, C. 1982. "Remedial Strategies for Age-Related Characteristics of Learning Disability." In *The Multi-Handicapped Hearing Impaired: Identification and Instruction*, eds. D. Tweedie and E. Shroyer. Washington, D.C.: Gallaudet College Press, 85-94.

Kasten, R. 1978. "Standards and Standard Hearing Aids." In *Handbook of Clinical Audiology*, 2nd edition, ed. J. Katz. Baltimore, MD: The Williams and Wilkins Company, 485-500.

Katz, J., ed. 1978. *Handbook of Clinical Audiology*. Baltimore, MD: The Williams and Wilkins Company.

Kenna, M. and Stool, S. 1983. "Hearing Aid Battery Ingestion in the Child." *Hearing Instruments* 34:21-22.

Klaus, M. and Kennell, J. 1976. *Maternal-Infant Bonding*. St. Louis, MO: The C. V. Mosby Company.

Kubler-Ross, E. 1969. *On Death and Dying*. New York: Macmillan Publishing Company, Inc.

Lehane, S. 1976. *Help Your Baby Learn: 100 Piaget-Based Activities for the First Two Years of Life*. Englewood Cliffs, NJ: Prentice-Hall, Inc.

Levine, E. 1976. *Lisa and Her Soundless World*. New York: Human Sciences Press.

Lewis, M. and Harlan, E. 1980. "Your Baby's Well-Being: A Lifetime Involvement." *Mothers' Manual*. Sept/Oct:22-26.

Ling, A. 1974. "Sequential Processing in Hearing-Impaired Children." *Proceedings of the International Conference on Auditory Techniques*, ed. C. Griffiths. Springfield, IL: Charles C. Thomas, 97-106.

Ling, A. 1977. *Schedules of Development in Audition, Speech, Language, Communication for Hearing-Impaired Infants and Their Parents*. Washington, D.C.: Alexander Graham Bell Association for the Deaf, Inc.

Ling, D. 1976. *Speech and the Hearing-Impaired Child: Theory and Practice*. Washington, D.C.: Alexander Graham Bell Association for the Deaf, Inc.

Ling. D. 1978. *Teacher/Clinician's Planbook and Guide to the Development of Speech Skills* and *Cumulative Record of Skill Acquisition*. Washington, D.C.: Alexander Graham Bell Association for the Deaf, Inc.

Ling, D. June 1981. "Keep Your Hearing Impaired Child Within Earshot." *Newsounds*. Washington, D.C.: Alexander Graham Bell Association for the Deaf, Inc.

Ling, D., ed. 1984. *Early Intervention for Hearing Impaired Children: Oral Options* and *Early Intervention for Hearing Impaired Children: Total Communication Options*. San Diego, CA: College Hill Press.

Ling, D. and Ling, A. 1978. *Aural Habilitation: The Foundations of Verbal Learning in Hearing-Impaired Children*. Washington, D.C.: Alexander Graham Bell Association for the Deaf, Inc.

Linkletter, A. 1978. *The New Kids Say the Darndest Things!* Aurora, IL: Caroline House Publishers, Inc.

Litchfield, A. 1976. *A Button In Her Ear*. Niles, IL: Albert Whitman and Company.

Loeb, R. and Sarigiani, P. 1986. "The Impact of Hearing Impairment on Self-Perception in Children." *Volta Review* 88:89-100.

Lotterman, S. and Kasten, R. 1967. "The Influence of Gain Control Rotation on Nonlinear Distortion in Hearing Aids." *Journal of Speech and Hearing Research* 10: 593-599.

Luterman, D. 1979. *Counseling Parents of Hearing-Impaired Children*. Boston, MA: Little, Brown and Company.

McCandless, G. 1973. "Loudness Discomfort and Hearing Aids." Cited in Ross, M. 1978. "Hearing Aid Evaluation." In *Handbook of Clinical Audiology*, ed. J. Katz. Baltimore, MD: Williams and Wilkins Company, 524-542.

McCollum, A. Spring 1985. "Grieving Over the Lost Dream." *The Endeavor*. Silver Spring, MD: International Association of Parents of the Deaf, Inc.

McCormick, L. and Noonan, M. 1984. "A Responsive Curriculum for Severely Handicapped Preschoolers." *Topics In Early Childhood Special Education* 4:79-96.

McDonald, J. 1985. "Language through Conversation: A Model for Intervention with Language Delayed Infants." In *Teaching Functional Language*, eds. S. Warren and A. Rogers-Warren. Austin, TX: Pro-Ed, Inc.

McElroy, D. and Bernstein, H. 1976. "The Role of Parents in Developing Self Esteem in a Hearing Impaired Child." *Volta Review* 78:219-223.

McInnes, J.M. and Treffry, J.A. 1982. *Deaf-Blind Infants and Children: A Developmental Guide*. Buffalo, NY: University of Toronto Press.

McKeever, P. 1983. "Siblings of Chronically Ill Children: A Literature Review with Implications for Research and Practice." *American Journal of Orthopsychiatry* 53:209-217.

McLean, J., Snyder-McLean, L., Rowland, C., Jacobs, P., and Stremel-Campbell, K. 1981. *Generic Skills Assessment Inventory*. (Experimental Edition). Bureau of Child Research, Lawrence, KA: University of Kansas.

McNeill, D. 1966. "The Capacity for Language Acquisition." *Volta Review*. Reprint 852:5-21.

Mahoney, T. 1984. "High Risk Hearing Screening of Large General Newborn Populations." In *Seminars in Hearing: Early Identification of Hearing Loss in Infants*, Vol. 5, No. 1, eds. J. Northern and W. Perkins. New York: Thieme-Stratton, Inc., 25-37.

Manolson, A. 1985. *It Takes Two to Talk*. Toronto, Ontario: Hanen Early Language Resource Center.

Marmor, G. and Petitto, L. 1979. "Simultaneous Communication in the Classroom: How Well is English Language Represented?" *Sign Language Studies*, Vol. 23.

Mathy-Laikko, P., Ratcliff, A., Villarruel, F., and Yoder, D. 1986. "Augmentative Communication Systems." In *Communication Development in Young Children with Deaf-Blindness: Literature Review II*, ed. M. Bullis. Monmouth, OR: Teaching Research Division, 183-209.

Mavilya, M.P. 1969. "Spontaneous Vocalization and Babbling in Hearing Impaired Infants." Ph.D. Dissertation, Columbia University, New York.

Meadow, K. 1980. *Deafness and Child Development*. Berkeley, CA: University of California Press.

Mendelsohn, J. 1984. "Don't Forget the Sibs!" *What's Happening*, Vol. 3, No. 3. Los Alamitos, CA: Modern Signs Press.

Miller, K. and Simmons, F.B. 1984. "A Retrospective and An Update in the Crib-O-Gram Neonatal Hearing Screening Audiometer." In *Seminars in Hearing: Early Identification of Hearing Loss in Infants*, Vol. 5, No. 1, eds. J. Northern and W. Perkins. New York: Thieme-Stratton, Inc., 49-56.

Miller, S. 1985. "Siblings." *Sibling Information Network Newsletter*, Vol. 4, No.3. Storrs, CT: University of Connecticut.

Mindel, E. and Vernon, M. 1971. *They Grow In Silence: The Deaf Child and His Family*. Silver Spring, MD: National Association of the Deaf.

Minton, C., Kagan, J., and Levine, J. 1971. "Maternal Control and Obedience in the Two-Year-Old." *Child Development* 42:1873.

Morse, P.A. 1972. "The Discrimination of Speech and Nonspeech Stimuli in Early Infancy." *Journal of Experimental Child Psychology* 14:477-492.

Moses, K. 1979. "Parenting a Hearing-Impaired Child: An Interview with Ken Moses." *Volta Review* 81:73-80.

Moses, K. 1982. "Brothers and Sisters of Special Children." A reprint from Waisman Center Inter-actions. Madison, WI: University of Wisconsin.

Moses, K. 1985. "Infant Deafness and Parental Grief: Psychosocial Early Intervention." In *Education of the Hearing-Impaired Child*, eds. F. Powell, T. Finitzo-Hieber, S. Friel-Patti, and D. Henderson. San Diego, CA: College Hill Press.

Musselwhite, C. and St.Louis, K. 1982. *Communication Programming for the Severely Handicapped: Vocal and Non-Vocal Strategies*. San Diego, CA: College Hill Press.

Nienhuys, T., Horsborough, K., and Cross, T. 1985. "A Dialogic Analysis of Interaction Between Mothers and Their Deaf or Hearing Preschoolers." *Applied Psycholinguistics* 6:121-140.

Nittrouer, S. and Hochberg, I. 1985. "Speech Instruction for Deaf Children: A Communication-Based Approach." *American Annals of the Deaf* 130:491-495.

Northcott, W., ed. 1977. *Curriculum Guide, Hearing-Impaired Children — Birth to Three Years — and Their Parents*. Washington, D.C.: Alexander Graham Bell Association for the Deaf, Inc.

Northcott, W., ed. 1980. *I Heard That!: A Developmental Sequence of Listening Activities for the Young Child*. Washington, D.C.: The Alexander Graham Bell Association for the Deaf, Inc.

Northern, J. and Downs, M. 1984. *Hearing In Children*, 3rd edition. Baltimore, MD: Williams and Wilkins.

Northern, J. and Perkins, W., eds. 1986. *Seminars in Hearing: Cochlear Implants in Children*, Vol. 7, No. 4. New York: Thieme Medical Publishers.

Novelli-Olmstead, T. and Ling, D. 1984. "Speech Production and Speech Discrimination by Hearing-Impaired Children." *Volta Review* 86:72-80.

Pappas, D. and Houston, D. June 1984. "The Post Meningitis Hearing-Impaired Child: Otological, Audiological and Educational Management." A paper presented at the Alexander Graham Bell Association for the Deaf Convention, Portland, OR.

Peterson, J. 1977. *I Have a Sister, My Sister Is Deaf*. New York: Harper and Row, Publishers.

Piaget, J. and Inhelder, B. 1969. *The Psychology of the Child*. New York: Basic Books, Inc.

Pollack, D. 1984. "An Acoupedic Program." In *Early Intervention for Hearing-Impaired Children: Oral Options*, ed. D. Ling. San Diego, CA: College Hill Press, 181-253.

Pollack, D. 1985. *Educational Audiology for the Limited-Hearing Infant and Preschooler*, 2nd edition. Springfield, IL: Charles C. Thomas.

Pollack, M. 1975. "Electroacoustic Characteristics." In *Amplification for the Hearing-Impaired*, ed. M. Pollack. New York: Grune and Stratton, 21-80.

Powell, T. and Ogle, P. 1985. *Brothers and Sisters — A Special Part of Exceptional Families*. Baltimore, MD: Paul H. Brooks Publishing Company.

Quigley, S.P., Steinkamp, M.W., Power, D.J. and Jones, B.W. 1978. *Test of Syntactic Abilities*. Beaverton, OR: Dormac, Inc.

Radcliffe, D. 1984. "The Cochlear Implant: Its Time Has Come." *The Hearing Journal* 37: 7-15.

Reichle, J. and Keogh, W. 1985. "Communication Instruction for Learners with Severe Handicaps: Some Unresolved Issues." In *Education of Learners with Severe Handicaps*, eds. R. Horner and L. Meyer. Baltimore, MD: Paul H. Brooks Publishing Company, 189-219.

Robbins, N. and Stenquist, G. 1967. "The Deaf-Blind 'Rubella' Child." Perkins Publication, No. 25. Watertown, MA: Perkins School for the Blind.

Roberts, G. 1979. "Early Cognitive Development in Deaf Children." *Young Children* 34:53-59.

Robinson, C. and Fieber, N. 1974. "Development and Modification of Piagetian Sensorimotor Assessment and Curriculum for Developmentally Handicapped Infants." *MCRI Working Papers, No. 1*. Meyer Children's Rehabilitation Institute, Omaha, NE: University of Nebraska Medical Center.

Robinson, C. and Robinson, J. 1983. "Sensorimotor Functions and Cognitive Development." In *Systematic Instruction of the Moderately and Severely Handicapped*, 2nd edition, ed. M. Snell. Columbus, OH: Charles E. Merrill.

Rogers, C. 1951. *Client-Centered Therapy*. Boston, MA: Houghton Mifflin.

Ross, M. 1975. "Hearing Aid Selection for the Preverbal Hearing-Impaired Child." In *Amplification for the Hearing Impaired*, ed. M. Pollack. New York: Grune and Stratton, 207-242.

Ross, M. 1978. "Hearing Aid Evaluation." In *Handbook of Clinical Audiology*, 2nd edition, ed. J. Katz. Baltimore, MD: The Williams and Wilkins Company, 524-542.

Ruben, R.J. and Rapin, I. 1980. "Plasticity of the Developing Auditory System." *Annals of Otolaryngology* 89:303-311.

Schaeffer, B. 1982. "Linguistic Functions and Language Intervention: Part I, Concepts, Evidence and Instructional Sequence." *The Journal of Special Education* 16:289-308.

Schaeffer, B. 1982. "Linguistic Functions and Language Intervention: Part II, Special Topics." *The Journal of Special Education* 16:401-411.

Schafer, D.S., Moersch, M., and D'Eugenio, D., eds. 1985-86. *Developmental Programming for Infants and Young Children*, 5 volumes. Ann Arbor, MI: University of Michigan Press.

Schein, J. 1984. "Cochlear Implants and the Education of Deaf Children." *American Annals of the Deaf* 129:324-332.

Schildroth, A. 1986. "Hearing-Impaired Children Under Age 6: 1977 and 1984." *American Annals of the Deaf* 131:85-90.

Schlesinger, H.S. 1985. "Deafness, Mental Health, and Language." In *Education of the Hearing Impaired Child*, eds. F. Powell, T. Finitzo-Hieber, S. Friel-Patti, and D. Henderson. San Diego, CA: College Hill Press.

Schlesinger, H.S. and Meadow, K.P. 1972. *Sound and Sign: Childhood Deafness and Mental Health*. Berkeley, CA: University of California Press.

Schweigert, P. 1986. "Contingency Intervention." In *Communication Development in Young Children with Deaf-Blindness: Literature Review II*, ed. M. Bullis. Monmouth, OR: Teaching Research Division, 167-182.

Seligman, M. 1975. *Helplessness: On Depression, Development and Death*. San Francisco, CA: W. H. Freeman.

Shah, C.P., Chandler, D., and Dale, R. 1978. "Delay in Referral of Children with Impaired Hearing." *Volta Review* 80:206-215.

Sharp, E. 1970. *Thinking Is Child's Play*. New York: Avon Books.

Shepherd, B. 1973. "Parent Potential." In *The Hearing-Impaired Child in a Regular Classroom*, ed. W. Northcott. Washington, D.C.: Alexander Graham Bell Association for the Deaf, Inc. 239-243.

Shontz, F. 1965. "Reactions to Crisis." *Volta Review* 67:364-370.

Siegal-Causey, E., Sims, C., Ernest, B., and Guess. D. 1986. "Elements of Prelanguage Communication and Early Interactional Processes." In *Communication Development in Young Children with Deaf Blindness: Literature Review II*, ed. M. Bullis. Monmouth, OR: Teaching Research Division, 59-83.

Simmons-Martin, A. 1978. "Early Management Procedures for the Hearing Impaired Child." In *Pediatric Audiology*, ed. F. Martin. Englewood Cliffs, NJ: Prentice-Hall, Inc.

Singer, D. and Lenahan, M. 1976. "Imagination Content in Dreams of Deaf Children." *American Annals of the Deaf* 121:44-48.

Sisco, F., Kranz, P., Lund, N., and Schwarz, G. 1979. "Developmental and Compensatory Play: A Means of Facilitating Social, Emotional, Cognitive, and Linguistic Growth in Deaf Children." *American Annals of the Deaf* 81:850-857.

Sonnenschein, M. 1986. "Cochlear Implant Update." *Shhh Journal* May/June. Bethesda, MD: Self-Help for Hard of Hearing People, Inc., 16-19.

Sonquist, H. and Kamii, C. 1967. "Applying Some Piagetian Concepts in the Classroom for the Disadvantaged." *Young Children* 22:231-246.

Spring, D. and Dale, P. 1977. "Discrimination of Linguistic Stress in Early Infancy." *Journal of Speech and Hearing Research* 20:224-232.

Stillman, R., ed. 1978. *Callier-Azuza Scale*. Dallas, TX: Callier Center for Communication Disorders.

Stone, P. 1980. "Developing Thinking Skills in Young Hearing-Impaired Children." *Volta Review* 82:345-352.

Stovall, D. 1982. *Teaching Speech to Hearing-Impaired Infants and Children*. Springfield, IL: Charles C. Thomas.

Swisher, M.V. and Thompson, M. 1985. "Mothers Learning Simultaneous Communication: The Dimensions of the Task." *American Annals of the Deaf* 130:212-217.

Talbott, C.B. June 1984. "A Longitudinal Study Comparing Infants' Responses to Pure Tones Using Two Behavioral Test Paradigms." A paper presented to the Audiology Update: Pediatric Audiology Conference, Newport, RI.

The Endeavor May/June 1985. Silver Spring, MD: International Association of Parents of the Deaf, 6-7.

Therrien, V. 1984. *For the Love of Siblings Who Cope with Special Sisters and Brothers*. Hookset, NH: Association for Retarded Citizens.

Thoman, E. and Trotter, S. 1978. "Introduction." In *Social Responsiveness in Infants*, eds. S. Trotter and E. Thoman. Skillman, NJ: Johnson and Johnson Baby Products Company, xvii-xx.

Thompson, G. and Wilson, W. 1984. "Clinical Application of Visual Reinforcement Audiometry." In *Seminars in Hearing: Early Identification of Hearing Loss in Infants*, Vol. 5, No. 1, eds. J. Northern and W. Perkins. New York: Thieme-Stratton, Inc, 85-99.

UCPA, 1982. "Cerebral Palsy — Facts and Figures." New York: United Cerebral Palsy Association, Inc.

Ungerer, J. and Sigman, M. 1984. "The Relation of Play and Sensori-Motor Behavior to Language in the Second Year." *Child Development* 55:1448.

University of Bristol School of Education, 1978. "Language at Home and At School." Unpublished summary of findings. University of Bristol, England: Center for the Study of Language and Communication.

Uzgiris, I. and Hunt, J. 1975. *Assessment in Infancy: Ordinal Scales of Psychological Development*. Urbana, IL: University of Illinois Press.

Vernon, M. 1982. "Multi-Handicapped Deaf Children: Types and Causes." In *The Multi-Handicapped Hearing-Impaired: Identification and Instruction*, eds. D. Tweedie and E. Shroyer. Washington, D.C.: Gallaudet College Press, 11-28.

Vernon, M. and Koh, S. 1970. "Effects of Manual Communication on Deaf Children's Educational Achievement, Linguistic Competence, Oral Skills and Psychological Development." *American Annals of the Deaf* 115:527-536.

Wallin, J.L. 1965. "Freeing and Binding Responses." *Curriculum on Interpersonal Communication*. Portland, OR: Northwest Regional Educational Laboratory.

Warren, M. and Cunningham, D. (no date). "Can Your Baby Hear?" Washington, D.C.: Alexander Graham Bell Association for the Deaf, Inc.

Warren, S. and Rogers-Warren, A. 1985. *Teaching Functional Language*. Austin, TX: Pro-Ed, Inc.

Watson, J.S. 1966. "The Development and Generalization of 'Contingency Awareness' in Early Infancy: Some Hypotheses." *Merrill-Palmer Quarterly* 12:123-135.

Watson, J.S. and Ramey, C.T. 1972. "Reactions to Response-Contingent Stimulation in Early Infancy." *Merrill-Palmer Quarterly* 12:123-135.

Webster's New Collegiate Dictionary, 1974. Springfield, MA: G. and C. Merriam Company.

Whetnall, E. and Fry, D.B. 1966. *The Deaf Child*. London: The Whitefriars Press, Ltd.

Wiesel, T.N. and Hubel, D.H. 1965. "Extent of Recovery from the Effects of Visual Deprivation in Kittens." *Journal of Neurophysiology* 28:1060-1072.

Wilbur, R. 1979. *American Sign Language and Sign Systems*. Baltimore, MD: University Park Press.

Wolff, P.H. 1963. "Observations on the Early Development of Smiling." In *Determinants of Infant Behavior*, Vol. II, ed. B.M. Foss. New York: Wiley.

Yoshinaga-Itano, C. and Snyder, L. 1985. "Form and Meaning in the Written Language of Hearing-Impaired Children." *Volta Review* 87:75-89.

INDEX